Religious Pluralism, Globalization, and World Politics

EDITED BY THOMAS BANCHOFF

OXFORD

UNIVERSITY PRESS

2008

OXFORD

UNIVERSITY PRESS

Oxford University Press, Inc., publishes works that further
Oxford University's objective of excellence
in research, scholarship, and education.

Oxford   New York
Auckland   Cape Town   Dar es Salaam   Hong Kong   Karachi
Kuala Lumpur   Madrid   Melbourne   Mexico City   Nairobi
New Delhi   Shanghai   Taipei   Toronto

With offices in
Argentina   Austria   Brazil   Chile   Czech Republic   France   Greece
Guatemala   Hungary   Italy   Japan   Poland   Portugal   Singapore
South Korea   Switzerland   Thailand   Turkey   Ukraine   Vietnam

Copyright © 2008 by Oxford University Press, Inc.

Published by Oxford University Press, Inc.
198 Madison Avenue, New York, New York 10016

www.oup.com

Oxford is a registered trademark of Oxford University Press

All rights reserved. No part of this publication may be reproduced,
stored in a retrieval system, or transmitted, in any form or by any means,
electronic, mechanical, photocopying, recording, or otherwise,
without the prior permission of Oxford University Press.

Library of Congress Cataloging-in-Publication Data
Religious pluralism, globalization, and world politics /
edited by Thomas Banchoff.
    p. cm.
Includes bibliographical references and index.
ISBN-13: 978-0-19-532340-5; ISBN-13: 978-0-19-532341-2 (pbk.)
1. Religions—Relations. 2. Religious pluralism. 3. Globalization.
4. International relations. I. Banchoff, Thomas F., 1964–
BL410.R44 2008
201'.5—dc22   2008002473

9 8 7 6 5 4 3 2 1
Printed in the United States of America
on acid-free paper

Acknowledgments

Few issues are more important and less understood than the role of religion in world affairs. Religious diversity has long been a fact of life in national and international politics. But the eruption of religious issues and actors into the public sphere—a trend accelerated in the aftermath of September 11, 2001—caught many observers by surprise, scholars included. Religious pluralism that goes beyond mere diversity to encompass the interaction of religious communities in society and politics is deepening in the context of globalization. It is sparking new forms of conflict and collaboration at the intersection of the religious and the secular. And it is reframing old questions about religion's impact on peace and violence, democracy and human rights, and economic and social development—questions that will remain on the global agenda for decades to come.

This book brings together leading scholars across disciplines to address some of those questions. It grows out of the conference "The New Religious Pluralism in World Politics," held in March 2006 in Washington, D.C., and sponsored by the Berkley Center for Religion, Peace, and World Affairs at Georgetown University. The friendly and pointed exchanges at the conference, and the willingness of the participants to revise their papers substantially for publication, made this book possible. It is the second of two volumes, based on Berkley Center conferences, that explore the dynamics of religious pluralism in today's world. The first, *Democracy and the New Religious Pluralism* (Oxford University Press, 2007), focused on the transatlantic experience.

This exploration of religious pluralism, globalization, and world politics has benefited greatly from the invaluable criticisms and suggestions of many colleagues inside and outside Georgetown, including Liz Bucar, José Casanova, Thomas Farr, Michael Kessler, Katherine Marshall, Tulasi Srinivas, and Chris Vukicevich. Kyle Layman, Luis Felipe Mantilla, and Amy Vander Vliet provided indispensable editorial assistance in preparing the manuscript. Theo Calderara of Oxford University Press generously supported the project from start to finish.

This book is dedicated to the memory of Father Robert Drinan, S. J., a tireless human rights advocate during his years in Congress and later as a member of the Georgetown University Law Center faculty. Father Drinan was an inspirational presence at the March 2006 conference that gave rise to this volume.

Contents

Contributors

Kwame Anthony Appiah is the Laurance S. Rockefeller University Professor of Philosophy and the University Center for Human Values at Princeton University.

R. Scott Appleby is Professor of history and Director of the Joan B. Kroc Institute for International Peace Studies at the University of Notre Dame.

Thomas Banchoff is Associate Professor of government and Director of the Berkley Center for Religion, Peace, and World Affairs at Georgetown University.

Aaron P. Boesenecker is a doctoral candidate in government at Georgetown University.

Jean Bethke Elshtain is the Laura Spelman Rockefeller Professor of Social and Political Ethics at the University of Chicago Divinity School.

Katherine Marshall is a Senior Fellow and Visiting Associate Professor at the Berkley Center for Religion, Peace, and World Affairs at Georgetown University.

Pratap Bhanu Mehta is President and Chief Executive of the Centre for Policy Research, New Delhi.

Thomas Michel, S. J., is the Secretary of Interreligious Dialogue for the Society of Jesus in Rome.

Elizabeth H. Prodromou is Assistant Professor of international relations and a Research Associate of the Institute on Culture, Religion and World Affairs at Boston University.

Leslie Vinjamuri is Lecturer in international relations, Department of Politics and International Studies at the School of Oriental and African Studies, University of London.

John O. Voll is Professor of Islamic history and Associate Director of the Prince Alwaleed bin Talal Center for Muslim-Christian Understanding at Georgetown University.

John Witte Jr. is Jonas Robitscher Professor of Law and Ethics and Director of the Center for the Study of Law and Religion at Emory University.

Religious Pluralism, Globalization, and World Politics

I

Introduction: Religious Pluralism in World Affairs

Thomas Banchoff

To think religion and world politics is often to think violence. The attacks of September 11, 2001, suicide bombings in the Middle East, sectarian clashes in Kashmir, civil war in the Balkans, bloodshed in Nigeria and Indonesia—these are prominent associations. In these cases and others, links between religion and violence are not hard to find. Political commitments with divine sanction often brook no compromise. For fanatical religious minorities, violence for a higher cause has a ready-made justification. And members of the wider community who identify with the grievances of militants often lend their support, overt or tacit, to the use of force. Religion is never the sole cause of violence. It intersects in explosive ways with territorial disputes; unstable and oppressive institutions; economic and social inequalities; and ethnic, cultural, and linguistic divisions. But today as in previous eras, passionate religious identities and commitments have often served to exacerbate tensions and promote bloodshed.[1]

Less visible, but no less significant, is the peaceful engagement of religious communities in contemporary world affairs. At a declaratory level, leaders drawn from the world's leading religious traditions—Christian, Muslim, Jewish, Hindu, and Buddhist—have long endorsed ideals of peace, human dignity, equality, freedom, and solidarity. Today, more than at any time in history, exponents of these and other traditions are promoting conflict resolution, human rights, and economic and social development in practice—within national borders but also across them. The Good Friday agreement in Northern Ireland, the resolution of Mozambique's civil war, and support for the Millennium Development Goals—all provide examples of transnational religious engagement, not in isolation but through interaction with other religious and secular actors in state and society. Riding the wave of globalization, religious actors have deployed new communications technologies and invoked human rights norms to mobilize public support, reframe debates, and support winning political and policy coalitions. Peaceful engagement of this kind should not be confused with harmony. It can oppose different interests and ethics, generating competition and controversy. But it is nonviolent. Less likely to make the newspapers, it has a far-reaching, if underappreciated, impact.

This book examines the intersection of religious pluralism, globalization, and world politics from a variety of disciplinary and analytical perspectives. It brings together social and legal theorists, historians, political scientists, and practitioners to explore the contours of religious pluralism in world affairs across traditions, regions, and issue areas, including peacebuilding, transitional justice, economic development, and bioethics. Taken as a whole, the volume does not depict religion as inherently more peaceful than violent—either in theory or in practice. That long-running dispute will not be conclusively resolved one way or the other. Instead, the essays deepen our understanding of the constructive role played by religious actors in world affairs, in its various dimensions. The volume provides a broader overview of engagement in our post–September 11, 2001, world—one that can inform new, collaborative efforts to meet pressing global policy challenges.

The balance of this chapter sets out a working definition of religious pluralism in world affairs, discusses its relationship with globalization, and explores six of its related dimensions: fragile identity politics, strong ethical commitments, international-national-local linkages, interfaith and intrafaith dynamics, religious-secular interaction, and the centrality of the United States. The overview of these dimensions serves to introduce the individual essays, compare their arguments, and sketch the overall contours of religious pluralism, globalization, and world politics in the contemporary era.

Religious Pluralism in World Politics

"Religious pluralism" is a contested concept across national, political, and disciplinary contexts. In theology the term often suggests harmony, convergence, or compatibility across religious traditions—in opposition to religious exclusivism. In sociology, pluralism can refer to the diversity of different religious traditions within the same social or cultural space.[2] As deployed in this volume, religious pluralism refers to patterns of peaceful interaction among diverse religious actors—individuals and groups who identify with and act out of particular religious traditions. Religious pluralism, in this definition, does not posit different religions on diverse paths to the same truth, as it does in some theological contexts. And the term implies more than the social and religious diversity explored in much sociological analysis. Religious pluralism is the interaction of religious actors with one another and with the society and the state around concrete cultural, social, economic, and political agendas. It denotes a politics that joins diverse communities with overlapping but distinctive ethics and interests. Such interaction may involve sharp conflict. But religious pluralism, as defined here, ends where violence begins.

This conception of religious pluralism maps best onto national democratic contexts. Where state institutions guarantee individual freedoms, majority rule, and constitutional order, the interaction of diverse religious communities is more likely to remain peaceful. Recourse to the sword to settle disputes is effectively outlawed. Religious conflict can be fierce and has the potential to erupt into civil disorder that threatens democratic stability. But day to day, a national democratic and constitutional order provides a framework for peaceful interaction within and across religious and secular communities. This has been the dominant experience of North Atlantic and other democracies for decades. Today, greater religious diversity and the growth of Muslim communities in Western Europe, in particular, are generating divisive controversies about how best to combine political and social cohesion with respect for minority rights. But with few exceptions, those controversies are playing out peacefully, through the push and pull of democratic politics.[3]

World politics is different. The absence of a sovereign authority at a global level makes religious pluralism a more fragile construct. Neither the United Nations nor the United States nor any group of states can impose the equivalent of a constitutional order or maintain a monopoly on the legitimate use of violence. Al-Qaeda's emergence and survival over the past decade make that clear. The weakness of many states and the persistence of autocracy across the globe also undermine religious pluralism in world affairs. Failed states cannot provide effective protection for religious minorities or transnational religious communities. Nor can they prevent religious differences from spilling over into bloodshed—as is evident in Iraq, Somalia, and elsewhere. At the same time, nondemocracies, while they may keep the peace and afford minorities some protection, will often favor some religious communities over others (as in Iran) or marginalize religion in the public sphere (as in China). Political conditions across much of the globe militate against national religious mobilization or transnational religious activity. Religious pluralism might therefore appear a limited phenomenon in world politics, localized within established democracies—and challenged even there.

To see religious pluralism only within the democratic national context is to miss one of the most salient trends of the last two decades—the emergence of more agile transnational religious actors, including a global papacy, Evangelical networks, the Jewish Diaspora, and a panoply of organizations with roots in the Muslim world.[4] Faith communities, which claim about four-fifths of humanity as adherents, have attained more organizational strength and transnational reach since the 1980s. They have not displaced secular states and international institutions as key actors in world affairs—nor are they likely to in the foreseeable future—but they have begun to interact more with one another and with secular forces within state and society across multiple issues.

For example, the Roman Catholic Church, the world's largest religious organization, with more than 1 billion members, has become a much more visible actor on the world stage since the 1980s. Long international in scope, the Church first took up global issues of peace, human rights, and development with the Second Vatican Council (1962–1965). Under John Paul II (1978–2005), the papacy emerged as a force in international affairs, through personal diplomacy, clearly articulated policy positions, and growing engagement within UN institutions. Far from a monolith, the Church is home to a variety of religious orders (including the Society of Jesus) and lay organizations (including the Rome-based Community of Sant'Egidio) that have been particularly prominent in pursuit of peace and social justice agendas in Africa, Latin America, and around the world.[5]

Protestant and Orthodox churches, with combined adherents of just under 1 billion, have also increased their involvement in world affairs in recent decades. The World Council of Churches, founded in 1948, has grown in terms of membership to some 340 churches and has expanded its cultural, social, and political agenda and policy interaction with governments and international organizations. Evangelical Christianity has grown sharply in the developed and developing worlds. Widely associated with missionary activities and traditional values, Evangelical congregations have increasingly carved out policy stances on issues ranging from HIV/AIDS to global poverty to global warming. Since the fall of the Soviet empire in 1989–1991, Orthodox churches, too, have emerged as more independent political actors. Based in Russia, Eastern Europe, and the Middle East and linked to global diasporas, they have increased in size, strength, and visibility around issues including education and minority rights.[6]

Islam, the world's second-largest religion, with about 1.3 billion adherents, has also emerged as a more powerful transnational force. Islamic militants, and Al-Qaeda in particular, have commanded the most media attention.

But the vast majority of Muslims and Muslim organizations are committed to peaceful engagement in social and political affairs—and increasingly organized in their pursuit. The last two decades have seen the expansion of Muslim social movements and nongovernmental organizations (NGOs) and a much higher profile for the Organization of the Islamic Conference (OIC). The OIC, founded in 1969, brings together fifty-seven countries with majority or significant minority Muslim populations to articulate shared positions on a range of global issues including, but going well beyond, ongoing conflicts in the Middle East. While Islam lacks any strong centralizing authority, and the OIC itself is not a religious actor in any narrow sense, Muslim voices have grown more prominent in world politics since the end of the cold war.[7]

The third of the Abrahamic traditions, Judaism, while small by comparison—a community of about 15 million worldwide—has a vital international role grounded in the strength of the state of Israel and the importance of the Jewish Diaspora. A regional power in military-territorial conflict with its neighbors, Israel is both a besieged Jewish state and a successful pluralist democracy. The Jewish Diaspora, anchored in the United States and Western Europe, has a robust transnational identity and organizational expressions, including the World Jewish Congress. It provides financial and political support for Israel and broader causes, including the Middle East peace, global economic and social development, and the struggle against anti-Semitism and all forms of racism.[8]

Hinduism, the world's third-largest religious community, while less geographically dispersed, is also a growing force in world affairs. With perhaps 800 million adherents, Hinduism is the least monolithic and most internally diverse of the world's major religious traditions. There is nothing even approaching an actor or organization that can speak for a tradition marked by a rich multitude of beliefs and practices. At the same time, however, Hindu nationalism—the political identification of Hinduism with the Indian nation—has been on the rise since the 1980s. While the media have focused on outbreaks of Hindu-Muslim violence, including the 2002 riots in Gujarat, the growth of the Hindu nationalist parties and civic associations and the rise of pan-Islamic sentiment among the country's 150 million or so Muslims mark a deeper transformation of political culture in India, one with far-reaching transnational and international implications, given the size of the Indian diaspora and the country's emergence as a world power.[9]

Buddhism, with about 400 million adherents, is also an internally diverse tradition with few authoritative organizations. Concentrated in varied forms across a range of Asian and Southeast Asian countries, Buddhism has long been engaged in politics, as historical interactions between monks and monarchies in Cambodia, Thailand, Burma, and elsewhere attest. For much of the twentieth century, colonialism and its legacies, autocratic military rule, and Buddhism's own traditional concern with the enlightenment of the individual have limited political engagement around national and international issues. Over the last two decades, however, the global diplomacy of the Dalai Lama, the exiled spiritual leader of Tibetan Buddhism, and the "engaged Buddhism" of monks in Cambodia and Burma struggling for human rights and social justice have altered this picture. Transnational networks involving many Buddhists in North America and Europe have become more active around a host of global issues, ranging from the struggle for democracy in Asia to equitable social and economic development and climate change.[10]

This sketch of religious communities active in world affairs is far from comprehensive. Other traditions, including Sikhs and the Baha'i, play an important national and international role. Moreover, none of the five leading traditions outlined—the three Abrahamic faiths, Hinduism, and Buddhism—represents a single monolithic actor in world affairs, or anything approaching one. Particular religious actors should not be confused with whole religions that are internally diverse along lines of geography, class, race, ethnicity, and gender. With this caveat in mind, one can explore the increasing global role of religious actors, defined as individuals and groups who identify with and act out of religious traditions in the public sphere, nationally and internationally.

The Dual Impact of Globalization

What, if anything, is new about religious pluralism in world affairs? Religion has long had a transnational dimension. Major world religions have grown and changed as they have spread across borders, generating far-flung networks with varied regional and local expressions. The migration of Buddhism out of India and extended kinship ties within Judaism suggest there is nothing radically new about religion's transnational reach. Islam and Christianity, in particular, have long been global movements. During the Middle Ages and the early modern period, first Islam and then Christianity became an intercontinental force. Muslim expansion from the Middle East into North Africa and Europe and across much of South, Central, and Southeast Asia preceded the conquest of the New World and the spread of Christianity to the Americas, Africa, and parts of Asia centuries later. The frequent recourse to violence in this process of expansion and interaction, most notable in the initial Muslim conquests and the Crusades, might appear to draw a sharp line between religious dynamics in the past and religious pluralism today. In point of fact, the spread of religion by peaceful means, and the nonviolent coexistence of different traditions characterized much of the world over long stretches of time. Medieval Spain and the Ottoman empire, for example, were marked by significant periods of peaceful coexistence among Muslims, Jews, and Christians.

If pluralism defined as peaceful interaction is not new in world affairs, neither is its political dimension—interaction that engages state power and issues of governance. Religious beliefs and practices, embodying certain understandings of right human conduct, inevitably intersect with questions about how power should be organized and exercised justly. Church-state struggle in Christian Europe and secular-religious interaction in the Muslim world, South Asia, and China constitute historical legacies of transnational political engagement. "Religion and politics have been tied together from the beginning," Anthony Appiah reminds us in this volume. "Athens and Rome had state religions, cults of divinities with special importance for the city or the empire. Many places, from Pharaonic Egypt on, have had divine kingship. The major empires of Eurasia—Mongol, Mughal, Manchu, Roman, Ottoman, British—all took religion with them." These political-religious dynamics continued into the modern imperial era. During the nineteenth century, John Voll points out in his essay, transnational religious engagement was evident in "missionary activity and the influence of religious organizations on early international advocacy campaigns like the one to abolish slavery."

If contemporary international and political manifestations of religious pluralism are not completely unprecedented, they do mark a break with the post-1945 era. The growing salience of religion in international affairs contrasts sharply with the cold war's four decades of secular and ideological superpower competition. In retrospect one can see the beginning of a shift in the late 1970s, with the Iranian revolution, the prominence of Evangelicals in U.S. politics, and the onset of John Paul II's international papacy. With the collapse of the Soviet empire and the end of East-West ideological competition, transnational religious communities emerged more clearly as sources of identity and engagement in world affairs. The spread of Evangelical social and political movements in Latin America, Africa, and Asia attests to this dynamic, as do the rise in Muslim middle-class participation in politics and new crises at the intersection of the religious and the secular, such as the Muhammad cartoon controversy of early 2006 and reactions to Pope Benedict XVI's remarks on Islam later that year. The media and the academy have focused on the violent campaigns of Al-Qaeda, the U.S.-led counteroffensive, sectarian violence in Iraq, and the Israeli-Palestinian struggle. But the reemergence of religious actors in world politics is part of a broader, predominantly peaceful trend.

The return of religion is not simply a result of the collapse of the postwar order and its secular, ideological frame of reference. It does not simply take us back to an earlier era. While linked to long-established religious traditions, religious pluralism in world affairs is propelled forward by the contemporary dynamics of globalization. It is sometimes argued that globalization is neither new nor all-encompassing. By some measures, transnational flows of people, goods, and capital are comparable to the pre–World War I era. And by other measures, nation-states have gained, not lost, political and economic leverage in dealing with domestic and international forces.[11] But two dimensions of globalization are undeniably new: the near-instantaneous worldwide sharing of information through modern communications technology, and the global spread and institutionalization of the idea of universal human rights. One has connected and mobilized far-flung communities more effectively, while the other has enlarged the space for their cultural, social, and political engagement, both nationally and internationally.[12]

Since the 1980s the proliferation of telephone, fax, television, and Internet technologies has fostered the survival and growth of transnational religious networks and diaspora communities. With the papacy of John Paul II global media and personal diplomacy strengthened transnational Catholic identity and helped to unravel the Soviet empire in Eastern and Central Europe. Over the same period, radio and television were instrumental in the growth of Evangelical Christianity in Latin America, Africa, and Asia, and the associated spread of American-style individualism and consumer culture and a "Gospel of Prosperity." Global travel and communications have strengthened ties among Jews inside and outside Israel and increased support for the Jewish state in the United States. And in the Islamic context, the Internet has proved a particularly powerful medium in the creation and contestation of transnational identities. Within Islam, inexpensive and instantaneous communications are forging virtual communities in the absence of transnational, hierarchical structures of authority. Here, Al-Qaeda is one example of a broader trend that is dominated by nonviolent Muslim groups, including the Gülen movement explored by Thomas Michel in his chapter.[13]

New communications technologies not only enable the creation and sustenance of transnational religious communities, thereby sustaining a high degree of religious pluralism in world politics, but also foster an internal diversification of religious traditions. The individualization of religious—or, better, spiritual—identities, a trend parallel to the expansion of global consumer culture, is a striking development of recent decades. Suspicion of religious authority and formal institutions, evident in public opinion polls and in some declines in attendance at religious services, is on the rise.[14] The wavering strength of many mainline religious organizations, measured in terms of members and resources, is undeniable. At the same time, however, new and reformed religious communities are thriving—including Evangelical groups that build on an individualized ethos and Muslim organizations that provide an anchor for identity within a churning world. A loose amalgam of faith-inspired groups, aligned with but not identical to larger religious communities, is emerging to meet the demand to translate spiritual and ethical values into social and political action in areas such as poverty relief, the HIV/AIDS crisis, and environmental protection. The same communications technologies that advance transnational mobilization, then, are promoting a high level of internal diversity and the reformulation of religious identities and ethical commitments at a global level.

The geographic extension and mobilization of religious communities through communications technologies also deepen their interaction with one another—in society, culture, and politics. And much of that interaction is competitive. "The impact of globalization on religious pluralism is most evident in that the quest for religious recognition and competition among religious groups has become truly global," Pratap Mehta writes in this volume. "Transnational linkages of religious groups add to local competition and put a strain on local patterns of accommodation." John Witte argues in his essay that we are seeing a "new war for souls"—in the former Soviet Union, for example, where a revitalized Orthodoxy confronts Catholicism, Protestantism, and Islam; in Latin America, where an entrenched Catholic Church faces inroads from Evangelicals; and in parts of Africa and Asia, where Christian and Muslim missionaries compete.[15] This competition has a theological dimension; it is a confrontation among beliefs and practices. But it is also a political struggle, as different sides seek to mobilize state power, secure rights and resources for themselves, and restrict those of national and international rivals.

The existence of this (mainly) peaceful competition points up the salience of a second, legal-political dimension of globalization—the spread of democracy and the institutionalization of a global human rights regime. The conviction that all human beings possess an inherent dignity and equality, fundamental freedoms, and the right to democratic self-governance is more widespread today than at any time in history. It is evident at the level of global public opinion, where support for democracy and individual rights continues to grow. It finds expression in interfaith documents and initiatives, including the much-cited Declaration of the Parliament of the World's Religions (1993). And it is set down in international declarations and legal instruments endorsed by the vast majority of the world's governments, beginning with the Universal Declaration of Human Rights (1948). The international human rights regime, however fragmented and imperfect, creates a political space for the free exercise of religion, including the opportunity to organize and mobilize in the public sphere around policy issues.[16] Global norms of human dignity and human rights dovetail with the ethical commitments of majority or mainstream religious traditions. And they make it harder for governments to suppress or co-opt religious actors—local, national, and transnational. "The modern human rights revolution," John Witte points out in his essay, "has helped to catalyze a great awakening of religion around the globe." In regions now marked by democracy and human rights, "ancient faiths once driven underground by autocratic oppressors have sprung forth with new vigor."

The emergent global human rights regime should not be confused with a constitutional order. In the absence of a global sovereign, there is no monopoly on the legitimate use of violence and no way routinely to punish human rights violations on the national model. Legal instruments including the Universal Declaration of 1948, the International Covenant on Civil and Political Rights (1966), and the Declaration on the Elimination of All Forms of Intolerance and of Discrimination Based on Religion or Belief (1981) establish rights to have and manifest one's religion. But they bind only their signatories. Some Muslim-majority countries, including Saudi Arabia, have refused to endorse certain of them. And most include clauses that permit exceptions under certain circumstances, such as threats to public order. Still, the growing body of human rights law does have considerable moral, and therefore practical, force. Governments often feel constrained to abide by declarations and treaties endorsed by the international community. Accusations of violations are met with efforts to explain and justify state actions. To flout international law is to risk political isolation, which entails political costs. It is likely, for example, that hard-liners in Russia and India would pursue tougher policies against Christian missionaries in the absence of a significant, if still fragmentary and contested, global human rights regime.

More than the abstract endorsement of human rights, the global trend toward democracy has created greater leeway for religious communities in national and international affairs. Where rights to religious freedom and practice are not just articulated but set down in constitutions and laws backed by effective state power, religious actors have more freedom of maneuver. The wave of democratization in Latin America that began in the 1980s loosened ties between the Catholic hierarchy and government officials in many countries, creating larger political openings for Evangelicals. New democracies in Central and Eastern Europe—and a more precarious democracy in Russia—created space for indigenous and outside religious communities to strengthen their positions. In Turkey, democratization has gone hand in hand with the rise of a moderate Muslim party and its successful transition into government. Similar dynamics are evident in parts of Africa and Asia. And in the Arab Middle East, limited trends toward economic and political liberalization have enabled a growing educated, pious, and powerful middle class to engage more fully in civil society and public affairs. These trends are not universal. In Saudi Arabia, for example, non-Wahhabi Muslims face discrimination, and in Burma (Myanmar), the junta crushed the protests of Buddhist monks in late 2007. Globally, however, the pronounced trend toward democracy has enhanced opportunities for religious communities, both national and transnational, to organize and enter the public sphere.

Whether global levels of religiosity or spirituality are rising, declining, or steady in today's world is difficult, if not impossible, to determine. But the social and political expressions of religion have clearly increased overall, if unevenly, over the past several decades. Globalization's dual impact—through communications technologies and legal-political shifts—has facilitated the mobilization of religious communities, within and across countries, and their engagement at the level of society and the state. The essays in this volume explore those patterns of mobilization and engagement across regions, traditions, and issue areas. Together they point to six dimensions of religious pluralism in world affairs: fragile identity politics, strong ethical commitments, international-national-local linkages, interfaith and intrafaith dynamics, secular-religious interaction, and the centrality of the United States.

Fragile Identity Politics

Religious pluralism in world politics is an increasingly salient backdrop for national identity politics, defined as struggles over representation and recognition in multicultural contexts.[17] Historically, where one religion has dominated a nation-state—or when an equally dominant secularist ideology has taken its place, as in parts of Western Europe—religious pluralism has not always proved divisive. The majority tradition, religious or secular, has determined the rules of the game and imprinted the national identity, the dominant norms and narratives that bind citizens to the state and one another. Today, transnational religious activity, carried by globalization, can generate perceived threats to national identity overlaid with emotional passion. Global flows of people and ideas unsettle majority traditions and create space for political challenges by minority communities that invoke human rights. The presence of growing Muslim minorities in Denmark and the Netherlands, for example, has generated sustained controversies about national identity in both countries. The perceived threat posed by an immigrant and transnational religious community has become an axis of conflict, enflaming passions around critical events, including the murder of filmmaker Theo van Gogh by a Muslim extremist in

the Netherlands in November 2004 and the publication of Muhammad cartoons in Denmark a year later.

In his essay, Anthony Appiah asks why domestic and international political
disputes are so difficult to resolve once they have religious stakes. His answer
centers on the centrality of religious identity and its role in integrating other
aspects of personal identity, underwriting ethical commitments, and defining
the national community. When it is a salient identity marker, religion is difficult to sacrifice or compromise. The political explosiveness of religious identity
and national identity is heightened in a world where globalization is unsettling
the latter. "Nationality—its meaning for each citizen—is the result of cultural
work, not a natural and preexisting commonality," Appiah writes. This creates
"a place for the politics of national identity" in which it matters "very much
how the nation is conceived, including religiously." When the contestation of
national identity is inflected by religious questions, as is increasingly the case
in today's world, a divisive identity politics can result. "Once you want your
national identity to cohere with your religious identity," Appiah notes, "you will
aspire for its rituals to become national rituals, its morals to be embodied in
law, its gods to be honored in public ceremonial."

Mehta's exploration of the Indian case illustrates these dynamics. About
80 percent of the country's more than 1 billion citizens are classified as Hindus, but Hinduism itself is marked by incredible regional and ethnic diversity
that encompasses a significant global diaspora. The country is also home to the
third-largest Muslim population in the world (behind Indonesia and Pakistan)
and has significant Christian and other religious communities that are part of
wider global networks. The growth of Hindu nationalism, evident in the rise
of the Bharatiya Janata Party, is an assertion of a constructed Hindu national
identity against perceived threats, external and internal, including the rising
social and political engagement of a growing Muslim middle class, itself part
of a global trend. Tensions are most evident in ethnic and religious violence in
Kashmir on the Pakistani frontier and have flared up periodically, most recently
in Gujarat in 2002, where hundreds of Hindus and Muslims were killed in
communal bloodshed. India remains a success story—the world's largest democracy managing religious difference in the context of globalization—but its
religious pluralism goes hand in hand with a fragile identity politics.[18]

In their essays both Appiah and Mehta propose ways of managing religious pluralism. Neither suggests removing religion or religious claims from
the public sphere. That recommendation, associated with John Rawls and other
classic liberal theorists, flies in the face of the pervasive and inevitable intersection of religion and politics in today's world. Appiah's solution is to call for
the cultivation of a cosmopolitan ethos centered on the dignity and freedom

of all human beings. Such an ethos, he argues, is best cultivated not against but within religious traditions. Dialogue between cosmopolitan adherents of different communities—those who read their traditions as compatible with human dignity, human freedom, and respect for the dignity and freedom of others—is the best way to manage religious diversity and avoid violence. Mehta makes a compatible institutional recommendation; he calls for a clear separation of religious identity from political *representation*. "A political order can give space for religious freedom of individuals," he writes, "but if the political order is required to be representative of religious communities," polarization and paralysis are the likely result. In the interest of political stability under religious pluralism, groups should "give up the aspiration that a political order will represent *them*, qua religious groups in some respect." Mehta invokes the example of contemporary Iraq as a critical country wrestling with these issues.

Appiah and Mehta focus on the fragile politics of national identity. Jean Bethke Elshtain and John Witte, in their essays, address a related, and especially sensitive, issue at the intersection of religious pluralism and identity politics—international religious freedom and proselytism. The growth of missionary activity in the context of globalization, originating mainly in the United States and several other countries, including South Korea, and supported by worldwide communication networks, has sparked national, regional, and global reactions. "Beneath shiny constitutional veneers of religious freedom for all and unqualified ratification of international human rights instruments," Witte writes, "several countries of late passed firm new antiproselytism laws, cult registration requirements, tightened visa controls, and various other discriminatory restrictions on new or newly arrived religions." Anticonversion laws in Indian states directed against Southern Baptists, described by Mehta, are a prominent example, as are Russian regulations designed to protect the predominance of the Orthodox Church. Such conflicts between national and regional authorities, on the one hand, and transnational religious communities, on the other, are increasingly overlaid by international diplomacy. The U.S. International Religious Freedom Act of 1998, described by Elizabeth Prodromou in her essay, makes upholding religious liberty an avowed national foreign policy priority. Subsequent annual reports sponsored by the U.S. government have criticized China, Saudi Arabia, Russia, and other states for not living up to their obligations under international law—and often sparked critical and dismissive reactions.[19]

Where the exercise of religious freedom ends and inappropriate or illicit proselytism begins is a hotly contested international issue. Witte expresses overall support for the U.S. government position: "Religious expression inherent in proselytism is no more suspect than political, economic, artistic, or other forms of expression and should, at minimum, enjoy the same rights protection." But he also acknowledges the complexity of the issues raised by efforts at conversion and how, in some cases, they can threaten existing religious and political identities. International covenants reference not only the rights to freedom of expression but also rights to have and to hold one's own religious convictions. For Witte this encompasses the duty to "respect the religious dignity and autonomy of the other, and to expect the same respect for one's own dignity and autonomy." In light of these competing principles, he urges "all parties, especially foreign proselytizing groups, to negotiate and adopt voluntary codes of conduct of restraint and respect of the other." There is no legal basis or political imperative for the restriction of proselytism from sender countries, but transnational religious groups should recognize and respect anxieties in target countries, especially when they come in with superior material resources, and may be perceived as an extension of U.S. foreign policy. "Moratoria on proselytism might provide temporary relief," he concludes, "but moderation by proselytizers and proselytizees is the more enduring course."

Jean Bethke Elshtain is less concerned about negative national or international political fallout from proselytism. For her, freedom of religion and the freedom to proselytize are inseparable. For religious pluralism to be robust it must not just encompass religious diversity and interaction but also include efforts to knowingly and determinedly set out to change someone else's mind about something basic to his or her identity and self-definition. Drawing on Charles Taylor, Elshtain argues for a "deep pluralism" that includes the possibility of the transformation of the self and the other through dialogical encounter.[20] "Any strong articulation of a powerful religion or a powerful political position is going to make somebody somewhere uncomfortable," she maintains. Does opposition to proselytization "mean we are all reduced to bleating at one another across a vast distance?" For Elshtain that would be unacceptable. She acknowledges the power imbalances and mutual suspicions that accompany efforts to win converts through transnational activity. But she argues that to restrict proselytism, through mandatory or self-imposed measures, is to restrict free speech. Nothing should compromise open dialogue within and across traditions in a spirit of truth.

Religious pluralism, then, poses a double challenge for identity politics. Domestically, it can unsettle identification of the nation-state with the predominant religious or secular tradition. In the face of economic and cultural globalization—including penetration by new religious ideas and groups—majority traditions can strive for a closer identification of religious and national identity, with divisive political consequences. Internationally, states sometimes restrict transnational religious communities as perceived threats to national and local identities, effectively curtailing their presence and proselytizing activities. In the process they internationalize their national identity politics, with consequences for international diplomacy—particularly as the world's leading power, the United States, has made religious freedom an express foreign policy priority. These dynamics were illustrated in the 2006 controversy surrounding Abdul Rahman, a citizen of Afghanistan threatened with capital punishment for converting from Islam to Christianity. U.S. diplomatic pressure and judicial discretion ultimately led to Rahman's release and forced emigration. But the case revealed explosive tensions between Afghanistan's identity as an Islamic republic, on the one hand, and the principle of international religious freedom and its advancement by the United States, on the other.

Strong Ethical Commitments

A focus on identity politics highlights tensions at the intersection of religious pluralism and national and international politics—tensions that most often play out nonviolently through the push and pull of politics and diplomacy. Religion is more, however, than a powerful source of individual and collective identity. It also grounds strong ethical commitments that inform particular actions. For some radical minorities, open to the use of violence, the survival and strength of the community itself is the ethical good that trumps all others under all circumstances. But for the religious mainstream across the Abrahamic traditions, Hinduism, and Buddhism, other ethical commitments are also in play. The flourishing of the community is a positive good, but so are values of human freedom, equality, solidarity, and peace. Multiplying interfaith initiatives have pointed to ethical commonalities alongside theological differences, most notably the Declaration on a Global Ethic endorsed by participants in the Parliament of the World's Religions in 1993. Ethical and not just theological questions continue to divide religious traditions, as ongoing controversies about the rights of women and homosexuals attest, but some convergence across a range of overlapping ethical commitments is undeniable.[21]

In the context of religious pluralism and globalization, the common ground increasingly extends from discourse to practice. Exploiting global communications and national and local trends toward greater respect for democracy and human rights, communities across traditions are grappling with core issues of conflict, human rights, and economic and social development. Leaders as diverse as the American Evangelical Rick Warren, Anglican archbishop Desmond Tutu of South Africa, and Egyptian preacher Amr Khaled are mobilizing faith communities in the face of policy challenges at home and abroad. Personal agendas and organizational interests certainly shape such engagement. But one should not downplay the psychological force and political effectiveness of ethical commitments to peace, human dignity, and human equality grounded in particular religious traditions. Secular institutions such as national governments, the United Nations, and nonreligious NGOs share many of those same basic commitments. They often have more resources at their disposal and still play the predominant role in formulating and implementing policy. But they can rarely invoke embedded ethical traditions or appeal to particular communities as effectively as religious counterparts.

Conflict resolution is perhaps the most significant area of religious engagement. In his essay, Scott Appleby takes up the question of peacebuilding: the construction of a sustainable peace in societies divided or threatened by deadly conflict.[22] He examines three cases spanning three religious traditions and three parts of the world: the Catholic lay movement of Sant'Egidio's engagement in Africa; Buddhist activism in support of human rights in Cambodia; and religious engagement in both Sunni and Shiite Muslims across the war-torn Middle East. An exploration of these cases points to the central role of core ethical convictions in driving the pursuit of peace. The experience of several decades, Appleby argues, shows that religious peacebuilding works through the agency of long-term actors dedicated to the (re)construction of civil society and the strengthening of relationships across ethnic and religious boundaries. Religious groups have also grown more adept at collaborating with secular actors—international organizations, governments, and NGOs—in advancing a peacebuilding agenda.

In their essay, Leslie Vinjamuri and Aaron Boesenecker take up a related issue at the intersection of peace and human rights: the achievement of transitional justice. Truth commissions, war crime trials, lustration, and amnesty are all strategies that states have pursued following regime transitions and civil wars.[23] Religious communities, local, national, and international, have been key players in efforts to break with an oppressive and violent past, in countries ranging from South Africa to East Timor. One distinguishing characteristic of such engagement has been a particular conception of justice anchored in religious ethics, in particular the emphasis placed on forgiveness and reconciliation. Differences in religious and secular approaches to transitional justice should not be overdrawn, Vinjamuri and Boesenecker argue. But a focus on dialogue and restorative justice—alongside and, in some cases in place of, traditional ways to punish evildoers—is a proven way to heal wounds in the wake of some divisive civil conflicts.

Thomas Michel, in his essay, draws our attention to the peacebuilding resources in the Muslim tradition, what he refers to as "Qur'anic pacifism." Most media attention has centered on the activities of a violent Muslim minority; larger Islamic movements, dedicated to the principle of nonviolence, have garnered much less of the spotlight. Michel examines three such movements in detail—their historical origins, ethical commitments, and social and political practices. Two of the movements, centered around the teachings of Said Nursi and Fethullah Gülen, have emphasized the importance of education, dialogue, and service to the poor as imperatives in a modern, globalizing world. A third movement, the Asian Muslim Action Network (AMAN), pools resources and expertise across a range of local and national partners in the region and supports concrete educational and development initiatives, as well as efforts to monitor human rights across East, South, and Southeast Asia. "Precisely because such transnational movements unequivocally and emphatically reject and condemn violence and even incline toward a radical Qur'anic pacifism," Michel argues, "they tend to be overlooked in analyses of contemporary Islamic currents of thought, organization, and activity."

In her essay, Katherine Marshall focuses on religious involvement in the world of economic and social development. Here the large faith-inspired development organizations, including Catholic Caritas International, Protestant World Vision, and Islamic Relief, have long combined an ethical commitment to serve the poor and disadvantaged with transnational activities. Churches and Islamic charities, and other religious networks, have sustained networks of schools and hospitals. The past two decades have seen two new trends. The first is greater breadth of participation. In the context of globalization, more and more religious groups anchored at the local and national level are now active internationally. The catalyst is often a particular disaster that triggers relief efforts, such as the tsunami of 2004 or the Pakistan earthquake of 2005. The second trend concerns the scope of engagement. Faith-inspired groups are increasingly moving beyond humanitarian relief, education, and the provision of health care into new issue areas traditionally dominated by secular actors and organizations, such as women's rights, human trafficking, the HIV/AIDS crisis, and global warming.[24]

It is difficult to generalize about distinctive characteristics of religious actors in world affairs in the context of peacebuilding, human rights, and development. They are marked by tremendous diversity in terms of size and approach to the translation of ethical commitments into action. One pattern that emerges across the essays is that of relatively low levels of formal organization. In general, religious groups have fewer administrative resources at their disposal than states and international organizations. With exceptions that include the Catholic Church and major faith-inspired development agencies, religious groups lack extensive transnational bureaucracies and chains of command. In such circumstances, the strength of collective identity and the depth of ethical commitments can help to hold together far-flung communities.

Michel makes this point in his analysis of the Nursi and Gülen movements, which originated in Turkey and now encompass international networks with millions of members marked by common vision and shared fields of activities, but no central organization. The World Jewish Congress (WJC), mentioned by Vinjamuri and Boesenecker in their essay, provides another example. Founded in 1936, the WJC represents Jewish communities in almost 100 countries. Organizational ties and shared resources buttress its support for Israel and other policy agendas, but a shared Jewish religious and cultural identity, the historical legacy of the Holocaust, and an ethical commitment to human dignity and equality grounded in tradition are also keys to the WJC's global reach and policy effectiveness.

Ethical commitments anchored in religious traditions not only sustain communities across space, sometimes compensating for a lack of high levels of formal organization. They can also sustain long-term strategies around issues of peacebuilding, human rights, and development. Where ethical commitments constitutive of collective identity inform policy, that policy can be easier to maintain in the face of short-term setbacks. Said Nursi's commitment to nonviolence and dialogue amid the hostility of Atatürk's secular regime in Turkey provides an example of steadfastness in the face of adversity. The patient growth of the Fe y Alegría program of Jesuit support for primary education in poor Latin American communities, described by Marshall, is another. In their survey of transitional justice, Vinjamuri and Boesenecker argue that the depth of identity and shared commitment to ethical principles often informs "inclusiveness, community involvement, and long-term commitment" and an "ability to sustain engagement on a personal and spiritual level." Attention to long-term processes of reconciliation, they argue, has become a "hallmark of religious actors engaged in transitional justice."

If religious engagement in world affairs is growing, and ethical commitments serve to cement transnational efforts and maintain involvement over time, why have religious communities not had more of an impact on global policy agendas? A first, obvious reason has to do with competitive dynamics— Witte's "war for souls." Religious communities struggling for adherents, and against one another, in Africa, Latin America, or elsewhere, have less energy and resources to devote to peaceful engagement with social, economic, and political problems. And where they combine such engagement with proselytism— or are perceived to be doing so—they can limit their own impact. When in 2003 Franklin Graham's Samaritan's Purse organization distributed care packages to suffering Iraqi families along with material on salvation through Jesus Christ, he was roundly criticized in the media of Muslim-majority countries— and in the United States. And Saudi-based religious charities that support a network of schools, including the Al Haramain Islamic Foundation, have been accused by the U.S. government and others of spreading a hateful, anti-Western and anti-Semitic strain of Islam.

There is another reason for this limited impact of religious actors: their local center of gravity. In the context of peacebuilding, Appleby points out that local religious leaders often lack the practical expertise of secular counterparts and, just as significantly, often do not have the time or the inclination to acquire it. The core work of most religious organizations is pastoral—tending to the spiritual and material needs of their adherents. Here, demand almost always exceeds supply, leaving limited energies for activities external to the community, including support for broader national and international initiatives. In some cases, a failure to move beyond the local, Vinjamuri and Boesenecker point out in their essay, is one reason why the work of religious actors on transitional justice has gained relatively little attention from secular groups, the media, or the academy. The next section explores the intersection of local, national, and international dynamics as both a catalyst and a constraint on religious actors in world affairs.

International-National-Local Linkages

Even amid globalization, linkages between the local and the international are mediated at the national level. States remain the key actors in world affairs—as a locus of national identity and political legitimacy and a frame for civil society, including religion. As the same time, however, as John Voll points out in his essay, "Globalization has challenged the familiar national/international polarity by transforming relationships between what were considered 'global' and 'local' aspects of politics, culture, and society." Members of the same religious community, anchored in different parts of the world, have greater capacity to increase their cultural, social, and economic links with one another and with other religious and secular partners in other parts of the world. They can jump beyond the local—a pattern evident in the global reach of the Community of Sant'Egidio in Rome, the National Cathedral in Washington, D.C., and Al-Azhar University in Cairo. Efforts to reach out to global networks within a tradition or to extend influence and activity to other parts of the world are often constrained by a preoccupation with local concerns, by limited resources, and by national laws and regulations at home and abroad. But examples of local-national-international uplinks are plentiful.

Linkages also run from the international to the national and local level, as governments, international organizations, and transnational religious actors look for allies to mobilize resources, gather knowledge, and implement policies. Local religious actors embedded within communities can often draw on a reservoir of trust not available to secular actors. Because religion typically cuts across class, ethnic, generational, and cultural divisions, religious leaders can sometimes serve an important, if informal, representative function. "The social location and cultural power of religious leaders," Appleby notes, "make them potentially critical players in any effort to build a sustainable peace." Vinjamuri and Boesenecker acknowledge the importance of trust and networks but also underscore the local knowledge that makes religious groups valued partners for national and international actors. Local actors, they argue, "often possess specific characteristics that allow them to mobilize support for transitional justice strategies, including intimate knowledge of language and culture, access to firsthand information, political expertise, and long-term vision."

Specific cases outlined in the volume illustrate the dynamics of links up from and down to the local level. Marshall's essay examines the Aga Khan Foundation's support of preschools in Tanzania and its successful efforts to apply international educational standards across varied local conditions. The Fe y Alegría educational network reaches more than a million people across sixteen Latin American countries and emphasizes the Jesuit ideal of ethical leadership in service to the wider community. Marshall also mentions Jubilee 2000, an effort to advocate for debt forgiveness for poor countries grounded in religious ethics that began at the local level, morphed into a global network of like-minded religious and secular activists, and ultimately impacted governments and international institutions. Another of her examples, the work of the World Faiths Development Dialogue, points to efforts of national and international faith leaders, in conjunction with the World Bank, to reach down to and support local economic and social development agendas in conjunction with the United Nation's Millennium Development Goals.

The global engagement of religious communities, evident in complex international-national-local linkages, does not leave their internal structures untouched. Religious identity can serve as a powerful bond amid the vicissitudes of globalization—a bond reinforced by ethical commitments embedded within a particular tradition. At the same time, the spread of individualism—a cultural thrust of globalization—encourages religious adherents to exercise freedom in choosing and defining their religious identity. The individualist ethos does not necessarily undermine religion or spirituality, but it does undercut established religious authorities. A local imam, the Pope, and the Archbishop of Canterbury—all must compete more than ever within traditions for loyal followers exposed to new religious ideas, practices, and actors, through an admixture of global communications and transnational activities. Within the Church, as Appleby points out, "Catholics publicly and vehemently oppose other Catholics over everything from birth control to liberation theology and armed resistance to political oppression and human rights abuses." And the Archbishop of Canterbury, the head of the global Anglican Communion, has recently confronted a diverse community sharply divided on homosexuality and by transnational alliances of conservative and progressive forces.

Of these three examples, the local imam is perhaps in the most dynamic position. Islam does not have a clearly defined clerical leadership. Adherence to the Qur'an, the Sunna, and the Sharia is common to the Sunni and Shia communities, but it allows for a range of religious expressions, ranging from mystical Sufism to puritanical Wahabbism. For Islam, globalization means the further decentralization of an already decentralized religious tradition. The multiplication of new ideas and new leaders, buttressed by the Internet and other communications technologies, has led to new, unstable authority structures linking individuals and religious leaders locally, nationally, and internationally. Efforts to define Islam in Europe are a potent example of this trend. Tariq Ramadan, a Swiss citizen of Egyptian descent who teaches at Oxford University, has emerged as a very influential exponent of an Islam that embraces a centuries-old tradition, on the one hand, and contemporary norms of freedom, equality, and rule of law, on the other. Unbound by any local, national, or international religious authority, Ramadan articulates an Islam that endorses religious pluralism in a democratic context—provoking criticism from those, within and outside the Muslim fold, for whom Islam and democracy are incompatible.[25]

Ironically, as Voll points out in his essay, the rise of religious pluralism amid globalization has also strengthened the hand of Muslim leaders such as Osama Bin Laden, intent on destroying pluralism altogether. Al-Qaeda preaches peace but glorifies violence. It claims to be acting in self-defense against the imperialist encroachments of the West but endorses suicide bombing—in violation of long-standing Muslim teaching. Bin Laden's view that violent jihad is an obligation on individual believers isolates him from leading Muslim scholars and jurists. Still, he has been able to gather and hold a sizable following, through dramatic actions, but also through the very same communications technologies that drive religious pluralism in world affairs. While hostile to non-Muslim traditions, both religious and secular, Osama Bin Laden and his lieutenants embrace and exploit the global diversity *within* Islam. Mehta echoes Voll's argument: "If Al-Qaeda calls into question the authority of the sovereign state, it equally calls into question any conception of religious authority."

International-national-local linkages, then, not only empower religious communities but also can dilute their authority structures and undermine them internally. Although they are increasingly influential actors in world affairs, religious communities are not about to displace states as a repository of both collective identity and political authority. Nation-states, not the international community, remain the primary locus of organization for religious communities—including those, like the Muslim *umma* and the Catholic Church, whose self-image is transnational. Two of the largest Muslim organizations in the world, Voll points out, are national in orientation: Indonesia's Muhammadiyya (founded in 1912) and Nahdatul Ulama (founded in 1926). The Muslim Brotherhood, sometimes viewed as a prototypical global network, remains predominantly organized at the national level in Egypt, Jordan, and elsewhere. Even the Catholic Church has powerful national forms of organization. National Bishops Conferences established in the wake of Vatican II have partially succeeded in maintaining a degree of autonomy vis-à-vis Rome.

Of the essays in the volume, Thomas Banchoff's exploration of the global politics of cloning provides the clearest example of the continued primacy of states and national identities in the context of religious pluralism. Scientific and bioethical questions, by definition, have a universal and transnational impetus. Scientific knowledge flows across borders, and basic questions about the dignity and protection of human life are a universal concern. In the case of the struggle in the UN from 2001 to 2005 over whether to ban human cloning, however, arguments from national interest trumped ethical commitments embedded in diverse religious and secular traditions. In the years before the UN took up the issue, religious communities staked out positions on stem cell and cloning research at the national level and began to articulate them in international forums. Within the UN context, the Catholic Church and the administration of George W. Bush, committed to a ban on both reproductive and therapeutic cloning, could not win the support of the Muslim-majority countries represented by the OIC. But they also ran up against arguments from national interest articulated by secular West European countries and scientific powers in Asia. Ultimately it was an insistence on national sovereignty—on a country's right to decide sensitive ethical questions for itself—that carried the day. Religion was able to inflect policy in different ways, but more at the national than at the international level.

Interfaith and Intrafaith Dynamics

As religious traditions mobilize more globally, within and across nation-states, they interact increasingly with one another. The result is a complex mix of competitive and cooperative dynamics. Over the past two decades, a sharpened struggle for adherents and resources has emerged alongside interreligious dialogue designed to find common ground. The struggle contributes to fragile national identity politics and stokes international controversy. But what of interreligious dialogue? The largest international gathering in recent memory was the Parliament of the World's Religions of 1993, convened a century after the first such parliament was held at the Chicago world's fair. Thousands of representatives and adherents of the world's diverse faith traditions convened to explore common ground and discuss world affairs, an exercise repeated on a somewhat smaller scale in Cape Town (1999) and Barcelona (2004). Other significant gatherings include the Assemblies of the World Conference of Religions for Peace and Sant'Egidio's International Prayer for Peace, which traces its origins back to a multifaith gathering hosted by John Paul II in Assisi in 1986. The gathering of religious leaders at the UN in September 2000 to mark the turn of the millennium was a further important milestone.

The essays in this volume point beyond interfaith dialogue to interfaith interaction around global policy challenges. The call for dialogue in the Nursi and Gülen movements that Michel describes goes beyond abstract commitments; it finds expression in school curricula and educational projects in both Muslim-majority and non-Muslim-majority countries that emphasize tolerance and mutual respect. Transitional justice after civil conflict or repressive regimes offers another occasion for concrete interfaith collaboration. Vinjamuri and Boesenecker provide the example of the truth and reconciliation process in South Africa. Interfaith work joining traditional African insights into shared humanity with Christian perspectives on forgiveness enabled a choice against what Archbishop Tutu called "justice with ashes" and for "amnesty with the possibility of continuing survival for all of us." The World Faiths Development Dialogue described by Marshall is aimed precisely at the mobilization of faith communities around concrete development challenges. Appleby gives the concrete example of Muslim and Catholic leaders cooperating in the context of the UN Population Summit held in Cairo in 1994, and again during the UN World Conference on Women held in Beijing the following year. Here, shared ethical commitments solidified a conservative alliance in opposition to women's reproductive rights favored by progressive forces, both religious and secular.

As the Cairo and Beijing examples make clear, interfaith interaction should not be equated with cooperation. Conflicting interests, ethics, and identities can divide traditions internally and from one another. And sensitive issues ranging from abortion and female circumcision to capital punishment and global warming can and do generate crosscutting alliances of religious and secular forces. Contemporary world politics, Appleby points out, "might feature Catholics, Mormons, Jews, Muslims, agnostics, and atheists forming an ethical alliance against a rival bloc of Catholics, Mormons, Jews, Muslims, agnostics, and atheists." In the case explored by Banchoff, the alliance forged by the Vatican and Muslim-majority countries in the mid-1990s fragmented on the issues of cloning and stem cell research. Here, efforts to forge common ground came up against irreducible differences in moral theology with deep roots in opposing traditions—the Catholic view that the embryo should be treated as a person from conception, and the Muslim view that full humanity sets in weeks later. Both traditions were home to different interpretations of the cloning issue, creating some space for interfaith work for or against the projected UN ban. But dominant positions within each tradition did impose some constraints.

As the cloning example illustrates, patterns of scripture, tradition, and ethical reflection internal to religious communities can inform different approaches to global policy challenges. The key problem is how to keep the negotiation of difference, and the conflict it entails, from breaking down into discord and violence. For Appiah, keeping the negotiation of difference peaceful requires the cultivation of cosmopolitanism—an openness to other traditions and what they can teach us. He suggests that "decent, respectful engagement" with the cosmpolitans of a given tradition can "help them in their struggle to bring more of their coreligionists to the side of toleration, just as their conversation strengthens our own search for modes of productive cohabitation." Ultimately, however, the course of dialogue *within* traditions between proponents and opponents of intolerance and violence may be decisive. Appleby cites Khaled Abou El Fadl, for whom "the burden and blessing of sustaining that moral trajectory—of accentuating the Qur'anic message of tolerance and openness to the other—falls squarely on the shoulders of contemporary Muslim interpreters of the tradition."[26] A parallel burden falls on leaders and interpreters of other traditions, whether Christian or Jewish, Hindu or Buddhist.

Religious-Secular Interaction

Interfaith and intrafaith debates do shape religious engagement in world affairs. But religious-secular interaction is probably more important. Secular actors tend to set the global agenda. Relations among states, international institutions, markets, and corporations—almost exclusively nonreligious actors—determine the overall direction of world politics. The main lines of conflict and cooperation within and across them provide the context for religious involvement in the public sphere. The U.S.-led invasion of Iraq and the unresolved Israeli-Palestinian conflict have an adverse impact on Christian-Muslim-Jewish collaboration on peace, human rights, and development agendas. And the failure of the World Trade Organization to achieve breakthroughs on agricultural subsidies and tariff schedules that impede international trade adversely affects efforts to build coalitions between religious organizations in the global North and South. Struggles for power and wealth inflect the course of religious pluralism in world politics.

Within this broader constellation, it is hardly surprising that most religious organizations engage other faith traditions far less than they do secular actors ranging from local governments and civil associations through international organizations. Secular-religious interaction encompasses efforts to win resources and protection from government authorities. But it also includes collaboration across multiple issue areas. In Cambodia, Appleby points out, Buddhist monks worked with secular NGOs with expertise in organizing peaceful movements for social and political change. Appleby notes that such partnerships pool expertise but also can support political coalitions for policy change. Marshall's essay also includes several examples of positive religious-secular cooperation. The World Faiths Development Dialogue (WFDD) has served both as a forum for religious leaders and as a partner for the World Bank, which was dedicated, under its president, James Wolfensohn, to deeper interaction with faith communities around its poverty reduction agenda.

Religious-secular collaboration in these cases and others is marked by two kinds of tension. One might be termed "cultural suspicion"—anxiety among religious groups about secular organizations, and vice versa, based on their very different core identities and beliefs. Appleby notes that Cambodian monks marching for democracy and justice were initially averse to accepting the secular support that eventually contributed so much to their success. The mixed record of the WFDD–World Bank partnership in practice derives in part from a clash of cultures: the prevalent view of religion, among World Bank officials, as irrational, parochial, and therefore dangerous, and hostility in some religious circles toward a perceived technocratic, pro-market bias within global economic and financial institutions. Such a culture clash can also carry over into different strategies and tactics. Tensions between forgiveness and retribution in the context of transitional justice provide an example. "Strategies pursued especially by religious capacity-builders," Vinjamuri and Boesenecker point out, have "provided a significant counterweight to the legalism embraced by many large international human rights organizations."

Related religious-secular tension is sometimes also manifest at the institutional level. As noted previously, religious communities often lack the formal organization of governments and established secular NGOs. They tend to rely more on diffuse identities and shared ethical commitments to mobilize members for action. As a result, when it comes to following through on particular initiatives, such groups do not always have the organizational means or specialized knowledge necessary to be effective partners on human rights and development issues. Efforts to increase professionalism can improve the prospects for effective collaboration with secular actors in practice. Vinjamuri and Boesenecker outline the efforts of the Mennonite Central Committee—one of the best-organized religious peacebuilding organizations—to build institutional capacity in Latin America through the systematic training of local actors over time.[27] Marshall notes another success story, the collaboration of the World Bank and Sant'Egidio to improve the treatment of HIV/AIDS in three African countries. Here high levels of professionalism on both sides helped to defuse religious-secular tensions—cultural suspicions that a Catholic group might push treatment to the exclusion of prevention, and an institutional concern about its ability to implement programs on the ground.

The future of religious-secular interaction will depend in no small part on how these cultural and institutional tensions are negotiated across traditions, regions, and issue areas. Much will turn on whether religious organizations develop a pragmatic problem-solving ethos that does not foreground theological claims or proselytism, and on the development of the organizational capacity and professional skill set to implement particular programs. Here, the Mennonite Central Council, Sant'Egidio, World Vision, and other established groups provide a model. Another key issue is whether secular actors and institutions can abandon views of religion as a purely private affair or as a necessarily divisive and destructive force, and acknowledge its powerful and productive role across a range of policy challenges, including human rights and economic and social development. Religious-secular collaboration is no substitute for governance in the public interest, at the level of states or international institutions. In the light of growing religious pluralism in world politics, and the passions it can enflame, it is critical that the exercise of public authority be oriented by concern for the common good. At the same time, however, where religion enters the public sphere in a significant way, only political authorities that reach out to religious communities and tap their ethical commitments and enthusiasm will be able to build sustainable coalitions and govern effectively.

The Centrality of the United States

This picture of the new international constellation is incomplete in one major respect—it does not acknowledge the vast power asymmetries that frame and inform the intersection of religious pluralism, globalization, and world politics. States remain the most important actors in world politics, and the United States towers above the rest in terms of its economic and security influence.[28]

The fact that the United States is a Christian-majority country with a significant Jewish community has a global impact. For while one might be able to distinguish between the United States and Christianity (or the Judeo-Christian) at an analytical level, the juxtaposition and interpenetration of material power and religious tradition inflect world politics at the level of perceptions. Most citizens in Muslim-majority countries, for example, view the United States as a Christian nation. Many further view Christian relief and development organizations as extensions of U.S. power—even when their activities have no clear link back to U.S. national interests. (The lens works in reverse as well. Citizens in the United States and Europe tend to view the foreign policies of Pakistan and Egypt, not to mention Saudi Arabia and Iran, through a religious lens. Perhaps because religious identity is foundational for so many, it becomes a handy category for analyzing interstate affairs, whether it maps on to reality or not.)

By its sheer economic, political, and military weight, the United States does multiply the influence of Christianity and Judaism as forces in world affairs. This happens at the level of civil society, where Protestant missionary efforts have been centered for more than a century; where the Catholic Church, which accounts for about a fifth of the U.S. population, has a disproportionate influence on the evolution of the global Catholic community; and through the national Jewish community, which provides much of the leadership for its international counterpart. Increasingly, as Elizabeth Prodromou argues in her essay, the intersection of religion and American power is evident not just at the level of society and its transnational engagement, but at the level of government and policy. Under the presidency of George W. Bush, an Evangelical, religious identities and ethical commitments had a significant impact on U.S. foreign policy—and an even greater impact on perceptions of that policy abroad.

Prodromou discusses two key historical junctures in U.S. policy: the International Religious Freedom Act of 1998 and the attacks of September 11, 2001. With the collapse of the Soviet empire in 1989–1991 and the acceleration of globalization, religious mobilization in U.S. politics coincided with heightened awareness of religious persecution across many countries, and the Sudan in the particular. Political entrepreneurs put together a powerful, multifaith, religious-secular, and bipartisan coalition to secure the passage of the 1998 legislation. Religion moved up the U.S. foreign policy agenda, even if it did not play a central role in overall U.S. diplomacy around the world.[29] The attacks of September 11, 2001, and the U.S.-led invasion of Afghanistan and then Iraq reinforced this religious turn. The struggle against Islamic radicalism—what Bush, starting in 2004, termed "Islamofascism"—became both a foreign policy priority and a rallying cry in U.S. domestic politics. The worldwide perception of a religious impetus in U.S. foreign policy was reinforced by Bush's injudicious use of the term "crusade" and multiple references to the divine as an ally in U.S. efforts to rid the world of evil. One result of this trend, as John Voll reminds us, was erosion of U.S. cultural influence and an increase in the "soft power" of Osama Bin Laden and other radicals, that is, their ability to persuade others to join their cause.[30]

Overall, U.S. domestic politics and foreign policy under Bush have shaped religious pluralism in world politics along multiple dimensions. Identity politics in the United States, already fragile in the context of the multiculturalism debates and culture wars of the 1980s and 1990s, has grown more fractious in the wake of September 11, 2001. Rhetoric about the United States as a Christian or a Judeo-Christian nation under siege by the forces of secularism, on the one hand, and by Islam, on the other, punctuates American politics. And the Muslim minority, 1 to 2 percent of the population, has faced growing harassment and discrimination. In the new millennium U.S.-based religious groups are at the center of international-national-local linkages that support both missionary activity and transnational mobilization around global challenges such as HIV/AIDS and global warming. Christian and Jewish groups are active in interfaith initiatives and religious-secular partnerships around the world. Across these varied dimensions of religious pluralism and world affairs, U.S. influence and globalization feed off each other, as global communications and an emphasis on the rights of individuals strengthen U.S.-anchored agendas around the world and across issues.

If the United States, as the world's only superpower, both exemplifies and strengthens religious pluralism in the world arena, it also threatens to undermine it. The recourse to military force, in Iraq in particular, has deepened mistrust between the West and the Islamic world, complicating Christian-Muslim-Jewish efforts to address common policy agendas. And the U.S. emphasis on international religious freedom, when combined with support for Christians in the Muslim world, China, India, and elsewhere, evokes the specter of a superpower throwing its military, economic, and political resources behind a particular religious agenda. U.S. officials can and do claim that the war in Iraq is about peace, stability, and democracy—not about repressing and dividing Islam—and that support for religious freedom is best understood as support for universal human rights, not the advancement of a worldwide Christian agenda. But in a world marked by sharp power asymmetries, colonial and postcolonial legacies, a festering Israeli-Palestinian conflict, and the current reality of U.S. troops invading and then occupying two Muslim-majority countries, the perception of a U.S.-led international crusade is difficult to counteract.

Prodromou ends her analysis on a hopeful note. Despite its weakened moral authority, she maintains that "the United States possesses material resources that could serve to strengthen international law and global governance in a post–cold war order marked by a resurgence of ethnic and religious differences and greater cultural and religious pluralism." The United States will remain a Christian-majority nation with a religious political culture. And it will not soon be eclipsed as the leading power on the world stage. Tensions at the intersection of religion and world politics will continue, as transnational religious mobilization anchored in the United States and American support for international religious freedom generate hostility and resistance in some quarters. "But a positive redirection of the role of religion in U.S. foreign policy—in the service of durable forms of global governance and robust democratic regimes—is possible," Prodromou argues. For her it "presupposes a break with the destructive combination of religion, unilateralism, and resort to force that characterized U.S. foreign policy under the presidency of George W. Bush."

Conclusion

The essays in this volume cannot provide a comprehensive overview of religious pluralism at the intersection of globalization and world politics. That terrain is too vast. The complexity of the topic also militates against the development of a comprehensive theory of religion and world affairs that might map on to or explain an emergent international constellation. The ambitions of this essay have been correspondingly modest—to define key concepts, including religious pluralism and globalization, and to explore their interaction with world politics across a variety of traditions, regions, and issue areas addressed in the volume. That exploration reveals six interrelated dimensions of religious pluralism in world affairs that will likely persist into the foreseeable future: fragile identity politics, strong ethical commitments, international-national-local linkages, interfaith and intrafaith dynamics, religious-secular interaction, and the centrality of the United States.

None of those six dimensions is isolated from the other five, as the preceding analysis makes clear. The fragile politics of national identity in India, for example, is shaped by international-national-local linkages, including economic globalization and the efforts of Christian missionaries. Strong ethical commitments grounded in religious traditions, such as the universal norm of human dignity, can sharpen identity politics but also form a basis for interfaith and intrafaith collaboration. The potential for collaboration around economic and social development agendas is conditioned by religious-secular interaction, in particular the policies and priorities pursued by states, international organizations, and nonreligious NGOs. And the United States, with its preponderant military and economic power, can shape identity politics within other countries—most dramatically today in Afghanistan and Iraq—and, through its diplomacy around human rights and religious freedom, mold the evolution of international-national-local linkages within and across increasingly transnational religious communities.

Two overarching themes that emerge at the intersection of these six dimensions are the centrality of states and the problem of violence. Religious pluralism in world affairs is a fragile construct because of the decentralized structure of the state system. In the absence of a global sovereign, religious groups often depend on states for protection and resources. In fact, as Pratap Mehta reminds us in his essay, the state determines what counts as religion within a particular territory and political domain. Happily, the running debate about globalization has moved beyond claims and counterclaims about the demise of the state. In the religious context and others, the key issue is not whether the state can survive globalization but how it is reacting and changing in response to it. Religious-political conflict and cooperation at the level of the state—and not an amorphous clash or dialogue of civilizations—will drive the future trajectory of religious pluralism in world politics.[31] From this perspective, the United States is a particularly critical player. But other emergent world powers, including China and India, will have a decisive impact on the trajectory of religious pluralism internationally in the years to come.

A second overarching theme, with which this essay began, is the problem of violence. Religious pluralism in this volume is defined by an *absence* of violence, as the peaceful interaction of religious actors with one another and secular actors in the public sphere. The chapters point up the growth of religious pluralism in world politics, as religious communities have become more global in their outlook and activities across issues including human rights and economic and social development. The spread of religious ideas and movements, dramatically accelerated by globalization, is remarkable for its predominantly peaceful character. Even proselytism, which engages passions and can provoke political tensions, rarely generates bloodshed.

Even as religious pluralism flourishes in the context of globalization, its very success poses a double threat. On the one hand, the open encounter of religious perspectives, on the Internet in particular, provides an opening for extremists to preach hatred, intolerance, and violence. Opponents of religious pluralism like Osama Bin Laden can exploit pluralism in their efforts to destroy it. On the other hand, as religion figures more prominently in the public sphere around the world, it presents opportunities for political leaders to stir up passions and exacerbate conflicts in an effort to consolidate power at home and extend it abroad. Neither threat to religious pluralism—extremist ideas and political manipulation—is likely to disappear. Violent religious ideologies, however reprehensible, cannot be effectively suppressed, and the surge of religion into public life, with its divisive potential, looks to be part of a long-term trend. Under these circumstances, whether religious pluralism in world politics survives and thrives will depend in large part on interreligious and religious-secular dialogue and engagement and its capacity to strengthen those within and across traditions commited to peaceful coexistence.

NOTES

1. On religion and violence in contemporary world affairs, see Mark Juergensmeyer, *Terror in the Mind of God: The Global Rise of Religious Violence* (Berkeley: University of California Press, 2003); Bruce Lincoln, *Holy Terrors: Thinking about Religion after September 11th* (Chicago: University of Chicago Press, 2003).

2. For an influential theological approach to religious pluralism, see John Hick, *An Interpretation of Religion: Human Responses to the Transcendent* (New Haven, CT: Yale University Press, 2004). Sociological approaches to religious pluralism include Robert Wuthnow, *America and the Challenges of Religious Diversity* (Princeton, NJ: Princeton University Press, 2005); and Diana L. Eck, *A New Religious America: How a "Christian Country" Has Become the World's Most Religiously Diverse Nation* (San Francisco: HarperSanFrancisco, 2002).

3. For an exploration of the new religious pluralism in the transatlantic context, see Thomas Banchoff, ed., *Democracy and the New Religious Pluralism* (Oxford: Oxford University Press, 2007).

4. On the resurgence of religion in world affairs, see José Casanova, *Public Religions in the Modern World* (Chicago: University of Chicago Press, 1994); Susanne Hoeber Rudolph and James Piscatori, eds., *Transnational Religion and Fading States* (Boulder, CO: Westview Press, 1997); Peter L. Berger, *The Desecularization of the World: Resurgent Religion and World Politics* (Washington, DC: Ethics and Public Policy Center, 1999); Eric O. Hanson, *Religion and Politics in the International System Today* (Cambridge: Cambridge University Press, 2006); and Daniel Philpott, "Explaining the Political Ambivalence of Religion," *American Political Science Review* 101, no. 3 (August 2007): 505–525.

5. Daniel Philpott, "The Catholic Wave," *Journal of Democracy* 15, no. 2 (April 2004): 32–46; Eric O. Hanson, *The Catholic Church in World Politics* (Princeton, NJ: Princeton University Press, 1987).

6. Zoe Knox, *Russian Society and the Orthodox Church: Religion in Russia after Communism* (New York: Routledge, 2005); Paul Freston, *Evangelicals and Politics in Asia, Africa, and Latin America* (Cambridge: Cambridge University Press, 2001).

7. Olivier Roy, *Globalized Islam: The Search for a New Ummah* (New York: Columbia University Press, 2004); Giles Kepel, *Jihad: The Trail of Political Islam* (Cambridge, MA: Belknap Press of Harvard University Press, 2002).

8. Yossi Shain, *Kinship and Diasporas in International Affairs* (Ann Arbor: University of Michigan Press, 2007).

9. Thomas Blom Hansen, *The Saffron Wave: Democracy and Hindu Nationalism in Modern India* (Princeton, NJ: Princeton University Press, 1999); Adrian Hastings, *The Construction of Nationhood: Ethnicity, Religion and Nationalism* (Cambridge: Cambridge University Press, 1997).

10. Christopher Queen, Charles Prebish, and Damien Keown, eds., *Action Dharma: New Studies in Engaged Buddhism* (London: Routledge, 2003); Charles F. Keyes, Laurel Kendall, and Helen Hardacre, eds., *Asian Visions of Authority: Religion and the Modern States of East and Southeast Asia* (Honolulu: University of Hawaii Press, 1994).

11. For examinations of globalization as a concept, see Roland Robertson, *Globalization: Social Theory and Global Culture* (London: Sage, 1992); David Held, Anthony McGrew, David Goldblatt, and Jonathan Perraton, *Global Transformations: Politics, Economics, and Culture* (Stanford, CA: Stanford University Press, 1999); and Benjamin Barber, *Jihad versus McWorld: Terrorism's Challenge to Democracy* (New York: Ballantine Books, 2001).

12. Secular organizations, too, have exploited globalization to mobilize on a transnational scale. They are the focus of Margaret Keck and Kathryn Sikkink, *Activists beyond Borders: Advocacy Networks in International Politics* (Ithaca, NY: Cornell University Press, 1998); and Sidney Tarrow, *The New Transnational Activism* (Cambridge: Cambridge University Press, 2005).

13. These dynamics are explored by Roy, *Globalized Islam*. Important discussions in the Christian context include David Stoll, *Is Latin America Turning Protestant?* (Berkeley: University of California Press, 1990); and Paul E. Sigmund, ed., *Religious Freedom and Evangelization in Latin America: The Challenge of Religious Pluralism* (Maryknoll, NY: Orbis Books, 1999).

14. Ronald Inglehart and Pippa Norris, *The Sacred and the Secular: Religion and Politics Worldwide* (Cambridge: Cambridge University Press, 2004).

15. John Witte Jr. and Michael Bourdeaux, eds., *Proselytism and Orthodoxy in Russia: The New War for Souls* (Maryknoll, NY: Orbis Books, 1999); John Witte Jr. and Johan D. van der Vyver, eds., *Religious Human Rights in Global Perspective*, 2 vols. (The Hague: Martinus Nijhoff, 1996); Abdullahi Ahmed An-Na'Im, *Proselytization and Communal Self-Determination in Africa* (Maryknoll, NY: Orbis Books, 1999).

16. See, for example, Derek H. Davis and Gerhard Besier, eds., *International Perspectives on Freedom and Equality of Religious Beliefs* (Waco, TX: Baylor University Press, 2002).

17. See, for example, Amartya Sen, *Identity and Violence: The Illusion of Destiny* (New York: Norton, 2007); Kwame Anthony Appiah, *The Ethics of Identity* (Princeton, NJ: Princeton University Press, 2005); and Charles Taylor, *Multiculturalism* (Princeton. NJ: Princeton University Press, 2004).

18. On Hindu-Muslim relations in India, see Ashutosh Varshney, *Ethnic Conflict and Civil Life: Hindus and Muslims in India* (New Haven, CT: Yale University Press, 2002).

19. For an overview of the politics of international religious freedom, see Thomas F. Farr, *World of Faith and Freedom: Why Religious Liberty Is Vital to American National Security in the 21st Century* (Oxford: Oxford University Press, 2008).

20. For an extended discussion of Taylor's views on pluralism, see Ruth Abbey, ed., *Charles Taylor* (Cambridge: Cambridge University Press, 2004).

21. Hans Kung, *A Global Ethic: The Declaration of the Parliament of the World's Religions* (London: Continuum, 1994).

22. On religion and peacebuilding, see R. Scott Appleby, *The Ambivalence of the Sacred: Religion, Violence, and Reconciliation* (Lanham, MD: Rowman and Littlefield, 2000); Harold Coward and Gordon S. Smith, eds., *Religion and Peacebuilding* (Albany: State University of New York Press, 2004); Marc Gopin, *Between Eden and Armageddon: The Future of World Religions, Violence, and Peacemaking* (Oxford: Oxford University Press, 2000); John Paul Lederach, *Building Peace in Divided Societies* (Syracuse, NY: University of Syracuse Press, 1997); Mohammed Abu-Nimer, *Nonviolence and Peace Building in Islam: Theory and Practice* (Gainesville, FL:University Press of Florida, 2003).

23. A. James McAdams, ed., *Transitional Justice and the Rule of Law in New Democracies* (South Bend, IN: University of Notre Dame Press, 1997); Martha Minow, ed., *Breaking the Cycles of Hatred: Memory, Law, and Repair* (Princeton, NJ: Princeton University Press, 2002).

24. Katherine Marshall and Lucy Keough, *Mind, Heart and Soul in the Fight against Poverty* (Washington, DC: World Bank, 2004); and Katherine Marshall and Marisa Van Saanen, *Development and Faith: Where Mind, Heart and Soul Work Together* (Washington, DC: World Bank, 2007).

25. Tariq Ramadan, *Western Muslims and the Future of Islam* (Oxford: Oxford University Press, 2004).

26. A key text is Khaled Abou El Fadl, *The Great Theft: Wrestling Islam from the Extremists* (New York: HarperSanFrancisco, 2005).

27. John Paul Lederach and Cynthia Sampson, eds., *From the Ground Up: Mennonite Contributions to International Peacebuilding* (Oxford: Oxford University Press, 2000).

28. For reflections on the role of religion in U.S. foreign policy, see Madeleine K. Albright, *The Mighty and the Almighty: Reflections on America, God, and World Affairs* (New York: HarperCollins, 2006). On the religion–foreign policy nexus more broadly, see Douglas Johnston and Cynthia Sampson, eds., *Religion: The Missing Dimension of Statecraft* (New York: Oxford University Press, 1994); and Douglas Johnston, ed., *Faith-Based Diplomacy: Trumping Realpolitik* (New York: Oxford University Press, 2003).

29. On the politics of the International Religious Freedom Act, see Allen D. Hertzke, *Freeing God's Children: The Unlikely Alliance for Global Human Rights* (Oxford: Rowman and Littlefield, 2004).

30. On soft power, see Joseph S. Nye Jr., *Power in the Global Information Age: From Realism to Globalization* (London: Routledge, 2004).

31. Samuel Huntington, "The Clash of Civilizations?" *Foreign Affairs* 72, no. 3 (Summer 1993): 22–49.

BIBLIOGRAPHY

Abbey, Ruth, ed. *Charles Taylor*. Cambridge: Cambridge University Press, 2004.
Abu-Nimer, Mohammed. *Nonviolence and Peace Building in Islam: Theory and Practice.*
    Gainesville, FL: University Press of Florida, 2003.

Ahmed An-Na'Im, Abdullahi, *Proselytization and Communal Self-Determination in Africa*. Maryknoll, NY: Orbis Books, 1999.

Albright, Madeleine K. *The Mighty and the Almighty: Reflections on America, God, and World Affairs*. New York: HarperCollins, 2006.

Appiah, Kwame Anthony. *The Ethics of Identity*. Princeton, NJ: Princeton University Press, 2005.

Appleby, R. Scott. *The Ambivalence of the Sacred: Religion, Violence, and Reconciliation*. Lanham, MD: Rowman and Littlefield, 2000.

Banchoff, Thomas, ed. *Democracy and the New Religious Pluralism*. Oxford: Oxford University Press, 2007.

Barber, Benjamin. *Jihad versus McWorld: Terrorism's Challenge to Democracy*. New York: Ballantine Books, 2001.

Berger, Peter L., ed. *The Desecularization of the World: Resurgent Religion and World Politics*. Washington, DC: Ethics and Public Policy Center, 1999.

Casanova, José. *Public Religions in the Modern World*. Chicago: University of Chicago Press, 1994.

Coward, Harold, and Gordon S. Smith, eds. *Religion and Peacebuilding*. Albany, NY: State University of New York Press, 2004.

Davis, Derek H., and Gerhard Besier, eds. *International Perspectives on Freedom and Equality of Religious Beliefs*. Waco, TX: Baylor University Press, 2002.

Eck, Diana L. *A New Religious America: How a "Christian Country" Has Become the World's Most Religiously Diverse Nation*. San Francisco: HarperSanFrancisco, 2002.

El Fadl, Khaled Abou. *The Great Theft: Wrestling Islam from the Extremists*. New York: HarperSanFrancisco, 2005.

Farr, Thomas F. *World of Faith and Freedom: Why Religious Liberty Is Vital to American National Security in the 21st Century*. Oxford: Oxford University Press, 2008.

Freston, Paul. *Evangelicals and Politics in Asia, Africa, and Latin America*. Cambridge: Cambridge University Press, 2001.

Gopin, Marc. *Between Eden and Armageddon: The Future of World Religions, Violence, and Peacemaking*. Oxford: Oxford University Press, 2000.

Hansen, Thomas Blom. *The Saffron Wave: Democracy and Hindu Nationalism in Modern India*. Princeton, NJ: Princeton University Press, 1999.

Hanson, Eric O. *The Catholic Church in World Politics*. Princeton, NJ: Princeton University Press, 1987.

———. *Religion and Politics in the International System Today*. Cambridge: Cambridge University Press, 2006.

Hastings, Adrian. *The Construction of Nationhood: Ethnicity, Religion and Nationalism*. Cambridge: Cambridge University Press, 1997.

Held, David, Anthony McGrew, David Goldblatt, and Jonathan Perraton. *Global Transformations: Politics, Economics, and Culture*. Stanford, CA: Stanford University Press, 1999.

Hertzke, Allen D. *Freeing God's Children: The Unlikely Alliance for Global Human Rights*. Oxford: Rowman and Littlefield, 2004.

Hick, John. *An Interpretation of Religion: Human Responses to the Transcendent.* New Haven, CT: Yale University Press, 2004.

Huntington, Samuel. "The Clash of Civilizations?" *Foreign Affairs* 72, no. 3 (Summer 1993): 22–49.

Inglehart, Ronald, and Pippa Norris. *The Sacred and the Secular: Religion and Politics Worldwide.* Cambridge: Cambridge University Press, 2004.

Johnston, Douglas, ed. *Faith-Based Diplomacy: Trumping Realpolitik.* New York: Oxford University Press, 2003.

Johnston, Douglas, and Cynthia Sampson, eds. *Religion: The Missing Dimension of Statecraft.* New York: Oxford University Press, 1994.

Juergensmeyer, Mark. *Terror in the Mind of God: The Global Rise of Religious Violence.* Berkeley: University of California Press, 2003.

Keck, Margaret, and Kathryn Sikkink. *Activists beyond Borders: Advocacy Networks in International Politics.* Ithaca, NY: Cornell University Press, 1998.

Kepel, Giles. *Jihad: The Trail of Political Islam.* Cambridge, MA: Belknap Press of Harvard University Press, 2002.

Keyes, Charles F., Laurel Kendall, and Helen Hardacre, eds. *Asian Visions of Authority: Religion and the Modern States of East and Southeast Asia.* Honolulu: University of Hawaii Press, 1994.

Knox, Zoe. *Russian Society and the Orthodox Church: Religion in Russia after Communism.* New York: Routledge, 2005.

Kung, Hans. *A Global Ethic: The Declaration of the Parliament of the World's Religions.* London: Continuum, 1994.

Lederach, John Paul. *Building Peace in Divided Societies.* Syracuse, NY: University of Syracuse Press, 1997.

Lederach, John Paul, and Cynthia Sampson, eds. *From the Ground Up: Mennonite Contributions to International Peacebuilding.* Oxford: Oxford University Press, 2000.

Lincoln, Bruce. *Holy Terrors: Thinking about Religion after September 11th.* Chicago: University of Chicago Press, 2003.

Marshall, Katherine, and Lucy Keough. *Mind, Heart and Soul in the Fight against Poverty.* Washington, DC: World Bank, 2004.

Marshall, Katherine, and Marisa Van Saanen. *Development and Faith: Where Mind, Heart and Soul Work Together.* Washington, DC: World Bank, 2007.

McAdams, A. James, ed. *Transitional Justice and the Rule of Law in New Democracies.* South Bend, IN: University of Notre Dame Press, 1997.

Minow, Martha, ed. *Breaking the Cycles of Hatred: Memory, Law, and Repair.* Princeton, NJ: Princeton University Press, 2002.

Nye, Joseph S., Jr. *Power in the Global Information Age: From Realism to Globalization.* London: Routledge, 2004.

Philpott, Daniel. "The Catholic Wave." *Journal of Democracy* 15, no. 2 (April 2004): 32–46.

———. "Explaining the Political Ambivalence of Religion." *American Political Science Review* 101, no. 3 (August 2007): 505–525.

Queen, Christopher, Charles Prebish, and Damien Keown, eds. *Action Dharma: New Studies in Engaged Buddhism.* London: Routledge, 2003.

Ramadan, Tariq. *Western Muslims and the Future of Islam*. Oxford: Oxford University Press, 2004.

Robertson, Roland. *Globalization: Social Theory and Global Culture*. London: Sage, 1992.

Roy, Olivier. *Globalized Islam: The Search for a New Ummah*. New York: Columbia University Press, 2004.

Rudolph, Susanne Hoeber, and James Piscatori, eds. *Transnational Religion and Fading States*. Boulder, CO: Westview Press, 1997.

Sen, Amartya. *Identity and Violence: The Illusion of Destiny*. New York: Norton, 2007.

Shain, Yossi. *Kinship and Diasporas in International Affairs*. Ann Arbor: University of Michigan Press, 2007.

Sigmund, Paul E., ed. *Religious Freedom and Evangelization in Latin America: The Challenge of Religious Pluralism*. Maryknoll, NY: Orbis Books, 1999.

Stoll, David. *Is Latin America Turning Protestant?* Berkeley: University of California Press, 1990.

Tarrow, Sidney. *The New Transnational Activism*. Cambridge: Cambridge University Press, 2005.

Taylor, Charles, et al. *Multiculturalism*. Princeton, NJ: Princeton University Press, 2004.

Varshney, Ashutosh. *Ethnic Conflict and Civil Life: Hindus and Muslims in India*. New Haven, CT: Yale University Press, 2002.

Witte, John, Jr., and Michael Bourdeaux, eds. *Proselytism and Orthodoxy in Russia: The New War for Souls*. Maryknoll, NY: Orbis Books, 1999.

Witte, John, Jr., and Johan D. van der Vyver, eds. *Religious Human Rights in Global Perspective*. 2 vols. The Hague: Martinus Nijhoff, 1996.

Wuthnow, Robert. *America and the Challenges of Religious Diversity*. Princeton, NJ: Princeton University Press, 2005.

PART I

Challenges of Religious Pluralism in a Global Era

2

Causes of Quarrel: What's Special about Religious Disputes?

Kwame Anthony Appiah

Tantum religio potuit suadere malorum.

Lucretius, *De Rerum Natura* Book 1, 1. 101

Memories of Córdoba

In the month of Ramadan in the year 851 c.e., Christian hagiographers tell us, there was a disturbance in the splendid city of Córdoba in Moorish Spain. A Christian monk—Perfectus, by name—violated an unchallengeable edict of Muslim rule: he denounced Muhammad, publicly reviling him as a lecher, a pervert, a false prophet. The punishment for such an offense in Al-Andalus, he knew, was death. He was brought before the Islamic judge, or *qadi*, along with many witnesses to his blasphemous invective.[1] Yet the authorities declined to exact immediately the only possible penalty. Perhaps, the *qadi* ventured, the monk had been provoked by the crowd. Perfectus, it seemed, sought martyrdom. Instead, he was offered mercy.

More than a millennium later, the politics of blasphemy still proves troublesome. Early in 2006, thousands of protesters through-out the Middle East took to the streets to denounce a Danish newspaper's publication of cartoons depicting Muhammad. Danish (and, for that matter, Norwegian) embassies were torched and besieged, Danish workers threatened, Danish goods boycotted. Some imams called for the cartoonists to be beheaded.

These violent protests were, on their face, somewhat puzzling. For one thing, the cartoons were not *aimed* at those they offended; and so, while they may have been derogatory, they were not strictly speaking, an *insult*, since insults have to be targeted at those they affront. What is more, creeds do not, as a rule, expect outsiders to respect their own taboos. (Nor are images of the Prophet anathematized in all Islamic traditions; you can find Islamic depictions of him in classical illustrated manuscripts in the Topkapi Sarayi library of Istanbul, as well as in collections of Islamic art in the West.)[2] And it was not entirely clear whether the objection was to depictions of the Prophet, as such, or to the association of him, in a couple of the cartoons, with suicide bombings—bombings that, after all, many in the rioting crowds would sometimes have supported.

Plainly, then, the cartoon riots must be understood politically, not just religiously. Danish imams launched a campaign to internationalize the offense, hoping to make an issue in Denmark of Western hostility toward Muslims. Then broadcast television based in Saudi Arabia and the United Arab Emirates—countries where elites of doubtful godliness legitimize their rule by displays of piety—brought it to the masses. In Syria it suited an Alawite regime to be seen supporting Muslim orthodoxy. But the fury swiftly passed beyond the control of those who had sought to orchestrate it, confirming, therefore, rather than confronting, Europe's anti-Muslim prejudices.

In most cross-cultural conversations about a moral affront, there is a simple, powerful move to make. You try to find a cultural equivalent: *If you want to understand how we feel, imagine how you would feel if. . . .* Yet the turn-it-around approach was, as you might have anticipated, a striking failure in this case. Trying to conjure up something that the Danes would find comparably offensive, one mujahid[3] commentator wrote, "The Muslims could have made satirical cartoons of Danish men and women fornicating openly like the beasts in the jungle, reflecting their crass culture of porn and Viking heritage."[4] Well, quite, if they wanted to try their hand at storyboarding the next Lars von Trier film. (In 2005, after all, the mayoral candidate in Copenhagen for the right-wing nationalist Danish People's Party had been, as she freely admitted, a "pornographic starlet" in her youth.)[5] When an Iranian paper proposed to match the offense by running cartoons about the Holocaust, the *Jyllands-Posten* editor, Flemming Rose, who had published the original cartoons, asked if he could run them, too. He might also have pointed out that those cartoons would not have been the first; or that, on the whole, the response of most Europeans to anti-Semitism is moral revulsion, not personal affront. Denmark's problem with Islam (like Holland's) is that it is a largely secular country that has inherited a Protestant understanding of religion. As a result, Danes would be appalled by attempts to enforce religious notions by way of the state.

One difficulty was that the concept of blasphemy has relatively little purchase on the contemporary European mind. (Imagine how *Catholics* would feel if, say, someone published a book with the incendiary premise that Jesus married Mary Magdalene, and a powerful Vatican faction had been killing people to cover up the truth! Oops. They did. Yet somehow the Holy See contented itself with bland cautions that *The Da Vinci Code* should be read as fiction. No riots there.) In the United States attempts at blasphemy seldom prompt much more than reproachful words and fulminations about National Endowment for the Arts funding practices. The issue is not so much religious obligation as good manners. Blasphemy, Americans think, should not get government subsidy. Beyond that, it is between you and the neighbor you offend by it (who will nevertheless be arrested if he assaults you in response) or, I suppose, between you and the God you dishonor (who, if he exists, has considerably more resources with which to punish you than even the mightiest government in the history of the world).

The key to the cartoon riots is to see that they reflect a sense of relative powerlessness among many people of Muslim identity. As that mujahid commentator maintained, "A tiny nation like Denmark would not antagonise a population of over one billion, unless it knew that it can do it with impunity."[6] That is what feeds the fury. And that is why the turn-it-around efforts fail to persuade. It is just easier to shrug off expressions of contempt when you are feeling powerful. That is one lesson from ninth-century Córdoba. There, Muslims were an advanced, regionally dominant, and self-confident civilization. Like many Westerners today, they had the magnanimity of the mighty.

But even such tolerance has its limits. A few days later, when Perfectus let loose another tirade against the Prophet, the authorities reluctantly gave him his martyrdom, a fate they had then to confer over the next decade on dozens of others who, beginning in the summer of 851, were apparently inspired by his example. To the emir and the *qadi*, Perfectus and his fellow martyrs were fanatics, extremists, even lunatics. To the Catholic Church, he is a saint—though most of the Catholic bishops of Córdoba seem to have regarded people who behaved like him not as martyrs (good) but as troublesome suicides (bad).

The tale of the Martyrs of Córdoba raises a general question. Why are many moral and political disputes across nations, as within them, made so difficult to resolve once they have religious stakes? I want to tell a story that weaves together three relatively independent strands. One burden of my analysis will be that the problem has taken a new shape in the modern world, one that requires new solutions. What Perfectus was doing was different from most modern forms of religious politics: he was bearing witness for Christ, but he was not trying to change Cordovan state practices. It was precisely because Rome had to deal with the politics of *this* world that the official Catholic Church ended up trying to discourage the Christians of Córdoba from offering themselves up for execution. In coming to terms with religious differences in the modern world, and the problems they pose, I will be exploring a particular set of challenges that arise for that combination of universalism and tolerance that we can call—following Diogenes of Sinope—cosmopolitanism. Since Diogenes began a tradition that came to infuse various strains of the Abrahamic monotheisms, as we will see, talk of such cosmopolitanism places us not outside of religious discourse but within it.

Materials for an Analysis I: Religion as Social Identity

Three strands, then. Here is the first. Religion is an important crucible of *social identity*. Along with Catholic faith, Catholic practice, and Catholic institutions, there are *people* who think of themselves—and are thought of—as Catholic; so too, mutatis mutandis, for the great number of other religious traditions human beings have come up with. The extent of this phenomenon is a novelty. In the past, in places where there was one dominant religious tradition, religion as such was not an important source of social identity.

In Asante, in the mid–nineteenth century, for example, when my great-grandmother was young, people had all sorts of beliefs about Nyame (the sky god), Asaase Yaa (the earth goddess), and other spirits of diverse kinds. Still it would never have occurred to people to define themselves by an identity based in those beliefs. They might have identified *others* in this way—"Kramo" is an old word for Muslim in our language—but precisely because the traditions were so widely shared, there was nothing salient for social life about participation in these various religious forms, except when it came to those few, mostly strangers, who diverged from them. Being Asante was a serious identity, and Asantes shared these "religious" beliefs and engaged in these "religious" practices. But "Asante religion" was a constituent of Asante-ness, not an independent source of identity; indeed, you would be hard put to find a word in nineteenth-century Asante-Twi (as in most of the world's languages then) to translate the word "religion" (or, of course, "identity").

But most religious people in the world today live in societies where there are significant numbers of people of *other* religions, and even when they do not, they mostly know they live in a *world* of other religions. Let us say that a collection of people is *religiously diverse* when

1. its members adhere to a number of distinct religious traditions, and
2. more than one of those traditions has adherents who make up a significant minority of the population, and
3. none of the traditions is adhered to by an overwhelming majority.

I am going to keep the word "diverse" to refer to this sort of situation and keep "pluralism" for later use as the name of an ideology. America is obviously diverse in this way: no Christian denomination makes up more than half of the U.S. population, and there are many non-Christian denominations whose numbers make them a significant presence in public life. Other cases are harder. Is Denmark, home to those planet-circling cartoons, religiously diverse? Not if you believe the *CIA World Factbook*, which tells us that 95 percent of Danes are Evangelical Lutheran.[7] But one scholar argues, after reviewing the recent literature, that anywhere from 2.3 to 4.3 million of the 5.5 million or so Danes are, in fact, atheists or agnostics.[8] So, while a vast majority is formally Lutheran, most are not practicing, and perhaps 15 percent are avowedly atheist. Lutherans are not, in fact, an *overwhelming* majority, then. There are all those agnostics, along with the Catholics, Jews, and Muslims, as well as various other kinds of Protestants and the odd Buddhist, Hindu, and Taoist; but there *are* also some real Lutherans—believers—as well, and together these people make up enough of the population to guarantee that agnosticism, which is the commonest position on religious matters, does not overwhelm this diverse group of believers.[9]

Because religious differences go with differences in behavior—some of which is open to public scrutiny—most religious people today, unlike my Asante forebears, have religious *identities* as well as religious habits and beliefs. What Frederick Barth argued for ethnic identities—that they are the product of processes of social boundary formation—is largely true of modern religious identities, too.[10] While the content of the identity is hugely important for many of those who hold it, its social function depends mostly on its distinguishing other people as either in-group members (coreligionists) or out-group members (infidels, heretics, gentiles). I will come back to what I mean by religious identity and why it is a source of so many troubles. Before I do, however, I want first to sketch in the two other elements of my analysis.

Materials for an Analysis II: Religion as Psychologically Integrative

Sir Edward Tylor began the modern anthropology of religion by borrowing the word "animism" to discuss a "general belief in spiritual beings." Animism provides, as he famously put it, the "minimum definition" of religion.[11] There is, no doubt, much this proposal misses. But I am going to proceed in a roughly Tylorian vein, stipulating that the religions I am interested in involve a belief in a world beyond the everyday world and a being or beings whose power transcends the quotidian powers of ordinary people.

But what matters most about religions in answering the questions we are pursuing is not their Tylorian core. It is, rather, what I am going to call—this is the second strand of my analysis—the *integrative* character of religious world-views. This is the one part of the analysis that has to do with something that is *not* new in religious life. The basic insight here is Durkheim's, but a more influential formulation these days is Clifford Geertz's, in his well-known essay "Religion as a Cultural System":

> Sacred symbols [he writes] function to synthesize a people's ethos—
> the tone, character, and quality of their life, its moral and aesthetic
> style and mood—and their world view—the picture they have of the
> way things in sheer actually are, their most comprehensive ideas of
> order. . . . Religious symbols formulate a basic congruence between a
> particular style of life and a specific (if, most often, implicit) meta-
> physic, and in so doing sustain each with the borrowed authority of
> the other.[12]

This integration of the cognitive and the affective, the moral and the meta-physical, is part of what makes the symbolic dimensions of religion a particular challenge for modern politics. And it is the only one of the three features of religion today that is not new.

Materials for an Analysis III: Religion and Epistemological Dissensus

The third and final strand of the analysis has to do with the social context of the claims made by contemporary religions, claims I have just suggested give religions their distinctive psychological power. The point is a simple one: distinc-tively religious claims—about the nature of God (or gods) and the demands he (or they) makes upon our behavior—are not nowadays widely thought to be sus-ceptible to confirmation by the ordinary empirical means that we can appeal to in trying to persuade fellow citizens of claims about the world. The God of modern Christianity does not show up in obvious ways in photographs or X-rays; you can-not ask him a question and expect everyone to hear the same answer. He speaks to you *in pectore*, and so only you hear him. Or he speaks through the church's magisterium, but its authority is doubted by outsiders. This, like the pervasive-ness not of religion but of religious identities, is a modern phenomenon.

Theological claims could once be settled in many societies by methods that were relatively uncontroversial. Oracles and other sacred texts might require interpreting, but that they mattered was not in doubt. The epistemic authority of priests was not widely doubted either, which did not mean you could always be sure they were truthful. There is an old Asante proverb, whose point is that some things are completely obvious: *No one,* it says, *needs to show God to a child* (Obi nkyerē abōfra Nyame). The existence and character of divinities is no longer a paradigm of the self-evident. And, equally important, because of the context of diversity, disputes about religious matters are carried on without shared standards for the evaluation of claims.

Many past religious disputes—including those that led to some of the bloodiest conflicts in the last millennium—were about the meaning of texts that all parties agreed were sacred. If the text required something, everyone thought, that was indeed a valid command. But a great deal of religious dispute today in the United States, as in the world, is different. Everyone knows there is massive disagreement among the majority who believe in traditional texts about which texts have authority. The Bhagavad Gita? The Torah? The Talmud? The Qur'an? The New Testament? The Book of Mormon? The Gospel of Thomas? Having picked our texts, we will swiftly run into disagreement over how they should be interpreted. Some people, meanwhile—at least 40 percent of Danes, for example—doubt that there *are* authoritative texts or sources of revelation, publicly available mechanisms for adjudicating religious claims, at all.

Those, then, are the three elements of the analysis: religion as (1) a basis of social identity; (2) an integrative system of symbols, and (3) a source of claims that have to be evaluated without socially shared epistemological standards. Once we see what social identities are and why they create political problems, we can go on to say something about what is distinctive about religious identities, which is where the other two strands of analysis will come into their own.

A Theory of Identity

I think the best account of social identities proceeds by explaining how social *labels* operate, rather than by trying to say more directly what the identity itself is.[13] Take some identity label. Let's call it "R," for "religion." The proposal has four parts:

> "R"—the label—will have *criteria of ascription*; some people will
> *identify* as Rs; some people will *treat* others as Rs; and being-an-R
> will entail *norms of identification*.

I want to make a few brief points about each of these italicized phrases.

So far as the application of religious labels goes, the key point is that *criteria of ascription* can be contested; there may not be consensus about who falls under the label. Now, as in the past, contest over labels is a central source of social conflict: between Sunni and Shia, between Protestants and Catholics, between some Evangelicals and the so-called mainstream churches. In these cases people are particularly contemptuous of those who make a claim on the label they claim for themselves—here, Muslim or Christian—but disagree with them over matters of morals or religious practice or doctrine.

What makes a classification a social identity of the relevant kind is not just that some people are called "Rs," however, but the way being-an-R figures in their thoughts, feelings, and acts. *Identification* of this kind is central to the dynamics of social identity. When a person thinks of herself as an R in the relevant way, she *identifies as an R*, which means she sometimes *feels like* or *acts as an R*. Some American Christians, for example, support attempts to redeem slaves in the Sudan because they think (misleadingly, at best, in my view) of the slaves as fellow Christian victims of Muslim slavers.

But identity labels do not only figure in how we think about ourselves. They matter, too, to how we treat others. To *treat someone as an R* is just to do (or abstain from doing) something to her *because she is an R* (where her being-an-R is one of your reasons for treating her that way). Kindness to people who share the label is a common form of *treatment* directed toward in-group members, people seen as sharing a social identity. Indifference and many more actively hostile forms of behavior are equally frequent forms of treatment directed toward out-group members. Here is room for politics as people try to use the government to enforce their likes and dislikes. And the politics can be very serious: think of the struggle against apartheid in South Africa or the Catholic civil rights movement in Northern Ireland.

Now, identities are useful, in part, because once we ascribe an identity to someone, we make predictions about her behavior on that basis. This is not just because the criteria of ascription entail that members of the group have, or tend to have, certain properties. People who identify as Rs do things because they are Rs, as we saw, and what they do for this reason is not just an individual matter. There are *norms of behavior* for Rs. People do not only do and avoid doing things because they're Rs; often they do them because they—and most other people in their society—believe there are things that, as Rs, they ought and ought not to do. The "ought" here is not some special moral one, and examples are easy to come by. Negatively: Muslims ought not to eat pork. Positively: Muslims ought to make the hajj. To say these norms exist is not to endorse them. The existence, in a particular society, of a norm that Rs ought to do x amounts only to its being widely known that many people think Rs ought to do x.

The Politics of Identity

Political philosophers have written a good deal recently about one particular way in which social identities have figured in politics, namely, in what is called the "politics of recognition." The responses of other people obviously play a crucial role in shaping one's sense of who one is. Unfortunately, our societies have not treated certain individuals with respect because they were, say, homosexuals or Catholics. Because our identities are "dialogically" shaped, as Charles Taylor puts it, people who have these characteristics find them central—often negatively central—to their identities. The politics of recognition starts when we grasp that this is wrong. One response involves seeing these collective identities anew, not now as sources of limitation and insult but as valuable parts of one's identity. And so people move next to demand social recognition *as* homosexuals or Catholics. It is a short step to asking to be respected *as* gays or *as* Catholics.

This is a demand that others may or may not accede to personally: I do not mind calling social negotiations of this sort a kind of micropolitics. But what, if anything, does it have to do with the state? Well, there can be laws against hate speech or verbal harassment in the workplace, state education for tolerance, public celebrations of the heroes of the formerly oppressed. But it is important to see that, while members of previously disadvantaged groups may indeed need new social practices in order to flourish, what they are seeking is not always *recognition*. When the largely Catholic civil rights movement in Northern Ireland made claims for Catholics, it was not that they were asking for positive recognition as Catholics in public life. They were asking to be treated by the state *without* regard for their identity as Catholics: they wanted, for example, to be eligible for government jobs that had largely been reserved for Protestants. Being seen as Catholic by state officials—policemen and civil servants—was a large part of the problem; they wanted to be seen less as Catholics, more as citizens. They wanted *less* recognition, not more. And to the extent that they did care about recognition, it was because they were asking for respect in response to the years of contempt. The point is not just that recognition is not all that matters. It is, rather, that we can be confused about our overall interest when we focus too narrowly on our need for recognition. One obvious example is this: the politician whose identity we share is not necessarily going to pursue the politics we care for.

We identify with people and parties for a variety of reasons, including identifications of this prepolitical sort, and then we are rather inclined to support all the policies of that person or party. This is, in part, for a good reason: sensible people have better things to do than work out by themselves what the proper balance should be between, say, property, sales, and income taxes; and people sufficiently like you may actually pick policies, when they do think about them, that you would pick, if you had the time. That used to work by creating political identities—left, right, small-l liberal, Labour, Tory, big-l Liberal, Democrat, Republican, Christian Democrat, and Marxist. But in many of the advanced democracies, party affiliations are less strong than they used to be, and other identities are bearing more political weight. That is in part because many of the older party affiliations were class-based, and social class as defined by one's work has declined in significance in people's identifications. In that very profound way a new kind of identity politics, based in the declining social salience of class, has been on the rise since the 1960s. And the politics of both gay activists and Evangelical conservatives fits right into that trend.

Now, as I said at the start, my first answer to the question why religion poses problems for politics is that religious identity can raise political problems in all the ways that other social identities do. We have identified at least six such ways already: let me itemize them and offer examples of their application to religious identities.

1. There are political conflicts about who is in and who is out, the politics of ascription. If you want a religious example, consider the Israeli debate about whether the Ethiopian Jews—the Beta Israel or Falasha—were really Jews. Yes (which, it turned out, was the winning answer) meant they had the right of aliyah (emigration to Israel).

2. Politicians can mobilize identities, shaping norms of identification. A religious example: Sri Lankan Buddhism has been mobilized to shape Sinhalese identity, which is part of why the Tamil resistance is deliberately conceived by the Tamil Tigers in ethnic and not religious terms. Although most Tigers are Hindus, some of their intellectual leaders have been Christian, a fact to which they like to draw attention.[14]

3. States can behave differently toward people of distinct identities. We can call this "the politics of treatment." I have already offered the example of Northern Ireland in the period up to the early 1970s.

4. People can pursue a politics of recognition. A religious example: lesbian and gay Episcopalians seek acknowledgment within the Anglican Communion.

5. There can be a social micropolitics enforcing norms of identification. A religious example: Jewish groups that aim to draw secularized Jews

back to a more religious life. "Are you Jewish?" they ask. And if you *are*, they want to persuade you that you have obligations to return to orthodox practice.

6. There are inherently political identities like party identifications, social identities that are about our relationship with the state, entailing commitments as to what the state should and should not be doing. There are many religious examples in Lebanon, where almost all the political parties are associated with religious identities: Catholic, Sunni, Shia, Maronite, Druze, and so on.

The first step, I have claimed, in understanding how religion gets to be so regular a source of difficulty in political life is to see it as a form of social identity and to apply the general account of why social identities are important. In the cases I have just offered, religion as social identity serves two deep functions central to all forms of social identity. One is the strategic function of providing bases for pulling together, for forming coalitions in pursuit of resources. The second is the ethical, psychological function of underpinning what I earlier called "identification." Religious identities serve both these functions very well. But the first, strategic, function is of particular importance in contexts of scarcity, where working with some and against others is the only way to acquire resources.[15] It is not surprising that religious identities resurfaced in the Balkans just as the Yugoslav economy collapsed.

One final point about what I just called identity's strategic function: religious identities are normally acquired through families. Even in traditions—like the Mennonites—that insist on adult baptism, the values, beliefs, practices, and attachments that go with the identity are acquired at home or in churches and temples whose membership is shared with parents and siblings. Religion provides, in most places, what we might call a *default* identity: you get your family's religious identity unless something special happens to interfere. So, obviously, one shares one's religious identity with the people with whom one has the most intimate and enduring relationships, and religious practices are invested with the distinctive emotional aura of family life. Since the family is the basic institution of solidarity—the basic coalition and the basic center of relationship—religious affiliations are always likely to be salient when it comes to seeking a group with which to identify for struggles over resources. And, if you have a religious identity and are engaged in a struggle for resources in a context of religious diversity, it is likely to be one of the first to suggest itself.

The Specificities of Modern Religious Identity:
The Connection with Nationalism

We need, now, to take the next step and see why religious identities are an especially important source of political conflict in the contemporary world. The general considerations I have so far offered do not, as I said, distinguish religion from race or ethnicity—and, as everybody knows, all three of these kinds of identity are associated with long histories of political trouble. Race and ethnicity, too, are inherited in families and are associated with the distinctive emotional aura of the familial. Both can be the bases of coalitions and sources of ethical rewards. But I want now to suggest that it is features that they do not share with these and other social identities that help to explain why religious identities have their current salience, even in societies, like our own, that are plural but whose politics is not dominated by scarcity of resources.

Of course, religion and politics have been tied together from the beginning. We started with the example of Córdoba, which was in the end a caliphate, where religious and political authority were united. But Athens and Rome had state religions, cults of divinities with special importance for the city or the empire. Many places—from Pharaonic Egypt on, have had divine kingship. The major empires of Eurasia—Mongol, Mughal, Manchu, Roman, Ottoman, British—all took religion with them. But to understand what is distinctive about the modern situation of religious identities, you need to start with something that is modern. And that is the combination of religious diversity with modern nationalist politics.

It requires a spectacular feat of imagination to step outside the framework of modern nationalism. Almost everyone, everywhere today on the planet lives with a picture of the world in which it is as natural as could possibly be that the world is divided into a couple of hundred nation-states.[16] But the idea in fact took form only slowly and only recently. The Treaty of Westphalia of 1648 essentially turned the Holy Roman Empire into a collection of states, each with its own sovereignty; in so doing, it set in motion a significant shift in the heart of Europe. These newly independent states inherited the principles of religious freedom established in the Reformation by the Peace of Augsburg (1555), which granted each ruler the right to determine his own sovereign religious affiliation. And so we speak of a Westphalian model, where each nation-state has its own sovereign, subject to no higher secular authority, independent both of the empire and of Rome. The Westphalian settlement did not, by itself, produce the modern nation-state. For that at least one more development was crucial: what Arjun Appadurai calls "the idea of a national ethnos" had to take hold. And that is new. "No modern nation," Appadurai says, "however benign its political system and however eloquent its public voices may be about the virtues of tolerance, multiculturalism, and inclusion, is free of the idea that its national sovereignty is built on some sort of ethnic genius."[17]

The thought is one that was first philosophically developed in the European Enlightenment in the writings of Johann Gottfried Herder. What Appadurai calls the "ethnic genius" of the nation, Herder called its *Volksgeist*: the spirit of its people. And Herder taught that every member of a people shared that spirit with every other. That spirit found its expression above all in the language and the literature of the *Volk*: its poetry and song, its tales and myths, as well as in the music, art, and literature produced both by the common people and by its leading creative spirits. It was in the name of recording the spirit of the German people that the Brothers Grimm set out to collect those German fairy tales the world now knows; it was with the aim of recording, preserving, and purifying the spirit of the German language—its *Sprachgeist*—that they began the great German dictionary, the *Deutsche Wörterbuch*. And a nation, with its shared mental life, was the natural unit of government.

So far, though, this was all the doings and saying of intellectuals. The material preconditions for giving reality to the *idea* of the national ethnos—and for its uptake by ordinary people—were complex. But, as Benedict Anderson points out, a critical factor was the rise of print. Books, which formerly had required a great deal of time and money to copy—and had therefore been limited to the possessions of governmental and ecclesiastical institutions and the very rich—were now accessible to a wider public, and that led to an explosion of works in the vernacular languages of Europe.

Once a text like, say, the Luther-Bibel (1534), the King James Bible (1611), or the Bible de Port-Royal (1693) became more widely available, there developed in popular consciousness the idea of the community of its readers. Print also created pressure to develop standardized versions of languages like French and German and English, which had hitherto been collections of often mutually unintelligible dialects. And that in turn made possible the rise of modern mass media—the institution, in the first case, of newspapers and magazines—in which speakers of a printed language could read of the doings of their nation. Britain or France or Spain could become protagonists in a narrative of world history. It also allowed rulers to address vast national publics, almost directly—or, at any rate, more directly than ever before. Modern national identity was born.

This is the picture it takes a great leap of imagination to escape. And the fact that it *is* hard to escape should be puzzling. Literature and music and mass-mediated culture are all, in fact, quite transnational in their influences and their effects. History left us a world in which hardly any nation-states fitted the

Herderian picture of the homogeneous monocultural nation living under a single government. Those few states that do fit roughly have usually been forced into it over a couple of centuries of violent civil strife: the homogeneous nation is the result, not the precondition, of modern statehood. Eugen Weber taught a generation of students of French history that as late as 1893, roughly a quarter of the then 30 million citizens of metropolitan France had not mastered the French language. So much for the *Sprachgeist*.[18] Linda Colley argued somewhat later in her marvelous book *Britons: Forging the Nation*, "The sense of a common identity here did not come into being, then, because of an integration and homogenization of disparate cultures. Instead, Britishness was superimposed over an array of internal differences in response to contact with the Other, and above all in response to conflict with the Other."[19] So much for the *Volksgeist*. There are no doubt candidates for Herderian states. I will give you Japan, where 99 percent of the population identify as Japanese—though I cannot forbear adding that their script is Chinese, their largest religion Indian, and ethnologue.com lists fifteen Japanese languages, including Japanese sign language. By and large, people do not live in monocultural, monoreligious, monolingual, nation-states, and, by and large, since large states arose, they never have.

On the one hand, then, nationality, for better or worse, has become an increasingly central feature of the identities of modern men and women; but, on the other, the content of nationality—its meaning for each citizen—is the result of cultural work, not a natural and preexisting commonality. That means there is a place for the politics of national identity. And once people care about their nationality, it matters to them very much how the nation is conceived, including religiously. Once you want your national identity to cohere with your religious identity, you will aspire for its rituals to become national rituals, its morals to be embodied in law, its gods to be honored in public ceremonial. Even in the agnostic haven of Denmark, many people cannot imagine their nationality clothed in Muslim garb.

Epistemological Dissensus

It is here that the third strand of the analysis comes into its own, as we turn to the peculiar cognitive situation religions face in the contemporary world. Let me say first, however, that it is important not to describe this situation in ways that beg the question on substantive religious claims. Some people think, for example, that the difficulty with religious identities is the irrationality of religious belief. Of course, they will say, you cannot have reasonable discussions about which moral prescriptions should be enforced by the state with people who think that the truth about those questions can be settled by interpreting texts they think were dictated by a god, who, in fact, is not there. If the gods do not exist, the mechanisms for determining what they want are bound to be unreliable. I think there are at least three reasons for not basing an analysis on claims like these. One is political. These are issues we want to be able to discuss in our political life, at least if religious disputes are causing problems. But you cannot have a respectful civic exchange on this basis. A second reason is that irrationality is simply not the prerogative of the religious. And a third is that whether these claims are reasonable depends on what the truths are about these metaphysical questions: and metaphysical questions are very difficult. Fallibilism about our own views on these matters is very much in order. So there is much to be said, as John Rawls, for one, famously argued, for getting on without controversial metaphysical presuppositions if we can.

The key insight, I believe, is not about the difficulty of rational debate about religious matters. It is, rather, that modern societies are not only diverse (this is not historically unusual) but also ideologically pluralistic. It is now widely accepted—for a great variety of different reasons—that even where a society has a majority of one religious identity, it does not follow that all questions should be settled according to the view of that religious tradition. More than this, in the world as a whole, it is understood that no religious group has the power to settle things on its own terms; even more interestingly, most people do not think that they *should* be settled that way even if they could. I know that there are people who deny this and places where this is not a mainstream view. One kind of modern fundamentalism aims to force a universal Christianity or Islam (in each case of a particular sect) or atheism (of their own particular variety) on the world. But many people, in religious majorities *and* in religious minorities, believe in an ideological religious pluralism that does not accept—as majorities in the past from Córdoba to Amsterdam demanded and minorities conceded— giving a dominant place to the religion of the majority.

That, I believe, is the new situation. The emir of Córdoba tolerated Christians and Jews no doubt in part for reasons of policy. (The people who apparently goaded Perfectus into his first blasphemies did not share that official tolerance.) But he could tolerate them—provided they did not blaspheme— because there was a Muslim reason to do so: they were Ahl al-Kitâb, People of the Book, for whom, as the Holy Qur'an says, there should be "no compulsion in religion." Toleration of people of minority religious identities began in places where the majority religion recommended it, and the minorities, though grateful, never expected religions to be treated equally. Once the Christians took over in Spain, in fact, they treated Muslims and Jews with a great deal less tolerance than the infidels had once offered *them*. As in ninth-century Córdoba, so in Rembrandt's Amsterdam, where modern Jewish toleration first emerged in western Europe.[20] Because Protestantism taught that only the confession of a free conscience was worth anything, coercing religious conformity was pointless. So, as I say, as in Córdoba, it was possible to give an account in terms of the dominant religion of why the minorities should be tolerated. Locke's Protestant toleration of Catholics was similarly grounded in Anglican moral theology; and even Voltaire's toleration was based in his substantive religious view, which was a kind of skeptical deism, and endorsed a state religion with civic disabilities for those who were not Catholic.

The example of Asante, which I mentioned earlier, underlines the relative modernity in global terms of the "institution" of religion: of the self-conscious church. The ancient Israelites did not have "religion"; they had a form of life, which was self-consciously different from other forms of life they were familiar with. They had a cult with temples, in which certain acts of propitiation were to be performed. They had domestic rituals. But there was not agriculture and textile weaving here, and religion over there. As with the Asante in more recent times, Hebrew was who they were, not (save derivatively) what they did. Toleration finally requires that other religions be recognized as religions, not just heresies, delusions, defections from the true path. It requires the degree of abstraction that allows you to see that other people's views and practices (wrong as they may be) are *alternatives* to your religion: that what they have is relevantly like what you have.[21] And that requires recognizing yourself as having a religion first. But toleration can be combined, as it was in Holland and England and in the American colonies, with establishment and the political dominance of one religion. Now, however, we live in a world where tolerance has made the further step to pluralism: to the view that people with different religions must still be equal as citizens—equal, that is, in the eyes of the state.

Once you have the pluralistic ideology, though, against the background of the sociological fact of modern religious diversity, you have the beginnings of a substantial problem. Because now the mere fact that the majority believes something is right for religious reasons will not do as a political reason: and so you must discuss what is right across religious traditions within a single political order. And how can you do this reasonably when—to invoke the third strand of my analysis—the religious claims that ground people's ambitions to identify nation and religion have to be evaluated without socially shared epistemological standards?

Sir Edward Evans-Pritchard, one of the greatest anthropologists of the twentieth century, wrote a wonderful book called *Witchcraft, Oracles and Magic among the Azande*, about a people of that name who live largely in the Sudan. Having explained their ideas about witchcraft in great detail, he observes at one point that sometimes, in the evenings, when he saw a flash of flame in the bush around the Azande settlement where he was living, he found himself thinking, "Look, a witch." Of course, he did not believe it, really. He knew it was probably someone from the village going off to relieve himself, carrying a flaming torch to guide him on his way. But what he was teaching us is that what you see depends on what you believe. What it is reasonable for you to think, faced with a particular experience, depends on what ideas you already have.

This is a fortiori true when it comes to the sorts of beliefs that are central to religion. Suppose I pray each evening and, as it seems to me, God answers. How are you going to persuade me that I have got the wrong God? And if God's answer to my prayerful reflection on his Holy Book is that a man that lies with a man "as with a woman" should be put to death (as it seems to say pretty clearly in Leviticus 20), how will you (who have other texts or other interpretations) persuade me that this should not be the law of the land?[22]

The problem is deepened by what I called the integrative character of religion, the way in which it coheres psychologically. The picture of the world and the prescriptions as to how we should behave come together, work together, and together help make sense of the universe and my place in it. Giving up a sincerely held element of the picture or a practice that the picture underwrites will be hard. Racial and ethnic identities, by contrast, do not attach to integrative symbolic systems in the way that religions do; and so, unless the ethnicity is itself conceived in religious terms, disentangling them from political positions is easier, at least in principle. And so, while the identities themselves are often the source of deep commitments, they do not usually generate the difficulty for public deliberation that religions do.

The Persistence of Religious Difference

In spite of what so many Enlightenment thinkers would have predicted, religious identities are still central to ethical identity. And there is a profound political fact about that centrality: it is extremely hard for states to change. In the period after the Peace of Augsburg, when the principle *cuius regio, eius religio* governed relations between the Holy Roman Emperors, on the one hand, and the Protestant German princes and free cities, on the other, sovereigns of various sorts—from the republic of Geneva to the papacy to the kingdom of France—attempted to enforce religious uniformity. Notwithstanding the Saint Bartholomew's Day massacre of thousands of Huguenots; the burning of Servetus at the stake (by Calvinist Geneva) and in effigy (by the Inquisition in France); the repeated expulsions of Jews and the disabilities imposed

on Catholics and non-Conformists in England—notwithstanding a long succession of such enormities—men and women stuck stubbornly to faiths their
states abhorred. *Cuius regio* was proposed as a normative principle; as a description it was always preposterous. This obstinate fact of religious obstinacy is what
makes sense of the view that, where possible, we should tolerate other religions
rather than trying to bring people over to ours. It is largely a matter of accepting the inevitable. Outside Scandinavia, there are only three countries in which
scholars largely agree that a majority of the population is atheist or agnostic: two
of them—Vietnam and Japan—have long histories of Buddhism (which makes
doctrinal adherence to atheism consistent with a religious identity), and in one,
the Czech Republic, where 54 percent of people in one survey denied believing
in God, only 20 percent of people were willing to call themselves "atheist."[23]

Accepting that Enlightenment practice of toleration in the contemporary
world—a world of empirical diversity and ideological pluralism—requires us all
to try to persuade people not to rely on controversial religious claims in political
argument within or across societies. Here the real divides are not between one
religion and another but between what you might call cosmopolitan and countercosmopolitan forms of religiosity. And by cosmopolitanism I mean only this: an
attitude that combines moral concern for all people with a willingness to let others live their own lives. Universality plus difference is the cosmopolitan slogan.

Developing cosmopolitan responses to countercosmopolitan tendencies
requires detailed engagement with the particulars of a tradition; that is why the
best chance of moving the countercosmopolitans is often to get their cosmopolitan coreligionists to begin the conversation. We live in a world in which
various countercosmopolitan fundamentalisms—Buddhist, Christian, Hindu,
Jewish, and Muslim—are at work in religious traditions that also have cosmopolitan adherents and traditions. It is this fact that gives me hope that we can
work our way toward a world in which diversity and pluralistic tolerance are
possible both within and among nations.

For the problem I have identified—that disputes grounded in controversies
about metaphysics are unlikely to be resolved—has been solved in the past in
part because ordinary believers were willing to live without worrying about the
theoretical resolution of the contradictions. A life can be psychologically integrated by religious narratives and practices without being logically integrated.
Attendance at church (or temple or mosque) and prayer in everyday life can go on
in company and harmony with others of different faiths. Historically, what has
made the growth of toleration in the Christian West possible has not been the
growth of agreement about the metaphysical claims of religion. Protestant toleration of Catholics and Catholic toleration of Jews, for example, developed in contexts where there was a continuing conviction of the error of the tolerated: that is

why it was a form of *toleration*, of bearing with others despite their failings. Nor has toleration required the explicit abandonment of the authority of scripture. Many contemporary Christians insist still on the authority of scripture, even on biblical inerrancy. As a result, many of them, taking this claim seriously, know, for example, that Exodus 22:18 says: "Thou shalt not suffer a witch to live." This may lead them to worry about their children participating in Halloween festivities. Nevertheless, it does not lead them to go out looking for followers of Wicca to lynch. Similarly, those Anglican congregations that have welcomed gay priests could hardly be unaware that there are passages that suggest that (at least some kinds of) sex between men is an "abomination."

In understanding the possibilities of cosmopolitan cohabitation with people of different faiths, we need always to recall that toleration is a practice, and that, like most practices, it can survive despite theoretical incoherence. Given the actual texts and the actual histories of most of the world religions, people consumed by religious certainty and bent on coherence will likely find themselves unable to live at peace with others because they will insist that everyone ought to recognize a singular truth. But if we look at the religions that face each other in our country or our world, we see that each of them has resources—in its moral and textual traditions—for underwriting a life in peace with neighbors whose faiths are different.

Of course, they also have the resources for underwriting wars of conversion or massacres of unbelievers. But it is foolish to point to bellicose passages in the texts of one religion and declare it, and all its sects, essentially anticosmopolitan, when there are also such passages in the texts of other religions, which have sects that practice toleration. By themselves these passages enforce nothing, just as the more pacific passages require uptake if they are to do their cosmopolitan work. It is, no doubt, an entertaining parlor game for outsiders to point to passages in people's scriptures that they do not seem to live by: in the First Epistle to the Corinthians 11:14, Saint Paul writes, "Doth not even nature itself teach you, that, if a man have long hair, it is a shame unto him?" which is something that might have surprised you if you hung out, as I did, in the sixties with Christian hippies. Knowing this, why think that because some Muslim texts explicitly require women to cover their faces no devout Muslim woman could enter the public world unveiled?

Taking up the cosmopolitan texts and traditions requires more than just pointing to them. It requires, as the peacemakers of every tradition know, courage, persistence, and appeals to those elements of human psychology that draw us to kindness and concern for others and away from cruelty. Practicing toleration ourselves, putting it into practice as those peacemakers seek to do, helps create a global community each of whose local branches strengthens the work of the others. There is little hope for direct dialogue with the anticosmopolitans of any faith. They are against conversation save in the service of conversion. But we can be in touch with them indirectly through our dialogue with their more cosmopolitan brethren. And we strengthen the hands of the cosmopolitans by our decent, respectful engagement with them; we help them in their struggle to bring more of their coreligionists to the side of toleration, just as their conversation strengthens our own search for modes of productive cohabitation.

Identifying the resources for peaceful coexistence requires what I just now called a "detailed engagement with the particulars" of each of the traditions of faith with which we live. I want to insist, in closing, against those who regard religion itself as the problem, on the cosmopolitan traditions of Christianity and Islam, whose struggle with each other is seen by many as the greatest religious challenge faced by politics today. The first person we know to call himself *kosmou polites* (a citizen of the world) was, as previously mentioned, Diogenes of Sinope, Sinope being a trading city on the Black Sea founded by the Ionians. It was he, as I say, who began a tradition in the classical world that was inherited by both Hellenized Judaism and Christianity, and thus, later, by Islamic philosophy.

Nor is Muslim cosmopolitanism something that existed only among its philosophers. The history of Islam includes the sixteenth-century Mughal emperor Jalaluddin Muhammad Akbar—a descendant both of Timur or Tamburlane, the fourteenth-century lord of Central Asia, and (it is said) of Genghis Khan, the twelfth- to thirteenth-century Mongolian emperor—in whose capital there was a flourishing culture of intellectual debate with infidel traditions. Over the last two centuries, one can identify distinguished Islamic scholars who have engaged seriously with ideas from outside Islam.[24] Ahmed al-Tayeb, president of Al-Azhar, the world's oldest Muslim university (in fact, the oldest university, period), has lent the Archbishop of Canterbury his pulpit. And he has said, "God created diverse peoples. Had He wanted to create a single *ummah*, He would have, but He chose to make them different until the day of resurrection. Every Muslim must fully understand this principle."[25]

Christianity, too, from its earliest days, echoes Stoic cosmopolitanism. You hear it in the language of the Greek-speaking Saul of Tarsus, another town in Asia Minor, in what is now southern Turkey, about halfway between Sinope and Jerusalem. Saul was a Hellenized Jew and a Roman citizen—known to history as Saint Paul, the first great institutional architect of the Christian church. Here is a typical passage: "There is neither Jew nor Greek, there is neither bond nor free, there is neither male nor female: for ye are all one in Christ Jesus" (Galatians 3:28). Much of Saint Paul's evangelism took place in Asia Minor, where he was born. These well-known lines are from the Epistle to the Galatians.

Here is a fact you could not make up: Sinope, Diogenes' hometown, was in Galatia. So Saint Paul, when he wrote those very cosmopolitan words, was writing to Diogenes' people—to the very people who gave the world the first known cosmopolitan.

NOTES

Epigraph Note. "So much of evil could religion urge," http://perseus.uchicago. edu/hopper/text.jsp?doc=Perseus:text:1999.02.0130:book=1.

1. I first learned of the martyrs of Córdoba many years ago in reviewing Norman Daniel's *The Arabs and Mediaeval Europe*, 2nd ed. (London: Longmans, 1979). See my "Mediaeval Misunderstandings Explained," *Voice of the Arab World* 90, no. 2 (1979): 6. Even the standard Christian version of the story has Perfectus condemning the Prophet for the first time only after he was asked by a group of Muslims specifically what he thought and was given an undertaking that they would not turn him in. A few days later, when they apparently no longer felt governed by their undertaking, they did report him to the *qadi*, who invited Perfectus to retract, gave him time to think about his refusal to do so (it was during Ramadan), and finally ordered the execution when he persisted in his claim that Muhammad was a false prophet.

2. See, for example, *The Ascent of the Prophet to Heaven*, a mid-sixteenth-century Safavid painting in the collection of the Smithsonian; http://www.asia.si.edu/ collections/zoomObject.cfm?ObjectId=22226.

3. For the meaning of this term, see http://www.usc.edu/dept/MSA/reference/ glossary/term.MUJAHID.html: "Someone who is active and fights for Islam."

4. Yamin Zakaria, "Freedom for Danish Bacon Part One," (February 9, 2006) http://www.jihadunspun.com/index-side_internal.php?article=106166&list=/home. php&. Accessed March 29, 2008.

5. "Pornographic Past Catches Up with Candidate," *Copenhagen Post Online* (November 14, 2005), http://www.cphpost.dk/get/92160.html. Accessed March 29, 2008.

6. Ibid.

7. https://www.cia.gov/cia/publications/factbook/fields/2122.html.

8. Phil Zuckerman, "Atheism: Contemporary Numbers and Patterns," in *The Cambridge Companion to Atheism*, ed. Michael Martin (Cambridge: Cambridge University Press, forthcoming), 47–68, http://www.pitzer.edu/academics/faculty/ zuckerman/atheism.html.

9. The problem that not everyone who identifies as Lutheran should count as an adherent arises for the other religious traditions, too, of course.

10. Frederik Barth, "Ethnic Groups and Boundaries," in *Theories of Ethnicity: A Classical Reader*, ed. Werner Sollors (New York: New York University Press, 1996), 294–324.

11. Sir Edward B. Tylor, *Primitive Culture: Researches into the Development of Mythology, Philosophy, Religion, Language, Art and Custom* (New York: Henry Holt, 1899), 424. "And although it may seem to afford a bare and meager definition

of a minimum or religion, it will be found practically sufficient; for where the root is, the branches will generally be produced." Ibid., 426.

12. Clifford Geertz, *The Interpretation of Cultures: Selected Essays* (London: Fontana Press, 1993), 89–90. The elided passage runs: "In religious belief and practice a group's ethos is rendered intellectually reasonable by being shown to represent a way of life ideally adapted to the actual state of affairs the world view describes, while the world view is rendered emotionally convincing by being presented as an image of an actual state of affairs peculiarly well-arranged to accommodate such a way of life. This confrontation and mutual confirmation has two fundamental effects. On the one hand, it objectivizes moral and aesthetic preferences by depicting them as the imposed conditions of life implicit in a world with a particular structure, as mere common sense given the unalterable shape of reality. On the other, it supports these received beliefs about the world's body by invoking deeply felt moral and aesthetic sentiments as experiential evidence for their truth." A *religion*, he goes on to say, offering a now-famous definition, is "(1) a system of symbols which acts to (2) establish powerful, pervasive, and long-lasting moods and motivations in men by (3) formulating conceptions of a general order of existence and (4) clothing these conceptions with such an aura of factuality that (5) the moods and motivations seem uniquely realistic." Ibid., 90.

13. So the account is, as philosophers say, "nominalist" rather than realist.

14. Question 4 on the FAQ on the Web site www.tamiltigers.net is "Is the LTTE a religious organization?" The answer begins with a laconic, if emphatic, "No." http://www.tamiltigers.net/faq/faq04.html.

15. Given the human propensity to desire social standing, one kind of scarcity is inevitable, namely, the scarcity of positions at the top of hierarchies of social status. This is what Hobbes meant when he called "glory," in chapter 13 of *Leviathan*, one of the three "principall causes of quarrell" (in the phrase that gave me my title.) What he does not there notice is the connection between social identity, as we have been discussing it, and glory.

16. There are 192 UN members plus the Vatican, Taiwan, Palestine and Western Sahara, minus the United Kingdom plus England, Scotland, Wales, and Northern Ireland. (If you thought the UN had 191 members, you did not notice the accession of Montenegro in June 2006, after its separation from Serbia.)

17. Arjun Appadurai, *Fear of Small Numbers: An Essay on the Geography of Anger* (Durham, NC: Duke University Press, 2006), 3.

18. See Eugen Weber, "Who Sang the Marseillaise?" in *My France: Politics, Culture, Myth* (Cambridge, MA: Belknap Press, 1991), 92–102.

19. Linda Colley, *Britons: Forging the Nation, 1707–1837* (New Haven, CT: Yale University Press, 1992), 6.

20. Steven Nadler, *Rembrandt's Jews* (Chicago: University of Chicago Press, 2003).

21. There is a crucial difference between forms of worship as a feature of a way of life and a polity, on the one hand, and "religions" as something that a state, empire (e.g., Constantine's), or community might promulgate: self-conscious churches are often the remnants of extinct polities. And so a fraught relation between church and state is pretty much built into the system.

22. Lying with a man as with a woman is said to be "toeba" (TO VE BAH), an "abomination," a term used also of many activities from religious offenses, like idol worship (Deuteronomy 7:25), to the observance of taboos against eating seafood such as lobster and crab (Leviticus 11:10) and other biblically unclean animals (Leviticus 20:25), to obvious moral offenses like lying (Proverbs 12:22), using rigged weights (Deuteronomy 25:13–15, Proverbs 11:1), and cheating in business more generally (Proverbs 20:10 and Proverbs 20:23), to remarrying an ex-wife who has since been married to someone else (Deuteronomy 24:4).

23. See the sources cited in Zuckerman "Atheism."

24. For Sayyid Ahmad Khan, see the essay by Javed Majeed, "Nature, Hyperbole, and the Colonial State: Some Muslim Appropriations of European Modernity in Late Nineteenth-Century Urdu Literature," in *Islam and Modernity: Muslim Intellectuals Respond*, ed. John Cooper, Ronald Nettler, and Mohamed Mahmoud (London: I. B. Tauris, 2000), 10–37; for Taha, see the essay by Mohamed Mahmoud, "Mahmud Muhammad Taha's Second Message of Islam and His Modernist Project," in *Islam and Modernity: Muslim Intellectuals Respond*, ed. John Cooper, Ronald Nettler, and Mohamed Mahmoud (London: I. B. Tauris, 2000), 105–128; there are references to Muhammad 'Abduh throughout the book. Tariq Ramadan, *Western Muslims and the Future of Islam* (New York: Oxford University Press, 2003); Khaled Abou El-Fadl, *The Place of Tolerance in Islam* (Boston: Beacon Press, 2002).

25. See the interview by Rania Al Malky in *Egypt Today* 26, no. 2 (February 2005).

BIBLIOGRAPHY

Al Malky, Rania. Interview with Sheikh Ahmed El-Tayeb. *Egypt Today* 26, no. 2 (February 2005), http://www.egypttoday.com/article.aspx?ArticleID=2292. Accessed March 29, 2008.

Appadurai, Arjun. *Fear of Small Numbers: An Essay on the Geography of Anger*. Durham, NC: Duke University Press, 2006.

Appiah, Kwame Anthony. "Mediaeval Misunderstandings Explained." *Voice of the Arab World* 90, no. 2 (1979): 6.

Barth, Frederik. "Ethnic Groups and Boundaries." In *Theories of Ethnicity: A Classical Reader*, ed. Werner Sollors, 294–324. New York: New York University Press, 1996.

CIA World Factbook. https://www.cia.gov/cia/publications/factbook/fields/2122.html.

Colley, Linda. *Britons: Forging the Nation, 1707–1837*. New Haven, CT: Yale University Press, 1992.

Copenhagen Post Online. "Pornographic Past Catches Up with Candidate," November 14, 2005. http://www.cphpost.dk/get/92160.html.

Daniel, Norman. *The Arabs and Mediaeval Europe*. 2nd ed. London: Longmans, 1979.

El-Fadl, Khaled Abou. *The Place of Tolerance in Islam*. Boston: Beacon Press, 2002.

Geertz, Clifford. *The Interpretation of Cultures: Selected Essays*. London: Fontana Press, 1993.

Hobbes, Thomas. *Leviathan*. Cambridge: Cambridge University Press, 1904.

Lucretius. *De Rerum Natura*. Book 1, l. 101. http://perseus.uchicago.edu/hopper/text.jsp?doc=Perseus:text:1999.02.0130:book=1.

Mahmoud, Mohamed. "Mahmud Muhammad Taha's Second Message of Islam and His Modernist Project." In *Islam and Modernity: Muslim Intellectuals Respond,* ed. John Cooper, Ronald Nettler, and Mohamed Mahmoud, 105–128. London: I. B. Tauris, 2000.

Majeed, Javed. "Nature, Hyperbole, and the Colonial State: Some Muslim Appropriations of European Modernity in Late Nineteenth-Century Urdu Literature." In *Islam and Modernity: Muslim Intellectuals Respond,* ed. John Cooper, Ronald Nettler, and Mohamed Mahmoud, 10–37. London: I. B. Tauris, 2000.

Nadler, Steven. *Rembrandt's Jews.* Chicago: University of Chicago Press, 2003.

Ramadan, Tariq. *Western Muslims and the Future of Islam.* New York: Oxford University Press, 2003.

Tylor, Sir Edward B. *Primitive Culture: Researches into the Development of Mythology, Philosophy, Religion, Language, Art and Custom.* New York: Henry Holt, 1899.

USC-MSA Compendium of Muslim Texts. http://www.usc.edu/dept/MSA/.

Weber, Eugen. *My France: Politics, Culture, Myth.* Cambridge, MA: Belknap Press, 1991.

Zakaria, Yamin. "Freedom for Danish Bacon Part One." *Jihad Unspun,* February 9, 2006. http://www.jihadunspun.com/newsarchive/article_internal.php?article=106166&list=/newsarchive/index.php&.

Zuckerman, Phil. "Atheism: Contemporary Numbers and Patterns." In *The Cambridge Companion to Atheism,* ed. Michael Martin, 47–68. Cambridge: Cambridge University Press, forthcoming. http://www.pitzer.edu/academics/faculty/zuckerman/atheism.html.

3

On the Possibility of Religious Pluralism

Pratap Bhanu Mehta

One of the great perplexities of our age is this: we seem to think that religion matters a great deal to politics but are unsure about just why it matters, how it matters, or indeed even what religion is. Certainly, reference to religious language seems to pervade politics, moral argument, and social conflict around the world. But what are we to make of this "return" of religion? Is it merely "flotsam on the sea of a post-religious age," to use a phrase of Charles Taylor's?[1] Or does the rise of religion represent something more fundamental? What would count as evidence for or against these views? Religion is a trope around which a good deal of conflict seems to be organized; but it is equally true that for every conflict that is attributed to "religion," there is a rival explanation that traces the root of the conflict to some other cause altogether: misdirected class conflict, failed states, incomplete nationalisms, repressed sexual needs, or even unmet social aspiration.

We are, at one level, profoundly ambivalent in how we understand the place of religion in collective life. We premise a justification of liberal society on the thought that it allows different religions to flourish, but worry about the limits that need to be placed on what thus flourishes. While the social functions of religion seem to dissolve, in that religion cannot order the world as an unbroken totality, its subjective functions seem to acquire a new intensity. In an age of subjectivism, we want to grant religion some special status—we want to affirm it as something important, an act of choice that is somehow more significant than choosing between flavors of ice cream—but are unsure about how to affirm its status. We want to be open to the possibility that religion will be a source of meaning, yet at the same time worry if the needs and demands of society are subject to any imperatives that come from outside the realm of the social, something that subordinates the social to something perhaps more transcendent. Religion is something we cannot seem to affirm or disavow. We are not sure quite what to do with it.

This dilemma over the status of religion may be endemic to modernity. But two particular historical developments make this dilemma existentially more vivid for citizens of modern democracies. The first is the challenge of pluralism, the fact that many liberal democracies are now composed of citizens who profess a variety of beliefs. In a way, there is nothing new about this predicament. But the challenge of pluralism is exacerbated by the fact that there is a fairly thick range of normative restrictions on the kinds of argument that are acceptable when accommodating diversity. Many early modern societies have a wonderful history of toleration, with different faiths and ways of life coexisting, sometimes even intermingling. But this toleration usually exhibited two features. First, it was hierarchical, with the political superiority of one or another of the faiths being openly acknowledged. The second feature was that this form of toleration was what might be called segregationist: different ways of life were given their own space and domain, without it being assumed that members of different groups would speak a language of common citizenship. The modern challenge arises because all citizens have to be treated equally— prima facie hierarchical conceptions of toleration are suspect—and because all modern states have a conception of common citizenship that involves citizens making decisions over collective life together. Therefore, "to each community its own practices," is not always a normatively viable solution. The challenge for modern democracies is not pluralism per se but reconciling pluralism with a common political identity.

The second source exacerbating the dilemma of religion is globalization. Globalization and the challenge of pluralism are connected most straightforwardly in many ways. Patterns of migration have made the dilemma of pluralism more urgent; transnational religious movements are possible in a new and unprecedented way. But perhaps most important, globalization has created all kinds of identity dilemmas in which religion plays a complicated part. In short, the functions that religion or religious identity perform in the public sphere have been made vastly more complicated as a result of globalization. It makes rather more complicated questions such as Is religion about belief? Is it about a way of life? Or is it a marker of identity? Or what combination of the three? This observation is the starting point of this essay.

A first section problematizes the concept of religion, not with a view to debunking the concept but in order to underscore that it is not always clear what we are invoking when we invoke "religion" in contemporary argument. A set of distinctions about what is at stake in religious pluralism provide a starting point. A corollary of these distinctions is that the line between religious and secular can often be a function of politics and not at all self-evident. The second section argues that what counts as a religious motive is indeterminate, but that is the source of religion's potency in politics. It is precisely because religion is not easily available as a way of life that it becomes a self-conscious ideology. The third and final section of the essay takes up the case of India in order to illustrate the complex relationship between religious pluralism, globalization, and world politics in the contemporary era.

The Stakes of Religion

What is at stake in invoking religion? Is it a way of life or a "true belief"? Perhaps the best introduction to these issues is provided by two classic passages from antiquity that lay out the stakes.

In the first century B.C.E., Cicero wrote in *De Natura Deorum*:

> for *religion has been* dissociated from superstition not only by philosophers but by our own ancestors as well. I may mention as to these two terms that men who used to spend whole days in prayer and sacrifice in order that their children might survive them (*essent superstites*), were called *superstitiosus,* a title which afterwards extended more widely, while such as heedfully repeated and, as it were, "regathered" (*relegerent*) everything that formed a part of divine worship, were named *religiosus* from *relegere,* in the same way that *elegans* is derived from *eligere, diligens* from *diligere,* and *intellegens* from *intellegere,* for in all these words the force of *legere* is the same as in *religiosus*. It was in this way that with the words *superstitiosus* and *religiosus* the one became the designation of a fault, the other of an excellence.[2]

Lactantius, a Christian writing more than three centuries later, responded:

> We are fastened and bound to God by this bond of piety, where religion itself takes its name. The word is not as Cicero interpreted it from "re-reading," or "choosing again" (*relegendo*). . . . We can know from the matter itself how inept this interpretation is. For if superstition

and religion are engaged in worshipping the same gods, there is light or rather no difference . . . because religion is a worship of the true; superstition of the false. And it is important, really, why you worship, not how you worship, or what you pray for. . . . We have said that *the name of religion is taken from the bond of piety, because God has bound and fastened man to Himself of piety, since it is necessary for us to serve Him as Lord and obey Him as father. . . . They are superstitious who worship many and false gods; but we, who supplicate the one true God, are religious.*[3]

The contrast could not be more striking.[4] For Cicero, religion is more akin to tradition, a body of practices inherited from ancestors. It is an ongoing way of life. For Lactantius, religion is ultimately about worshiping the correct God in the appropriate way. It involves two thoughts. First, that the believer be sincere in his belief for it to qualify appropriately as religion. Second, mere worship is not enough: the God being worshiped must be the true God, not any God but one who is truly our creator. For Lactantius, the distinction between *religio* and *superstitio* is marked by the opposition between true and false. This distinction is not particularly germane to Cicero's understanding of religion. Like the Romans, he too contrasts *religio* and *superstitio*, but the grounds of the distinction are quite different. The relevant contrast is not between true and false but between excess and moderation. For him *superstitio* consists in an act of not choosing rightly from tradition; it does not refer primarily to belief. For Lactantius, the focus of religion primarily is: *Whom* do you worship? For Cicero, it is almost as if the real question is: *How* do you worship?

It is often thought that a religion more concerned with truth will lend itself to persecutory ideologies. But this claim should not be overstated. Pagan religions like that of Rome, or occasionally religions like Hinduism can generate their own politics of persecution. But the grounds of these ideologies are surely different. It is unlikely that Roman religion or Hinduism is worried about the falsity of other religions. What are a few more Gods among the numerous that already exist? They rather become persecutory when they link the presence of rival doctrines as a palpable threat to their way of life. In other words, the boundaries between doctrines, practices, and beliefs that are tolerated and those that are not are marked politically rather than theologically. Whereas for Lactantius, those boundaries of toleration are clearly marked theologically, for Cicero they were more political.

These contrasts have great consequences for how the distinction between the religious and the nonreligious gets drawn. For Lactantius, this distinction marks the boundary between Christians and others, especially pagans. But this rather commonplace observation poses a serious challenge. Can the boundary between the religious and the nonreligious be derived independently of particular theologies? Does the term "religion" pick out a universal domain of experience? Is it possible to have a "religion" and for it not become your "identity"? What is the relationship between identity and belief, and which way does the causation run? Conversely, is it possible for a "religion" to become your identity without subscription to any particular set of beliefs? This is the phenomenon known as the ethnicization of religion, where participants come to participate and share in a religious group identity in an abstract sense. I identify as a Hindu or Sikh or whatever without any beliefs associated with a religion whatsoever. (In Cicero's case this was clearly a possibility: he could disbelieve Roman theology yet practice Roman religion—most commentators see this as an instance of Cicero being inauthentic in the profession of his priestly duties. But why do we suppose that that relation between belief and practice has to correspond to a classical Christian model?)

Perhaps we are living in an age where the two models of religion that Cicero and Lactantius represent are no longer available to us as distinct models. In part this is because even the so-called customary itself is, in some sense, an act of choice, governed by complex principles and considerations; it is subject to the demands of justification and can no longer claim authority on the ground that it is customary. It seems no longer possible to identify religion with a particular way of life, or a set of customs; nor can our usage simply restrict it to identification with a true theology. Arguably, the term "religion" is invoked because neither custom nor theology is self-validating, as they were for Cicero and Lactantius, respectively. So what are we talking about when we invoke religion?

Attempts to define religion often miss an interesting question. Who draws the boundaries around what counts as religious? What makes something religious rather than not religious?[5] Can the concept of religion be used across traditions? Can the concept be taken to refer unproblematically to the same phenomenon? It seems here that there are two options that are tempting but pose problems. The first option is an expansive notion of religion that makes it almost synonymous with culture. It was this sort of definition that would allow scholars to assert things like: For Hindus all aspects of life are religiously regulated. But if a religion can pervade the entire domain of activity of a particular culture, the whole concept becomes meaningless. On the other hand, if we define religion by listing certain essential attributes, it is not always clear by whose authority a particular set of attributes are thought to be essential to a definition of "religion." Why should we include beliefs but not moods and motivations? How do we classify particular acts as being religious?

In contemporary discussions of the challenges posed by religious pluralism, many different things are at stake. At a first approximation we should distinguish three different issues. The first issue is this: What are the *grounds* for belief? For liberal theory, such as that of John Rawls, this is the central issue. Should reasons derived from religious conceptions be acceptable in the public sphere, given that not all citizens can subscribe to those grounds for belief? Are such reasons compatible with the idea of citizenship based on reciprocity and fairness? The first line of contest is therefore this: Should arguments based on appeals to religion be legitimized in the public sphere? Or should conceptions of political morality always depend upon freestanding arguments? This is a large philosophical question that is perhaps more germane to academic discussions of secularism than to the global politics of religion and pluralism.

The second set of controversies arises from the *scope* of religious belief. There are some religious movements where religion has been more effectively privatized. This does not mean that beliefs are not sincerely held, or important to their adherents. It simply means that these beliefs do not apply to vast areas of social life. The extent to which religion poses a challenge depends upon how much area of social life comes under its jurisdiction. The more the religion is an effective way of life rather than simply a set of beliefs, the more germane this issue. Typically matters pertaining to the "family" are the last to be emancipated from religious jurisdiction. Many of the conflicts are over issues such as: Should family law or gender relations still be governed by religious precepts? Who decides where the boundaries lie? How far can religion dilute its scope without being rendered irrelevant? On this view the issue is not the legitimacy of religious argument; it is the scope of these arguments. This is a question haunting many religious adherents and is discussed at greater length in the next section.

The third set of controversies arises from the *intensity* of religious belief. This has two aspects. The first is the thought that there is often a passion associated with religious belief that is the source of political instability. This passion itself may immobilize reason and civility. Here the issue is not so much philosophical as psychological, rooted in the Enlightenment fear of what the eighteenth century called "enthusiasm." The second aspect has to do with identity. The passions associated with religious belief can be particularly destructive when religions construct images of nonadherents that are often the source of conflict. Under modern conditions of globalization, these images may have less to do with actual beliefs or ways of life. Rather, members of a particular religion are marked out as posing a threat because of who they are. This intensity of distrust of members of other religions is often exacerbated where religion becomes the basis of a national identity that marks out other religions as a possible threat. A prominent example of this is interreligious violence in India. This has less to do with disputes over the grounds of belief, or the scope of religion. But it has more to do with the fact that some groups want to make religion the basis of national identity. These sorts of disputes have more to do with particular histories of nationalism than religious arguments as such.

It is important to keep these distinctions in mind, since they require different sorts of responses. The challenge posed by religion to liberal theory is not exactly the same as the challenge that arises out of the conjunction of nationalism and religion.

Whatever one's views on defining religion, there is something useful in thinking of religion as a politically constructed category. A full-blooded nominalist line on religion has its advantages: what religion is depends upon who is defining it. Hobbes made the persuasive suggestion that the line between the religious and the secular is itself a function of sovereign power. Hobbes's radicalism was not simply to subordinate religion to politics; it was to assert emphatically that what counts as religious was itself a function of political power. The issue then becomes not "What is religious?" but "What is at stake in marking something as 'religious'?" Is it a stratagem to marginalize an argument, or a device to claim authority for it? Perhaps rather than obsessing with what religion is, we should be more attentive to the contexts in which the term is invoked and the purposes it serves. Perhaps we should look for its effects rather than its essence.

Hobbes may have been right that the distinction between the sacred and secular emerges only as a result of the advance of sovereign power. But this claim has two enormous consequences to which we have not paid sufficient attention. First, if this claim is correct, then there is something profoundly misleading about the dominant "church-state" metaphors we use to describe the relationship between religion and politics. Our prevalent metaphors for talking about regimes of religious toleration often disguise the stakes. No secular state, as is now familiar, can be neutral or impartial among religions because the state determines the boundaries within which neutrality must operate. Similarly, another metaphor used by Amy Gutmann, which describes the separation of church and state as a two-way accommodation whose purpose is to protect religion from the state as much as it is to protect the state from religion, does not adequately acknowledge the fact that the two-way accommodation metaphor works only when vast areas of what might be considered religious have already been ceded to the state, arguably to the point where religious practice becomes socially less consequential.[6]

The two-way accommodation metaphor also belies the fact that all states extensively regulate religion; one might say that they define the normatively permissible boundaries of religion. Particular aspects of religion are given protection, recognition, and support; others are the subjects of indifference, and many aspects are curtailed and proscribed. But the most crucial point is that the boundaries between the permissible and impermissible will be set by the state. It is therefore a little misleading to argue that the point of normative theory is to figure out the balance between "two realms," where religion does not encroach upon politics, or politics does not encroach upon religion. There is no such thing as "two realms" independent of where politics draws the lines.

If this is indeed the case, then it calls into question at least one move that liberal theorists are inclined to make in response to challenges from "religion." This is to invoke what you might call the sovereignty of the political. This is the idea that there is some freestanding realm of the political, which trumps the claims of the so-called comprehensive views that characterize religions. But invoking the political does not answer the question about who draws the boundaries of the political. This itself is a political question, in that there is no self-validating answer to it. The return of "religious" politics can therefore be read another way: When religion challenges politics, it is not so much a way of the transcendent disrupting the social as it is simply a reminder of the inherent instability of the political. Religion is invoked to destabilize the boundaries, and the secular is invoked to secure them. But can either realm be self-referential, self-instituted, self-sufficient, and self-validating?

But we can look at the problem from the reverse angle as well. If politics is not a self-validating realm, neither is religion. The sense in which the distinction between the secular and the sacred, or the religious and the nonreligious, has become problematic is this: Our dominant picture of talking about this relationship comes from thinking of the "church" and "state" as two different and independently identifiable institutions. But modern politics is characterized by a profound fragmentation of authority. Yes, institutions like the church—or their functional equivalents in other "religions"—still exist, but none can be unproblematically identified as a locus of authority within the religions they came to represent. In a way, it is characteristic of our times that the contest over authority goes all the way down, even within so-called religiously inspired movements. It has been argued, with some plausibility, that Al-Qaeda, far from being a return to religion in any conventional sense, represents the breakdown and a perverse kind of democratization within Islam. For what it has done is called into question the whole idea of authority within Islam. But if there is no locus of authority, how can the boundaries of the "religious" be defined? When George Bush claims that he has some intimations of God's plan for the world and his own role in those plans, what conception of God's authority is being invoked? If the political is not a self-validating realm, neither is religion. Perhaps it is not an accident that we are tying ourselves in knots trying to characterize contemporary religious movements. If Al-Qaeda calls into question the authority of the sovereign state, it equally calls into question any conception of religious authority. Perhaps it is not an accident that we are endlessly searching for what Islam or Hinduism or Christianity's true teaching is, trying valiantly to assure ourselves that Islam or Hinduism does not really teach this or that. This search, as a response to political challenges, is distinctly odd because it is premised upon the hope that there is a necessary truth of a religion, that this truth will be benign, and that this necessary truth once apprehended will move those who claim adherents of that religion. But the fact that we are engaged in this search itself suggests that the question of authority in matters "religious" has been opened up to an unprecedented degree.

The point of the foregoing is found in the following thought: what marks our predicament is not the return of the religious but the fact that neither so-called politics nor so-called religion appears to carry self-validating authority. What we can expect, therefore, is not the conflict between religion and politics but a deep politicization of fundamental questions all the way down; not a contest of authority between "religion" and "politics," as two identifiable realms, but as an unsettling of authority that cuts deep into both politics and religion.

This interpenetration of religion and politics is evident in the rhetoric of Osama Bin Laden himself. As Charles Glass has argued,

> His message is plain: leave the Muslim world alone, and it will leave you alone. Kill Muslims, and they will kill you. "America won't be able to leave this ordeal unless it pulls out of the Arabian Peninsula, and it ceases its meddling in Palestine, and throughout the Islamic world," bin Laden told the *al-Jazeera* correspondent Taysir Alluni six weeks after the 11 September attacks. "If we gave this equation to any child in any American school, he would easily solve it within a second." When Bush said in 2004 that his was "a war against people who hate freedom," bin Laden responded: "Perhaps he can tell us why we did not attack Sweden, for example."[7]

Of course Bin Laden is, to put it mildly, being disingenuous, but quite revealing as well. Is this a religious argument or a political one? Or both? What will hang on this classification? The same question can be posed for literally any phenomenon. Is the headscarf affair in France a religious or a political affair? Is Falun Gong a religious or a political movement? When Hindu nationalists mobbed a fifteenth-century mosque, was it a religious frenzy or an articulation of a warped kind of political nationalism? The very fact that in all these instances the line between the political and the religious remains precarious suggests that religion is also an extremely politicized concept: it is not a natural kind.

What Is a Religious Motive?

If the question "What is a religion" is difficult to answer, determining what exactly a "religious motive" is, is even more so. David Hume thought that the peculiarity of religious politics stemmed from just this fact. How can religiosity be embodied in this world? What counts as a display of *religion*? Hume thought that religious believers would be consistently haunted by this anxiety. Most human beings conduct their ethical lives according to a variety of motives drawn from different sources: self-interest, social relationships, and so forth. A truly virtuous man might be drawn to righteousness as a matter of duty. But they might all still worry whether they had acted *religiously*, acted, that is, from a special motive that was an expression of their genuine piety toward God or fidelity toward their faith.

One might be tempted to think that the search for a *religious* motive is akin to what Gilbert Ryle once called a "category mistake." It is a bit like a man who, having visited all the Oxford colleges, asked where Oxford University was. A religious motive, it might be said, is not a special kind of motive. It is simply a functional ordering of all our normal motives; it does not pick out a special class of actions as much as a form of organizing all our actions. This leaves open the possibility that one could be religious, as it were, without acknowledging oneself to be such. But Hume suggested that this answer would not suffice, at least for those who were superstitious about their religion. Hume wrote:

> He considers not that the most genuine method of serving the divinity is by promoting the happiness of creatures. He still looks out for some immediate service for the Supreme Being in order to allay those terrors with which he is haunted. And any practice recommended to him, which either serves no purpose in life, or offers the strongest violence to his natural inclinations; that practice he will most readily embrace, on account of those very circumstances which should make him absolutely reject it. It seems like the more purely religious, because it proceeds from no mixture of any other consideration.[8]

For Hume this quest to prove that one was acting on a purely religious motive, undistorted by any other consideration, led to the most unnatural and self-denying behavior. This is what prompts the religious to extreme austerity and sacrifice, to look for a site where his devotion or piety can be embodied. Ordinary actions and morality are not sufficient because a religious person thinks he is bound to perform them—as everybody else does—irrespective of God. On the other hand, as Hume put it, "If he fast a day or give himself a sound whipping," this has, in his opinion, direct reference to the service of God.

For Hume the problem with the quest to embody a religious motive is this: other motives have a clearly specified objective. Someone who wants to make money makes money, even though he can engage in an excess of it. In our motives, the objects that will satiate them are clearly defined. But how exactly would a *religious* motive manifest itself? Hume thought such a motive was a motive necessarily without a specified objective, or at least without an objective that can be clearly specified. Second, this is precisely what makes a religious motive protean: it can express itself in serene self-possession or an anxious drive to mastery; a religion of *momento vivere* or a religion directed toward some future world. Third, this motive was insatiable, in that there were no limits to what would count as fulfilling it. Thus the minute persons become anxious about whether or not they are being *religious*, that anxiety will weigh pitilessly upon those unfortunate enough to be under its grip. It will saturate their lives with great exaction. (Perhaps that is why Nietzsche was to say that the love of one thing is bad—even or especially God.)

This piece of moral psychology is pertinent to understanding what we normally call religious politics. In some ways the anxiety "Am I being religious?" would not occur in quite the same way when the social order or natural world is seen teleologically as embodying God's purposes. It is possible to imagine social structures where God's presence is palpable and direct in every aspect of social relations: the quest for a religious life finds social expression in an ongoing way of life. But when social life is not itself structured by religious rhythms and teleologies, when it is difficult to comprehend the world as a single religious totality, the question of where religion is embodied becomes more insistent. This is not to suggest that it is impossible to hold on to the view that the social world is or ought to reflect God's purposes. But under conditions of modernity, endowing an ongoing way of life with religious significance is an altogether more abstract gesture. As many observers have noted, religious identities are no longer connected to participating in distinct cultural practices. In fact, cultures and nations have, for good or for ill, ceded so much space to the modern economy, the modern state, and often the egalitarian aspirations of modernity that it is more difficult to hold on to a sense of difference that is embodied in a concrete way of life. Or to put it slightly more precisely, much of the realm of public collective action, especially the polity and the economy, is not the site for expressing such differences in ways that become the cornerstone of identities. Rather, the differences are expressed more in private spaces or social spaces.

It is precisely because substantive values and horizons of meaning are shrinking that greater and inordinate weight is placed on markers of difference. As Valentine Daniel put it, "Nationalism is the horripilation of culture in insecurity and fright." Finally, in the realm of culture, it is often argued that culture is to be valued because it is constitutive of someone's identity. This alignment of culture with identity can be misleading in a couple of ways. First, the minute we are talking of identity, we are talking of difference rather than diversity. It is possible for individuals or groups who are more like each other in most respects to have a profound sense of having a different identity, a different sense of who they are. Indeed, as many have argued, we see more and more identity conflicts not because of the objective diversity between people but because of their increasing likeness. Stress on difference becomes a way of defining identity in the face of narrowing differences in other spheres of life.

It is a commonplace experience of the modern world that, contrary to what Arjun Appadurai argues, culture, politics, and economy get disembedded from each other. After all, it is not an accident that when defending religious diversity very few are defending the right of a society to be governed by a Hindu view of the division of labor, or for central banks to run on Islamic principles of usury or power to be allocated by Confucian conceptions of elite. While it is true that religion is not simply an add-on to material resources, it is palpably misleading to argue that the culture, economy, and politics cannot to some degree be disembedded from each other. This is a greater functional differentiation that modern societies produce.[9] In this context, it is quite possible that individuals and groups are sharing more and more; they are embedded in similar matrices of political and economic institutions, yet want to assert their sense of difference. In fact, as Michael Ignatieff has argued, following Freud's insight that conflicts born of the "narcissism of small differences are most acute," identity differences do not by themselves signal greater diversity. Rather, invocation of identity may be a sign that diversity is decreasing.

This is an old anxiety about modernity. Bhudev Mukhopadhyaya, the nineteenth-century Bengali poet, enjoined Indians to strenuously hold on to their toilet habits because in the long run this would be the only site at which they could assert a real sense of a different religious identity. This was a bit indelicately put, but not far off the mark. If the economy and politics are governed by their own logic and imperatives, where in concrete ways of acting will a religious life be embodied? This is a pressure that most religiously based conceptions of identity are facing under conditions of globalization and modernity. It is not an accident that almost all religions of the world—Christianity, Islam, Hinduism, Judaism, Buddhism—have constructed a narrative for themselves, in which they appear beleaguered, as ways of life get more disembedded from their dictates. There is an old saying that "we put ourselves under God's yoke most when we feel his presence least." And there is something to the thought that effective secularization of society will increase religiously based assertions. In a world where it is no longer clear how one's convictions can be embodied as a way of life in large spheres of social action, people look toward willful acts of assertion to embody those convictions. This quest can take many forms: it can take the return to a nonpolitical orthodoxy that many religious groups all over the world are experiencing. If our customary social practices differentiate us less, more observances are called for. So the heroism of religion consists in a strict private regimen of observances. Or it can take a more overt political form: an attempt to endow forms of collective existence with religious significance. Arguably, the United States is undergoing such a political phenomenon, even though its full strength is mitigated by the enduring power of American institutions. I mention this only to signal the fact that the politics of religious assertion is likely to remain a feature of organized political life in many countries, and India is no exception. But as religion ceases to be called upon to control directly the natural and social world, as many vital areas of activity lose their religious coloration, Hume's question becomes more rather than less pressing: Where concretely can a religious motivation be embodied? Is it enough to hold on to it as a matter of private belief or personal sensibility? But if not, where will religion express itself?

Another way in which this struggle for affirming the status of religion is expressed is philosophical. What does it mean to affirm the status of religion under the conditions of pluralism? Ask a value pluralist the question: What makes something valuable? The difficulty in answering this question is not because there is not much to be said on this score. One can give a whole range of answers. A given practice may contribute to human flourishing, or the satisfaction of desire, or it may be intrinsically a good and so on. But none of these considerations are decisively authoritative for any given individual. For any individual can deny that those reasons are authoritative for *him or her*. Ultimately the value of an action or a practice will be due not to its intrinsic properties but to the valuation of the one who puts value upon them.

Thus liberal society is left in the awkward position of saying that the value of religion—or most other things that are valuable—will ultimately depend upon the individual who values it. In short, such valuation will be subjective. The experience of pluralism may lead not just to the realization that one's conception of the good is simply one good among many; it may threaten the authority of the idea of the "good" itself.

So it would be futile for liberal societies to pretend that they can protect and respect anything other than the rights of individuals, within certain limits, to value whatever it is that they value. This is why there is something awkward about a public discourse that claims to "respect" religion; one can respect the rights of individuals who made particular choices, but it seems that it will be impossible to affirm some special epistemic status for "religion."

This point is important because, there has been something of an inflation in the expectations about what liberal societies can do for religion. Obviously, by preventing persecution, they can make room for all kinds of individual practices, beliefs, and faiths. But this is no more than the freedom given to every individual compatible with a similar freedom to all others. But many believers are coming to the view that while a liberal society acknowledges *them* qua individuals, it does not adequately acknowledge the force of their *beliefs*. Take, for instance, the controversies around free expression, when religious sentiments are ostensibly offended. More than an affirmation of rights, the believer looks for respect of his beliefs. But it is not easy to articulate what exactly counts as giving such respect. It has been said, not entirely without justification, that liberal societies take the right to expression seriously, but only by not taking expression itself seriously; similarly, it has to be said that liberal societies can do no more than take the right to religion seriously, but in the end religion will be nothing more than one among many choices its citizens make.

So whatever the doctrinal content of a religion, it will hugely underdetermine its relationship to the world. A religious consciousness often tries to fulfill itself, practically speaking, in visible, historical, and concrete ways and cannot remain purely at the level of intellectual abstraction or personal piety. In a way, the conjunction of religion and political formations should not therefore surprise us. Apart from the fact that often religious identities, in their ethnicized forms, are markers around which there is a legacy of social and historical subordination, a religion that tries to express itself materially will relate to the institutional formations of its time. Christian fundamentalism in the Untied States latches on to the mythology of America as the chosen nation, just as Hindu nationalism can harp on the theme of an Indian exceptionalism. The question of the relationship between religion and the world will likely be negotiated through a complicated set of lived experiences, not argumentative refinement.

Religion, Pluralism, and Globalization in India

India is, at first glance, a wonderful illustration of the ways in which these larger trends in the global politics of religion are playing out. India has always been at the forefront of the conjuncture between religious pluralism and globalization. Although more than 80 percent of its citizens are legally classified as Hindu,

India is also the second-largest Muslim country in the world, with a sizable number of Christians and members of other communities. Indeed, it could be argued that its identity has been profoundly shaped by the conjuncture of globalization and religion in its successive formations. It was one of the earliest countries to receive Christian missionaries, and the expansion of Islam and the formation of successive Muslim empires have left a deep imprint on Indian culture. The onset of modern colonialism brought a heady mix of Evangelical Christianity, Enlightenment values, and a modern state. And alongside all this, there remains the continued vitality, inventiveness, and adaptability of Indic religions. It is a hugely successful liberal democracy, but also one that has experienced intense religious violence. How is this complicated landscape being shaped by contemporary globalization? What are some of the emerging fault lines?

Most scholars would agree that in India religious conflict has arisen not from disputes over permissible grounds of belief in the public sphere, or even because of deep conflicts over ways of life. In Indian history, there is a striking absence of any articulated discourse of *intolerance*, the idea that the state can legitimately persecute someone for his beliefs. The reasons for this are complex. In part they turn on the character of Hinduism as a religion, which has never had a single locus of authority or ideas about the relationship between belief and salvation that would give succor to persecutory ideologies. Islam in the Indian subcontinent has had a varied history, but it too has experienced the imprint of India's religious pluralism, accommodating itself to the imperatives of a plural society. This mode of religious accommodation was not liberal in the sense of acknowledging the worth of individuals as free and equal citizens; yet it allowed groups not only to pursue their ways of life (with all their internal contradictions) but also to generate creative new synthesis as well. *Therefore, the challenge to religious pluralism has seldom come from persecutory religious ideologies.*

Despite this propitious cultural ground for accommodating religious pluralism, India has experienced serious conflict among religious groups. What is the source of this conflict? How has globalization exacerbated it? To answer these questions we need to reexamine the way in which modernity itself has shaped the character of religious conflict. The discussion focuses first on structural dilemmas that the modern conception of citizenship brings forth for religious pluralism and then on ways in which globalization is mutating religious identities.

Religious Conflict and Citizenship

The first and perhaps most paradoxical fact we have to acknowledge is that challenges of religious pluralism in India are shaped profoundly by modern conceptions of citizenship in at least two different ways. The modern conception of citizenship shapes religious conflict by posing two pointed questions. First, what should be the *scope* of religious belief or ways of life? Second, how can religious differences be made compatible with modern ideas of representation?

Modern conceptions of citizenship raise the question of the scope of belief in the following way. Much of the legitimacy of the modern state is founded on the fact that it liberates individuals from oppressive intermediate communities. But in order to do so, it has to take more and more domains of social life under its sovereignty. The most common example of the state expanding its sovereign domain over social life is its attempt to delegitimize a whole series of personal laws that, say, govern marriage and inheritance. Modern states argue that laws that violate gender equality, for instance, or institutionalize practices that do not acknowledge that all citizens are free and equal, should be proscribed. Like many liberal constitutions, the Indian constitution was premised upon progressively moving toward a condition where the more morally egregious aspects of social life (caste, or gender inequality) would no longer get legal recognition. The process by which this social reform was carried out, first under the aegis of the colonial state, and then under a liberal constitution, is a complicated story. But the central point was that the state had to assert authority over areas of social life that traditional religious practices had claimed as their own. So the state could intervene and abolish the practice of disallowing untouchables from entering temples, or reform personal laws to bring them more in line with a liberal egalitarianism. The immediate question that this program of social reform raised was *how* should the state claim authority over these domains of social life? Legislatures and courts, dominated by Hindus, could at least claim a modicum of authority in relation to Hindu practices. They could argue that the legislature was the institution through which Hindus were collectively and democratically reforming their traditional practices. In the absence of any authoritative source to settle questions of reform, Hindus had opted to democratically reform their institutions.

But it was difficult to apply the same logic to reform of Muslim personal laws. Would a legislature dominated by Hindus have the same authority in relation to Muslim laws as it did in relation to Hindu laws? It was partly in recognition if this conundrum, and also because of the imperative of reassuring Muslims about their place in independent India, that the state came up with a modus vivendi. It deferred the question of the reform of Muslim Personal Law. The courts incrementally tried to reform these laws, and there have been important attempts by the Muslim Personal Law Board to reform laws relating to marriage, divorce, and property. But state authority over Muslim personal law remains largely undefined. This issue remains very much alive in Indian politics. Right-wing Hindu groups charge the state with double standards: too ready to intervene in Hindu laws, but reluctant to assert authority over Muslim law. On the other hand, from the point of view of Muslim identity there is the reverse dilemma. If the state exercises sovereignty over a domain that was left for Sharia, where would Muslim identity be embodied? The issue is not so much what the content of Sharia should be. The issue is, rather, should the scope of state sovereignty be extended over a domain traditionally reserved for Sharia? This conundrum has not been formally resolved.

But this brief illustration is instructive for the relationship between religious pluralism and globalization in the following way. On the one hand, it highlights the way in which the modern discourse of equal citizenship requires the state to enlarge the scope of its authority to all domains of social life. This has the potential for creating new forms of social conflict. On the other hand, the dilemma for religious groups is this. If they cede even these remaining areas governed by traditional laws to the state, where will vestments of their identity be embodied? This is the process of disembedding religion from thick ways of life addressed earlier. What would the authority of Sharia mean? And what would remain of Muslim identity without the Sharia? It is perhaps not an accident that many states, from Europe to India, are experiencing a version of this dilemma.

The second and related way in which modern conceptions of citizenship can produce a crisis of citizenship is around the issue of representation. The introduction of representative government introduces a large question. How is this representation going to be organized? This question becomes more rather than less acute under conditions of universal suffrage. If there is a significant minority, with some legitimate vestment in its identity, it fears being swamped by simple numerical majority rule. It therefore seeks forms of representation that can protect its interests, or give expression to its identity. But here arises a dilemma. If minorities are given representation in excess of their numbers or some special protections, there is the danger of a majority backlash. The majority fears the entrenchment and institutionalization of what it thinks are unfair concessions to the minority. Minority representation turns out to be in tension with the majority's vestments that the state be its own. Take, for instance, the case of prepartition India.

What we think of as Hindu-Muslim politics in India was born squarely in the crucible of representative politics—an underappreciated fact. To simplify a complicated story for the purposes of illustration, Syed Ahmed Khan had early on sensed that the gradual introduction of representative government might prove to be a threat to Muslims, because it would naturally advantage Hindus numerically. Thus began a complex debate over Muslim representation that was never quite resolved. Various proposals were floated: separate electorates, the grouping of Muslim-majority provinces, and so forth. But in retrospect it is clear that no stable solution to this conundrum was forthcoming. Any "extra" concessions to safeguard minority interests would provoke a backlash from some section of the Hindus. Why give Muslims representation in excess of their numbers? This was the crux of the Hindu Mahasabha's and the Congress Party's own right-wing critiques of various representative schemes. A different, more regionally oriented solution was also proposed. This was premised on something like a mutual hostage theory. The interests of Muslims in Hindu-majority provinces would be safeguarded by the fact that there would be a Hindu minority in Muslim-majority provinces. But the question then arose: What about the center? If Muslims did not have something close to parity or some veto power at the center, would not the center be partial to Hindus? But if some such provisions were made for Muslims, some cried back, would not that violate some principle of equality, giving Muslims special status in excess of numbers? Why should they get parity at the center?

And so the argument went back and forth. Whatever one may think of the history of Hindu-Muslim relations, the almost sixty years of negotiations did not produce a single representative scheme that was internally stable and fair, that did not run the risk of leaning in one direction or the other. Meanwhile, the aspiration had been unleashed that the state that succeeds empire be representative. But who shall it represent? "All Indians" would be an obvious answer. But that answer would not solve the problem: How would the identities that differentiate Indians be represented, at least along this axis? Partition was a nonsolution, but a nonsolution to a problem that had proved insoluble. That it resulted in the context of an empire of long duration, and on the backs of a nationalist movement as liberal and progressive as they come, does not augur well for similar problems elsewhere. Alfred Cobban's pithy formulation—India could be neither united nor divided—remains an unassailable account of the postcolonial condition, from Cyprus to India, from Iraq to Sri Lanka.

Contemporary Iraq is an uncanny rerun of an analogous dilemma. One can take chapter and verse from royal commissions from the 1920s—the Donoughmore Commission for Sri Lanka, for example—and find the same issues at play, in more or less the same terms. To simplify a bit, the dilemma is structurally the same. The Shia majority want numerical democracy because it favors them; too many veto powers to the Sunnis (and Kurds), and the Shias cry discrimination. Too little veto power to the Sunnis, and their interests in a numerical arithmetic are not protected. This arithmetic may be made all the more precarious by the fact that Sunnis might be targets of resentment. It is true that the added fear is that Shias want a more orthodox regime, but even if that were not the case, the dilemma of minority representation would remain. In short, the dilemma is the same: If special provisions are granted to protect minorities, the majority uses a simple notion of one person one vote to cry discrimination; if, however, we go for a simple rule such as one person, one vote, the minority remains unprotected.

There is a cautionary tale in all this. It has proved to be almost impossible to find a solution to the conundrum of representation in societies where groups think of themselves as permanent majorities or permanent minorities and demand that representation protect the vestments of these identities. Can there be representative arrangements that allow all parties concerned to feel that those arrangements are, in some senses, their own, and protect the vestments they have in their identities? Unfortunately, the only stable answer to this question turns out to be paradoxical. Representative institutions function best when there are no permanent identities to be protected, when the question of identity becomes detached from the question of citizenship. Structures of representation can be most trusted when they are least tested by the burden of identities. From India to Iraq, from Fiji to Sri Lanka, the structure of the dilemma is uncannily the same. There are many paths to the detachment of identity from citizenship: sheer coercion, gradual evolution, or forced territorial consolidation that makes the question of representation irrelevant by completely fusing identity and citizenship. But none of them has ever been brought about by a straightforward democratic solution.

The lesson for religious pluralism is this. A political order can give space for religious freedom of individuals, but if the political order is required to be representative of religious communities, then there is no solution to the problem of representation. In short, conditions of modernity entail that religious groups give up the aspiration that a political order will represent *them*, qua religious groups in some respect.

Independent India is, in some senses, struggling between two competing questions. On the one hand, there is the modern aspiration that what rights people have should be independent of any religious identity they may have; on the other hand, identities should be given political recognition. What India has produced in the process is a messy but workable modus vivendi that sometimes breaks down (as it did horrifically in the Gujarat riots of 2002). But the crucial point is that Hindu-Muslim conflict emerged out of the crucible of modern politics itself in a contest over the scope of the authority of the state, and in a contest over the terms of fair representation. Both Hindu nationalism and Muslim nationalism in India were offshoots of this conflict. Interreligious tension has less to do with disputes over beliefs. It has something to do with the conflicts over where the boundaries of the state should be, that is, over the scope of religious authority. But it has more to do with the fact that some groups want to make religion the basis of national identity. These sorts of disputes have more to do with particular histories of nationalism than religious arguments as such.

Religion and Political Identity in an Era of Globalization

Globalization has exacerbated the structural dilemma inherent in modern conceptions of citizenship in at least three ways that are profoundly impacting politics. The impact of globalization on religious pluralism is most evident in that the quest for religious recognition and competition among religious groups has become truly global.

Transnational linkages of religious groups add to local competition and put a strain on local patterns of accommodation. All three of India's largest religious groups are experiencing versions of this phenomenon. Hindu nationalism, for instance, draws support and sustenance from the Hindu diaspora; Christian groups are often very much allied to funding sources from abroad; and various pan-Islamic groups have been growing in strength. It would be a bit of an exaggeration to say that this competition would not exist without these transnational linkages. But these linkages help in two crucial respects. They provide a broader context for the mobilization of resources, and they set parameters for new forms of ideological conflict.

Two examples from the Indian context illustrate this dynamic. The Indian state has always been wary of proselytizing. This wariness is rooted in a number of causes, including a sense of vulnerability among some Hindus that lower castes would be an easy target for conversion and a historical association of missionary activity with forms of imperialism. Formally, the Indian Constitution guarantees freedom to propagate religion. But the Indian Supreme Court has held valid laws that aim at regulating propagation that is undertaken with the intent of conversion. The philosophical basis of this position is deeply problematic, but what is of interest is that a number of states, ruled by both the Congress Party and the Hindu nationalist Bharatiya Janata Party, have passed legislation with the intent of regulating conversion. The ostensible rationale given is heightened evangelical activity that traces its roots to Southern Baptists in the United States. Certainly Christian groups in India receive a large proportion of the funding that comes through official channels under the Indian Foreign Contribution Regulation Act. Whether such regulation can be normatively justified is a matter for another occasion, but there is an invocation of transnational linkages of these groups as a ground for anxiety.[10]

The transnational linkages of Islam in India present an even more complex picture. Indian Islamic groups have had all kinds of transnational links, and there is a sense in which Islamic identity still has recourse to a community and political imagination that transcends the boundaries of the nation-state. India has been one state that has been the *object* of terrorism, with foreign militant groups targeting it. But until recently, there was a sense that a lot of militancy directed against India was rooted squarely in the geopolitical imperatives of the region, including the movement in Kashmir and strategic objectives of Pakistan. Indeed, India prided itself on the fact that despite such a thicket of transnational linkages, it was one of the few places where Al-Qaeda found no recruits whatsoever.

But there is a sense that this is changing for two reasons. First, the riots in Gujarat, in which Muslims were the principle targets, may have radicalized a section of the Muslim middle class. But second, the U.S. invasion of Iraq has once again brought international issues to the forefront of Muslim consciousness in India. After independence, for a variety of reasons, pan-Islamism had very little foothold in India. But there is growing evidence that pan-Islamic issues and identities are once again beginning to cast a shadow on Indian politics.

The growth of pan-Islamism in India is interesting for two reasons. First, it is a reminder that globalization is perceived by many to be not a seamless and open interchange but something driven by the strategic imperatives of the United States. In short, the renewed allegiance being given to transnational forms of Muslim identity draws aid and succor from the conduct of U.S. foreign policy. In other words, the way in which globalization shapes religious identities and conflict will very much depend upon the fate of U.S foreign policy. There will be a political imperative to how identities are formed. Second, managing the growth of radical Islam, which challenges the nation-state form as the most important locus of political allegiance, will pose new challenges for religious pluralism.

Globalization has managed to produce an uncanny crisis of religious identity in India. This might seem a strong claim in face of the fact that religious identities seem resurgent. But across the world, adherents of many faiths have now internalized a narrative of victimhood. On this narrative, Hindus have been for centuries at the receiving end of onslaughts from others, the Christians and Muslims. Hindutva, for many who have internalized this narrative, represents a coming to grips with history, an assertion of the will that will finally put Hindus in charge of their own destiny, invulnerable to takeover or corrosion by outside forces. To be fair, this is a narrative to which there are analogues in most religions, insofar as they have political leanings. Versions of Islam tout the same sentiments vis-à-vis the West. There is a real sense that pan-Islamism has been nurtured on the idea of a Muslim community that has been at the receiving end of the grand geopolitical designs of the last century. Even the

Christian Right in the United States draws some of its support from presenting Christianity as beleaguered, though mostly at the hands of liberals! These
narratives represent a wider failure of these religions to give a meaning or tele-
ology to everyday life under the complex conditions of modernity, and to their
inability to accept the facts of difference.

In the Indian context, this narrative not only sustains groups like the Hindu
nationalist Vishva Hindu Parishad and the Rashtriya Swayamsevak Sangh. It
also makes even those otherwise ambivalent about those groups hesitant in
their denunciations. In fact, the crisis of Hinduism is signified by the fact that
so much of contemporary Hindu identity is vested in this narrative. This is not
to deny that we often witness genuine acts of faith, or a religiosity that runs
deep, or even that Hinduism provides an astonishing grammar with which to
comprehend life and creation. But, increasingly, being a Hindu is coming to
be identified with participation in the creation of a communal identity that can
now fully, and often furiously, discharge its role in history. It is an identity constituted by a sense of injury, a sense of always having been on the losing side, a
sense of innocent victimhood. This narrative strings together Islamic Mughal
rule in the early modern period with the loss of territorial integrity during post–
World War II partition. It draws sustenance from the threat of international
militant jihadi Islam and plays upon the sentiment that modern secularism
itself is a contrivance to favor minorities. Much of the understanding of history that sustains this sense of injury is simplistic if not often false. Of greater
import is the fact that Hindu identity, in so many ways, is coming to rest upon
a sense of resentment. All religions may be undergoing a version of this crisis.
But a religion that requires the ghosts of imagined injuries to sustain itself is
conspiring to create darkness where we will not be able to recognize each other
as citizens, as human beings. Instead, we will be defined by our resentments
rather than achievements, by our willfulness rather than the moral quality of
the objectives to which our will is directed.

An identity constituted by a sense of injury will inherently be a fragile
one, constantly looking to secure itself through clear benchmarks of what
makes that identity what it is. Under such conditions it will draw the boundaries between insiders and outsiders more sharply and will render invisible the
claims of all those who might appear different. There is a sense in which underlying the resurgence of religious nationalism is a crisis of genuine religious
faith. How will, how *can* religiosity express itself, when it has ceded control of
so many domains of collective life? All that remains are totems of identity, han-
kering for a political project to get attached to. For some, like Hindu nationalists, giving the nation-state in India a Hindu hue is the project; for others like
the Christian Right, there is also the quest for some acknowledgment of its

primacy within the American context. For others still, like Islam, that political project may be fighting what it thinks of as imperialism.

Conclusion

There are four general lessons I want to highlight from the overall discussion and the Indian example. First, the distinction between what is religious and what is not is regulated by state power; it is not a self-evident distinction. Second, much of the investment of modern states in the religious-secular dichotomy—increasingly cast as a way of managing cultural and religious diversity—may exist because a focus on religion exempts secular movements like nationalism from political scrutiny. Indeed, the threats posed to a civil liberal order in India and elsewhere are less from disputes over religious beliefs and more from the conjunction of nationalism and religion. This makes religion a site of destructive passion. Third, in the contemporary era of globalization, marked by greater religious pluralism, all states have to operate with a regulative idea of religion; the boundaries within which it can operate are the function of state power.

This inevitable politicization of religion—of where it begins and ends and how it relates to state authority—suggests a way forward for the study of religion, globalization, and world politics. Rather than worrying about defining religion and politics as independent realms of activity, it might be better to focus on their effects. What are the circumstances in which they are invoked? Who invokes them, and for what purposes? For in the final analysis our concern over religion and politics cannot but reflect the profound dualism of modernity: we think religion is important enough that it should be given space, but at the same time it is a threat that needs to be contained. As an alternative to religion, we laid faith in a self-validating sphere of the political. But while the return of religion signifies the waning of the political, religion needs politics to shore up its authority as well. The return of religion to politics is at the same time an affirmation of the politicization of religion. Perhaps religion and politics are leaning on each other because it is the twilight of both. Will there be a new dawn?[11]

NOTES

1. Charles Taylor, "Foreword" to Marcel Gauchet, *The Disenchantment of the World* (Princeton, NJ: Princeton University Press, 1999), xv.

2. Cicero, *De Natura Deorum* (On the nature of the gods), trans. Francis Brooks (London: Methuen, 1896), 2: 272.

3. Lactantius, *The Divine Institutes*, trans. Sister Frances Mary McDonald (Washington, DC: The Catholic Press of America, 1964), 318–320.

4. After writing about the dispute between Cicero and Lactantius, I discovered a remarkable book: S. N. Balagangadhara, *"The Heathen in His Blindness . . .": Asia, the West and the Dynamic of Religion* (Leiden: Brill, 1994). The following two paragraphs are deeply indebted to his work.

5. After all, as Eliot once said, someone can be religious because of the quality of his doubt; while conversely, as Wittgenstein suggested, someone can be irreligious because of the profession of his faith.

6. Amy Gutmann, "Religion and the State in the United States: A Defense of Two-Way Protection," in *Obligations of Citizenship and Demands of Faith: Religious Accommodation in Pluralist Societies*, ed. Nancy Rosenblum (Princeton, NJ: Princeton University Press, 2000), 127–164.

7. Charles Glass, "Cyber Jihad," *London Review of Books* 28, no. 5 (March 9, 2006), 12–16.

8. David Hume, *Writings on Religion*, ed. Anthony Flew (Chicago, IL: Open Court, 1992), 177.

9. Niklas Luhmann, *Observations on Modernity* (Stanford, CA: Stanford University Press, 1998); Pratap Mehta, "Cosmopolitanism and the Circle of Reason," *Political Theory* 28, no. 5 (October 2000): 619–639.

10. For my critique, see "Passion and Constraint," Seminar 521 (January 2003): 22–28.

11. I would like to acknowledge my deep debt to Tom Banchoff, not just for inviting me to write this paper, but for substantive editorial and intellectual suggestions that went way beyond his call of duty.

BIBLIOGRAPHY

Balagangadhara, S. N. *"The Heathen in His Blindness . . .": Asia, the West and the Dynamic of Religion*. Leiden: Brill, 1994.

Cicero. *De Natura Deorum* (On the nature of the gods). Translated by Francis Brooks, 2:272. London: Methuen, 1896.

Gauchet, Marcel. *The Disenchantment of the World*. Princeton, NJ: Princeton University Press, 1999.

Glass, Charles. "Cyber Jihad." *London Review of Books*, March 9, 2006, 12–16.

Gutmann, Amy. "Religion and the State in the United States: A Defense of Two-Way Protection." In *Obligations of Citizenship and Demands of Faith: Religious Accommodation in Pluralist Societies*, ed. Nancy L. Rosenblum, 127–164. Princeton, NJ: Princeton University Press, 2000.

Hume, David. *Writings on Religion*, ed. Anthony Flew, 177. Chicago, IL: Open Court, 1992.

Lactantius. *The Divine Institutes*. Translated by Sister Frances Mary McDonald. Washington, DC: The Catholic Press of America, 1964.

Luhmann, Niklas. *Observations on Modernity*. Stanford, CA: Stanford University Press, 1998.

Mehta, Pratap. "Cosmopolitanism and the Circle of Reason." *Political Theory* 28, no. 5 (October 2000): 619–639.

———. "Passion and Constraint." Seminar 521 (January 2003), 22–28.

4

Toleration, Proselytizing, and the Politics of Recognition

Jean Bethke Elshtain

I propose to examine toleration and proselytization within a framework of "the politics of recognition" associated with the work of the philosopher Charles Taylor. Proselytizing—preaching the "good word"—is central to some religious traditions: my specific focus is Christianity. The first "great commission," as it is known, spoken by Christ in the Christian narrative, is a call to "go forth" and preach the gospel to all lands. This is to be done peacefully, but it is to be done. One does not impose one's faith, in this vision, but one makes it manifest, preaches it, calls upon others to consider it. So one question that occurs immediately is whether this call to "preach" is compatible with what we ordinarily take "toleration" to be. I insist that it is and that we need not hunker down encased in our own belief systems. We may be called to share them joyfully but diligently. A decent, tolerant society should have no problem with this. Nor should the international community.

As one examines this call to preach the word, one must do so with an eye to the historic insistence that a democratic polity requires something like an informal "civic" faith. Of course, official state-based religions, mandated from the top, are incompatible with toleration and with the freedom to proselytize for one's faith without fearing crackdown and persecution. That is the easy part. Harder by far is to sort out how religious toleration has been understood in the Western democracies; to examine assaults on the very idea of toleration from some quarters; and to unpack the claim that public freedom to proselytize is part and parcel of a robust regime of toleration, one that I call *deep toleration*, based on the insistence that we can, at one and the same time, tolerate religious pluralism and advocate for the truths of our own faiths.

By way of introduction, I must put just a few other issues on the table. The story of the emergence of a regime of toleration is a long and complex one. Suffice to say that a certain *privatization* of religion was part of the deal, most notably in western Europe, where one found the odd combination of private belief but state support. One worshiped publicly, in a sense, but the whole thing came down, finally, to what my own conscience tells me, thereby assuming much of what needs to be understood and explained, namely, the formation of conscience itself: an issue I must set aside in the interest of space, but the question of formation lurks throughout. How are people formed such that conscience even matters? What sustains and supports "faithfulness"? And so on.

This privatization invited a further subjectivization and interiorization of religion: you have your "spirituality" and I have mine. We prescind from claims that there are strong warrants for truth in a faith tradition based on "faith seeking understanding" (the Augustinian credo). If faith is narrowed to the pinpoint of one, proselytizing comes to seem a violation of toleration, as if toleration means I expect no one—ever—to challenge *my* faith, my spirituality, and so forth. Why? Well, precisely because it is mine. So we collapse coercion, manipulation, and persuasion into one unsavory mix and spit them all out: all become forms of imposition.

A second major issue, and I will take it up, in part, in my longer treatment to follow, holds that the entire notion of toleration is puny: "I do not want toleration, I want recognition"—recognition of the sort that eschews normative distinctions as between beliefs and ways of being in the world. *Equal normative acceptance*, one might call this, and in this world toleration is always "mere" as in "mere toleration"—toleration is not enough. Those criticizing toleration from this allegedly radical direction forget what a precious and fragile achievement toleration is, even as they decamp from the necessary debates any decent society must have about what is good, what is true, what is workable, and so on. Defenders of toleration, understood robustly, myself included, insist that it is foolish to the point of suicidal for those who are in a minority—in any sense—to undermine toleration. Toleration is their best bet as a world of indistinguishable "difference" is an illusion. But a commitment to deep toleration should not be grudging and instrumental, at base. For deep toleration speaks to the respect for persons that lies at the heart of democratic possibility and should inform international community.

Charles Taylor on Selves as "Strong Evaluators"

With that general introduction, let me now turn directly to a philosopher who helps us to appreciate what is at stake in toleration understood robustly, namely, Charles Taylor. Taylor first became known to many of us through his profound and important essays challenging the regime of behavioralism in the human sciences. For those like myself who were clinging to the hope that there would be room for scholars who were not committed to a positivist epistemology and to the behavioralist outcropping in departments of political science, Taylor was a lifeline. He helped many whose training was not in philosophy proper but in the political theory variant to appreciate the distinctive quality of the *Geisteswissenschaften* and to fight back when we were told that the *only* way to do things was to abandon the ground of meaning and values; to embrace a narrow science of verification; to ignore ontological or anthropological questions altogether; and to hold epistemological debates at arm's length as well. Taylor's resounding claim, backed up with richly elaborate and elegant argument, that the human sciences cannot be *wertfrei*, or value-free, because "they are moral sciences" whose subject matter is that "self-interpreting animal," the human person, helped to put many of us on our own scholarly paths.[1] Taylor's monumental *Sources of the Self* added much needed richness and nuance to the question of identity, displaying in full Taylor's historic acumen and knowledge. This volume signaled Taylor's move toward that phase of his career associated with "the politics of recognition," very much linked to questions of identity and current, often heated, debates about multiculturalism.

I mention this because it is the Taylor of the politics of recognition I hope to engage in dialogue around the problematic of toleration and proselytization and what this says about regnant understandings of the self. Taylor's politics of recognition raises questions about the liberal regime of toleration and about the dynamics of proselytization. Proselytization takes place when I knowingly and determinedly set out to change someone else's mind about something basic to his or her identity and self-definition, like religious belief. Toleration requires that I learn to live with deep differences even though I may disagree profoundly with another's beliefs and identity. Here are the key questions to engage within a broad framework of Taylor's politics of recognition: Is toleration pallid and inadequate stacked up against the politics of recognition? Is proselytization fully compatible with the politics of recognition and a regime of toleration or a challenge to it? I take up these matters because (1) they are intrinsically interesting, and (2) they are in need of clarification given certain current forms of identity politics at odds with Taylor's perspective. A Taylorian politics of recognition, in other words, can, and should, be brought to bear against that form of identity and recognition politics that pushes either in a narrowly "essentialist" (we are hardwired all the way down) or strongly deconstructionist (we are not wired at all) direction. The heart of the matter is our understanding of the human person and in what the dignity of persons consists.

For Taylor, the self cannot exist absent his or her immersion in an inescapable framework. It is within such frameworks that we establish our orientation to the good; that our moral intuitions are engaged and formed to become solid habits; and that these moral instincts go on to become our mode of access to a world in which certain ontological claims serve as a "background picture" against which our own understandings and intuitions are articulated. Taylor argues that such background frameworks may be implicit or explicit, but we can never escape them; we can never step outside them or shed them.[2] Without these frameworks, we would plunge into a kind of abyss, described by Taylor in dire terms: "a kind of vertigo, terrifying emptiness, anomie, lack of purpose," and the like.[3]

One such framework, for citizens of liberal societies, has been a political ethic of toleration. Selves oriented to this ethic learn to live and let live, if not approve of deep commitments different from their own. Being formed in this framework means being taught that, if one is part of the majority religious or political orientation, or ethnic group, or race, one must imagine what it would be like to be part of, or belong to, a minority. This, in turn, spurs appreciation of the necessity of a regime of toleration. If in the majority now, one might find oneself in a minority position one day. Because selves are, to a greater or lesser extent, self-interested, many argue that prudence alone suffices to buttress a regime of toleration. The Golden Rule is likely evoked here, or a secular variant of it. In its classical form, the regime of toleration did not require suspending judgment as between contrasting beliefs, identities, and way of being; rather, it required not coercing those whose orientations one might find unintelligible, even distasteful, so long as these orientations neither posed a threat to public safety nor undermined the overarching orienting framework of toleration itself. Because human beings are, on Taylor's understanding, "strong evaluators," to call for persons to suspend judgment about right and wrong, or better and worse, is to call for them to suspend a constitutive feature of their moral personality.

There is, of course, a story behind the classical liberal regime of toleration, and it is one that speaks to dangers that are assumed to exist *should* selves locate themselves within orienting frameworks that make it impossible, or very difficult, to speak across frameworks. In a sense, the strong evaluations of selves become too strong. What Taylor calls the "qualitative discriminations" push in exclusionary directions. The upshot, again so the story goes, is suspicion, fear, if not outright enmity and war. Lost along the way is a humbler epistemological stance (so to speak), lodged in a recognition of human fallibility and what theologians call "the noetic effects of sin." To really examine what Taylor's strong politics of recognition does to, or for, standard frameworks of toleration, it will help if a more complete unpacking of the received story of toleration is proffered.

Why Toleration Emerged and Why It Is Necessary for Selves to Coexist: The Standard Narrative

The standard version of the story goes something like this: mandated liberal toleration saved religion from its own excesses and absolutist demands. By forcing a regime of toleration on religion, liberalism in its constitutional forms demanded that religion act more tolerantly. And so it came to pass that both "sectarian" groups (meaning religious groups, of course) and nonsectarian groups (all others organized along the lines of the liberal mandate) would learn to live happily or, if not that, at least peacefully with and among one another. This truce is insistently represented as a fragile one by contemporary civil libertarians and the most ardent secularists. If religion threatens to get out of hand, it must be beaten back. Often the Spanish Inquisition is trotted out in argument as if this were a serious historic possibility in twenty-first-century Western societies.

This is the regnant story. Of course, there are other ways to tell the tale. One would be to take note of the fact that were one to do something as unseemly as a body count of victims, the antireligious ideologies of the twentieth century would win that contest hands down. Murderous intolerance leading to a quest to silence or, worse, to eliminate those who challenge one's own views is no exclusive purview of those with religious convictions. To this would be added details of the many ways that the regime of liberal tolerance has imposed real hardships on the free exercise of religion. These restrictions on free exercise derive from the suspicion that religious intolerance is more to be feared than anything else and that such intolerance is to be found lurking in the interstices of even the most benign forms of religious expression. One way or the other, this rebuttal would hold, religion per se is not the primary problem in the late modern Western democracies but, rather, a dogmatic, highly ideological disparagement of religions and their faithful as an in situ threat to constitutional order.

If one traces the beginning of liberal toleration from John Locke's classic *Letter Concerning Toleration*, one discovers that in order for religion to be tolerated it must be privatized. There is a realm of private soulcraft, and a realm of public statescraft, and never the twain shall meet.[4] In the religious domain, one answers God's call. In the civic realm, God does not figure directly anymore. One's fidelity is pledged to what Locke calls the "magistracy." Should the magistracy egregiously overstep its bounds, there is always the "appeal to heaven" and the possibility of revolution. All religions—save atheism and Roman Catholicism—are to be tolerated. Constitutional scholar Michael McConnell observes: "Locke's exclusion of atheists and Catholics from toleration cannot be dismissed as a quaint exception to his beneficent liberalism; it follows logically from the ground on which his argument for toleration rested. If religious freedom meant nothing more than that religion should be free so long as it is irrelevant to the state, it does not mean very much."[5] How so? Because religion has been privatized and its meaning reduced to the subjective spiritual well-being of religious practitioners. This move toward subjectivism is a general, and troubling, feature of modernity (and the constitutive episteme of modern selves, one might say), observed by Taylor over and over in his work. One strong example is the conclusion of his essay "Language and Human Nature," in which he describes the "rotten" compromise (intellectually speaking), in which crass scientism and "the most subjectivist forms of expressivism" coexist.

Religious faith has not escaped this subjectivist-expressivist juggernaut. If I am right, Locke did his part to put Western selves—Protestant selves, initially, as Catholics were omitted from his regime of toleration—on the pathway toward privatizing whatever grates, or is discordant with reference to, the dominant liberal, eventually market, paradigm. Taylor notes the struggle "between technocracy and the sense of history or community, instrumental reason versus the intrinsic value of certain forms of life, the domination of nature versus the need for reconciliation with nature."[6] Whether one casts the battle lines this way or not, it is undeniably the case that that which was privatized over time became subjectivized and reducible to private experience. This undermines any robustness to the notion of a community of faith having a form of membership that exerts strong claims on its members. But back to the main story.

This privatizing, even subjectifying, of religion feeds into the bad odor currently surrounding any hint of proselytization. Proselytizing seems at its best bad manners; at its worst, it is a way to try to force something on me that I do not want, am not interested in, but may be gulled or intimidated into accepting. The general animus against proselytizing flows from a conviction that those driven in that direction will, almost invariably, be persons of overly strong religious conviction; those, therefore, who, should they become dominant, would move to end the very toleration that has made their open proselytizing possible. (The association of the word, and process, with religion does not help, of course. Somehow no one speaks of proselytizing when I try to convince you to change your political party. But if I urge you to change your religion, I am engaged in proselytizing and fall under suspicion.) So, in the name of preserving a regime of toleration, we must not tolerate unrestrained proselytization.

A whiff of this intolerance for proselytizing comes through in the comments of one of Alan Wolfe's respondents in his book *One Nation after All*. One "Jody Fields" is quoted as saying: "If you are a Hindu and you grew up being a Hindu, keep it to yourself. Don't impose your religion, and don't make me feel bad because I do this and you do this."[7] Embedded in this comment is an intolerance of religious pluralism should that pluralism reveal itself in a robust, public way. Telling a Hindu to hide being Hindu is scarcely a picture of liberal pluralism: or so, at least, one would think. One way or the other, the continuing privatizing of religion—or the view that that is what it is all about—means that when religion shows its face, it must not take the form of actually trying to persuade someone else of the truth of the religious beliefs being displayed. "Keep it to yourself."

Toleration Challenged

As if this were not enough to mull over, let us add a more recent trend to the mix. I have in mind the attack on the very notion of tolerance and toleration emanating from a postmodern direction and from those most tied up in the identity politics tendency. The argument goes roughly like this: toleration was always a sham, a way to enforce a particular Eurocentric, patriarchal, heterosexist, Christian worldview. It was a cover story for hegemony. (And, of course, there is always just enough truth to be found in such blanket charges that one cannot simply dismiss them out of hand.) What atheists, or pagans, or non-Western religious devotees, those with once-hidden sexual orientations, those who are "third world" or nonwhite, seek is not toleration but equal normative acceptance. This equal acceptance will be attained only when the society—any society—refuses to make any normative distinctions between and among any and all comprehensive understandings of what makes a life good, or worthy, or a belief true, or a way of structuring families better than some other, and so forth. Laws, public policies, the cultural ethos must practice total nondiscrimination, in the sense of refraining from making any normative distinctions as between modes of belief and ways of life. Thus, for example: sexual sadomasochism between consenting adults is not to be construed as a problematic way of ordering a human existence by contrast to a faithful monogamous relationship between adults.

All in all, we are enjoined to abandon orienting frameworks that offer criteria whereby we can, and are obliged to, make qualitative distinctions as between

alternative orientations. Taylor's insistence that human beings cannot but ori-
ent themselves to the good is stoutly denied: we not only can but we *should* if
we are going to move beyond toleration to validation of the "free choices" made
by selves; if we are going to resist being "judgmental"; if we are going to affirm
and "validate" without distinction any and all (or nearly so) ways of being in the
world. Those pressing the antitoleration argument see toleration as negative, a
grudging thing. They want "validation" and approval—even as they simultaneously proclaim the radical and dangerous nature of what it is they are saying or
doing, as if one could have full societal validation and yet remain a permanent
voice of radical dissent—but that is another issue.

Those who defend toleration point out that the alternative to toleration
historically has not been a happy pluralism where we are all equally delectable
peas in the pod but, instead, very unhappy, unpluralistic orders in which religious minorities and dissenters were exiled or tortured or forced to conform;
in which political dissenters often faced similar assaults; in which any inkling
of a sexual orientation other than that which is considered normal was grounds
for imprisonment or worse, and so on. The defenders of toleration would argue
that it is foolish to the point of suicidal for those who are a minority—in any
sense—to undermine support for toleration. Toleration is their best bet as the
world of indistinguishable "differences" is a chimera. There never has been
such a world and never will be.

This, of course, still leaves open the matter of just how tolerant of pluralism the defenders of toleration are. There are, after all, among some of our
legal thinkers, arguments that favor increased government regulation of "sectarian" bodies in order to make them conform to standard liberal modes of
representation and legitimation in their internal ordering on the view that all
associations in a constitutional order must sprout analogous forms of administration. Authentic tolerance based on a recognition of deep, not superficial,
differences here gives way before an attempt to normalize along the lines of
forcing Catholic hospitals to perform abortions on pain of punitive measures,
or requiring the Catholic and Orthodox communities to ordain women, and
so on. This latter attack on pluralism is mounted in the name of a strong nor-
mativity that dictates in what equality between men and women consists that
extends to every dimension of human life. It is a view of equality that is taken as
the view of equality rather than as one among a number of competing views of
equality, including those that do not demand homologous internal structures
in all of the institutions internal to a society—a position that would destroy
plurality in the name of equality.

How does Taylor help to adjudicate this knotty matter? Laying out his position is by no means simple, as what he offers or, better said, what he believes

human selves simply are within as the constitutive terms of their very existence, is deep involvement in complex anthropological circumstances. Different aspects of our embodied and intrinsically social selves are engaged with particular features of equally complex cultures and orienting frameworks. So when Taylor argues that a rightly oriented culture is one that promotes identity recognition, what exactly does that mean? What ethical practices are presupposed or called for? Is respect the same as approval or "validation" for a "lifestyle choice"? Surely not, but working out the details is not easy. One may be obliged to recognize another as a being of equal worth even as one repudiates that being's choices as unworthy and demeaning precisely to one whose worth is given by virtue of his or her humanness.

Those of us who grew up in Christian households will recall the times a mother or father said we were to "love the sinner but hate the sin," or to "walk around in the other person's shoes for a while" and then our hearts would unlock to pity, not as a sickly attitude of paternalism but as a humble recognition of the humanity of another self. Perhaps something like that is implicated here. We need to recognize the worth of another in order to be motivated to deepen our awareness of human commonalities. This awareness of commonalities, through dialogical possibilities, will highlight particular and individual qualities that we do not want swamped by the commonalities: "I want to be me," and so does he, and she.

Perhaps I am simply redescribing the problem. Using Taylor's essay "Self Interpreting Animals," let us try again. Taylor describes the ways in which I can make claims on others and they, in turn, on me. He gives an example of a "felt obligation" in the Good Samaritan story. One is called upon to help the other— or so Jesus insisted—simply because this wounded and bleeding person is a child of God, a fellow creature, a moral being. To move on by, as several had done in the parable, because the man left dead by robbers and lying off the side of the road is a Samaritan and Israelites have nothing to do with Samaritans, is a sinful act of cruel negligence that narrows the boundaries of the moral life. Jesus lays on a strong obligation, clearly, and Taylor rightly names it as an obligation of charity.

One is called upon to *act*, not simply to *feel* the right way or think good thoughts. And we are called to act because we are creatures of a certain sort as is the one who makes a claim on our help. An ability to respond to the claim of the stranger presupposes moral formation of a certain kind, and Taylor stresses that identities can be forged in such a way that we experience felt obligations and act on them. Although Taylor really prescinds on the formation question, his entire argument is parasitic upon some such notion. No doubt there is some sort of bioevolutionary template for empathic response or the human species would not have survived. But we know well enough that fellow feeling can be frozen, rejected, or fail to develop in the first place.

Toleration and Power

Those who see toleration as just a puny thing, best exposed as bogus and done away with, construe any attempt to proselytize in negative terms because this is, by definition, an assault on someone else's identity. The issue of toleration and the complexities of proselytization have been heavily psychologized in our time. Whatever makes somebody else uncomfortable is to be eschewed. But, of course, any strong articulation of a powerful religion or a powerful political position is going to make somebody somewhere uncomfortable. Does this mean we are all reduced to bleating at one another across a vast distance, but that any attempt to persuade is cast as proselytizing and that is bad by definition?

Let us unpack this issue a bit. Somewhere along the line—certainly in the last thirty years or so—a view of power took hold that disdains distinctions between coercion, manipulation, and persuasion. If I change my mind about something after an encounter with you, or after having spent some time in your religious community, the presupposition is that I have been messed with: gulled or brainwashed or taken for the proverbial walk down the primrose path. It is an odd business, power, because when we say, as many do these days, that every encounter involves power, we make it harder to distinguish between instances of real intimidation and, by contrast, those of authentic persuasion.

In instances of intimidation, there is an implied threat of harm unless you convert to my point of view. In instances of manipulation, I sneakily get you on my side. Neither of these views respects you as a moral agent who can freely weigh alternatives and make up his or her own mind. Persuasion, by contrast, begins with the presupposition that you are a moral agent, a being whose dignity no one is permitted to deny or to strip from you, and, from that stance of mutual respect, one offers arguments, or invites your participation, your sharing, in a community and its rhythms and rituals. You do not lose something by agreeing. One never simply jettisons what one has believed before. But one may reject it. (And those are not identical.) Even among persons religious, however, proselytizing has come to have an unpleasant ring to it. Evangelizing sounds better. The picture of the proselytizer is of some latter-day Savonarola, severe and intimidating, or an "Elmer Gantry"–type huckster.

The upshot of all this would seem to be that both toleration and proselytizing are badly battered as concepts and as practices. Is there any way to redeem one, or the other, or both? I think there is. My example of redeeming both toleration and proselytization comes from Pope John Paul II's pastoral visit to Kazakhstan in September 2001. Something struck me in a report I read of that visit in which the pontiff, in his greeting to "Dear Young People!" last September 23 in the capital city, Astana, said:

> Allow me to profess before you with humility and pride the faith of Christians: Jesus of Nazareth, the Son of God made man two thousand years ago, came to reveal to us this truth through his person and his teaching. Only in the encounter with him, the Word made flesh, do we find the fullness of self-realization and happiness. Religion itself, without the experience of the wonderful discovery of the Son of God and communion with him who became our brother, becomes a mere set of principles which are increasingly difficult to understand, and rules which are increasingly hard to accept.[8]

I found this moving, and I want to explore why briefly. Certainly the combination of pride and humility is a part of it. One places before another, in all humility, one's most profound beliefs, beliefs one holds with pride—not boastful self-pride but with dignity—knowing that these beliefs may well be repudiated or ignored. Also powerful is John Paul's recognition that turning God into a metaphysical first principle is not only "increasingly difficult to understand" but "increasingly hard to accept." Here there is a fascinating dimension to his words to Kazak young people for he is also proselytizing to those who are already Christians, reminding them of what their profession is all about.

John Paul's words on this remarkable pastoral visit constituted an eloquent defense of toleration in another of his homilies in Kazakhstan:

> When in a society citizens accept one another [notice that what is being accepted is one another as citizens, in one's civic status] in their respective religious beliefs, it is easier to foster among them the effective recognition of other human rights and an understanding of the values on which a peaceful and productive coexistence is based. In fact, they feel a common bond in the awareness that they are brothers and sisters because they are children of the one God.

This is a reference to toleration among religious believers.

Unbelievers, presumably, have their own resources to draw upon to respect human rights, but the pontiff suggests that the bond of coexistence will have a different valence between believers and unbelievers than between believers and believers. He reminded his listeners that in Kazakhstan today there are "citizens belonging to over 100 nationalities and ethnic groups" and they live—they have no choice but to live—side by side. Coexistence is a necessity. But "bridges of solidarity and cooperation with other peoples, nations, and cultures" are an immanent possibility that should be realized even as the gospel in all its fullness is preached "in all humility and pride."

This is not pie-in-the-sky stuff at all but, rather, a filling out and in of what a commitment to authentic toleration means as a baseline that one is invited—or called to move beyond in the direction of equal affirmation—or not, as the case may be. Toleration rightly understood permits more robust ties of civic sisterhood and brotherhood to grow and to flourish, perhaps between religious believers whose comprehensive understandings differ but whose anthropologies overlap. Toleration also permits more distance when, for example, I simply cannot affirm your life choices and comprehensive views. I need not validate them at all. In fact, toleration means I may actively loathe them and argue against them. But, unless you threaten the civic order in a central way, I am not permitted to deny you your "free exercise."

Developing what it means to threaten the civic order in a central way is a topic for another essay, but it derives from Supreme Court justice Robert Jackson's rueful recognition that the Constitution is not a suicide pact. What is one to do with groups that use freedoms, claim tolerance, and set about proselytizing, and what they are proselytizing for is a future order that would immediately move to destroy all religious tolerance, to abolish constitutional protections, to establish a theocracy or a militant official atheism (as in twentieth-century communist regimes). Minimally it means that I am under no obligation, as one who supports constitutional guarantees of tolerance, to work up any respect for beliefs that deny the dignity of persons, preach hatred, and directly threaten me, my family, my faith, and my country. Making me uncomfortable is part of the deal. In the order I support the discomfiting attendant upon real toleration and pluralism is very different from a serious threat.

Taylor's Politics of Recognition as Deep Toleration

Taylor's politics of recognition encompasses in a single frame both proselytization and toleration, and the versions of each he provides for are robust, not anemic. Let's call Taylor's position one of *deep toleration*, a position whose starting point is his insistence on the dialogical character of human life. "One is a self among other selves" within a language community or "web of interlocution."[9] The dialogic position commits him to the view that all human beings are creatures of value; that relativism is bound to be self-defeating; that equal recognition does not demand that all positions are equal with respect to the distribution of, or understanding of, certain goods. One requires what Taylor calls a horizon of significance to sort this all out.

Deep toleration, to characterize the position schematically, does not require privatizing our deepest convictions. We live, therefore, in a dialogic community, and our selves are defined and refined within this web. That being the case, the dialogic nature of selves and communities means one always remains open to the possibility of proselytizing and being proselytized. The dialogic community in which deep differences become occasions for contestation with the ever-present possibility of persuasion is pluralistic without being fragmented. Taylor has made clear his position against fragmentation of the sort that takes as a starting point a kind of incommensurability as between positions; politically this means hard-edged identity politics of a kind that insists, "You just don't get it," as both the beginning and the end of conversation.

Taylor's position is, as he has argued, neither essentialist nor deconstructionist. Within the position of deep toleration I here articulate, the essentialist position is at odds with toleration, as is deconstructionism. Essentialism grates against toleration because differences are so hardwired, cut so deep, and define us so thoroughly that the dialogic nature of selves is denied. Denying that dialogic dimension to selves means one cuts off the possibility of a dialogic community. The irony, of course, is that one remains defined in important ways by the very community whose dialogic features one denies. Because deep toleration is open to proselytization and transformation of identity, the essentialist cannot go for it.

What of the deconstructionist? Here, too, deep toleration is opposed, oddly enough, because if there is no truth to be found there is nothing to have deep dialogue about and, further, because that which most deeply defines us is thinned out to consist in privatized ironies. If the beliefs that constitute the core of a dialogically understood self and community are privatized, it cuts off the dialogic moment. Deconstructionism, for all the talk of multiculturalism associated with it, seeks not toleration but validation of all positions absent an airing of what holds those positions together and whether each is equally worthy of endorsement. There are no shared standards for evaluation, in any case, on this view. So, each in its own way, both essentialism and deconstructionism, pushes in the direction of antidialogic monologism. This is not the stuff out of which deep toleration is made. I hope I have said enough to demonstrate that Taylor's view is not only capacious enough to encompass that which we tend to drive apart—efforts to proselytize and toleration—but that his argument helps to define and refine a position of *deep toleration*.

Deep Toleration in International Context

How relevant is deep toleration in the international sphere? Beyond the nation-state, it might be argued, historical legacies and power asymmetries rule out the kind of dialogical interaction at the heart of Taylor's vision. Critics of pros-elytization typically point to centuries of Christian missionary activity in Asia, the Middle East, Africa, and Latin America—an enterprise often backed by state power and the force of arms. Today, the international playing field remains unequal, as the United States and its allies—home to the wealthiest and most dynamic Christian communities—maintain a predominant position within the global political economy. Under such conditions, the critics charge, support for proselytization is support for the exploitation of the weak by the strong.

This argument is flawed. Deep toleration that allows for the possibility of persuasion and proselytization is more, not less, vital in the international con-text. At a most fundamental level, deep toleration resonates with the idea of universal human rights. Opposition to proselytization is opposition to a central dimension of religious freedom and therefore incompatible with a robust inter-national human rights regime. To draw a distinction between having a religion and sharing that religion with others is to truncate religious freedom. It is also to curtail freedom of expression, assembly, and political participation. A robust norm of international religious freedom, including the right to proselytize, is central to any coherent understanding of universal human rights.

The view that power asymmetries in world affairs rule out dialogical inter-action is also unpersuasive. Every human relationship, from the familial to the national and the international, is marked by unequal resource endow-ments. Perfect social equality is a chimera. If anything, it is the perennial fact of inequality that makes deep toleration more, not less, important. It is through exchanges of ideas, through argument and evidence, claim and counterclaim, that human beings in social settings engage in a search for truth—about what is important to them, about how to live together. The ability to think critically, to communicate, to persuade and be persuaded, is part of what defines our humanity. Historically, the freedom to speak one's mind—including religious witness—has proved a weapon of the weak in the face of the strong. Martin Luther King Jr. and the civil rights movement are a salient example. To restrict proselytization not only violates a basic human right; it also curtails an open exchange of ideas and a politics of recognition that may challenge (and not simply reinforce) existing power relationships.

What of the argument from history—that the legacy of missionary activ-ity advanced by state power makes it wrong for the United States and its allies to support proselytization? There may be prudential reasons for governments not to back proselytization efforts directly. State support for faith-based groups that combine poverty relief with the propagation of the gospel, for example, may generate a political backlash at home and abroad. But the argument that historical legacies should lead us away from robust support for the right to religious freedom makes little sense. In a world marked by unprecedented religious pluralism and interaction in the context of globalization, international legal restrictions on the right to proselytize threaten to choke off interreligious dialogue. Where violence and religion are joined in potent mix in the post–September 11, 2001, world, we should not abandon Taylor's ideal of dialogic community. Deep toleration—an encounter among religious individuals and groups that is open to transformation—represents a just and workable foundation for peaceful engagement in a spirit of truth.

NOTES

1. The two essays here referenced are, of course, Charles Taylor, "Interpretation and the Sciences of Man," in *Philosophical Papers: Philosophy and the Human Sciences* (Cambridge: Cambridge University Press, 1985), 2:15–57; quotation on page 57; and Taylor, "Self-Interpreting Animals," in *Philosophical Papers*, 1:15–44.

2. This is a brief summary of Taylor's opening and framing arguments in *Sources of the Self: The Making of Modern Identity* (Cambridge, MA: Harvard University Press, 1989), 3–20. I also draw on previous work that I have done on Taylor.

3. Ibid., 18.

4. John Locke, *Letter Concerningn Toleration* (Indianapolis, IN: Hackett, 1983). My argument is not that Locke was covertly irreligious or anything of the sort, or that he meant to do religion in. Indeed, he was seeking a free space for its exercise. But by shearing soulcraft from statescraft—making what was essentially a separate-spheres argument—he helped to alter a basic orienting framework in which ecclesia was the heart of existence, not at the margins, and was very much the public expression of a domain of inwardness, yes, but a domain of inwardness that required, in order that it remain robust and faithful, external signs, symbols, rituals, and participation.

5. Michael McConnell, "Believers as Equal Citizens," in *Obligations of Citizenship and Demands of Faith: Religious Accommodation and Pluralist Democracies*, ed. Nancy L. Rosenblum (Princeton, NJ: Princeton University Press, 2000), 90–110.

6. Charles Taylor, "Language and Human Nature," in *Philosophical Papers* (Cambridge: Cambridge University Press, 1985), 216–247.

7. Alan Wolfe, *One Nation after All* (New York: Viking, 1998), 63.

8. Pope John Paul II, "Allow Me to Profess before You with Humility and Pride the Faith of Christians," *L'Osservatore Romano* 39 (September 26, 2001): 5.

9. Taylor, *Sources of the Self*, 35.

BIBLIOGRAPHY

John Paul II. "Allow Me to Profess before You with Humility and Pride the Faith of Christians." *L'Osservatore Romano* 39 (September 26, 2001): 5.

Locke, John. *Letter Concerning Toleration.* Indianapolis, IN: Hackett, 1983.

McConnell, Michael. "Believers as Equal Citizens." In *Obligations of Citizenship and Demands of Faith: Religious Accommodation and Pluralist Democracies,* ed. Nancy L. Rosenblum, 90–110. Princeton, NJ: Princeton University Press, 2000.

Taylor, Charles. *Philosophical Papers: Philosophy and the Human Sciences.* 2 vols. Cambridge: Cambridge University Press, 1985.

———. *Sources of the Self: The Making of Modern Identity.* Cambridge, MA: Harvard University Press, 1989.

Wolfe, Alan. *One Nation after All.* New York: Viking, 1998.

5

The Rights and Limits
of Proselytism in the New
Religious World Order

John Witte Jr.

A "Dickensian Era" of Religion and Human Rights

"It was the best of times, it was the worst of times, it was the age of
wisdom, it was the age of foolishness, it was the epoch of belief, it
was the epoch of incredulity, it was the season of Light, it was the
season of Darkness, it was the spring of hope, it was the winter of
despair."[1] Charles Dickens penned these famous words to describe
the paradoxes of the late eighteenth-century French Revolution fought
for the sake of "the rights of man and citizen."[2] These same words
aptly describe the paradoxes of the world revolution fought two centuries later in the name of human rights and democratization for all.

The world has entered something of a "Dickensian era"[3] in the
past three decades. We have seen the best of human rights protections inscribed on the books, but some of the worst of human rights
violations inflicted on the ground. We have celebrated the creation
of more than thirty new constitutional democracies since 1980, but
lamented the eruption of more than thirty new civil wars. We have
witnessed the wisest of democratic statecraft and the most foolish of
autocratic belligerence. For every South African spring of hope, there
has been a Yugoslavian winter of despair, for every Ukrainian season
of light, a Sudanese season of darkness.

These Dickensian paradoxes of the modern human rights revolution are particularly striking when viewed in their religious dimensions. On the one hand, the modern human rights revolution has

helped to catalyze a great awakening of religion around the globe. In regions newly committed to democracy and human rights, ancient faiths once driven underground by autocratic oppressors have sprung forth with new vigor. In the former Soviet bloc, for example, numerous Buddhist, Christian, Hindu, Jewish, Muslim, and other faiths have been awakened, alongside a host of exotic goddess, naturalist, and personality cults.[4] In postcolonial and postrevolutionary Africa, these same mainline religious groups have come to flourish in numerous conventional and inculturated forms, alongside a bewildering array of traditional groups.[5] In Latin America, the human rights revolution has not only transformed long-standing Catholic and mainline Protestant communities but also triggered the explosion of numerous new Evangelical, Pentecostal, and Traditional movements.[6] Many parts of the world have seen the prodigious rise of a host of new or newly minted faiths—Adventists, Baha'is, Hare Krishnas, Jehovah's Witnesses, Mormons, Scientologists, Unification Church members, among many others—some wielding ample material, political, and media power. Religion today has become, in Susanne Rudolph's apt phrase, the latest "transnational variable."[7] Religious pluralism has become the latest local reality for all but the most insular communities.

One cause and consequence of this great awakening of religion around the globe is that the ambit of religious rights has been substantially expanded. In the past three decades, more than 200 major new statutes and constitutional provisions on religious rights have been promulgated—many replete with generous protections for liberty of conscience and freedom of religious exercise; guarantees of religious pluralism, equality, and nondiscrimination; and several other special protections and entitlements for religious individuals and religious groups.[8] These national guarantees have been matched with a growing body of regional and international norms, notably the UN Declaration on Religious Intolerance and Discrimination Based upon Religion and Belief (1981), the UN Declaration on the Rights of Persons Belonging to National or Ethnic, Religious and Linguistic Minorities (1992), and the long catalogue of religious-group rights set out in the Vienna Concluding Document (1989) and its progeny.[9]

On the other hand, this very same world human rights revolution has helped to catalyze new forms of religious and ethnic conflict, oppression, and belligerence that have sometimes reached tragic proportions. In the former Yugoslavia and Chechnya, for example, local religious and ethnic rivals, previously kept at bay by a common oppressor, have converted their new liberties into new licenses to renew their ancient hostilities, with catastrophic results.[10] In Sudan, Rwanda, Burundi, and the Central African Republic, ethnic nationalism and religious extremism have conspired to bring violent dislocation or death to hundreds of rival religious believers each year, and persecution, false imprisonment, forced starvation, and savage abuses to thousands of others.[11] In France, Belgium, Germany, and Austria, political secularism, laicization, and nationalism have combined to threaten civil denial and deprivation to a number of believers, particularly "sects" and "cults" of high religious temperature or of low cultural conformity. In the United States, political messianism and Evangelical fundamentalism have together embraced a "clash-of-civilizations" ethic that has encouraged bigotry against minorities at home and belligerence against the "axis of evil" abroad. In several communities from Asia to the Middle East, Christian, Jewish, and Muslim minorities have faced sharply increased restrictions, repression, and more than occasional martyrdom.[12] And, in many parts of the world today, barbaric Islamicist terrorists have waged a destructive jihad against all manner of religious, cultural, and ethnic enemies, real and imagined.

In parts of Russia, Eastern Europe, Africa, and Latin America, this human rights revolution has brought on something of a new war for souls between indigenous and foreign religious groups. This is the most recent, and the most ironic, chapter in the modern Dickensian drama. With the political transformations of these regions in the past two decades, foreign religious groups were granted rights to enter these regions for the first time in decades. Beginning in the early 1990s, they came in increasing numbers to preach their faiths, to offer their services, to convert new souls. Initially, local religious groups— Orthodox, Catholic, Protestant, Sunni, Shiite, and Traditional alike—welcomed these foreigners, particularly their foreign coreligionists with whom they had lost contact for many decades. Today, local religious groups have come to resent these foreign religions, particularly those from North America and Western Europe that assume a democratic human rights ethic. Local religious groups resent the participation in the marketplace of religious ideas that democracy assumes. They resent the toxic waves of materialism and individualism that democracy inflicts. They resent the massive expansion of religious pluralism that democracy encourages. They resent the extravagant forms of religious speech, press, and assembly that democracy protects.[13]

A new war for souls has thus broken out in these regions, a war to reclaim the traditional cultural and moral souls of these new societies, and a war to retain adherence and adherents to indigenous faiths. In part, this is a theological war, as rival religious communities have begun to demonize and defame each other and to gather themselves into ever more dogmatic and fundamentalist stands. The ecumenical spirit of the previous decades is giving way to sharp new forms of religious balkanization. In part, this is a legal war, as local religious groups have begun to conspire with their political leaders to adopt statutes and regulations restricting the constitutional rights of their foreign religious rivals. Beneath shiny constitutional veneers of religious freedom for all and unqualified ratification of international human rights instruments, several countries of late passed firm new antiproselytism laws, cult registration requirements, tightened visa controls, and various other discriminatory restrictions on new or newly arrived religions. Indeed, several parts of the non-Western world seem to be at the dawn of fundamentalist Islamic and Christian religious establishments.[14]

While some non-Western nations seem poised to reestablish old forms of religion, some Western nations seem ready to establish new forms of secularism. In the 1990s, France, Germany, Belgium, and Austria passed firm new anticult legislation that targeted a large number of new and traditional religious groups with a tone approaching xenophobia.[15] In more recent years, France, Belgium, and Turkey have begun to press aggressive new state policies of "laicization" and "secularization" that have resulted in growing restrictions on minority religious schools, charities, and sanctuaries and stronger policing of culturally different or deviant behavior.[16] The recent sensational Muslim headscarf cases in France and Turkey are only one illustration of bigger issues that culturally different religious minorities are now facing in many parts of Western Europe, as well as in Canada and other Commonwealth countries. The 2004 judgment of the European Court of Human Rights against the Turkish Muslim woman who sought religious freedom to wear her headdress in a public university has only encouraged nation-states to tighten their restrictions on religious and cultural minorities as part of a broader effort to create national solidarity on secular grounds.[17]

Variants on some of these same patterns are beginning to emerge in the United States as well. Using the vaunted principle of "separation of church and state," several recent federal courts have struck down public displays and expressions of religion as violations of the First Amendment establishment clause. This has renewed concerns among some commentators that American courts have embarked on a new campaign to privatize religion and to "establish a religion of secularism."[18] At the same time, the U.S. Supreme Court's dramatic weakening of the First Amendment free exercise clause in the case of *Employment Division v. Smith* (1990) has left religious and cultural minorities highly vulnerable to local prejudice.[19] To be sure, the U.S. Congress and various state legislatures have stepped into this breach by passing a number of special statutory protections for religious minorities.[20] But several federal agencies, notably the Internal Revenue Service and the Immigration and Naturalization Service, have not dealt kindly with religious and cultural groups that have proved critical of mainline religions or majoritarian politics, or aggressive in their attempts to expand their unpopular faith.

Hence the modern problem of proselytism: How does the state balance one person's right to exercise his or her faith versus another person's right to liberty of conscience, one group's right to religious expression and another group's right to religious self-determination? How does the state protect the juxtaposed rights claims of majority and minority religions, or of foreign and indigenous religions? How does the state balance its need to create national solidarity and peace with its duty to respect minority cultures and their need to dissent? How does the state craft a general rule to govern multiple theological understandings of conversion or change of religion? These are not new questions. They confronted the drafters of the international bill of rights from the very beginning. But some of the compromises of 1948 and 1966 have today begun to reveal their limitations.

The Problem of Conversion

One side of the modern problem of proselytism is the problem of competing theological and legal understandings of conversion or change of religion.[21] How does a state craft a legal rule that at once respects and protects the sharply competing understandings of conversion among the religions of the Book? Most Western Christians have easy conversion into and out of the faith. Most Jews have difficult conversion into and out of the faith. Most Muslims have easy conversion into the faith, but allow for no conversion out of it, at least for prominent members: indeed, to convert out of Islam is a capital crime.[22] Whose rites get rights? Moreover, how does one craft a legal rule that respects Orthodox, Hindu, Jewish, or Traditional groups that tie religious identity not to voluntary choice but to birth and caste, blood and soil, language and ethnicity, sites and sights of divinity?

On the issue of conversion or change of religion, the major international human rights instruments largely accept the religious voluntarism common among libertarian and Western Christian groups. The Universal Declaration of Human Rights (1948) included an unequivocal guarantee: "Everyone has the right to freedom of thought, conscience, and religion; this right includes *the right to change his religion or belief*" (Art. 18.1). The 1966 International Covenant on Civil and Political Rights (ICCPR), whose preparation was more highly contested on this issue, became a bit more tentative: "This right shall include freedom to have or adopt *a religion or belief of his choice*" (Art. 18.1). The Declaration on the Elimination of All Forms of Intolerance and of Discrimination Based on Religion or Belief (1981) repeated this same more tentative language. But the dispute over the right to conversion contributed greatly to the long delay in the production of this instrument, and to the number of dissenters to it. The Vienna Concluding Document (1989) did not touch the issue at all but simply confirmed "the freedom of the individual to profess or practice religion or belief" before turning to a robust rendition of religious group rights.

Today, this issue over the right to convert has become more divisive than ever as various soul wars have broken out, especially between and within Christian and Muslim communities around the globe. These tensions have been exacerbated by the U.S.-led wars on terror in Afghanistan and Iraq. Some hard-line Christian and Muslim fundamentalists have cast these wars as "crusades" not to end terror but to conquer Islamic cultures and convert Muslim souls. This image has only been encouraged by the sensational media case surrounding the Christian conversion of an Afghani man, Abdul Rahman, in the spring of 2006. Rahman had converted from Islam to Christianity and was seeking to gain custody of his two daughters. His wife's family counterclaimed that he was unfit to gain custody because of his crime of conversion. Following the 2004 constitution, which declares the supremacy of Islamic law, an Afghani court not only denied Rahman custody of his daughters but sentenced him to death for his crime of conversion contrary to Islamic law. Mr. Rahman was able to escape death only because of the intense media exposure of his case and diplomatic intervention at the highest levels. But he had to leave his daughters in Afghanistan and seek asylum in Italy.[23] Other converts to Christianity from Islam have not fared nearly so well, human rights watch groups regularly report.

"A page of history is worth a volume of logic," Oliver Wendell Holmes Jr. once said.[24] And, on an intractable legal issue such as this, recollection might be more illuminating than ratiocination. It is discomfiting, but enlightening, for Western Christians to remember that the right to enter and exit the religion of one's choice was born in the West only after centuries of cruel experience. To be sure, a number of the early church fathers considered the right to change religion as essential to the notion of liberty of conscience, and such sentiments have been repeated and glossed continuously over the centuries.[25] But in practice the Christian church largely ignored these sentiments for centuries. As the medieval Catholic Church refined its rights structures in the twelfth and thirteenth centuries, it also routinized its religious discrimination, reserving its harshest sanctions for heretics. The communicant faithful enjoyed full rights. Jews and Muslims enjoyed fewer rights, but full rights if they converted to Christianity. Heretics—those who voluntarily chose to leave the faith—enjoyed still fewer rights and had little opportunity to recover them even after full confession. Indeed, at the height of the Inquisition in the fifteenth century, heretics faced not only severe restrictions on their persons, properties, and professions but sometimes unspeakably cruel forms of torture and punishment. Similarly,

as the Lutheran, Calvinist, and Anglican churches born of the Protestant Reformation routinized their establishments in the sixteenth and seventeenth centuries, they inflicted all manner of repressive civil and ecclesiastical censures
on those who chose to deviate from established doctrine—savage torture and
execution in a number of instances.[26]

It was, in part, the recovery and elaboration of earlier patristic concepts
of liberty of conscience as well as the slow expansion of new Protestant and
Catholic theologies of religious voluntarism that helped to end this practice.
But, it was also the new possibilities created by the frontier and by the colony
that helped to forge the Western understanding of the right to change religion.
Rather than stay at home and fight for one's faith, it became easier for the dissenter to move away quietly to the frontier, or later to the colony, to be alone
with his conscience and his coreligionists. Rather than tie the heretic to the
rack or the stake, it became easier for the establishment to banish him quickly
from the community with a strict order not to return. Such pragmatic temper-
ing of the treatment of heretics and dissenters eventually found theological
justification. By the later sixteenth century, it became common in the West to
read of the right, and the duty, of the religious dissenter to emigrate physically
from the community whose faith he or she no longer shared.[27] In the course
of the next century, this right of physical emigration from a religious community was slowly transformed into a general right of voluntary exit from a
religious faith and community. Particularly American writers, many of whom
had voluntarily left their Europeans faiths and territories to gain their freedom,
embraced the right to leave—to change their faith; to abandon their blood, soil,
and confession; to reestablish their lives, beliefs, and identities afresh—as a
veritable sine qua non of religious freedom.[28] This understanding of the right
to choose and change religion—patristic, pragmatic, and Protestant in initial
inspiration—has now become an almost universal feature of Western Christian understandings of religious rights.

To tell this peculiar Western tale is not to resolve current legal conflicts over
conversion. But it is to suggest that even hard and hardened religious traditions
can and do change over time, in part out of pragmatism, in part out of fresh
appeals to ancient principles long forgotten. Even those schools of jurisprudence
within Shiite and Sunni communities that have been the sternest in their opposition to a right to conversion from the faith do have resources in the Qur'an,
in the early development of Sharia, and in the more benign policies of other
contemporary Muslim communities to rethink their theological positions.[29]

Moreover, the Western story suggests that there are halfway measures,
at least in banishment and emigration, that help to blunt the worst tensions
between a religious group's right to maintain its standards of entrance and

exit and an individual's liberty of conscience to come and go. Not every heretic needs to be executed. Not every heretic needs to be indulged. It is one thing for a religious tradition to insist on executing its charges of heresy, when a mature adult, fully aware of the consequences of his or her choice, voluntarily enters a faith and then later seeks to leave. In that case group religious rights must trump individual religious rights—with the limitation that the religious group has no right to violate, or to solicit violation of, the life and limb of the wayward member. It is quite another thing for a religious tradition to press the same charges of heresy against someone who was born into, married into, or coerced into the faith and now, upon opportunity for mature reflection, voluntarily chooses to leave. In that case, individual religious rights trump group religious rights.

Where a religious group exercises its trump by banishment or shunning and the apostate voluntarily chooses to return, he does so at his peril. He should find little protection in state law when subject to harsh religious sanctions— again, unless the religious group threatens or violates his or his family's life or limb. Where a religious individual exercises her trump by emigration, and the group chooses to pursue her, it does so at its peril. It should find little protection from state law when charged with criminal violations of the individual.

The Problem of Proselytism

The corollary to the problem of conversion is the problem of proselytism—of the efforts taken by individuals or groups to seek the conversion of another. On this issue the international human rights instruments provide somewhat more nuanced direction.

Article 18 of the 1966 ICCPR protects a person's "freedom, individually or in community with others and in public or private, *to manifest his religion or belief in* worship, observance, practice, and *teaching*" (Art. 18.1). But the same article allows such manifestation of religion to be subject to limitations that "are prescribed by law and are necessary to protect public safety, order, health, or morals, or the fundamental rights and freedoms of others" (Art. 18.3). It prohibits outright any "coercion" that would impair another's right "to have or adopt a religion or belief of [his or her] choice" (Art. 18.2). It also requires states and individuals to have "respect for the liberty of parents . . . to ensure the religious and moral education of their children in conformity with [the parents'] convictions" (Art. 18.4). This latter provision is underscored and amplified in more recent instruments and cases on the rights of parents and children, most notably the UN Convention on the Rights of the Child (1989).[30]

Similarly, Article 19 of the 1966 ICCPR protects the *"freedom to seek, receive, and impart information and ideas of all kinds,* regardless of frontiers, either orally, in writing, or in print, in the form of art, or through any other media of his choice" (Art. 19.2). But Article 19, too, allows legal restrictions that are necessary for "respect of the rights and reputation of others; for the protection of national security or of public order or of public health or morals" (Art. 19.3). As a further limitation on the rights of religion and (religious) expression guaranteed in Articles 18 and 19, Article 26 of the 1966 covenant prohibits any state discrimination on grounds of religion. And Article 27 guarantees to religious minorities "the right to enjoy their own culture" and "to profess and practise their own religion." These latter guarantees are amplified by the Declaration on the Rights of Persons Belonging to National or Ethnic, Religious, or Linguistic Minorities (1992). Distilling the international principle of "religious self-determination," the 1992 declaration recognizes that "the promotion and protection of the rights" of religious minorities is "an integral part of the development of a society as a whole and within a democratic framework based on the rule of law." Accordingly, it calls upon states to respect and to pass implementing legislation that protects and promotes the rights of cultural, religious, and linguistic minorities "to enjoy their own culture, to profess and practice their own religion, and to use their own language, in private and in public, freely and without interference or any form of discrimination."[31]

The literal language of the mandatory 1966 covenant (and its amplification in more recent instruments and cases) thus certainly protects the general right to proselytize—understood as the right to "manifest," "teach," "express," and "impart" religious ideas for the sake, among other things, of seeking the conversion of another. The covenant provides no protection for coercive proselytism. At minimum, this bars physical or material manipulation of the would-be convert, and in some contexts even more subtle forms of deception, enticement, and inducement to convert. The covenant also casts serious suspicion on any proselytism among children or among adherents to minority religions and indigenous cultures. But, outside of these contexts, the religious expression inherent in proselytism is no more suspect than political, economic, artistic, or other forms of expression and should, at minimum, enjoy the same rights protection. If Coca-Cola can hustle its fizzy sugar water, and Hollywood can broadcast its violent movies in a newly opened area of the world, then religious communities must be able to express their religious convictions as well.

Such rights to religion and religious expression are not absolute. The 1966 covenant and its progeny allow for legal protections of "public safety, order, health, or morals," "national security," and "the rights and reputation of others," particularly minors and minorities. But all such legal restrictions on religious expression must always be imposed without discrimination against any religion in violation of Article 26, and with due regard for the general mandates of "necessity and proportionality"—the rough international analogues to the "compelling state interest" and "least restrictive alternative" prongs of the strict scrutiny test of American constitutional law. General "time, place, and manner" restrictions on all proselytizers that are necessary, proportionate, and applied without discrimination against any religion might thus well be apt. But categorical criminal bans on proselytism, or patently discriminatory licensing or registration provisions on proselytizing faiths are prima facie a violation of the religious rights of the proselytizer—as has been clear in the United States since *Cantwell v. Connecticut* (1940)[32] and in the European community since *Kokkinakis v. Greece* (1993).[33]

To my mind, the preferred solution to the modern problem of proselytism is not so much further state restriction as further self-restraint on the part of both local and foreign religious groups. Again, the 1966 covenant provides some useful cues. Article 27 of the covenant, and its amplification in the 1992 minorities convention, reminds us of the special right of local religious groups, particularly minorities, "to enjoy their own culture, and to profess and practise their own religion." Such language might well empower and encourage vulnerable minority traditions to seek protection from aggressive and insensitive proselytism by missionary mavericks and "drive-by" crusaders who have emerged with alacrity in the past two decades. It might even have supported a moratorium on proselytism for a few years in places like Russia just after perestroika and glasnost so that local religions, even the majority Russian Orthodox Church, had some time to recover from nearly a century of harsh oppression that destroyed most of its clergy, seminaries, monasteries, literature, and icons. But Article 27 cannot permanently insulate local religious groups from interaction with other religions. No religious and cultural tradition has the right to remain frozen. For local traditions to seek blanket protections against foreign proselytism, even while inevitably interacting with other dimensions of foreign cultures, is ultimately a self-defeating policy. It stands in sharp contrast to cardinal human rights principles of openness, development, and choice. Even more, it belies the very meaning of being a religious tradition. As Jaroslav Pelikan reminds us: "Tradition is the living faith of the dead; traditionalism is the dead faith of the living."[34]

Article 19 of the 1966 covenant reminds us further that the right to expression, including religious expression, carries with it "special duties and responsibilities" (Art. 19.3). One such duty, it would seem, is to respect the religious dignity and autonomy of the other, and to expect the same respect for one's own dignity and autonomy. This is the heart of the Golden Rule. It encourages all parties, especially foreign proselytizing groups, to negotiate and adopt voluntary codes of conduct of restraint and respect of the other. This requires not only continued cultivation of interreligious dialogue and cooperation—the happy hallmarks of the modern ecumenical movement and of the growing emphasis on comparative religion and globalization in our seminaries. It also requires guidelines of prudence and restraint that every foreign mission board would do well to adopt and enforce: proselytizers would do well to know and appreciate the history, culture, and language of the proselytizee; to avoid Westernization of the gospel and First Amendmentization of politics; to deal honestly and respectfully with theological and liturgical differences; to respect and advocate the religious rights of all peoples; to be Good Samaritans as much as good preachers; to proclaim their gospel both in word and in deed.[35] Moratoria on proselytism might provide temporary relief; but moderation by proselytizers and proselytizees is the more enduring course.

NOTES

This chapter represents work in progress on a monograph tentatively entitled *Religion and Human Rights: Foundations and Frontiers.* It draws in part on John Witte Jr., "A Dickensian Era of Religious Rights," *William and Mary Law Review* 42 (2001): 707–770; and Witte, "A Primer on the Rights and Wrongs of Proselytism," *Cumberland Law Review* 31 (2001): 619–629.

1. Charles Dickens, *A Tale of Two Cities* (London: Chapman and Hall, 1859), 1.

2. "Declaration des droits de l'homme et du citoyen," in Léon Duguit, *Les constitutions et les principales lois politiques de la France depuis 1789* (Paris: Librairie Générale de Droit et de Jurisprudence, 1952), 1.

3. The phrase is from Irwin Cotler, "Jewish NGOs and Religious Human Rights: A Case Study," in *Religious Human Rights in Global Perspective*, ed. John Witte Jr. and Johan D. van der Vyver (The Hague: Martinus Nijhoff, 1996), 1:235–294.

4. See John Witte Jr. and Michael Bourdeaux, eds., *Proselytism and Orthodoxy in Russia: The New War for Souls* (Maryknoll, NY: Orbis Books, 1999); Zoe Knox, *Russian Society and the Orthodox Church: Religion in Russia after Communism* (New York: Routledge, 2005).

5. Abdullahi Ahmed An-Na'im and Francis M. Deng, eds., *Human Rights in Africa: Cross-Cultural Perspectives* (Washington, DC: Brookings Institution, 1990); Abdullahi Ahmed An-Na'im, ed., *Proselytization and Communal Self-Determination in Africa* (Maryknoll, NY: Orbis Books, 1999); Symposium: "The Problem of Proselytism in Southern Africa," *Emory International Law Review* 14 (2000): 491–1303.

6. Paul E. Sigmund, ed., *Religious Freedom and Evangelization in Latin America: The Challenge of Religious Pluralism* (Maryknoll, NY: Orbis Books, 1999).

7. Susanne Hoeber Rudolph, "Introduction" to Susanne Hoeber Rudolph and James Piscatori, eds., *Transnational Religion and Fading States* (Boulder, CO: Westview Press, 1997), 6.

8. See analysis in Natan Lerner, *Religion, Secular Beliefs, and Human Rights: 25 Years after the Declaration* (Leiden: Martinus Nijhoff, 2006), with sample documents collected in Ian Brownlie and Guy S. Goodwin-Gill, eds., *Basic Documents on Human Rights*, 5th ed. (Oxford: Oxford University Press, 2006), and in Tad Stahnke and J. Paul Martin, eds., *Religion and Human Rights: Basic Documents* (New York: Center for the Study of Human Rights, Columbia University, 1998).

9. Tore Lindholm, W. Cole Durham Jr., and Bahia G. Tahzib-Lie, *Facilitating Freedom of Religion or Belief: A Deskbook* (Leiden: Martinus Nijhoff, 2004); Malcolm D. Evans, *Religious Liberty and International Law in Europe* (Cambridge: Cambridge University Press, 1997); Bahia G. Tahzib, *Freedom of Religion or Belief: Ensuring Effective International Legal Protection* (The Hague: Martinus Nijhoff, 1996); John Witte Jr. and Johan D. van der Vyver, eds., *Religious Human Rights in Global Perspective*, 2 vols. (The Hague: Martinus Nijhoff, 1996).

10. Julie A. Mertus, *Kosovo: How Myths and Truths Started a War* (Berkeley: University of California Press, 1999); Paul Mojzes, *Yugoslavian Inferno: Ethno-religious Warfare in the Balkans* (New York: Continuum, 1995); Michael A. Sells, *The Bridge Betrayed: Religion and Genocide in Bosnia* (Berkeley: University of California Press, 1996).

11. Francis M. Deng, *War of Visions: Conflict of Identities in the Sudan* (Washington, DC: Brookings Institution, 1995), 9–31.

12. T. Jeremy Gunn, *Dieu en France et aux États-Unis: Quand les mythes font la loi* (Paris: Berg International, 2005); T. Jeremy Gunn, "Religious Freedom and *Laïcité*: A Comparison of the United States and France," *Brigham Young University Law Review* (2004): 419–506.

13. Symposium, "Pluralism, Proselytism and Nationalism in Eastern Europe," *Journal of Ecumenical Studies* 36 (1999):1–286.

14. See examples in Gabriel A. Almond, R. Scott Appleby, and Emmanuel Sivian, *Strong Religion: The Rise of Fundamentalism around the World* (Chicago: University of Chicago Press, 2003); Abdullahi Ahmed An-Na'im, *African Constitutionalism and the Contingent Role of Islam* (Philadelphia: University of Pennsylvania Press, 2006); W. Cole Durham Jr. and Silvio Ferrari, eds., *Laws on Religion and the State in Post-Communist Europe* (Leuven: Peeters, 2004).

15. The most comprehensive is the *Endbericht der Enquete-Kommission Sogennante Sekten und Psychogruppen, Deutscher Bundestag 13. Wahlperiode Drucksche 13/10950* (June 6, 1998). See Peter B. Clarke, ed., *New Religions in Global Perspective: A Study of Religious Change in the Modern World* (New York: Routledge, 2006); Elisabeth Arweck and Peter B. Clarke, *New Religious Movements in Western Europe: An Annotated Bibliography* (Westport, CT: Greenwood Press, 1997); Derek H. Davis and Gerhard Besier, eds., *International Perspectives on Freedom and Equality of Religious Beliefs* (Waco, TX: Baylor University Press, 2002).

16. See analysis in Symposium, "The Frontiers of Religious Liberty: A Comparative Law Celebration of the 25th Anniversary of the 1981 UN Declaration on Religious Intolerance," *Emory International Law Review* 21 (2007): 1–276.

17. *Re Sahin v. Turkey*, App. No. 44744/98 (Eur. Ct. H. R. June 29, 2004), available at http://www.echr.coe.int/Eng/Judgments.htm. See analysis of this and related

cases in Lerner, *Religion, Secular Beliefs, and Human Rights,* 181–200; Natan Lerner, *Group Rights and Discrimination in International Law,* 2nd ed. (The Hague: Martinus Nijhoff, 2003). For comparative analysis of recent limitations and restrictions on religious freedom in Europe, see Symposium, "The Permissible Scope of Legal Limitations on Freedom of Religion and Belief," *Emory International Law Review* (2005): 465–1320.

18. The phrase was made popular in a dissenting opinion by Justice Potter Stewart in *Abington School District v. Schempp,* 374 U.S. 203, 313 (Stewart, J., dissenting). See, further, John Witte Jr., "Facts and Fictions about the History of Separation of Church and State," *Journal of Church and State* 48 (2006): 15–46.

19. 494 U.S. 872 (1990).

20. See analysis of recent statutory protections of religious freedom in John Witte Jr., *Religion and the American Constitutional Experiment,* 2nd ed. (Boulder, CO: Westview Press, 2005).

21. See Lerner, *Religion, Secular Beliefs, and Human Rights,* 119–168; J. A. Walkate, "The Right of Everyone to Change His Religion or Belief," *Netherlands International Law Review* 2 (1983): 146.

22. Joel A. Nichols, "Mission, Evangelism, and Proselytism in Christianity: Mainline Conceptions as Reflected in Church Documents," *Emory International Law Review* 12 (1998): 563–656; David Novak, "Proselytism and Conversion in Judaism," in *Sharing the Book: Religious Perspectives on the Rights and Wrongs of Proselytism,* ed. John Witte Jr. and Richard C. Martin (Maryknoll, NY: Orbis Books, 1999), 17–44; Donna E. Arzt, "The Treatment of Religious Dissidents under Classic and Contemporary Islamic Law," in Witte and van der Vyver, *Religious Human Rights,* 1:387–453.

23. See report in "Kabul Judge Rejects Calls to End Trial of Christian Convert," *New York Times,* March 24, 2006, A3; "Italy Grants Asylum to Afghan Christian Convert," *New York Times,* March 30, 2006, A14.

24. *New York Trust Co. v. Eisner,* 256 U.S. 345, 349 (1921).

25. Brian Tierney, "Religious Rights: An Historical Perspective," in Witte and van der Vyver, *Religious Human Rights,* 1:17–46.

26. Perez Zagorin, *How the Idea of Religious Toleration Came to the West* (Princeton, NJ: Princeton University Press, 2003); R. W. Davis, ed., *The Origins of Modern Freedom in the West* (Stanford, CA: Stanford University Press, 1995); Noel B. Reynolds and W. Cole Durham Jr., eds., *Religious Liberty in Western Thought* (Grand Rapids, MI: Eerdmans, 1996).

27. The most famous formulation of the right, and duty, of the dissenter to emigrate peaceably from the territory whose religious establishment he or she cannot abide comes in the Peace of Augsburg (1555); its provisions are repeated in the Edict of Nantes (1598) and the Religious Peace of Westphalia (1648). See Sidney Z. Ehler and John B. Morrall, eds., *Church and State through the Centuries: A Collection of Historical Documents with Commentary* (Newman, MD: Burnes and Oates, 1964), 164–198.

28. Max L. Stackhouse and Deirdre King Hainsworth, "Deciding for God: The Right to Convert in Protestant Perspectives," in Witte and Martin, *Sharing the Book,* 201–230.

29. See discussion by Farid Esack, Richard C. Martin, and Donna E. Arzt in Witte and Martin, *Sharing the Book*, 79–144.

30. Convention on the Rights of the Child (November 20, 1989), 28 I.L.M. 1448; Symposium, "What's Wrong with Rights for Children?" *Emory International Law Review* 20 (2006): 1–239.

31. Preamble and Articles 1–2, reprinted by the Office of the United Nations High Commissioner for Human Rights, at http://www.ohchr.org/english/law/ minorites.htm See similar protections in the Indigenous and Tribal Peoples Convention (1989), Arts. 3.2, 5(a)–(c), at http://www.ohchr.org/english/law/indigenous.htm See, further, Johan D. van der Vyver, *Leuven Lectures on Religious Institutions, Religious Communities, and Rights* (Leuven: Peeters, 2004), 67–90.

32. *Cantwell v. Connecticut*, 310 U.S. 296 (1940). See analysis in Howard O. Hunter and Polly J. Price, "Regulation of Religious Proselytism in the United States," *Brigham Young University Law Review* (2001): 537–575.

33. *Kokkinakis v. Greece*, 260-A Eur. Ct. H. R. (ser. A) 18.

34. Jaroslav Pelikan, *The Vindication of Tradition* (New Haven, CT: Yale University Press, 1984), 69.

35. See Anita Deyneka, "Guidelines for Foreign Missionaries in the Soviet Union," in Witte and Bordeaux, *Proselytism and Orthodoxy in Russia*, 331–340; Lawrence A. Uzzell, "Guidelines for American Missionaries in Russia," in Witte and Bordeaux, *Proselytism and Orthodoxy in Russia*, 323–330.

BIBLIOGRAPHY

Almond, Gabriel A., R. Scott Appleby, and Emmanuel Sivian. *Strong Religion: The Rise of Fundamentalism around the World*. Chicago: University of Chicago Press, 2003.

An-Na'im, Abdullahi Ahmed. *African Constitutionalism and the Contingent Role of Islam*. Philadelphia: University of Pennsylvania Press, 2006.

———, ed. *Proselytization and Communal Self-Determination in Africa*. Maryknoll, NY: Orbis Books, 1999.

An-Na'im, Abdullahi Ahmed, and Francis M. Deng, eds. *Human Rights in Africa: Cross-Cultural Perspectives*. Washington, DC: Brookings Institution, 1990.

Arweck, Elisabeth, and Peter B. Clarke. *New Religious Movements in Western Europe: An Annotated Bibliography*. Westport, CT: Greenwood Press, 1997.

Arzt, Donna E. "The Treatment of Religious Dissidents under Classic and Contemporary Islamic Law." In *Religious Human Rights in Global Perspective*, ed. John Witte Jr. and Johan D. van der Vyver, 1:387–454. The Hague: Martinus Nijhoff, 1996.

Brownlie, Ian, and Guy S. Goodwin-Gill, ed. *Basic Documents on Human Rights*. 5th ed. Oxford: Oxford University Press, 2006.

Clarke, Peter B., ed. *New Religions in Global Perspective: A Study of Religious Change in the Modern World*. New York: Routledge, 2006.

Cotler, Irwin. "Jewish NGOs and Religious Human Rights: A Case Study." In *Religious Human Rights in Global Perspective*, ed. John Witte Jr. and Johan D. van der Vyver, 1:235–294. The Hague: Martinus Nijhoff, 1996.

Davis, Derek H., and Gerhard Besier. *International Perspectives on Freedom and Equality of Religious Beliefs*. Waco, TX: Baylor University Press, 2002.

Davis, R. W., ed. *The Origins of Modern Freedom in the West*. Stanford, CA: Stanford University Press, 1995.

Deng, Francis M. *War of Visions: Conflict of Identities in the Sudan*. Washington, DC: Brookings Institution, 1995.

Deyneka, Anita. "Guidelines for Foreign Missionaries in the Soviet Union." In *Proselytism and Orthodoxy in Russia: The New War for Souls*, ed. John Witte Jr. and Michael Bourdeaux, 331–340. Maryknoll, NY: Orbis Books, 1999.

Dickens, Charles. *A Tale of Two Cities*. London: Chapman and Hall, 1859.

Duguit, Léon. *Les constitutions et les principales lois politiques de la France depuis 1789*. Paris: Librairie Générale de Droit et de Jurisprudence, 1952.

Durham, W. Cole, Jr., and Silvio Ferrari, eds. *Laws on Religion and the State in Post-Communist Europe*. Leuven: Peeters, 2004.

Ehler, Sidney Z., and John B. Morrall, eds. *Church and State through the Centuries: A Collection of Historical Documents with Commentary*. Newman, MD: Burnes and Oates, 1964.

Evans, Malcolm D. *Religious Liberty and International Law in Europe*. Cambridge: Cambridge University Press, 1997.

Gunn, T. Jeremy. *Dieu en France et aux États-Unis: Quand les mythes font la loi*. Paris: Berg International, 2005.

———. "Religious Freedom and *Laïcité*: A Comparison of the United States and France." *Brigham Young University Law Review* 2004 (2004): 419–506.

Hunter, Howard O., and Polly J. Price. "Regulation of Religious Proselytism in the United States." *Brigham Young University Law Review* 2001 (2001): 537–575.

Knox, Zoe. *Russian Society and the Orthodox Church: Religion in Russia after Communism*. New York: Routledge, 2005.

Lerner, Natan. *Group Rights and Discrimination in International Law*, 2nd ed. The Hague: Martinus Nijhoff, 2003.

———. *Religion, Secular Beliefs, and Human Rights: 25 Years after the Declaration*. Leiden: Martinus Nijhoff, 2006.

Lindholm, Tore, W. Cole Durham Jr., and Bahia G. Tahzib-Lie. *Facilitating Freedom of Religion or Belief: A Deskbook*. Leiden: Martinus Nijhoff, 2004.

Mertus, Julie A. *Kosovo: How Myths and Truths Started a War*. Berkeley: University of California Press, 1999.

Mojzes, Paul. *Yugoslavian Inferno: Ethno-religious Warfare in the Balkans*. New York: Continuum, 1995.

Nichols, Joel A. "Mission, Evangelism, and Proselytism in Christianity: Mainline Conceptions as Reflected in Church Documents." *Emory International Law Review* 12 (1998): 563–656.

Novak, David. "Proselytism and Conversion in Judaism." In *Sharing the Book: Religious Perspectives on the Rights and Wrongs of Proselytism*, ed. John Witte Jr. and Richard C. Martin, 17–44. Maryknoll, NY: Orbis Books, 1999.

Pelikan, Jaroslav. *The Vindication of Tradition*. New Haven, CT: Yale University Press, 1984.

Reynolds, Noel B., and W. Cole Durham Jr. *Religious Liberty in Western Thought.* Grand Rapids, MI: Eerdmans, 1996.

Rudolph, Susanne Hoeber, and James Piscatori, eds. *Transnational Religion and Fading States.* Boulder, CO: Westview Press, 1997.

Sells, Michael A. *The Bridge Betrayed: Religion and Genocide in Bosnia.* Berkeley: University of California Press, 1996.

Sigmund, Paul E, ed. *Religious Freedom and Evangelization in Latin America: The Challenge of Religious Pluralism.* Maryknoll, NY: Orbis Books, 1999.

Stackhouse, Max L., and Deirdre King Hainsworth. "Deciding for God: The Right to Convert in Protestant Perspectives." In *Sharing the Book: Religious Perspectives on the Rights and Wrongs of Proselytism,* ed. John Witte Jr. and Richard C. Martin, 201–30. Maryknoll, NY: Orbis Books, 1999.

Stahnke, Tad, and J. Paul Martin, eds. *Religion and Human Rights: Basic Documents.* New York: Center for the Study of Human Rights, Columbia University, 1998.

Symposium. "The Frontiers of Religious Liberty: A Comparative Law Celebration of the 25th Anniversary of the 1981 UN Declaration on Religious Intolerance." *Emory International Law Review* 21 (2007): 1–267.

Symposium. "The Permissible Scope of Legal Limitations on Freedom of Religion and Belief." *Emory International Law Review* (2005): 465–1320.

Symposium. "Pluralism, Proselytism and Nationalism in Eastern Europe." *Journal of Ecumenical Studies* 36 (1999): 1–286.

Symposium. "The Problem of Proselytism in Southern Africa." *Emory International Law Review* 14 (2000): 491–1303.

Symposium. "What's Wrong with Rights for Children?" *Emory International Law Review* 20 (2006): 1–239.

Tahzib, Bahia G. *Freedom of Religion or Belief: Ensuring Effective International Legal Protection.* The Hague: Martinus Nijhoff, 1996.

Tierney, Brian. "Religious Rights: An Historical Perspective." In *Religious Human Rights in Global Perspective,* ed. John Witte Jr. and Johan D. van der Vyver, 1:17–46. The Hague: Martinus Nijhoff, 1996.

Uzzell, Lawrence A. "Guidelines for American Missionaries in Russia." In *Proselytism and Orthodoxy in Russia: The New War for Souls,* ed. John Witte Jr. and Michael Bourdeaux, 323–30. Maryknoll, NY: Orbis Books, 1999.

van der Vyver, Johan D. *Leuven Lectures on Religious Institutions, Religious Communities, and Rights.* Leuven: Peeters, 2004.

Walkate, J. A. "The Right of Everyone to Change His Religion or Belief." *Netherlands International Law Review* 2 (1983): 146–169.

Witte, John, Jr. "A Dickensian Era of Religious Rights." *William and Mary Law Review* 42 (2001): 707–770.

———. "Facts and Fictions about the History of Separation of Church and State." *Journal of Church and State* 48 (2006): 15–46.

———. "A Primer on the Rights and Wrongs of Proselytism." *Cumberland Law Review* 31 (2001): 619–629.

————. *Religion and the American Constitutional Experiment*. 2nd ed. Boulder, CO: Westview Press, 2005.

Witte, John, Jr., and Michael Bourdeaux, eds. *Proselytism and Orthodoxy in Russia: The New War for Souls*. Maryknoll, NY: Orbis Books, 1999.

Witte, John, Jr., and Richard C. Martin, eds. *Sharing the Book: Religious Perspectives on the Rights and Wrongs of Proselytism*. Maryknoll, NY: Orbis Books, 1999.

Witte, John, Jr., and Johan D. van der Vyver, eds. *Religious Human Rights in Global Perspective*. 2 vols. The Hague: Martinus Nijhoff, 1996.

Zagorin, Perez. *How the Idea of Religious Toleration Came to the West*. Princeton, NJ: Princeton University Press, 2003.

PART II

Religious Actors in World Politics

6

Building Sustainable Peace: The Roles of Local and Transnational Religious Actors

R. Scott Appleby

If globalization simultaneously stimulates both differentiation and homogenization, as Roland Robertson argues,[1] then we might assume that religions—"exhibit A" in the world's catalogue of internally plural social forces—are adapting readily, if not quite effortlessly, to its impact. Both the monolith and the chameleon are found on religion's coat of arms. They might as well be stitched onto the banner of globalization. In a world made increasingly uniform by the replicating effect of interactive nation-states, transnational trade, global communications, and cultural as well as economic interdependency, religion assumes the role of a stock character. Enter "The Evangelicals," stage right, to defend American exceptionalism and "the American way of life" from dilution in the multicultural, multinational brew. They are accompanied by "The Roman Catholics" and "The Mormons," allies in the struggle to preserve and protect "the traditional family" from the value-free science and wares of the free market. And so on.

But globalization adds twists to the familiar role of religion as monolithic moral arbiter. Islam can appear, somewhat unexpectedly, as situational ally to Roman Catholicism. At the United Nations summit on world population held in Cairo in 1994, for example, priests and mullahs locked arms to block the unrestricted application of reproductive technology. The supposed rivals again shared a pulpit, so to speak, a year later, during the United Nations World Conference on Women.

Even while fostering such unlikely alliances and clustering religious actors on sides of the ethical divide, globalization also promotes fragmentation and internal differentiation—another pattern familiar to the reactive, shape-shifting, fluid, anything-but-monolithic communities known as religions. Robertson coined the term "glocal" to refer to the resistance of ethnic, religious, and national groups required to conform to "universal" rights and codes. Hence we find religious actors among the antiglobalization movements. In short, "Jihad" faces off against "McWorld," the olive tree against the Lexus, and religious actors are found on both sides of the global-local divide.[2]

Internal disputes, purges, and civil wars are not unknown to the major religious traditions throughout their long histories, but contemporary globalization has seemed to intensify and accelerate the phenomenon. Catholics publicly and vehemently oppose other Catholics over everything from birth control to liberation theology and armed resistance to political oppression and human rights abuses. Secular and Orthodox Jews race to denounce and restrict each other in Israel. Sunnis murder Shiites (and vice versa) in an externally triggered Iraqi civil war that gives new, terrifying meaning to "glocal" dynamics.

Yes, the hands of religion are bloody. But globalization has also revealed and accelerated the evolution of a character trait that was always already present in the chronicles of religion: pacification. This chapter examines three of the myriad ways religions are acting as peacemakers under the aegis of globalization: as agents of national reconciliation (Cambodian Buddhists), mediators of peace agreements (the Catholics of Sant'Egidio), and pioneers of internal religious reform (the transnational network of Muslim peacebuilders). Religious traditions have always promoted the peaceful resolution of conflict, sanctified the practices of forgiveness and hospitality to the stranger, and produced saints—exemplary models of peace and justice. In our time, however, the phenomena gathered together under the label of globalization offer the agents of peace within the religious traditions new means to demonstrate that their religion favors peace over war, forgiveness over revenge, nonviolence over violence.

The "new means" includes new partners who come together in unprecedented transnational alliances enabled by the accelerated communication and mobility available in the era of globalization. In this regard, as Thomas Banchoff points out in his introduction to the present volume, "pluralism" refers not merely to diversity but to the interaction of diverse actors within the political sphere. Religious pluralism, he writes, "denotes a politics that joins diverse communities with overlapping but distinctive ethics and interests." The new global politics might feature Catholics, Mormons, Jews, Muslims, agnostics, and atheists forming an ethical alliance against a rival bloc of Catholics, Mormons, Jews, Muslims, agnostics, and atheists. (Often the first task of religious peacemakers is to challenge or otherwise neutralize their belligerent coreligionists.) In principle, the intense and increasing interaction within and across traditions that marks what we call globalization leaves no religious or secular tradition excluded from the mix: any number can play.

Part of the dynamism of globalization and the moral energy and excitement it generates lies precisely in the liberating awareness that no one is in control. Of course, this state of creative anarchy creates a considerable crisis for religion as monolith. Authority—and authoritarian male leaders—created and sustain the monolith. Speed and mobility make it exceedingly difficult, however, for the old boys to retain their firm grip on power. Unauthorized deals are being cut behind computer screens, on the Web, and in global forums. As Banchoff notes, religion is taking its place alongside the major secular forces of modernity—the state, democratic civil society, and the market. But it is, increasingly, a decentered religion. The polycentric and pragmatically collaborative religions and religious actors, that is, are finding surprising and consequential political openings at the international level. New possibilities for religion as an international and transnational actor abound. Transnational religious peacebuilding is one such possibility.

Religious Peacebuilding and Faith-Based Diplomacy: A Work in Progress

By now, twelve years after the publication of *Religion: The Missing Dimension of Statecraft*, which was followed by dozens of subsequent books and journal articles exploring the various roles of religious actors in conflict settings, one can summarize an initial set of findings regarding religious peacebuilding and faith-based diplomacy, as follows.[3]

Religious leaders are uniquely positioned to foster nonviolent conflict transformation through the building of constructive, collaborative relationships within and across ethnic and religious groups for the common good of the entire population of a region. In many conflict settings around the world, that is, the social location and cultural power of religious leaders make them potentially critical players in any effort to build a sustainable peace. The multigenerational local or regional communities they oversee are repositories of local knowledge and wisdom, custodians of culture, and privileged sites of moral, psychological, and spiritual formation. Symbolically charged sources of personal as well as collective identity, these communities typically establish and maintain essential educational and welfare institutions, some of which serve people who are not members of the religious community.[4]

Having earned a reputation for integrity and service, such indigenous religious communities have few rivals for the trust of the people. Moreover, their sacred narratives and practices give meaning and context to everyday life. Not least, politics is informed by religious culture. The religious imagination shapes the popular notion of the "nation" or "polis." Significantly, religions can and must abet the establishment and growth of the interethnic and interreligious institutions of civil society—the civic associations and cross-cultural partnerships dedicated to improving local schools, regulating health care, building libraries and other cultural centers, and so on. The political scientist Ashutosh Varshney has identified such multireligious civic associations as critical to the immunization of religiously and ethnically plural cities and villages in India from the provocation of political elites or gangs intent on sowing division and fomenting violence. Varshney is testing these findings in regions of Southeast Asia and Africa.[5]

No truly effective methods of conflict resolution can ignore the locally rooted markers of identity over which religions hold sway. Culture, history, memory, authenticity (often equated with the autochthonous, the "homegrown")—these are the currency of the local peacebuilder. Beyond the shorter-term goals of reducing violence and resolving disputed issues, the drive to build a sustainable peace in communities riven by deeply rooted tribal, ethnic, religious, or political animosities is unlikely to succeed, we now recognize, if religious leaders are ignored or otherwise excluded from the process.[6]

And yet, it remains true that the practice of religious peacebuilding is unknown, untested, or underdeveloped in most conflict- and violence-ridden societies. Two obstacles prevent or hinder the emergence and maturation of peacebuilding in religious communities.

The first is *the failure of religious leaders to understand and/or enact their potential peacebuilding roles within the local community.* Several factors come into play. Religious leaders who have official responsibilities for maintaining the institutional life and organizational resources of a religious community find their time and energies occupied less with stimulating the religious imagination than with meeting the next mortgage payment, less with the spiritual formation of their flock than with protecting the turf on which their churches, synagogues, or mosques stand. Religious leadership, in short, often requires a level of institutional stewardship that turns the gaze inward; survival, maintenance, the quotidian concerns command the attention. When the religious community or group finds itself at war, or victimized by war, religious leaders are constrained by the needs and passions of their flock; in such circumstances, interreligious dialogue, relationship-building, "forgiveness," "reconciliation" are not plausible responses.[7]

Tellingly, in ordinary time, when neither war nor survival dominates the consciousness, religious leaders do not naturally see themselves as called to build peace across communities or to act as cultural or civic leaders; they are pastors of their own people, offering comfort to their afflicted and counsel to their own congregants.

Exceptions to the pattern of indifference to, or ignorance of, the promise of religious peacebuilding are numerous. The exceptions have attained a certain prominence during the past decade through the efforts of scholars and religious activists who have chronicled and popularized the religious exemplars' bold advocacy for civil and human rights, leadership of postwar truth-telling commissions and memory projects, building of interreligious coalitions, and renunciation of revenge.[8]

A second obstacle to the realization of the peacebuilding promise of religious leaders and the communities they lead is *the insufficient exploitation of their strategic capacity as transnational actors*. As we shall see, there are notable exceptions to this general rule as well. But religious leaders committed to building a sustainable peace are still learning what it means to think globally while acting locally.

"Thinking globally," which Christianity and Islam have done for centuries, takes on specific contours in the age of globalization. The most powerful globalized or globalizing religious forces today are identity movements, such as the Islamic renewal movement Tablighi Jamaat, Christian Pentecostalists, and Mormon missionaries. Their transnational networks take full advantage of the latest communications technologies, enhanced mobility across borders, and specialized expertise.[9]

Truly *strategic* peacebuilding likewise requires the sharing and integration of expertise and resources across national boundaries and areas of specialization. Religious leaders, like other agents of change through civil society, are recognizing the need to forge partnerships with outsiders (including secular as well as faith-based nongovernmental organizations [NGOs]) in order to build capacity for effective problem solving and conflict resolution. Not least, such partnerships offer the religious communities basic knowledge of and access to international norms and institutions. Perhaps more surprisingly, such partnerships also deepen local or regional religious communities' awareness of and collaboration with members of their own religious tradition who are working in grassroots activism in other geographic and cultural settings.[10]

Local-Transnational Partnerships: Stimulating
"Buddhist Peacebuilding" in Cambodia

A case study from Cambodia illustrates the progress of religious communities in integrating the local and the global, and in exploiting the transnational nature of both their host religious traditions and the numerous humanitarian and human rights organizations available to them as partners.

In the spring of 1993, Samdech Preah Maha Ghosananda, the sixty-eight-year-old Buddhist primate of Cambodia, led hundreds of Buddhist monks, nuns, and laity on a dramatic monthlong march from Siam Reap in the northwest section of Cambodia throughout the central regions to the capital, Phnom Penh. Held on the eve of the UN-sponsored elections of a new National Assembly and government, this second annual Dhammayietra (Pilgrimage of Truth) Peace March traversed dangerous territory marked by land mines and firefights. The marchers hoped to build popular confidence in the elections and overcome the fear that had been aroused by Khmer Rouge threats of violence and disruption. By the time Maha Ghosananda and his supporters reached Phnom Penh, hundreds of thousands of Cambodians had encouraged the marchers along their path, and more than 10,000 people had joined their ranks. Ninety percent of the Cambodian electorate voted in the ensuing free and fair elections, the first in the country's history. While the United Nations Transitional Authority in Cambodia (UNTAC) had created the conditions necessary for the holding of the elections, many Cambodians and NGO workers attributed the extraordinary level of popular participation to the success of the Dhammayietra.[11]

A year later, on April 24, 1994, when Maha Ghosananda led Dhammayietra III, the political circumstances had changed. Held in support of national reconciliation, the 1994 march came less than a month after Khmer Rouge troops had recaptured their strategic stronghold and nominal "capital" of Pailin, a lucrative gem-mining area, and only days after peace talks between the Khmer Rouge and the coalition government (formed after the 1993 elections) had been postponed indefinitely. The marchers, scheduled to arrive at their destination one month later, on a Buddhist holy day, intended to plant trees along the way as a symbol of rebirth and reconciliation. Eight hundred people began the march, including 400 monks, 200 nuns, and a dozen NGO workers. On April 30, in the Bavel district about twenty-four miles northwest of the provincial capital of Battambang, the marchers were caught in a firefight between soldiers of the Royal Cambodian army and the Khmer Rouge guerrillas occupying territory near the Thai border. Despite the casualties sustained during the march, and a loss of nerve by some of Ghosananda's fellow pilgrims, the monk continued to lead the annual pilgrimages.[12]

The Buddhist peace marches were Ghosananda's response to nearly two decades of Cambodians slaughtering Cambodians, despite their shared religious and cultural heritage. From April 1975 until the Vietnamese invasion of Cambodia in December 1978, the government of what was known as Democratic Kampuchea under Pol Pot had attempted to create a "racially pure" society entirely shorn of its past. In this effort the Khmer Rouge killed nearly one-fifth of Cambodia's population of 8 million people, targeting not only ethnic minorities, such as the Chinese, the Vietnamese, and the Muslim Chams, but fellow Khmers as well. All traces of the pro-American Lon Nol government and the earlier rule of Prince Norodom Sihanouk were eradicated, as were institutions associated with the French colonists. Pol Pot's soldiers also attacked Khmer institutions from the precolonial past, including the *sangha*, the Buddhist order of monks. In a systematic manner the Khmer Rouge attempted to obliterate Buddhism from Cambodian society, destroying more than one-third of the country's 3,300 *wats* (Buddhist temple-monasteries) and killing thousands of monks and nuns.

Ironically, the Communist movement in Cambodia had its origins in the Buddhist nationalism of the 1940s; monks and former monks became prominent in the movement in the 1950s. The party began to distance itself from Buddhism in the 1960s, however, and the Pol Pot regime demonized the tradition as a prelude to executing more than half the monks of Cambodia. Although the Khmer Rouge vilified the monks as "worthless parasites" whose doctrine of Nirvana or self-extinction undermined economic productivity, Pol Pot's campaign against Buddhism cannot be explained merely by reference to Marxist slogans about religion being the opiate of the people. "As the Khmer Rouge have become better understood," anthropologist Charles Keyes writes, "it has become clear that the potency of their ideology derived in part from its relationship to Khmer Buddhist culture."[13] Pol Pot himself had lived for a brief time in a *wat*, and he fashioned the national Communist Party into the Angkar, a disciplined organization modeled in part on the *sangha* and designed to replace it as the ultimate source of moral authority in Khmer society. Visitors to the ruined remains of Phnom Penh and the converted school buildings that had served as Khmer Rouge torture chambers noted the close correlation between the techniques of torture that had been employed and those that are depicted in traditional descriptions of Buddhist hells.[14]

Buddhism was both a source of imitation and the enemy to be supplanted. "The Khmer Rouge conceived of a new order in which evil and good were fused in the Angkar and cadres were both subhuman beings with immense magical powers and morally superior beings equivalent to Buddhist monks," Keyes explains. "Organized Buddhism had to be eliminated for this new order to be established."[15]

The 1978 Vietnamese invasion forced the Khmer Rouge to retreat to the hilly areas along the Thai border, while 350,000 Cambodians crowded into Thai refugee camps and 200,000 fled the region altogether. The Vietnamese installed a new government in Phnom Penh under the name the People's Republic of Kampuchea (PRK). Although it proved less severe than the regime of Pol Pot, and gradually began to rebuild Khmer culture and reinstate Buddhism, the PRK government, due to its Vietnamese character, was not recognized by the United States, European nations, the People's Republic of China, or member countries of Association of South-East Asian Nations [ASEAN]. With support from China and Thailand, the Khmer Rouge regrouped and launched a guerrilla war against the PRK. In 1982, after prodding from the United States, China, and the ASEAN countries, two refugee-based movements—the Khmer People's National Liberation Front and a royalist party led by King Sihanouk's son, Prince Norodom Ranariddh—agreed to join the Khmer Rouge in the Coalition Government of Democratic Campuchea nominally headed by Sihanouk but controlled by the Khmer Rouge. Meanwhile, back in Phnom Penh, the PRK found in Buddhism a source of legitimacy that avoided the thorny question of the monarchy and Sihanouk's status—but it was a Buddhism restored only partially, and along the restrictive lines set down by the Vietnamese-led Communist state.

The situation of Cambodian Buddhism improved markedly after 1988, when the government announced a withdrawal of Vietnamese forces and Hun Sen, the PRK prime minister (and former Khmer Rouge officer), agreed in principle to the creation of a new government that would include the PRK and Prince Ranariddh. In order to bolster its popular appeal, the PRK stepped up its support of Buddhism, and Hun Sen publicly apologized for the government's previous "mistakes" toward religion. By 1989 there were 2,400 temple-monasteries in the country, or about two-thirds of the number of wats that had existed before 1970.[16] In April of that year the National Assembly voted to restore Buddhism as the national religion of Cambodia, apparently in hopes that Buddhist leaders would help create the stability needed for the rebuilding of the country's agriculture and economy. The government removed restrictions on the ordination of men under fifty, and the *sangha* grew dramatically, so that by 1990 there were 16,400 Cambodian monks, 40 percent of whom were novices. The government also removed a tax on *wats* and contributed monies for the construction of shrines, including some dedicated to those killed by the Khmer Rouge and built in the form of traditional Theravadin Buddhist funerary structures, or stupas, memorials in which the relics of the dead are preserved. The enduring appeal of Buddhism, in short, ensured its central role in any successful reconstruction.

When peace accords were finally signed in Paris in 1991 under the auspices of the United Nations, Hun Sen recognized Sihanouk as king and head of state. Buddhist monks performed important rituals in the festivities enthroning the king, who resumed his royal role as supreme patron of the *sangha*. Hundreds of monks and novices ordained outside of Cambodia returned from exile in Thailand.

The Paris peace accords created UNTAC, the United Nations peacekeeping team, which proceeded to spend more than $2 billion in 1992 and 1993 supporting 20,000 peacekeeping troops and 5,000 civilian advisers who promoted human rights, encouraged a free press, staged a massive repatriation of refugees from the Thai camps, and organized the 1993 elections bolstered by the Dhammayietra Peace March. The party, led by Prince Ranariddh, pledged "national reconciliation" and won 45 percent of the vote. Hun Sen would not step aside, however, and threatened civil war. With much of the army loyal to him and the UN unwilling to risk war, Sihanouk announced the formation of a provisional national government with Ranariddh as first prime minister and Hun Sen as second prime minister—an unlikely coalition between enemies under the umbrella of a constitutional monarchy.

One important sign of hope was the presence of more than 200 NGOs, many of which had arrived during the 1980s to provide emergency relief when the United States and other Western governments had refused to assist the PRK. Several of the most effective NGOs working in Cambodia were religiously sponsored and religiously motivated. These included Catholic Relief Services, Lutheran World Service, and the American Friends Service Committee. Like UNICEF (the largest relief organization in Cambodia, with more than 200 staff in the midnineties), some of the NGOs were large multiservice operations, while others focused in specific areas such as women's issues, demining operations, AIDS education and treatment, the provision of prosthetic devices for those who had lost limbs, agricultural development, and environmental protection. Without the substantial and sustained contributions that such NGOs made during the 1980s, "it is hard to see how this country, devastated by its own leaders in the immediate past, and almost completely ostracized by western governments, could have survived at all."[17]

Survival was a significant accomplishment for a country whose older generations had been virtually wiped out, leaving a society populated primarily by children and young adults; where property ownership remained in a state of confusion, and the capital city was largely in ruins despite the presence of isolated foreign embassies and businesses, royal residences, and tourist attractions; where starvation, disease, a growing traffic in narcotics, government corruption, and foreign corporate exploitation of Cambodia's rich natural resources were the most obvious legacies of the years of lawlessness. The brief presence of the UN peacekeeping teams, followed by the unraveling of the election results in a makeshift coalition government that exacerbated rather than solved Cambodia's systemic problems (and arguably created new ones such as the international drug trade and money laundering), led veteran Cambodia watchers to label the previously celebrated UN intervention "a sham."[18]

In this context the Western-based NGOs expanded their operations in the 1990s. Among their many services, they worked with Cambodians to build the foundations of a legal system, including local and national courts. Indigenous NGOs sprouted as well, relying on collaboration with the more experienced organizations.

For the first time Buddhist-affiliated groups were prominent in the reconstruction effort. Ghosananda's Dhammayietra Center in Phnom Penh and the Coalition for Peace and Reconciliation (CPR), run by a Catholic priest, Bob Maat, and a Jewish activist, Liz Bernstein, built upon the fame of the annual peace walks by enrolling Cambodians in conflict-prevention training programs. In Battambang in 1996, for example, the CPR established the Dhammayietra Peacemakers Program for Cambodian students from the ages of fifteen to thirty. Staffed by volunteer teachers who formed the embryonic cell of the Dhammayietra Volunteer Corps, the program offered short courses on the lives of peacemakers in world history. CPR recruited these students, and other Cambodians, to attend workshops in active nonviolence, Buddhist peacemaking skills, and conflict resolution; more than 700 people attended such workshops in 1996. Foreign NGOs contributed trainers for the workshops and provided financial support.[19]

These incipient networks took the first steps in addressing the structural impediments to stability, including the lack of monastic leaders trained in conflict resolution techniques, the weakness of monastic disciplines, and the absence of educational resources (both Buddhist and secular) following the Khmer Rouge destruction of Buddhist institutes, libraries, and manuscripts. For millions of Cambodians the Buddhist community, galvanized by Ghosananda's charismatic leadership, was a powerful source of hope that Cambodia might recover from a quarter century of violence and chaos, dating from the U.S. obliteration bombing during the Vietnam War.[20]

Ghosananda was in many respects an exemplary religious leader. Relentlessly he sought peace for all Cambodians, demonstrating extraordinary physical courage and self-sacrifice, set within an exacting regime of prayer, moral formation, and spiritual discipline to which Buddhist monks and nuns recommitted themselves in the 1980s. Ghosananda's critics in the international human rights community, however, were appalled at his willingness to forgive Khmer

Rouge generals without demanding reparation or restitution; they concluded that he was indifferent to the demands of justice or, worse, that he was using his cultural authority to establish minimal requirements for national reconciliation.[21]

Religious virtuosos such as Ghosananda, it may be argued, do not make competent policy makers. Nor are they, typically, accomplished organizational leaders. From the first Buddhist peace marches, it became apparent to workers from transnational NGOs stationed in Cambodia that the "Buddhist peacemakers" needed help. Maha Ghosananda's supporters in the NGO community criticized him not so much for his approach to fundamental issues of justice and reconciliation but for his seeming indifference to building social capital from his religious charisma. They saw their mission as translating Buddhist devotion and courage into structural change through organizational recruiting, training, management—in a phrase, resource mobilization.

During the early years of the Dhammayietra marches, the general sense of such concerns was that Ghosananda's movement, rooted in his militant religiosity and powerful moral example, was not being translated into enduring institutions and widespread social practices. Ghosananda did not participate in the day-to-day training of recruits in the methods of nonviolent conflict resolution, and the Buddhist trainers themselves remained too few in number. Philanthropic offers of computers were refused for lack of staff capable of using them. The Dhammayietra events suffered at times from poor planning and inadequate flow of information. Strikingly, there was little advance discussion of procedures to follow in case of violence, and inadequate provision of safe houses in which marchers could take refuge.[22]

As peacebuilders, in short, the Buddhists were not sufficiently organized or well equipped. This led them to rely heavily on foreign NGO workers and inhibited the growth of the indigenous expertise necessary to make peacebuilding a long-term social effort. The large number of NGOs in Cambodia was a mixed blessing, therefore, for they kept Cambodians in a state of dependence and even complacency. In addition, some NGOs replicated the condescending attitudes and relational patterns of colonists. United Church of Christ minister Peter Pond, who had been involved for decades in human rights and pro-democracy training in southeast Asia, contended that NGO workers should have been devoting a greater portion of their funds and energies to publicizing and building up the indigenous peacemaking efforts under way. The 500 Buddhist supporters of the Dhammayietra Center, he pointed out, could and should have been 5,000 in number. Greater visibility would allow the peace movement to attract external financial and organizational support to train Cambodians in conflict resolution techniques. The cost of such programs, Pond believed, would be minuscule in comparison to the benefit to be realized from the presence of thousands of trained indigenous peacemakers. "With no more than one million U.S. dollars per year for the training of indigenous, middle-level leaders, from mayors to school teachers," he insisted in 1998, "stability can be achieved within a decade and the foundations of lasting peace built over a fifty year period."[23]

Since Pond uttered these hopes and criticisms, collaboration between Cambodian Buddhist leaders and transnational organizations has led to greater participation by Buddhists from Southeast Asia. The trajectory of expansion began in 1995, when it became evident that the walks might become an annual event dedicated to the promotion of national nonviolent social change. With Ghosananda's blessing, Maat, Bernstein, and other NGO workers developed guidelines for the marches and introduced a public education element around the cause of increased awareness of public health concerns in Cambodia. As mentioned, they also established training programs at various sites for prospective pilgrims, who were required to study basic Buddhist concepts and their application to social reform, along with conflict resolution and peacebuilding techniques, including the philosophy and practice of nonviolence.

Gradually Cambodian Buddhists took leadership of the training and formation exercises surrounding the annual marches. In 2004 the Southeast Asia office of Non- Violence International, in conjunction with the European Centre for Conflict Prevention, reported that marchers were coming from several nations to participate in the Dhammayietras, in order to learn new methods of cultural and religious grassroots activism. By 2004 "thousands of people" had attended the training sessions, generating momentum for both local and regional efforts to prevent the outbreak of war.[24]

As a result of Buddhist networking across national boundaries, a development stimulated by Buddhist-NGO partnerships in the region, the Dhammayietra was transformed in two ways. First, it evolved, according to the anthropologist Monique Skidmore, into "a new cultural ritual of remembering," which, "through the creation of new collective memories is allowing some Cambodians to emerge from the culture of violence created by the last twenty years of war." Second, according to NGO officer Yeshua Moser-Puangsuwan, the annual marches had become a force that "generates solidarity actions by grassroots activists in other parts of the world."[25]

Religion Not Isolable: The Alliance Building of Sant'Egidio

In the new religious peacebuilding, religion relinquishes pretense to autonomy. As the case of Cambodia demonstrates, religion as peacebuilder is interactive,

The history and evolution of the community from a small band of Italian Catholics to a multinational association, and from a company of Christians working with the poor and dispossessed (including, especially, HIV/AIDS victims in Africa) to a transnational conflict mediator renowned for its critical role in negotiating a settlement to end the civil war in Mozambique, has been told elsewhere.[26] What matters for our purposes in this essay is the conviction of Riccardi and his colleagues that their Catholic identity is fully articulated in Pope John XXIII's dictum: "Let us stress what unites us, not what divides us." The movement they founded to give expression to this simple goal numbered approximately 15,000 members by the midnineties.

It began in the late sixties as a voluntary charitable organization through which members could express their Christian commitment to ecumenical and interreligious dialogue and social concern for the poor. Eventually, the Vatican provided a headquarters by donating the sixteenth-century Carmelite convent of Sant'Egidio, located around the corner from the Church of Santa Maria in the ancient Roman district of Trastevere, a neighborhood traditionally known as a meeting place of nationalities and cultures. The Italian government subsequently renovated the convent, transforming it into a complex of meeting rooms, offices, and reception areas. Thereafter the group took the name Comunità di Sant'Egidio. Their secular and religious sponsors foreshadowed a career in which the community would draw upon the vast multinational resources of both governments and the Roman Catholic Church.[27]

In practice Sant'Egidio members, most of whom are laypeople with their own families and professional careers in law, banking, education, government, and the like, strive to integrate their local and international presences; each local community seeks a way to serve the poor, even while expanding its contacts with other religious and political communities, and with states, as part of Sant'Egidio's worldwide mission. In Rome, for example, the community operates a home for abandoned children, a hostel and a school for foreign immigrants, a solidarity network for elderly people, communities for the homeless, health services for handicapped adults and terminal AIDS patients, and legal counseling services for the poor. The social services are central to Sant'Egidio's identity and evangelical mission, for they embody its challenge to civil society to commit its resources more fully to the urgent needs of the poor and marginalized.

Sant'Egidio's network of *scuole popolari* teaches volunteers that local problems are connected to regional stability, which is enhanced by equitable social policies. Accordingly, the community lobbies governments and policymakers. In the 1980s, for example, Sant'Egidio members living in Africa, who were already active in language training and health programs for the indigenous populations, founded the NGO Solidarietà con il Terzo Mondo (Solidarity with internally plural, socially fluid, interdependent—characteristics not always as sociated with "religion" in textbook and ideal-type presentations. Religions—or more accurately, sectors or groups within multinational religious communities— that recognize, acknowledge, and exploit their multicultural, transnational presences are also more likely to welcome and explore avenues toward collabora- tion with secular, nongovernmental, and intergovernmental agencies, lobbying groups, international human rights organizations, and the like.

The Cambodian Buddhist disciples of Maha Ghosananda, traumatized and plunged into national and cultural crisis by genocide and civil war, were gradu- ally awakened to the power of their identity as a regional as well as a national presence, and to their need to incorporate "secular" (i.e., non-Buddhist) conflict resolution and organizational management techniques into their religious sensibility and repertoire of cultural practices. The Buddhist convergence on peacebuilding as a practice or a set of practices commensurate with, but sepa- rate from, traditional Buddhist practices such as meditation and almsgiving was a pragmatic response to a traumatic disruption in Cambodian life. How deep or enduring the new "practice" will be remains to be seen.

By contrast, the Catholic Community of Sant'Egidio was born of a simple idea—an idea, hardened into a conviction, that eventually gave birth not only to a new lay religious community but also to a set of instantiating practices. The story lends nuance to our portrait of religious peacebuilding in an era of globalization, for the idea was that Christianity, in its deepest meaning, opens out to all people of goodwill, religious and secular alike, who are potential allies in humanitarian service to the world and in the building of sustainable peace through personal and organizational partnerships.

The Community of Sant'Egidio was established in the late 1960s in response to the growing awareness of its young Italian founders that hard- and-fast categories of "religious" and "secular," if still somewhat meaningful in the theological realm, were rapidly becoming barriers to the enactment of the Catholic faith they heard proclaimed at the Second Vatican Council. Vatican II, a gathering of the world's Catholic bishops held in Rome at the Vatican from 1962 to 1965, was *the* formative event in their religious maturation. To Andre Riccardi and his fellow collegians studying in Rome during the years imme- diately following the council, Vatican II's identification of the church's mission with the "joys and hopes, grief and suffering" of all the people of the world, coupled with its exhortation to seek peace and justice as a Christian vocation, meant that the global ("universal") character of the Roman Catholic Church was not merely a historical contingency but a providential gift, enabling new faith communities to find allies, both Catholic and non-Catholic, in virtually every conflict setting imaginable.

the Third World) to pursue dialogue and cooperation among peoples and governments for the purpose of economic development.[28]

Sant'Egidio's emergence as a faith-based peacebuilding organization was a natural development from the community's international humanitarian presence and its slyly religious commitment to a "disciplined friendship," as they put it, with a variety of local and transnational, secular and religious, governmental and nongovernmental organizations.[29] The intervention that put the community on the map of transnational conflict mediation occurred directly as a result of Sant'Egidio's humanitarian service, in this case to the African nation of Mozambique.

When the opposing parties in Mozambique's civil war—FRELIMO, the party of the government, and RENAMO, the rebel group—sought a mediator to host the rounds of peace talks, they turned to the familiar actors of Sant'Egidio, a local "foreign" presence whose good offices and representatives (hailing from the "glocal" church and civil society) reinforced the community's reputation for impartiality bolstered by "connections." At critical moments during the community's service as mediator of the peace talks, members of Sant'Egidio made successful appeals to the United States and to European governments for grain shipments, military intelligence, and logistical and financial support. Along the way, these quietly devout Catholics drew on personal friendships with Italian communist politicians, CIA operatives, and a Spanish archbishop working in the Vatican's Curia.[30]

After the peace accords were signed and the fighting ended, Sant'Egidio remained on the scene as a monitoring and pacifying presence—reassuring the ex-combatants, keeping the international community aware of the developments (including natural disasters) that affected the implementation and observation of the peace settlement, and orchestrating the national celebration of a decade of peace.

The community's simultaneous commitment to the local and the global was also on display during its intervention in the civil war raging in Algeria. Sant'Egidio excels in building up what it calls "networks for peace"—personal and organizational contacts across religious boundaries. Bolstering its humanitarian presence in Algeria was the strong reputation the community had established in the Islamic world through its programs on behalf of Muslim immigrants newly arrived in Rome and other European urban centers from the Middle East and North Africa. Building on that reputation, Sant'Egidio fostered Muslim-Christian interaction and collaboration in multiple settings in the Islamic world, including North Africa.

In November 1994, these efforts in the Muslim community yielded fruit when Sant'Egidio was invited to convene a meeting of delegates from the major political parties in Algeria. The country was then entering the second phase of a protracted civil war following the Front de Libération National government's cancellation of the results of the 1991 elections, which had carried the major Islamist party, the Islamic Salvation Front (FIS), to the brink of controlling the state. At the 1994 summit Sant'Egidio's representatives helped to create an atmosphere of trust that allowed both the Islamists and the secular parties to offer major concessions. The result was a platform signed by all parties in January 1995—an agenda to begin peace talks between the government and the parties.[31]

In light of the low-key approach Sant'Egidio takes to its Roman Catholic identity, one might ask how the movement differs from secular organizations specializing in conflict mediation. Like other religious actors, the Community boasts an unimpeachable record for integrity and good offices in the societies it comes to serve. Through various initiatives, from orchestrating international humanitarian relief to providing direct services to the needy, Sant'Egidio practices nonpartisan social action that underscores its equanimity and commitment to the common good. The Community does not seek political or economic power for itself. Heeding Pope John Paul II's call for Catholics to build up civil society, however, the members of Sant'Egidio reject any model of the church that would legitimate Catholic withdrawal from public life. Working with communists or Catholics, insurgents or government officials, the movement is "apolitical," however—nonpartisan as a matter of principle.

The apolitical, nonpartisan label is not unique among mediators; to succeed in outsider-neutral mediation, such groups must be perceived as neutral. Yet one might argue that Sant'Egidio raises this principle to an almost mystical (certainly a theological-ethical) level. The Community's approach to conflict is based on the gospel imperative "Love thy enemy." Sant'Egidio members believe that while the state has a right and duty to punish criminals, the religious community operates from a radically different perspective in which all people are sinners and judgment belongs to God. "As Christians, we believe we are obliged to respect the human dignity of a Slobodan Milosevic no less than that of people far less culpable for bloodshed," Sant'Egidio vice president Andrea Bartoli explains. "Our goal is to understand his point of view—not approve or condemn—but also to search out the grain of reason and goodness we believe persists in even the hardest criminal."

Their focus on establishing relationships with egregious sinners may disqualify Sant'Egidio members from serving in the judiciary, but it makes them effective mediators of conflict. The Community's constructive relationship with Serbian president Milosevic, for example, enabled it to intervene successfully in 1995 to temper Serbia's repressive educational policies toward the ethnic Albanians of Kosovo. In the Mozambican conflict, while RENAMO supporters saw the insurgency engaged in a war against the international communist threat, and FRELIMO supporters saw the conflict as part of the anti-apartheid campaign, the Sant'Egidio mediators treated each side with equal dignity and respect. Its first priority is always to bring the warring parties to an agreement—something that would only be made more difficult by engaging in moral recriminations and debates over how to apportion the blame or interpret the conflict. In Algeria, only Sant'Egidio, having established a reputation for integrity among the region's Muslims, was able to bring the conflicted parties to the negotiating table.

Exploiting Internal Pluralism: Building Foundations for Peace through Islamic Networks

Our review of various dimensions of religious peacebuilding conducted through local and transnational synergies is hardly comprehensive. The literature cited in this essay is rich in case studies and vignettes describing dozens of faith-based interventions designed to end fighting and transform conflicts. Rather than review the types of religious accompaniment, we have explored a case in which local religious actors and communities have been drawn into transnational collaboration through the agency of NGOs (Cambodian Buddhists), and a case in which the internal logic of a religious community has caused its members to build their own transnational network of religious and secular partners in peace (Sant'Egidio).

A third important pattern of internal religious evolution toward local-transnational peacebuilding comes from the Islamic world. Here we see a budding "glocal" movement that is cultural, intellectual, and—fundamentally—religious in inspiration and motivation. Its aim is the nonviolent engagement with, the resolution or transformation of, a series of disputes and confrontations roiling the Muslim world. The issues underlying these confrontations within the world of Islam, and between Muslims and non-Muslims, include, inter alia, the proper relationship of Islam to the modern nation-state, the integration of Muslims into Westernized societies, the agency and identities of women in Islamic societies, and the appropriate means of resistance to internal and external military and economic aggression.

The major figures engaged in this effort reside in Europe, the United States, the Middle East, Southeast Asia, and South Africa, and they hail from various points on the religious spectrum.[32] Perhaps only under the aegis of globalization would such a geographically scattered and culturally diverse set of intellectuals, religious scholars, cultural leaders, and public figures qualify as a social "movement" for reform. They are united by their common awareness of the harrowing violence employed and suffered by Muslims in recent years and the range of responses provoked by the violence and its causes. Some of these transnational actors are openly revisiting and in some cases reconceptualizing Islamic traditions of war, peace, and violence. Some are dedicated to identifying and fortifying Qur'anic and jurisprudential sources that provide guidelines for peace and justice activism. In this moment of crisis within the religious community, challenged by gross acts of terrorism on the part of movements and states, this company of Muslim scholars, cultural leaders, and public officials finds it necessary to develop a project that would place Islam in the vanguard of peace activism around the world.[33]

During the final decades of the twentieth century and the early years of the twenty-first, this "glocal movement" devoted attention to identifying the structural and political obstacles encountered by Muslims who would advance the concept and practice of peacebuilding or conflict resolution. Perhaps the most formidable of these obstacles, many note, is the acute technocratic and political stagnation apparent in both Sunni and Shia societies, a condition that is manifest in a dearth of imaginative and creative political leadership. Other obstacles include the struggle for physical survival, the hierarchical and patriarchal nature of Islamic societies, and the control systems maintained by political and religious elites in Muslim-majority states.[34]

Several commentators have placed hope in the rising generation of young Muslim professionals and aspirants to the middle class.[35] The very Muslim communities whose historical and contemporary political experience compels young people to seek alternatives to both political repression and violent revolution, however, are those whose religio-political leadership is most resistant to the development of transnational networks and coalitions for social change. Especially in settings where the religious clergy is associated with the ruling regime, young participants in peacebuilding training workshops provided by NGOs (the participants are often diplomats and foreign service officers) express "frustration over their supervisors' resistance to the application of peacebuilding skills."[36]

While acknowledging that Islamic traditions, religion, and culture are "potentially fertile sources of nonviolence and peacemaking," Mohammed Abu-Nimer, a Muslim scholar-practitioner who has written insightfully about Islam, violence, and peacebuilding, argues that the potential has gone unrealized in the modern era, largely because the struggle against colonialism framed Muslim engagement with outsiders in so many settings. Preoccupied with striving to create a decolonized, just, and peaceful world, Muslims interpreted the

classical, normative sources and historical experiences of their religious forebears within this sociopolitical context of anticolonialism/anti-imperialism.
The theoretical and conceptual horizons of an Islamic just peace rested on
these historically specific and relatively narrow foundations.[37]

The transnational network of reformers mentioned earlier, to which Abu-
Nimer belongs, might not agree on a word or concept to comprehend their various aims. Were they to agree on "peacebuilding" as a common denominator,
however, the definition would surely encompass the formulation of strategies
of resistance to oppressive and unjust powers, and the development of authen-
tically Islamic alternatives to misbegotten schemes of governance and development. In making a case for interpreting Islam as giving priority to "peacebuilding," thus defined, many of the reformers do, in fact, focus on establishing
and broadening the historic foundations for what Abu-Nimer and others call a
"just peace."[38]

In so doing, they draw upon the internal pluralism of Islam—the multi-
plicity of its scriptural verses, commentaries, traditional teachings, moral injunctions, and so on. Religious traditions are vast and complex bodies of wisdom
built up over many generations. Their foundational sources—their sacred
scriptures, doctrinal traditions, and practices—express and interpret the experiences of the sacred that led to the formation of the religious community. A religious tradition is no less than these sources, but it is always more. The deeper
meaning and significance of the sources continues to be revealed throughout
history. In each of the major religious traditions of the world, one finds episodic
accounts of prophets, theologians, sages, scholars, and simple believers striving to refine and deepen the tradition's practices and ethical teachings in support of peacemaking. To be "traditional" is, inter alia, to take seriously those
developments in the community's understanding of conflict and violence that
claim authoritative status because they probe, clarify, and develop insights and
teachings contained in the foundational sources.

The writings of the Islamic legal scholar Khaled Abou El Fadl illustrate
this central interpretive dimension of the peacebuilding project. He insists that
the long tradition of Islamic jurisprudence, crystallized in the medieval period
(or frozen, Abou El Fadl might say), must be subjected to a new and rigorous
critique in light of modern conditions and understanding, including understanding of the Qur'an itself. The Qur'an's teachings on tolerance, for example,
were inadequately theorized by later scholars, Abou El Fadl argues, most likely
because the superiority of medieval Islamic civilization, assumed by the juris-
prudents of the golden age of Islam, gave them no reason to explore the sacred
text on the nature and necessity of tolerance. Accordingly, Abou El Fadl provides a detailed critique of the classical renderings of the notion of tolerance

and offers his own interpretation of the meaning of such fundamental Qur'anic concepts as "transgression against religion," "tolerance," and "holy war."

A prominent critic of what he calls contemporary Islamic Puritanism, Abou El Fadl applies the following hermeneutic in addressing the controverted issues facing Islam: "Reclaim the 'moral trust' of Islam by recovering the Qur'an's universal principles from the historical and social context in which the text was received . . . [and] interpret the Qur'anic verses about the treatment of women and non-Muslims in light of scriptural passages that call for mercy, kindness, and justice, and that emphasize the essentially plural nature of the human community."[39] It would be disingenuous to deny that the Qur'an and other Islamic sources offer the possibility of legitimating intolerance, he admits. "Clearly these possibilities are exploited by the contemporary puritans and supremacists." But the text does not command such intolerant readings, he adds. "Historically, Islamic civilization has displayed a remarkable ability to recognize possibilities of tolerance, and to act upon these possibilities," he writes. "If we assess the moral trajectory of a civilization in light of its past record, then we have ample reason to be optimistic about the future. But the burden and blessing of sustaining that moral trajectory—of accentuating the Qur'anic message of tolerance and openness to the other—falls squarely on the shoulders of contemporary Muslim interpreters of the tradition."[40]

In charting its peacebuilding path, must Islam conform to the example set by other religious traditions, especially Christianity? The reformers' network thinks not. Islam does not need to be understood and interpreted as an "absolute pacifist" religion, for example, in order for Muslims to justify nonviolent resistance campaigns and activities. "There are abundant clues, symbols, values, and rituals in Islamic religion and culture that can provide policymakers and other people with the opportunity to pursue nonviolent options in responding to conflicts," Abu-Nimer writes. "The fact that certain groups and policymakers have chosen another path does not abrogate the possibilities for nonviolent practice among Muslims."[41]

Other agents within Islam are contesting the peacebuilding path followed by the reformers' network. Radical Islamists have emerged in reaction to the stifling atmosphere of many Muslim societies, and they have developed their own transnational networks that are open to technology and a form of participatory, inclusive decision making. These radicals are open to violence as a means of reform. In response the European intellectual Tariq Ramadan believes that Muslim societies must liberate their people from the either-or conundrum—either radical Islamism or quietism. To do so would be to empower the youth, who are oriented to the global exchange of ideas and resources, for the task of forming virtual cadres of true believers dedicated to peace and nonviolent social change. Young, educated Muslims are poised, he asserts, to become pillars of a transnational *umma* that could join in a multireligious, multinational movement to find constructive solutions to social problems plaguing developing countries around the world.[42]

The sobering challenge facing Abou El Fadl, Abu-Nimer, Ramadan, and their colleagues who seek peace through religious agency is to identify and implement the means by which this creative energy and talent may be liberated for the work of intrareligious and interreligious relationship-building. For such relationship-building is the sine qua non of sustainable peace in countless settings of deadly conflict.

Conclusion: Strengthening the Religious-Secular Partnership

Taken together, the three case study–based vignettes featured in this chapter illustrate an obvious but important point. Each local religious community, drawing on its own history and on the spiritual and intellectual resources of its host religious tradition and ethnic heritage, will meet the challenge of religious peacebuilding in its own way. Owing to the centrality of local knowledge in any effective resolution of conflict, no one model or approach will suffice universally. Maha Ghosnanda's eagerness to forgive the agents of genocide and seeming indifference to the moral calculus of others (e.g., an international tribunal) might employ in judging the crimes of Pol Pot and the Khmer Rouge struck a chord with the Cambodian people. Evangelical Christians, for example, would be expected to deploy a different standard in weighing guilt and innocence and in determining what counts as atonement. In cultural settings as diverse as Algeria, Mozambique, and Serbia, Sant'Egidio was content to play the (essential) part of host and moderator; "friendship" was and remains its mantra. Muslim reformers for a just peace, while recognizing the irreplaceable particularity of the Islamic law in its local application, nonetheless strive to establish universal methods governing the interpretation of the bedrock principles of the Sharia. Peacebuilding, in short, is an exact science and a local art. The autochthonous religions of the locale will be essential partners in any comprehensive and enduring peace.

Complicating but also adding promise to this picture are the presence and influence of secular actors, now active in many realms once occupied solely by the religious. In traditional arenas such as health care and other "works of mercy," the secular agencies will continue to learn from the religious actors. In the "new" arena of conflict resolution and transformation, with its global-local coordinates and transnational players, however, the religious actors must learn from the secular. Peacebuilding is an art, a cure of and for the soul, antithetical to technocracy. But it is also a profession, in much the same way that clinical-pastoral counseling became an integral part of the minister's professional calling in the 1960s and thereafter. Can people of faith, acting as people of faith, also become professional peacebuilders? The progress of societies toward prosperity and human flourishing may depend in part on their ability to realize this possibility.

NOTES

1. Roland Robertson, *Globalization: Social Theory and Global Culture* (London: Sage, 1992).

2. Benjamin Barber, *Jihad versus McWorld: Terrorism's Challenge to Democracy*, 2nd rev. ed. (New York: Ballantine Books, 2001); Thomas Friedman, *The Lexus and the Olive Tree* (New York: Anchor Books, 1999).

3. Douglas Johnston and Cynthia Sampson, eds., *Religion: The Missing Dimension of Statecraft* (New York: Oxford University Press, 1994). For the basic argument in favor of acknowledging religion's enduring role in international affairs, see Jonathan Fox and Shmuel Sandler, *Bringing Religion into International Relations* (New York: Palgrave Macmillan, 2004). On faith-based mediation, see Douglas Johnston, ed., *Faith-Based Diplomacy: Trumping Realpolitik* (New York: Oxford University Press, 2003). For the term "religious peacebuilding," see David Little and Scott Appleby, "A Moment of Opportunity? The Promise of Religious Peacebuilding in an Era of Religious and Ethnic Conflict," in *Religion and Peacebuilding*, ed. Harold Coward and Gordon S. Smith (Albany: State University of New York Press, 2004), 1–23. Little and Appleby write: "We use the term *religious peacebuilding* to describe the range of activities performed by religious actors and institutions for the purpose of resolving and transforming deadly conflict, with the goal of building social relations and political institutions characterized by an ethos of tolerance and nonviolence" (5).

4. R. Scott Appleby, *The Ambivalence of the Sacred: Religion, Violence, and Reconciliation* (Lanham, MD: Rowman and Littlefield, 2000).

5. Ashutosh Varshney, *Ethnic Conflict and Civil Life: Hindus and Muslims in India* (New Haven, CT: Yale University Press, 2002).

6. The point is made repeatedly in Marc Gopin, *Between Eden and Armageddon: The Future of World Religions, Violence, and Peacemaking* (New York: Oxford University Press, 2000). For confirmation of the essential role of religious leaders as mediators between elite and popular sectors of a society, within the broader scheme of strategic peacebuilding, see John Paul Lederach, *Building Peace in Divided Societies* (Syracuse, NY: University of Syracuse Press, 1997).

7. Donald W. Shriver Jr., *An Ethic for Enemies: Forgiveness in Politics* (New York: Oxford University Press, 1995); Miroslav Volf, *Exclusion and Embrace: A Theological Exploration of Identity, Otherness and Reconciliation* (Nashville, TN: Abingdon Press, 1996).

8. For examples, see Mohammed Abu-Nimer, *Nonviolence and Peace Building in Islam: Theory and Practice* (Gainesville: University Press of Florida, 2003); Daniel L. Buttry, *Christian Peacemaking: From Heritage to Hope* (Valley Forge, PA: Judson Press, 1994); Gregory Baum and Harold Wells, eds., *The Reconciliation of Peoples: Challenge to the Churches* (Maryknoll, NY: Orbis Books, 1997).

9. Mumtaz Ahmad, "Islamic Fundamentalism in South Asia: The Jamaat-i-Islami and the Tablighi Jamaat," in *Fundamentalisms Observed*, ed. Martin E. Marty and R. Scott Appleby (Chicago: University of Chicago Press, 1991), 457–530; David Stoll, *Is Latin America Turning Protestant?* (Berkeley: University of California Press, 1990); Patrick Mason, "A Tale of Two Jerusalems: Latter-day Saints, Sacred Spaces, and Holy Lands," unpublished manuscript, March 2006.

10. Eric O. Hanson, *Religion and Politics in the International System Today* (New York:Cambridge University Press, 2006).

11. The first part of this vignette is adapted from Appleby, *Ambivalence of the Sacred*, 123–129. On this point, see Bob Maat, "Dhammayietra, Walk of Peace," *Catholic Worker*, May 1995, 22. For a more critical appraisal of the 1993 elections, which charges "widespread political violence, in which hundreds of people were killed," see Amnesty International, "Kingdom of Cambodia: Grenade Attack on Peaceful Demonstration," press release, March 31, 1997, cited in Appleby, *Ambivalence of the Sacred*, 123.

12. Fatally wounded in the crossfire were two peace marchers—the Venerable Suy Sonna, a sixty-seven-year-old Buddhist monk, and Yieychii Voeung, fifty-five, a Buddhist nun, both from Battambang. Four marchers sustained wounds, and nine others, including six foreigners, were detained briefly by the guerrilla forces but were released unharmed after the Khmer Rouge realized they were involved in the Dhammayietra. *Providence Journal-Bulletin*, May 3, 1994, 7C; "Former R. I. Buddhist Leads Cambodia Walk," *Providence Journal-Bulletin*, May 6, 1995, 7C. The theme of Dhammayietra IV, in May 1995, was the need to end global land mine production. Having been nominated for the Nobel Peace Prize in 1994 (by U.S. senator Claiborne Pell, a Quaker), Ghosananda, now lauded as "the Gandhi of Cambodia," hoped that his greater visibility would help secure international help in removing the estimated 10 million mines in Cambodian soil that continued to kill or maim hundreds of farmers each year.

13. Charles F. Keyes, "Communist Revolution and the Buddhist Past in Cambodia," in *Asian Visions of Authority: Religion and the Modern States of East and Southeast Asia*, ed. Charles F. Keyes, Laurel Kendall, and Helen Hardacre (Honolulu: University of Hawaii Press, 1994), 55, quoted in Appleby, *Ambivalence of the Sacred*, 125.

14. Frank E. Reynolds and Winnifred Sullivan, "Report from Cambodia," *Criterion* 33, no. 3 (August 1994): 16–23, quoted in Appleby, *Ambivalence of the Sacred*, 125.

15. Keyes, "Communist Revolution and the Buddhist Past in Cambodia," 58.

16. William Shawcross, "Tragedy in Cambodia," *New York Review of Books*, October 18, 1996, 47. See also Steve Heder and Judy Ledgerwood, eds., *Propaganda, Politics and Violence in Cambodia: Democratic Transition under United Nations Peacekeeping* (Armonk, NY: M. E. Sharpe, 1996).

17. Reynolds and Sullivan, "Report from Cambodia," 22.

18. Benjamin Barber, "Cambodia Asks US for Arms against Khmer Rouge Threat," *Christian Science Monitor*, May 20, 1994, 5. See also Nate Thayer, "Medellin on the Mekong," *Far Eastern Economic Review*, November 23, 1995, 24–28.

19. "CPR Update: A Newsletter of the Dhammayietra Center," Coalition for Peace and Reconciliation, January 1997, 6. Catholic Relief Services provided seed money for, among other projects, the "Peace Is Possible" Health Care Messages Project, which distributed 30,000 one-page flyers a month to the rural populations in Banteay Meanchey and Battambang. The flyers, covering various topics including peace and reconciliation, human rights, land mines, AIDS, and domestic violence, were a "humble attempt to spark the moral imagination that 'Peace Is Possible,'" Ghosananda's slogan.

20. Those hopes were dashed in July 1997, when Hun Sen staged a coup against Prince Ranariddh, conducted a brutal purge of Ranariddh's supporters, and took sole control of the government. Foreigners fled the country, and the progress of the previous five years, reflected in the development of an energetic and courageous press, a growing cadre of young lawyers, and an expanding number of organizations dedicated to fostering human rights, seemed undone in a few short days. "I feel like this country had a real chance," one NGO worker said. "People were starting to plan a little; Cambodians hadn't been able to plan ahead for twenty years. Now, they have no confidence in the country, no confidence in the future. It's hard to imagine any scenario now in which you can restore hope." Seth Mydans, "Hundreds Are Fleeing Cambodia: Violence and Fear Cast Chill over the Capital," *New York Times*, July 10, 1997, A8.

21. Donald Wilson and David Henley, "Ordaining Pol Pot—a Very Cambodian Solution," *Nation*, November 11, 1996, n.p.

22. Kim Leng, a member of the Dhammayietra steering committee and a trainer in tactics of nonviolence, quoted in "CPR Update: A Newsletter of the Dhammayietra Center," 6.

23. Ghosananda himself—"the undisputed moral authority in Cambodia"— should have arranged for prominent regional and international religious leaders to participate in the marches, Pond believes, and King Sihanouk could have been involved from the beginning in the rebuilding of Cambodia: the monarchy remains on a par with Buddhism in cultural importance to Cambodians. Author interview with Peter Pond, March 28, 1998.

24. Paul Van Tongeren, Malin Brenk, Marte Hellema, and Juliette Verhoeven, "Step by Step on the Way to Peace: The Dhammayietra Peace Walk in Cambodia," in *People Building Peace II: Successful Stories of Civil Society*, ed. Paul van Tongeren, Malin Brenk, Marte Hellema, and Juliette Verhoeven (Boulder, CO: Lynne Rienner, 2005), 236.

25. Skidmore and Moser-Puangsuwan quoted in ibid., 237.

26. The vision animating Sant'Egidio is both grand and inclusive: "A traditional and historical area of Rome has been able to recreate itself as a place of welcome and solidarity," proclaimed the movement's inaugural newsletter, "thus becoming the start of a multiracial, multicultural city, open to different kinds of religious life." See Appleby, *Ambivalence of the Sacred*, 155–164.

27. Robert P. Imbelli, "The Community of Sant'Egidio," *Commonweal*, November 18, 1994, 20, quoted in Appleby, *Ambivalence of the Sacred*, 157.

28. Andrea Bartoli, "A Mediation Model beyond the United Nations," *CROSS-LINES Global Report* 12–13 (March 1995): 47–49; Sebastian Bakare and Roelf Haan, "Exposure Programme: 'Community of San Egidio,'" *Mission Studies* 6 (1989): 55–66.

29. "Slyly religious": The religious actor, to be an effective peacebuilder in a transnational, globalized world, must eschew this kind of "identity politics." This is not a counsel to abandon or even submerge one's religious profile, but to find expression of it precisely in the act of cross-religious and religious-secular cooperation. Much of the Community's vitality derives from its emphasis on "friendship"—characteristically, Sant'Egidio prefers to use secular-friendly or bridge terms to articulate convictions and principles with deep religious roots—and its attitude of openness, hospitality, and respect for all people. This ethos of friendship is also a spiritual discipline: it finds expression in practically every aspect of the members' individual lives and corporate life, including the Community's penchant for networking and establishing relationships with political and religious actors at every level. Thus Sant'Egidio has enjoyed close relations not only with the dispossessed but with numerous government officials in Europe and Africa, and with the Holy See. In 1986 Pope John Paul II, extolling Sant'Egidio's vocation to the poor and commitment to ecumenical and interreligious dialogue, granted it a special status within the church as a "lay international public association."

30. Cameron Hume, *Ending Mozambique's War: The Role of Mediation and Good Offices* (Washington, DC: United States Institute of Peace, 1994), 15–16. For general historical background on the conflict, see Marilyn Newitt, *A History of Mozambique* (Bloomington: Indiana University Press, 1995), 517–540; Hilary Anderson, *Mozambique: A War against the People* (New York: St. Martin's Press, 1992), 1–45; William Finnegan, *A Complicated War: The Harrowing of Mozambique* (Berkeley: University of California Press, 1992).

31. Subsequently, however, the government rejected the Sant'Egidio platform for peace talks. On Sant'Egidio's role, see Marco Impagliazzo and Mario Giro, *Algeria Held Hostage: The Army, Fundamentalism, and the History of a Troublesome Peace* (Notre Dame, IN: University of Notre Dame Press, 1999); Milton Viorst, "Algeria's Long Night," *Foreign Affairs* 76, no. 6 (November/December 1997): 96.

32. See, inter alia, Akmed An Na'im, "The Reformation of Islam," *New Perspectives Quarterly* (Fall 1987): 48–51; Khaled Abou El Fadl, *The Great Theft: Wrestling Islam from the Extremists* (New York: HarperSanFrancisco, 2005); Afkhami Mahnaz, ed. *Faith and Freedom: Women's Human Rights in the Muslim World* (Syracuse, NY: Syracuse University Press, 1995); Reza Afshari, "An Essay on Islamic Cultural Relativism in the Discourse of Human Rights," *Human Rights Quarterly* 16, no. 2 (1994): 235–276; C. Satha-Anand, "Core Values for Peacemaking in Islam: The Prophet's Practice as Paradigm," in *Building Peace in the Middle East: Challenges for States and Civil Society*, ed. E. Boulding (Boulder, CO: Lynne Rienner, 1994), 295-303; Hassan bin Talal, *To Be a Muslim: Islam, Peace, and Democracy* (Brighton, UK: Sussex Academic Press, 2004); Yetkin Yildirim, "Peace and Conflict Resolution in the Medina Charter," *Peace Review* 18, no. 1 (January–March 2006): 109–117.

33. For a rhetorical statement of the project, see Imam Feisal Abdul Rauf, *What's Right with Islam Is What's Right with America* (New York: HarperSanFrancisco, 2005).

34. Bassam Tibi, *The Crisis of Modern Islam: A Preindustrial Culture in the Scientific-Technological Age*, trans. Judith von Sivers (Salt Lake City: University of Utah Press, 1988).

35. Giles Kepel, *Jihad: The Trail of Political Islam* (Cambridge, MA: Belknap Press of Harvard University Press, 2002).

36. Abu-Nimer, *Nonviolence and Peace Building in Islam*, 23.

37. Ibid.

38. Ibid.

39. Joshua Cohen and Ian Lague, "Editor's Preface," in Khaled Abou El Fadl, *The Place of Tolerance in Islam* (Boston: Beacon Press, 2002), vii–viii.

40. Abou El Fadl, *The Place of Tolerance in Islam*, 23.

41. Abu-Nimer, *Nonviolence and Peace Building in Islam*, 181–182.

42. Tariq Ramadan, *Western Muslims and the Future of Islam* (Oxford: Oxford University Press, 2004).

BIBLIOGRAPHY

Abu-Nimer, Mohammed. *Nonviolence and Peace Building in Islam: Theory and Practice.* Gainesville: University Press of Florida, 2003.

Afshari, Reza. "An Essay on Islamic Cultural Relativism in the Discourse of Human Rights." *Human Rights Quarterly* 16, no. 2 (1994): 235–276.

Ahmad, Mumtaz. "Islamic Fundamentalism in South Asia: The Jamaat-i-Islami and the Tablighi Jamaat." In *Fundamentalisms Observed*, ed. Martin E. Marty and R. Scott Appleby, 457–530. Chicago: University of Chicago Press, 1991.

Amnesty International. "Kingdom of Cambodia: Grenade Attack on Peaceful Demonstration." Press release, March 31, 1997.

An Na'im, Akmed. "The Reformation of Islam." *New Perspectives Quarterly* (Fall 1987): 48–51.

Anderson, Hilary. *Mozambique: A War against the People.* New York: St. Martin's Press, 1992.

Appleby, R. Scott. *The Ambivalence of the Sacred: Religion, Violence, and Reconciliation.* Lanham, MD: Rowman and Littlefield, 2000.

———. "Religion as an Agent of Conflict Transformation and Peacebuilding." In *Turbulent Peace: The Challenges of Managing International Conflict*, ed. C. A. Crocker, F. E. Hampson, and P. Aall, 821–840. Washington, DC: United Nations Institute of Peace Press, 2001.

Arinze, Francis A. *Religions for Peace: A Call for Solidarity to the Religions of the World.* New York: Doubleday, 2002.

Bakare, Sebastian, and Roelf Haan. "Exposure Programme: 'Community of San Egidio.'" *Mission Studies* 6 (1989): 55–66.

Barber, Benjamin. "Cambodia Asks US for Arms against Khmer Rouge Threat." *Christian Science Monitor*, May 20, 1994, 5.

————. *Jihad versus McWorld: Terrorism's Challenge to Democracy.* 2nd rev. ed. New York: Ballantine Books, 2001.

Bartoli, Andrea. "A Mediation Model beyond the United Nations." *CROSSLINES Global Report* 12–13 (March 1995): 47–49.

Bartov, Omer, and Phyllis Mack, eds. *In God's Name: Genocide and Religion in the Twentieth Century.* New York: Berghahn, 2001.

Baum, Gregory, and Harold Wells, eds. *The Reconciliation of Peoples: Challenge to the Churches.* Maryknoll, NY: Orbis Books, 1997.

Buttry, Daniel L. *Christian Peacemaking: From Heritage to Hope.* Valley Forge, PA.: Judson Press, 1994.

Cobban, Helena. "Religion and Violence." *Journal of the American Academy of Religion* 73, no. 4 (Dec. 2005): 1121–1139.

Coffey, Joseph I., and Charles T. Mathewes, eds. *Religion, Law, and the Role of Force: A Study of Their Influence on Conflict and on Conflict Resolution.* Ardsley, NY: Transnational Publishers, 2002.

Cohen, Joshua, and Ian Lague. "Editor's Preface." In Khaled Abou El Fadl, *The Place of Tolerance in Islam.* Boston: Beacon Press, 2002.

Coward, Harold, and Gordon S. Smith, eds. *Religion and Peacebuilding.* Albany: State University of New York Press, 2004.

CPR Update: A Newsletter of the Dhammayietra Center. "Coalition for Peace and Reconciliation." January 1997, 6.

El Fadl, Khaled Abou. *The Great Theft: Wrestling Islam from the Extremists.* New York: HarperSanFrancisco, 2005.

Ellens, J. Harold, ed. *The Destructive Power of Religion: Violence in Judaism, Christianity, and Islam.* 4 vols. Westport, CT: Praeger, 2004.

Finnegan, William. *A Complicated War: The Harrowing of Mozambique.* Berkeley: University of California Press, 1992.

Fox, Jonathan, and Shmuel Sandler. *Bringing Religion into International Relations.* New York: Palgrave Macmillan, 2004.

Friedman, Thomas. *The Lexus and the Olive Tree.* New York: Anchor Books, 1999.

Frost, J. William. *A History of Christian, Jewish, Hindu, Buddhist, and Muslim Perspectives on War and Peace.* 2 vols. Lewiston, NY: Edwin Mellen Press, 2004.

Gopin, Marc. *Between Eden and Armageddon: The Future of World Religions, Violence, and Peacemaking.* New York: Oxford University Press, 2000.

————. *Holy War, Holy Peace: How Religion Can Bring Peace to the Middle East.* New York: Oxford University Press, 2002.

Haar, Gerrie ter, and James J. Busuttil, eds. *Bridge or Barrier: Religion, Violence, and Visions for Peace.* Boston: Brill, 2005.

Hanson, Eric O. *Religion and Politics in the International System Today.* New York: Cambridge University Press, 2006.

Hashmi, Sohail H., and Steven Lee, eds. *Ethics and Weapons of Mass Destruction: Religious and Secular Perspectives.* New York: Cambridge University Press, 2004.

Heder, Steve, and Judy Ledgerwood, eds. *Propaganda, Politics and Violence in Cambodia: Democratic Transition under United Nations Peacekeeping.* Armonk, NY: M. E. Sharpe, 1996.

Hoffman, R. Joseph, ed. *The Just War and Jihad: Violence in Judaism, Christianity, and Islam.* Amherst, NY: Prometheus Books, 2006.

Hume, Cameron. *Ending Mozambique's War: The Role of Mediation and Good Offices.* Washington, DC: United States Institute of Peace, 1994.

Imbelli, Robert P. "The Community of Sant'Egidio." *Commonweal,* November 18, 1994: 20–23

Impagliazzo, Marco, and Mario Giro. *Algeria Held Hostage: The Army, Fundamentalism, and the History of a Troublesome Peace.* Notre Dame, IN: University of Notre Dame Press, 1999.

Johnson, James Turner. *The Quest for Peace: Three Moral Traditions in Western Cultural History.* Princeton, NJ: Princeton University Press, 1987.

Johnston, Douglas, ed. *Faith-Based Diplomacy: Trumping Realpolitik.* New York: Oxford University Press, 2003.

Johnston, Douglas, and Cynthia Sampson, eds. *Religion: The Missing Dimension of Statecraft.* New York: Oxford University Press, 1994.

Jones, James William. *Terror and Transformation: The Ambiguity of Religion in Psychoanalytic Perspective.* New York: Brunner-Routledge, 2002.

Juergensmeyer, Mark. *Terror in the Mind of God: The Global Rise of Religious Violence.* 3rd ed. Berkeley: University of California Press, 2003.

———, ed. *Violence and the Sacred in the Modern World.* London: Frank Cass, 1992.

Kepel, Giles. *Jihad: The Trail of Political Islam.* Cambridge, MA: Belknap Press of Harvard University Press, 2002.

Keyes, Charles F. "Communist Revolution and the Buddhist Past in Cambodia." In *Asian Visions of Authority: Religion and the Modern States of East and Southeast Asia,* ed. Charles F. Keyes, Laurel Kendall, and Helen Hardacre, 43–74. Honolulu: University of Hawaii Press, 1994.

Lederach, John Paul. *Building Peace in Divided Societies.* Syracuse, NY: University of Syracuse Press, 1997.

Little, David. "Religion, Conflict and Peace." *Case Western Reserve Journal of International Law* 38, no. 1 (2006): 95–103.

Little, David, and Scott Appleby. "A Moment of Opportunity: The Promise of Religious Peacebuilding in an Era of Religious and Ethnic Conflict." In *Religion and Peacebuilding,* ed. Harold Coward and Gordon S. Smith. Albany, New York: State University of New York Press, 2004. 1–23

Maat, Bob. "Dhammayietra, Walk of Peace." *Catholic Worker,* May 1995, 22.

Mahnaz, Afkhami, ed. *Faith and Freedom: Women's Human Rights in the Muslim World.* Syracuse, NY: Syracuse University Press, 1995.

Mason, Patrick. "A Tale of Two Jerusalems: Latter-day Saints, Sacred Spaces, and Holy Lands." Unpublished manuscript, March 2006.

McTernan, Oliver. *Violence in God's Name: Religion in an Age of Conflict.* Maryknoll, NY: Orbis Books, 2003.

Mydans, Seth. "Hundreds Are Fleeing Cambodia: Violence and Fear Cast Chill over
    the Capital." *New York Times,* July 10, 1997, A8.
Newitt, Marilyn. *A History of Mozambique.* Bloomington: Indiana University
    Press, 1995.
Ramadan, Tariq. *Western Muslims and the Future of Islam.* Oxford: Oxford University
    Press, 2004.
Rauf, Imam Feisal Abdul. *What's Right with Islam Is What's Right with America.* New
    York: HarperSanFrancisco, 2005.
Reynolds, Frank E., and Winnifred Sullivan. "Report from Cambodia." *Criterion* 33,
    no. 3 (August 1994): 16–23.
Robertson, Roland. *Globalization: Social Theory and Global Culture.* London:
    Sage, 1992.
Sampson, Cynthia. "Religion and Peacebuilding." In *Peacemaking in International
    Conflict: Methods and Techniques,* ed. I. William Zartman and J. Lewis Rasmussen,
    273–316. Washington, DC: United States Institute of Peace, 1997.
Satha-Anand, C. "Core Values for Peacemaking in Islam: The Prophet's Practice as
    Paradigm." In *Building Peace in the Middle East: Challenges for the States and Civil
    Society,* ed. E. Boulding. Boulder, CO: Lynne Rienner, 1994. 295–303
Schwarz, Regina. *The Curse of Cain: The Violent Legacy of Monotheism.* Chicago: Univer-
    sity of Chicago Press, 1997.
Selengut, Charles. *Sacred Fury: Understanding Religious Violence.* Walnut Creek, CA:
    Altamira, 2003.
Seul, Jeffrey R. "'Ours Is the Way of God': Religion, Identity, and Intergroup Conflict."
    Journal of Peace Research 36, no. 5 (September 1999): 553–570.
Shawcross, William. "Tragedy in Cambodia." *New York Review of Books,* October 18,
    1996, 47.
Shriver, Donald W., Jr. *An Ethic for Enemies: Forgiveness in Politics.* New York: Oxford
    University Press, 1995.
————."Religion and Violence Prevention." In *Cases and Strategies for Preventive Action,*
    ed. Barnett R. Rubin, 169–195. New York: Century Foundation Press, 1998.
Smock, David R. *Perspectives on Pacifism: Christian, Jewish, and Muslim Views on
    Nonviolence and International Conflict.* Washington, DC: United States Institute
    of Peace Press, 1995.
————. *Religious Perspectives on War: Christian, Muslim, and Jewish Attitudes toward
    Force after the Gulf War.* Washington, DC: United States Institute of Peace,
    Perspectives Series, 1992.
Spaeth, J. Paul, ed. *Perspectives in Religion and Culture.* Cincinnati: Catholic Students
    Mission Crusade, Paladin Press, 1957.
Steffen, Lloyd. *The Demonic Turn: The Power of Religion to Inspire or Restrain Violence.*
    Cleveland, OH: Pilgrim Press, 2003.
Stoll, David. *Is Latin America Turning Protestant?* Berkeley: University of California
    Press, 1990.
bin Talal, Hassan. *To Be a Muslim: Islam, Peace, and Democracy.* Brighton, UK: Sussex
    Academic Press, 2004.

Thayer, Nate. "Medellin on the Mekong." *Far Eastern Economic Review*, November 23, 1995, 24–28.

Tibi, Bassam. *The Crisis of Modern Islam: A Preindustrial Culture in the Scientific-Technological Age*. Translated by Judith von Sivers. Salt Lake City: University of Utah Press, 1988.

Van Tongeren, Paul, Malin Brenk, Marte Hellema, and Juliette Verhoeven. "Step by Step on the Way to Peace: The Dhammayietra Peace Walk in Cambodia." In *People Building Peace II: Successful Stories of Civil Society*, ed. Paul Van Tongeren, Malin Brenk, Marte Hellema, and Juliette Verhoeven. Boulder, CO: Lynne Rienner, 2005.

Varshney, Ashutosh. *Ethnic Conflict and Civil Life: Hindus and Muslims in India*. New Haven, CT: Yale University Press, 2002.

Viorst, Milton. "Algeria's Long Night." *Foreign Affairs* 76, no. 6 (November/December 1997), 86–99.

Volf, Miroslav. *Exclusion and Embrace: A Theological Exploration of Identity, Otherness and Reconciliation*. Nashville, TN: Abingdon Press, 1996.

Wilson, Donald, and David Henley. "Ordaining Pol Pot—a Very Cambodian Solution." *Nation*, November 11, 1996.

Woodberry, J. Dudley, Osman Zumrut, and Mustafa Koylu, eds. *Muslim and Christian Reflections on Peace: Divine and Human Dimensions*. Lanham, MD: University Press of America, 2005.

Yildirim, Yetkin. "Peace and Conflict Resolution in the Medina Charter." *Peace Review* 18, no. 1 (January–March 2006): 109–117.

7

Religious Actors and Transitional Justice

Leslie Vinjamuri and Aaron P. Boesenecker

Networks of nonstate actors, secular and religious, have been at the forefront of a range of efforts to promote truth, advance reconciliation, and prosecute alleged war criminals in conflict situations. And yet, the work of many religious organizations has been overshadowed by the highly visible work of secular human rights organizations prominent in shaping international public policy debates concerning the role of accountability in ongoing and postconflict situations. Indeed, scholarship on the role of religious organizations engaged in transitional justice is also comparatively limited.[1] This chapter investigates the universe of nonstate religious actors engaged in transitional justice. Its aim is both to account for the range of nonstate actors in this arena and also to suggest the linkage between the beliefs these separate organizations embrace, the strategies they pursue, and the impact of these strategies on transitional justice. It demonstrates that religious actors form a pluralistic community of nonstate actors that diverge widely in their beliefs about the proper role of justice in conflict mediation and settlement, and in the strategies they pursue. While some religious actors have adopted strategies that distinguish them quite dramatically from the major international human rights nongovernmental organizations (NGOs), others embrace positions that make them natural partners of the most established players in the human rights arena.

The nonstate actors engaged in transitional justice hold varying beliefs about how accountability shapes efforts to achieve truth, justice, peace, and democracy. The sources of these beliefs vary—some are derived from international legal precepts, others from religious doctrine, and still others from local traditions, or social psychological understandings of conflict resolution.[2] In this chapter we refer to five distinct frameworks, or "logics of action," in which these different beliefs are embodied. Central to each of these logics is an actor's conception of justice, which plays an important role in shaping the strategies that nonstate actors adopt and seek to promote. After distinguishing five different logics of action, the chapter presents a typology of nonstate actors engaged in transitional justice. By placing conception of justice and organizational attributes at the center of its analysis of nonstate actors, the typology moves beyond a simplistic distinction based on religion or secularism. Both religious and secular actors are also differentiated on the basis of whether they represent cosmopolitan or communitarian interests, and whether they are organized to operate locally or transnationally.

Empirical examples explored in the second part of the chapter illustrate distinctions among several different categories of actors suggested by the typology: capacity-builders, peacebuilders, legalists, pragmatists, and traditionalists. The local peace and capacity-building work of the Mennonite Central Committee in Latin America, the mediation activities of the Catholic Community of Sant'Egidio in Mozambique, and the transnational engagement of the World Jewish Congress and the Organization of the Islamic Conference (OIC) suggest that while particular strategies reinforce the visibility of certain organizations, some strategies contribute to the silence, or invisibility, that surrounds other actors engaged in transitional justice. Organizations whose beliefs about justice have led them to pursue grassroots activities targeted at fostering intergroup reconciliation and forgiveness have sacrificed visibility at the international level for local impact. In some cases, such strategies may have limited their access to transnational networks of advocates engaged in accountability issues.[3] Other religious actors that have advocated national or international institutional strategies for achieving accountability have, like their secular counterparts, had greater influence and visibility internationally. These categories represent ideal-types. As such, many of the actors and strategies discussed below do not fit rigidly in a single category. Over time, actors may change or develop their conception of justice, their strategies, or the scale of their operations, and may be better represented in an alternate position on the typology. Nonetheless, the ideal-type categories provide a valuable starting point for mapping the landscape of nonstate actors engaged in transitional justice and structuring inquiry into the intersection of conceptions of justice held by nonstate actors and the strategies of justice they pursue.

This chapter contributes to our understanding of the role of religion in postconflict reconstruction and peacebuilding by examining the universe of religious organizations involved in transitional justice. It also seeks to avoid two common positions that scholars have sometimes taken in the literature on religion, either to claim that religious actors are unique and cannot be compared with those secular actors motivated chiefly by ideology or principles, or to treat religion as an identity that is manipulated for instrumental purposes.[4] The typology presented here also identifies potential synergies that may foster collective engagement and networking among secular and religious actors. Especially where religious and secular organizations share a conception of justice and have complementary organizational attributes, the opportunities for networking are enhanced.

Nonstate Actors, Transitional Justice, and Logics of Action

Nonstate actors engaged in issues of justice and accountability have pursued strategies for promoting transitional justice that reflect a particular conception of justice. The conception of justice that actors embrace is grounded in broader understandings, or "logics," about politics, especially the role of different values in shaping prospects for peace and democracy. Each of the logics of action here attempts to capture the understandings that different types of nonstate actors have of the importance of justice and accountability, and the role of these values in underpinning peace and reconciliation. These logics of action consist of causal beliefs about the relationship between essential values, and more general theories of change that actors' embrace, either implicitly or explicitly, and that shape their behavior.

A conception of justice is defined by a general set of principled and causal beliefs about the role of accountability and justice in political and social life. One element of this is how justice is most optimally achieved, and in particular how different accountability strategies affect reconciliation, democracy, and peace and stability in postconflict societies. More specifically, a "conception of justice" includes an actor's preference for the balance among restorative and retributive justice strategies; their understanding of reconciliation and the nature and duration of engagement necessary for achieving justice and/or reconciliation; and the particular place that social justice themes have in peacebuilding and transitional strategies.[5]

In general, retributive justice focuses on the punishment of the perpetrator and is usually carried out through trials and imprisonment, but it may also include reparations, restitution, or other sanctions placed on a perpetrator. Retributive justice mechanisms include elements of both punishment and public acknowledgment of the crime committed.[6] Restorative justice draws explicitly on faith traditions and notions of community justice and forgiveness; it seeks both recognition of wrongdoing and the reintegration of an individual offender into the larger community. Faith traditions include Christian ideals from the Sermon on the Mount and injunctions stressing the universality of human suffering and the power of forgiveness; ideas such as *shalom* (Hebrew) and *salaam* (Arabic) meaning "peace with justice"; Talmudic teachings on restitution and repair; and diverse local traditions and customs.[7] Truth commissions and public apology are common mechanisms for restorative justice, though they may be accompanied by limited punitive measures such as restitution or symbolic sanctions imposed by the wider community. The needs of the victim figure more prominently in restorative justice, but transforming the relationship between the victim and victimized (rather than just reversing it through retribution) together with long-term community reconciliation underpins restorative justice. As a result, socioeconomic and sociocultural conditions that generate conflict are also central concerns.[8]

The five "logics of action" outlined in this chapter include the "logic of faith," "logic of legalism," "logic of emotion," "logic of custom," and "logic of consequences."[9] For many religious actors, conceptions of justice are grounded in principles that emerge from a commitment to a particular doctrine or faith, that is, they follow a "logic of faith" that informs their strategies for pursuing justice and accountability. Similarly, the conception of justice that has shaped the strategies of many secular human rights organizations is grounded in international human rights law and norms and is heavily influenced by a "logic of legalism." The "logic of emotions" embodies beliefs about the relationship between truth, emotion, and reconciliation.[10] Conceptions of justice held by a number of highly localized actors have been inspired by indigenous traditions and customs, or a "logic of custom." Finally, actors driven by a "logic of consequences" are assumed to have clear, predefined preferences and outcomes and are instrumental in their use of a full range of material, institutional, and persuasive resources to achieve these objectives.[11]

These logics are useful analytic constructs for understanding and identifying the sources of different beliefs about important values in transitional justice. The logic of faith is compatible with elements of each of the other four logics discussed here. In practice, actors often embrace understandings and behaviors that sit easily within more than one of these logics. In some cases behavior motivated by a logic of tradition and one informed by faith are difficult to distinguish. The historical specificity of actors' motivations is crucial to differentiating among them, yet at the same time, the synergies between beliefs grounded in religion, emotion, and tradition suggest that secular and religious actors will be natural allies across a range of cases; factors outside of those specific to values and beliefs may be more significant in determining compatibility. The purpose of these logics is to identify the sources of beliefs and behaviors. Specific strategies may be replicated by a variety of sources.

Religious Actors and the Logic of Faith

For religious organizations engaged in transitional justice, faith, or religious doctrine, defines the logic that shapes preferred strategies for dealing with accountability. Causal beliefs about accountability come not from law, or understandings of social psychology, but rather from a commitment to a set of principles that derive from a broader doctrine, or faith. Religious doctrine not only defines what is right, just, or appropriate but also lays the foundation for understanding how responses to wrongdoings shape outcomes. Actors whose understandings of accountability, and especially its role in ameliorating conflict, come from their faith are by no means uniform in the causal beliefs they hold or the strategies they prefer. In this sense, the logic of faith embraces a far more differentiated landscape of actors than the other logics of action. Actors here differ in part depending on the faith traditions from which they emerge.

In many religious traditions, faith calls for forgiveness and reconciliation over retribution, and themes of forgiveness and apology appear together across a variety of faiths.[12] Even where retribution is preferred, it usually takes the form of reparations or restitution, in conjunction with apology, instead of punitive (and impersonal) trials as preferred by actors favoring legalist strategies. Writing from a general Christian ethics perspective, Shriver notes that "in the tension between justice in the present (e.g. imprisoning a perpetrator) and justice in the future (e.g. preventing a civil war) the decision should bend towards the latter."[13] Ultimately, the element of faith is critical in cases of both forgiveness and retribution, as religiously informed notions of justice are more generally underpinned by the firm belief that vengeance will take place at some point in time, though not necessarily in this world or by the hand of the victim.[14]

Concepts of reconciliation, healing, and forgiveness that are fundamental to many religious doctrines underpin the preference that many religious actors have for strategies that emphasize truth-telling. Formal trials or similar legal proceedings are seen to be woefully inadequate in addressing the needs of the victims and establishing "truth" in the wake of mass atrocities.[15] The facts permitted or relevant for a courtroom are not necessarily conducive to reconciliation, healing, or other postconflict goals espoused by religious actors, as "from the point of view of legal proceedings and due process for the accused, justice does not always correspond to, indeed is often in conflict with, the victims' sense of what is owed them and what conditions are necessary for repair. . . . responding adequately to victims may conflict with wider societal needs for fairness and formal justice."[16]

Those religious actors that favor comprehensive forms of reconciliation and/or truth-telling, such as some traditionalists and peacebuilders, have a natural likeness to secular actors guided by a logic of emotion. This natural symmetry of views enables religious and secular actors to work together in networks designed to promote particular strategies. Other religious actors, notably the Mennonite or Quaker capacity-builders, have strategies that set them apart. These actors prefer strategies that emphasize capacity-building within divided societies through the creation of networks of trust and personal relationships, paying attention to social justice issues and eliciting conflict resolution strategies from within (in the field) rather than prescribing them from the outside. The value attached to reconciliation and peace by certain religious actors, referred to here as religious pragmatists, is such that attachment to a specific strategy is replaced by a preference for that strategy that in a particular context has the capacity to bring about particular outcomes. Religious pragmatists, in this sense, should have an array of natural secular partners among those guided by a logic of consequences.

Despite their easy affiliations with particular secular actors, religious actors may have a natural advantage over their secular counterparts when operating in social contexts where religious norms are prevalent. This was the case with interfaith dialogues in Bosnia and Herzegovina. Religious norms create structures of opportunity for lodging certain types of appeals and give greater legitimacy to particular types of actors.[17] Religious actors may serve as "entrepreneurs" in leading efforts to remember past atrocities and create public or societal truth, thus moving beyond formal legal types of transitional justice, as seen in the role of the faith groups in the South African reconciliation process.[18] Attention to long-term comprehensive social reconciliation with a particular emphasis on postconflict structural change, either in lieu of or parallel to short-term justice mechanisms, has become a hallmark of religious actors engaged in transitional justice.[19] In this sense, many religious actors fully embrace the specific notion of "restorative justice" discussed earlier in this chapter.[20]

Legalists and the Logic of Legalism

The logic of legalism has shaped beliefs about accountability and informed international debate on the role of justice in postconflict situations more than any other logic of action. Secular human rights advocates have made arguments and pursued strategies that are grounded in this logic. At its core, the understanding of change that legalists embrace centers on the importance of rule-governed behavior and individual responsibility. Conflict ultimately is reduced, according to this logic, through the creation, articulation, and diffusion of a common set of rules, norms, and laws that govern behavior. In the domain of mass atrocities, this means that state and nonstate actors should follow rules that require individuals to be held legally accountable for their wrongdoings. These rules, legalists argue, contribute to peace by deterring future would-be perpetrators from committing crimes, and also by removing antagonisms between groups and focusing on individual accountability. While legalists recognize the significance of enforcement and compliance, they generally pay little attention to the role of force in shaping prospects for peace.

The conception of justice that follows from this logic is one that emphasizes retribution through criminal justice. The cosmopolitan worldview that secular legalists embrace is founded on a commitment to the idea of universal human rights. Legalists look to international humanitarian and human rights law to establish standards and codes of practice for ensuring that perpetrators of mass crimes are held accountable. The particular strategy for accountability that they promote is legal accountability or more specifically criminal justice and is grounded in the broader logic of a commitment to international humanitarian law. The value they place on prosecutions is grounded in a view that over the long term, legalist strategies of accountability should lead to the reduction of human rights abuses and the strengthening of the international human rights regime on a global as well as a local level. Trials for the perpetrators of mass crimes, they argue, deter future crimes and guarantee compliance with human rights norms. Similarly, they have a bias against strategies that circumvent the law such as truth commissions (if they supplant trials); amnesties for international crimes are vigorously criticized and opposed. Secular legalists are organized both transnationally and locally; the specific logic of legalism does not preclude either type of organization, but it does create avenues for networks between local and transnational actors in this category. Organizations such as Amnesty International, Human Rights Watch, and the International Criminal Court typify actors in the secular legalist category.[21]

Despite the apparently pure secular origins of many of the actors in this category, the historical precursors to many contemporary secular legalists were religious organizations. Peace societies with Christian roots as well as international Jewish organizations that lobbied for legal accountability during the Second World War were crucial in providing the momentum for the blossoming of international nongovernmental human rights organizations during the cold war. The potential networks between secular legalists and religious legalists may, however, be contingent on political, social, and historical context.

Truth Seekers and the Logic of Emotions

The logic of emotions embodies a set of causal beliefs about the relationship between truth, emotion, and reconciliation.[22] It emphasizes the importance of relationships between perpetrators and victims in managing the transition from war to peace. For some, reconciliation is a side benefit of accountability or a secondary concern; here it is the central concern. Social-psychological understandings of conflict and peace underpin theories of reconciliation that inform actors working within this logic. Without reconciliation, lasting peace is not possible. And reconciliation is seen as contingent on an emotional catharsis between victims and perpetrators. Truth-telling strategies become one of the most important means through which accountability can be achieved because they allow for a collective account of past atrocities, sometimes in a public forum that allows for an emotional exchange.

Actors that embrace this theory of conflict resolution, generally truth seekers, tend to grant importance not only to relations between individuals but also to intergroup dynamics. Unlike legalism, which assumes that conflict is defused by attributing guilt to individuals, emotional logics assume that conflict is defused by the experience of creating shared understandings of past crimes. Actors guided by a logic of emotions exhibit a strong preference for reconciliation over retribution. Most of the strategies that follow from this logic seek to engage individuals at the popular level and also look to foster public recognition of wrongdoings. The range of strategies they promote emphasize the need to create official memories and histories of past crimes through a strategy of uncovering and sharing the truth. It is through this sharing of the truth that groups are able to reconcile and lay the foundation for a lasting peace. Societal reconciliation, rather than just elite pacts, is deemed essential, yet such strategies do not specifically address the role of elite leadership in mass atrocities.[23]

Similar strategies have been adopted by actors that do not sit exclusively within this tradition. Many religious actors share the belief that strategies of reconciliation grounded in public forgiveness and truth-telling are critical to peace. Some traditionalist logics are also grounded in similar assumptions about the relationship between conflict, public truth-telling strategies, reconciliation, and peace. What distinguishes actors working within this tradition is their grounding, often implicit, in social-psychological theories of conflict resolution. This more comprehensive view of "reconciliation" informs the particular notion of restorative justice that draws on many elements of faith and tradition.[24]

Traditionalists and the Logic of Custom

Traditionalists embrace a set of principled and causal beliefs that are grounded in local customs, traditions, and practices. The specific beliefs these actors hold vary across localities, but in general they emphasize the importance of local origins and venerated religious or secular customs. Traditionalists value participation by all members of the local community and seek to give locals a prominent role in addressing questions of accountability and justice. These actors are nearly always organized on a local scale. The practices they pursue for justice and accountability depend on specific indigenous traditions rather than on a particular commitment to restorative or retributive justice, or a concern for other factors. Although the specific strategies vary from case to case, justice is viewed as local, public, and interpersonal, and in many cases emphasizes rituals of shame, as well as public apology and forgiveness. Rituals emphasizing or resulting in shame for the perpetrator are neither explicitly restorative nor retributive in nature but represent a distinct approach to justice and accountability under the logic of custom.

Sometimes the strategies that traditionalists promote have a strong likeness to strategies promoted by truth seekers. Especially where tradition and faith are deeply intertwined, the logic of faith and the logic of custom are difficult to distinguish. And yet, the logic of custom rests first and foremost on an assumption that conflict can only be assuaged if mechanisms for accountability are grounded in deeply rooted local practices. Social-psychological models imported from other states are likely to be seen as foreign, and unlikely to suffice at home. Faith is capable of generating sustained support for peace only if it has a deep-rooted local base and is deemed more fundamental than other customs. Local custom, rather than any general causal framework derived from external actors or norms, defines understandings and practices for linking accountability to peace. Actors that embrace a logic of custom thus look for all past atrocities to be addressed at the local and interpersonal level, and individual communities have an obligation to address both the needs of victims and the alleged crimes of perpetrators.

Secular traditionalists embrace an understanding of accountability and peace that is grounded in the logic of custom. Unlike other secular actors, traditionalists are primarily organized locally rather than transnationally. These actors tend to be immersed in indigenous traditions, and they look to these traditions to inform their strategies for dealing with accountability. Reconciliation efforts in East Timor (the *lisan* community reconciliation process), Somalia (utilizing traditional clan and elder networks in lieu of UN conflict resolution methods), Uganda, and Mozambique have all drawn on local customs practices of reconciliation, in some cases combining a logic of tradition with a logic of faith. Secular traditionalists have also advocated strategies such as the Rwandan *gacaca*, or community justice, process that stresses retributive justice; those deemed guilty of crimes were committed to prison sentences, labor, and also restitution.[25] While different from the "justice" activities of the international community (e.g., UN-sponsored trials in East Timor or the International Criminal Tribunal for Rwanda), these efforts speak to the convictions held by the particular local actors that long-term reconciliation among divided populations is, in fact, the nature of justice to be achieved.

Pragmatists and the Logic of Consequences

Pragmatists assess strategies for accountability in terms of their effects in the pursuit of other goals, whether these be peace, stability, justice, truth or a range of values.[26] Rather than committing to a particular strategy and promoting this across all cases regardless of particular circumstances, these actors are willing to select from a variety of strategies depending especially on their assessment of what will work. The actors in this category are by nature inclined to be adaptable and flexible and are likely to pursue different strategies depending on the local, national, and international context in which they are operating. They pay particular attention to local institutional capacity, opportunities for alliances and networks with other actors working on similar issues, and the likely impact of particular strategies on the balance of power among key groups in society. Actors that embrace this logic do not find themselves concerned exclusively or even primarily with adhering to (or promoting) specific norms and rules. Instead, they deploy the full range of resources at their disposal (material, institutional, normative) in a calculated effort to achieve their aims. However, the logic of consequences does not denote a strategy of achieving ends by any means. Instead, actors are pragmatic about their approach to transitional justice, weighing the feasibility of individual approaches (e.g., retributive or restorative justice) against the effects of their actions and the overall impact on postconflict societies and on the goals of transitional justice. In the absence of a stable balance among warring parties, the pursuit of retributive justice may be viewed as unwise. Pragmatic actors are likely to take special note of this and other contextual factors deemed crucial to the success of alternative strategies. Truth-telling strategies, for example, may be dismissed as potentially antagonizing intergroup relations unless they are pursued in combination with policies that can guarantee the safety and security of each group concerned.

Pragmatists often do not exhibit a strong a priori preference for either retributive or restorative justice. Actors whose understandings about the role of accountability follow this logic often may use accountability to strike bargains with potential spoilers and build coalitions in support of new institutional arrangements that can guarantee peace.[27] Secular pragmatists, unlike either the legalists or the truth seekers, are far less committed to a particular strategy than any other category of secular actors. The understanding of accountability that they exhibit is grounded in a logic of consequences. Hence, they are flexible in their preferences and may promote a range of instruments depending on which is most likely to enhance the conditions associated with peace and justice.

Groups vary in their pragmatism, and indeed those most informed by a logic of consequences are in fact state, rather than nonstate, actors who are necessarily required to balance a series of conflicting priorities. But other organizations, even those that have a commitment to transitional justice and accountability, may also be pragmatic in their approach to the variety of strategies available depending on underlying local conditions. Groups such as the Campaign for Good Governance in Sierra Leone (a local, cosmopolitan secular pragmatist) or East Timor and Indonesia Action Network (ETAN) in East Timor (a transnational, communitarian secular pragmatist) differ in their specific preference for justice and accountability, but they share an overall preference for achieving a lasting peace through means that are "workable" within a given society and political context. Similarly, the International Center for Transitional Justice and the International Committee of the Red Cross both represent transnational, cosmopolitan actors of this type.[28]

These five logics of action are crucial in elucidating the understandings of accountability and peace that inform the strategies and policies pursued by nonstate actors engaged in transitional justice. Even where the source of actors' beliefs differs, common or at least compatible beliefs about accountability and peace may emerge, producing natural synergies among diverse actors. Alternatively, actors whose beliefs stem from a logic of faith form a pluralistic group that may have natural affinities less with each other than with a variety of secular actors. The following typology suggests that the strategies these actors embrace are specific not only to religion but also to core organizational attributes and world views.

Shaping Strategies for Justice: A Typology

Secular and religious actors engaged in transitional justice can be categorized by several defining characteristics. Although the conception of justice that emerges from particular understandings of the relationship between accountability and peace is critical, it is not the sole factor that explains the strategies they embrace. Two additional factors are important: organizational scale and worldview. Overall, the conceptions of justice held by religious and secular actors *in combination with* their organizational scale and worldview bias them toward particular strategies.

Organizational scale has two important effects on actors. First, it shapes actors' preferences for particular types of strategies. Locally organized actors are more likely to have an interest in pursuing strategies that lead to increased harmony among groups because they are less able to remove themselves from their interactions with all parties to a conflict. For this reason, they tend to have a stronger preference for strategies of forgiveness, apology, and reconciliation over retributive justice. Second, organizational scale shapes an actor's capacity to influence strategies of transitional justice. For actors that operate on a local scale only, engaging in transnational networks becomes critical to influencing transitional justice outside of their locality. Networking with larger transnational actors that are able to bring more pressure to bear on public officials may also enhance their leverage over the course of action that is taken at home.[29]

A second critical factor, the worldview that an actor holds, defines the constituency or interests that are an object of concern. For both religious and secular actors one can distinguish two broad worldviews, the cosmopolitan and the communitarian. Actors with a cosmopolitan worldview seek to represent, in principle, the interests of all of humanity. Communitarian actors, by contrast, are committed to a particular group. Cosmopolitans may embrace strategies that emphasize retribution or reconciliation depending on their understanding of the conflict and the needs of the society in question. Strategies of reconciliation underpinned by the logics of faith, emotion, and custom are often attractive to cosmopolitan actors. Communitarians, however, are less likely to consider the interests of "the other" or of a postconflict society in a comprehensive sense, and therefore are less likely to support a strategy that takes relationships between groups as the most fundamental element of peace. Strategies of reconciliation that are underpinned by a logic of emotion should therefore be less attractive to communitarians. Moreover, communitarians who operate transnationally are less likely to embrace strategies of reconciliation than locally organized communitarians who are forced to confront those outside their own group on a daily basis.

The following typology categorizes nonstate actors according to the conception of justice they hold (whether favoring retributive or restorative justice), the scale of their organization (transnational or local), and their worldview (cosmopolitan or communitarian). It also identifies a few representative organizations for each category. While some of these organizations may fall into multiple categories, and others may move across categories over time, they have all been placed according to their dominant orientation within the category that they have historically inhabited.[30] The "conception of justice" that an actor holds is categorized as either "high" or "low" to denote the strength of conviction and attachment that an actor has to a particular strategy. For example, pragmatic actors do not have a high level of attachment to either reconciliation or retribution; they are willing to alternate strategies depending on a range of other factors. Legalists, on the other hand, have been highly committed to a conception of justice that emphasizes criminal justice. Each general category of actor is listed together with a few representative organizations; these examples are meant to be illustrative rather than exhaustive. General categories of actors *without* representative organizations (the "empty cells" of the typology) are notable in that they signify the absence of significant activity (or organization) in a particular category. Similarly, the absence of a category of actor within a given cell in the typology indicates that a particular type of actor is unlikely to exist at all.

Religious Actors and Accountability Strategies: Key Cases

The categories in the typology presented here typify the range of actors engaged in transitional justice. How have these actors shaped accountability strategies in practice? In particular, how have different categories of religious actors participated in the politics of accountability? The typology identifies five types of religious actors (capacity-builders, peacebuilders, legalists, pragmatists, and traditionalists) and four types of secular actors (truth-seekers, pragmatists, legalists, traditionalists) according to the strategies they pursue. Religious actors define themselves first and foremost on the basis of an identity grounded in a specific faith tradition. But as the typology demonstrates, the strategies that actors pursue are also shaped by their worldview, and the scale on which they are organized. The following section uses empirical examples to illustrate the different approaches to accountability and justice taken by religious actors.

Religious Capacity-Builders

Religious capacity-builders hold a highly distinctive view of reconciliation that sets them apart from other religious actors. The unique strategies pursued by

TABLE 7.1 Religious and Secular (Nonstate) Actors in Transitional and Postconflict Justice

	Organizational Type and Interest Representation			
	Communitarian		Cosmopolitan	
Conceptions of Justice	Transnational	Local	Transnational	Local
Strong preference for reconciliation	—	Religious Traditionalists (*African Independent Churches, Ubuntu*)	Religious Capacity-builders (*Mennonites, Quakers*) Secular Truth Seekers	Secular Truth Seekers
Pragmatic with preference for reconciliation	Religious Pragmatists (*U.S. Conference of Catholic Bishops, Organization of the Islamic Conference*)	Secular Pragmatists	Religious Peacebuilders (*Roman Catholic Church, Sant'Egidio*) Religious Pragmatists Secular Pragmatists (*International Center for Transitional Justice*)	Religious Peacebuilders (*Inter-Religious Council – Bosnia and Herzegovina*) Religious Pragmatists (*South African Conference of Churches*) Secular Pragmatists (*Campaign for Good Governance – Sierra Leone*)
Pragmatic with preference for retribution	Religious Pragmatists (*U.S. Conference of Catholic Bishops*) Secular Pragmatists (*ETAN – East Timor*)	Religious Pragmatists (*Denominational Churches*)	Secular Pragmatists (*Centre for Humanitarian Dialogue, Red Cross/Red Crescent*)	Secular Pragmatists (*Alliance Against Impunity – Guatemala*)
Strong preference for retribution	Religious Legalists (*World Jewish Congress, Islamic Human Rights Commission*)	Secular Traditionalists (*Gacaca*) Religious Legalists (*National Association of Evangelicals*) Secular Legalists (*Mothers of Srebrenica*)	Secular Legalists (*Human Rights Watch, Amnesty International*)	Secular Legalists (*LIPRODHOR – Rwanda*)

religious capacity-builders also distinguish them from secular actors. Paradoxically, these actors have had a significant effect in those areas where they have worked, yet their visibility has remained low, and their influence on global discussions of transitional justice is negligible. Guided by understandings that are grounded in both the logic of faith and emotion, these actors have a belief in the cathartic power of healing and reconciliation between victims and perpetrators. In a sense, healing human relationships (reconciliation) *is* justice for capacity-building actors. The faith traditions of capacity-building actors emphasize religious notions of humility, mercy, tolerance, and pacifism, as is typified by the peacebuilding activities of the Mennonite Central Committee (MCC) or of Quaker Peace and Social Witness (QPSW).[31] Deeply influenced by the quietist tradition, reconciliation work in the Mennonite community reflects a profound personal commitment on the part of the peacebuilder and a commitment to the community in question, owing to the "conviction that to be a peacemaker is the most fundamental religious injunction."[32] Similarly, John Paul Lederach, a Mennonite, advises: "Focus on people and their experience. Seek a genuine and committed relationship rather than results. Be willing to set aside what works for you in order to come along side the struggle of those in the setting. Be leery of quick fixes. . . . Never assume you know better or more than those you are with who are struggling with the process. You don't."[33]

Although religious capacity-builders such as the MCC or QPSW are organized transnationally, their particular worldview (cosmopolitan) and conception of justice (local reconciliation) lead them to focus on more labor-intensive activities such as grassroots capacity-building and empowerment of local actors. Capacity-building actors are unique in their long-term commitment to conflict and postconflict situations and in their strong preference for comprehensive reconciliation and social transformation strategies.[34] Key practices such as practicing nonviolence, leaving the process in the hands of local actors, confronting social inequality, and building relationships are hallmarks of their strategy.[35] Religious capacity-builders emphasize the need to balance various forms of transitional justice (e.g., trials, truth commissions, amnesties) oriented toward the past, with the imperative to move forward into the future (reconciliation), inspired by the notion of hope.[36] Over the long term, justice is achieved not through punitive measures but by gaining the trust of all parties and working for community reconciliation and the eradication of oppressor-oppressed relationships and other inequalities.[37] While international human rights NGOs benefit from connections to broader networks concerned with accountability and justice, less connected religious actors "may nonetheless have other extremely valuable assets: ties to local actors, credibility, trust" attributable to their religious nature.[38] Ultimately, the tendencies toward inclusiveness, community involvement, and long-term commitment demonstrated by religious capacity-builders, as well as their ability to sustain engagement on a personal and spiritual level, speak to their particular attributes in a postconflict situation.[39]

This distinct conception of justice is evident in the engagement of capacity-builders in Bosnia and Herzegovina in the mid-1990s. Transnational actors like World Vision and Catholic Relief Services lacked a specific focus on local populations and were criticized for pursing inflexible strategies that were out of touch with reality and instead focused on fulfilling quantitative benchmarking achievements. Empowering local populations and resolving conflict were simply not on their agenda: "Organizers recall that they directly avoided potentially dangerous discussions and feared confrontations between participants from different religious and ethnic communities."[40] In contrast, the commitment of the MCC and QPSW to strategies of reconciliation that emphasized local engagement garnered "immense credibility and trust" at the local level. These organizations were able to foster a feeling among locals that they would remain even as others departed due to time pressure, budgetary constraints, or violence.[41]

Religious capacity-builders also embrace a conception of justice that emphasizes social justice, or efforts to end economic, political, and social inequality and discrimination.[42] The amelioration of inequalities fits naturally within a cosmopolitan worldview and alongside a conception of justice focused on long-term reconciliation and capacity-building. Working with the poor and ordinary also means that progress toward justice comes in small increments over time: "In this view, peacebuilding does not occur only at the top but also comes from micro readjustments of power in the small spaces of everyday social life, accomplished one at a time in the lives of people in situations of conflict. Without local transformations, successful negotiations by top leaders will not produce peace."[43] The activity of the MCC throughout Latin American in the 1980s illustrates this commitment. Importantly, the commitment of the MCC to building social relationships between groups led it to partner with existing local actors (both secular and religious) rather than establish its own churches in the region.

MCC efforts across Latin America highlight most clearly the centrality of its long-term approach to building trust and local relationships as a means of transforming the social conditions that underpin conflict: "Zooming in from the outside for a short intervention produces limited results. The MCC Peace Portfolio proved to be effective because of its close relationships with local partners and on-the-ground presence of its workers."[44] The work of religious capacity-builders provides an example of restorative justice. In Colombia, the

MCC was active in promoting social justice issues as the route to conflict transformation and reconciliation. Acting in response to the civil conflict that began in the 1960s, the MCC's justice and reconciliation strategy drew on its fundamental beliefs concerning human rights, human freedom, community, and nonviolence.[45] The MCC focused on training and educating local populations, as "it is those who are immersed in a conflict who hold the keys to the ways through it, since it is they who know and understand the sociopolitical structures and dynamics."[46] The establishment of a justice and peace commission in 1990 (Justapaz) to address social justice themes underlying the civil conflict ultimately led to the participation of NGOs and community and religious leaders in government planning and decision making, as well as to the emulation of this reconciliation strategy across the region. In Nicaragua, addressing the underlying social and economic inequalities that contributed to civil conflict was a critical element to rebuilding relations among people who would have to live together on a daily basis. As one former combatant noted, "In the end, I guess we're all still a bunch of Nicaraguan peasants. That fact hasn't changed after all the fighting."[47]

Religious Peacebuilders

Peacebuilders constitute a second type of religious actors. Unlike capacity-builders, religious peacebuilders are attentive to social justice and reconciliation only in a more general sense and are primarily concerned with conflict settlement (e.g., achieving a cease-fire or overcoming the immediate crisis); their embrace of transitional justice is valued in part for its consequences on the more pressing concern with facilitating conflict resolution. This focus has made them more natural participants in the international politics of transitional justice and increased their visibility. Peacebuilders' embrace of reconciliation emerges, in part, from their faith. However, unlike capacity-builders, for peacebuilders, questions of transitional justice are important but not primary. Peacebuilders employ strategies to facilitate elite-level negotiations by providing good offices and mediation and facilitation services, but they refrain from taking an active stance in the negotiation process. Truth-telling activities are generally restricted to formal truth commissions, and social justice activism is pursued via elite negotiation instead of grassroots engagement. The peacemaking activities of the Roman Catholic Church and those of the Community of Sant'Egidio represent the views and strategies of justice pursued by religious peacebuilders.

The Roman Catholic Church's approach to transitional justice is influenced by the Catholic conception of justice and reconciliation, which in turn emphasizes "peace" as an overarching goal. The church's "theory of conflict resolution remains relatively underdeveloped as compared to its positive teaching on peace. The paradoxical result of a strong positive doctrine of peace and a less articulated doctrine of conflict resolution is that even as church leaders are thrown into the role of national conciliators . . . they find themselves bereft of tools and support."[48] As a result, individual bishops or church organizations are often very active in mediating a conflict settlement or advocating for an end to oppression or discrimination, but they are left without institutional support and resources to undertake comprehensive reconciliation efforts.[49] Although the Catholic Church and its associated organizations undertake a wide array of efforts in the area of peacebuilding, historically the emphasis of Catholic peacemaking has been focused on high-level mediation.[50] This emphasis may be changing, as seen in the more comprehensive approach to peacebuilding adopted by Catholic Relief Services (CRS) in the late 1990s.[51] This change in emphasis illustrates the manner in which actors may adapt their strategies over time. The examples provided here illustrate the approach of the Catholic Church towards questions of peace and justice through the 1990s.

In Guatemala, the church played an important high-level role in brokering the 1996 peace agreement that ended a long, brutal civil war. The peace agreement contained a limited amnesty (acts of torture, disappearances, and massacres were excluded from the amnesty) later formalized through the Law of National Reconciliation, but in the last stages of the peace process, the church issued a major document calling for repentance and forgiveness as a response to the past.[52] The overarching goal of attaining peace and securing justice not through retribution but through other forms of reconciliation such as truth recovery reflected the particular conception of justice held by the church. In response to the amnesty law, the church instituted the Project for Recovering Historical Memory (Recuperación de la Memoria Histórica, or REMHI) to document human rights abuses in the conflict, even though those identified as perpetrators (mostly military personnel) were protected by the amnesty. The church dismissed any notion of a real conflict and implicitly embraced the possibility that the success of REMHI may have rested on amnesty when it stated: "We wanted the report to create a social reconstruction, not be a cause of conflict."[53]

The church's embrace of a conception of justice that focused on human rights, social justice, and truth recovery was also evident in its engagement against dictatorships and promotion of truth-telling in Chile and Brazil.[54] Similarly, in the Philippines the church acted as a high-level mediator between opposition forces and the Marcos regime not through virtue of an official church position but through the entrepreneurial efforts of the local clergy (notably,

Cardinal Sin). In aiding the ouster of Marcos, the church based its engagement on the fight against the political and social oppression of local populations.[55]

The peacemaking activities of the Catholic lay Community of Sant'Egidio are also representative of those pursued by religious peacebuilders. Sant'Egidio has been intimately involved in numerous high-level negotiation and mediation processes, most notably the peace process that lead to the 1994 General Peace Agreement in Mozambique. As in Guatemala, the peace agreement that emerged from these negotiations incorporated an amnesty and a "general trend of integration without individual punishment for acts perpetrated during the war."[56] Although criticized by the secular human rights community, religious actors supported this in the spirit of redemption, forgiveness, and reconciliation that allows even for a criminal to be reintegrated into society. The mediation efforts of Sant'Egidio, shaped by a religious identity founded on prayer, service to the poor, and friendship, were crucial to negotiating the General Peace Agreement and establishing an environment for reconciliation.[57] The role of Sant'Egidio was not to impose solutions but to facilitate constant contact (not just formal dialogue) among the parties. The relationship of trust between Sant'Egidio and all parties was based a longer history of aid and assistance to local communities, and provided a conduit to the mood or underlying current in the Mozambican population at large.[58]

Religious Legalists

In stark contrast to both capacity-builders and peacebuilders, religious legalists hold a strong preference for retributive justice. Although the understandings that these actors embrace about accountability and peace bear some similarities to those of secular legalists, their conception of justice and the strategies they pursue are defined not by international human rights law but by a commitment to a particular faith and a particular community that shares that faith. Religious legalists are typically communitarian actors. Unlike their cosmopolitan counterparts, communitarians limit their focus to those individuals and groups that share a particular faith. Although forms of retributive and restorative justice may be combined in some form, the communitarian orientation shapes the bias toward trials, as the primary concern becomes achieving "justice" for one particular group engaged in a conflict—a group that is often viewed as victims. Thus, when religious communitarian actors perceive a threat to groups or individuals sharing their faith, they tend to support the justice-minded strategies of secular human rights organizations. Unlike the secular legalists, however, their arguments for supporting retribution do not stem from general theories of law and the role of individual accountability in deterring future conflict.

During the Second World War, the World Jewish Congress (WJC) actively lobbied the War Crimes Commission to prosecute those responsible for the Holocaust. More specifically, it pressed for the extension of the concept of "war crimes" to cover the atrocities being committed against European Jews.[59] Initially, the British and American governments drew a distinction between "atrocities committed against Allied nationals and those directed against Axis citizens," whereas the WJC maintained "that the Jews 'form a special class of victims,' as the crimes against them were being committed only by reason of their connection with the Jewish faith and race."[60] The WJC did not link these to broader notions of universal human rights, but specifically advanced a claim for their particular constituency. Peacebuilding and justice strategies among these actors tend to focus on elite-level engagement and negotiation, with limited grassroots involvement.

Religious Pragmatists

In contrast to other types of religious actors, religious actors that are purely pragmatic are rarer. Most religious actors prefer some form of reconciliation, though in varying degree. Even when religious actors are willing to trade off accountability for the sake of securing peace, their understanding of these trade-offs is frequently grounded in the notion that justice will come in another life, or that forgiveness is essential to reconciliation. There is, however, variability among religious actors in their willingness to negotiate among strategies based on the anticipated impact of these strategies on peace. Those religious actors that have been more willing to "negotiate" accountability have had increased opportunities for forming alliances both with secular actors and with other religious actors with whom they might take a similar stand on particular cases. The U.S. Conference of Catholic Bishops has adopted a range of strategies depending on local circumstances. In Darfur, it lobbied for peace, and for justice or accountability to the extent it could be achieved. Elsewhere, it has advocated for fair and ethical treatment of war crimes detainees or promoted social justice.[61] Similarly, the Organization of the Islamic Conference actively promotes a conception of justice based primarily on Islamic traditions of tolerance, but it also campaigns specifically for the defense and independent rights of Muslim peoples.[62] In particular, the OIC has taken a more retributive stance in the Israeli-Palestinian conflict, invoking international law in calls for the establishment of an International Criminal Court to prosecute "Israeli war criminals" while at the same time defending the rights of the Palestinian people to self-determination.[63] In this sense, the OIC highlights a combination of religious pragmatism with a communitarian worldview. Finally, the South African Conference of Churches espoused first and foremost a strategy of peace and national reconstruction for South Africa, but it accepted that this might be accomplished by a combination of particular justice strategies.[64]

Religious Traditionalists

Religious traditionalists, much like their secular counterparts, draw on specific local customs and traditions, as well as their own faith, to inform their conception of justice. Actors in this category exhibit a wide range of individual approaches to justice and accountability. Religious traditionalists tend to favor reconciliation and even comprehensive restorative justice strategies over the retributive justice preferred at times by secular traditionalists. By definition, traditionalists operate at a local level and pursue justice according to specific indigenous traditions. Although religious traditionalists often possess only limited (material) resources and/or few connections to broader networks, these local actors often possess specific characteristics that allow them to mobilize support for transitional justice strategies, including intimate knowledge of language and culture, access to firsthand information, political expertise, and long-term vision; "because they are closer to the scene of events, at ease with many actors, and familiar with the language and the issues at stake, religious leaders may offer important interpretive frameworks."[65] In addition, the fundamental human need for community to overcome hatred and terror places religious actors in an advantageous position to facilitate healing and reconciliation.[66]

Religious traditionalists often resemble religious capacity-builders in their types of activity, though they are more often organized locally, and their approach is shaped by particular local traditions. The East Timorese Community Reconciliation Process (CRP) was the main grassroots initiative in the reconciliation process that followed the violent conclusion to Indonesian occupation of East Timor in October 1999. The CRP was underpinned by norms of truth-telling and community reconciliation. Designed to reintegrate individuals who had committed less serious crimes into their communities, the CRP utilized a combination of local traditions (*lisan*) together with criminal and civil law.[67] The *lisan* system itself is a community-based dispute resolution tradition governed by elders and spiritual leaders and employing local rituals and symbols as part of the adjudication process. The vast majority of East Timorese people also belong to the Catholic Church, and accordingly the linkage between *lisan* and Catholic doctrines of absolution and confession added to the legitimacy of the CRP process.[68] Hearings opened with collective prayer, the wider community questioned both the deponent and victims, and the elders consult both the victim and deponents in deciding upon appropriate "acts of reconciliation" for the deponents.[69] The perpetrator is required to submit a public apology, and according to *lisan* tradition, this is given with the utmost gravity and viewed as binding.[70] Designed to represent the deponent's commitment to reconciliation with both the victim and the wider community, these acts are more symbolic than punitive. The use of ritual and tradition in the *lisan* process gave credence to the CRP. The success of the CRP also worked to reduce the appeal of an amnesty; some actors argued that "amnesty was the only option for dealing with the massive number of unresolved 'less serious crimes.'"[71] In contrast, secular and religious actors together crafted a transitional justice mechanism grounded in local norms and religious traditions that resonated with the local population as legitimate and appropriate.

In South Africa, local religious pragmatist and traditionalist actors thus drew on numerous local and religious norms and traditions to construct a transitional justice mechanism that was consistent with the notion of justice as reconciliation held by the population and reflected in local norms. The combined power of religiosity and local religious norms is evident in the combination of the African *ubuntu* tradition with a Christian (and interfaith) dimension in the reconciliation process.[72] Although the religious character of the Truth and Reconciliation Commission (TRC) drew some criticism, it was one of the most powerful forces for legitimating and mobilizing continued support for the TRC.[73] The combination of *ubuntu* and reconciliation was also central to the acceptance of an amnesty as part of the TRC process; Archbishop Tutu posed the options as "'justice with ashes' against 'amnesty with the possibility of continuing survival for all of us.'"[74] The concept of *ubuntu* is drawn from a longer phrase meaning "a human being is a human being because of other human beings" and thus expresses ideas of humanity, group solidarity, and morality.[75] *Ubuntu* was used to emphasize "the priority of 'restorative' as opposed to 'retributive' justice" and helped lend legitimacy and acceptance to the overall TRC strategy because most South Africans were comfortable with concepts such as reconciliation, storytelling, and the search for truth as a community.[76] These norms helped to create a shared narrative and memory in the TRC process.

This combination of storytelling, apology, forgiveness, and restitution represents a unique "package" of justice mechanisms embraced by religious actors whose beliefs about justice and peace are grounded in logics of faith, emotions, and tradition. To begin with, "the religious environment created by religious peacemaking can be conducive to expressions of apology, repentance, and forgiveness. . . . Such personal expressions are much less likely to occur in secular than in religious contexts."[77] Forgiveness itself stems from storytelling that promotes the (re)establishment of human connections and understanding and respect for the position of the other.[78] The additional components of apology, forgiveness, and restitution are also linked, as an apology is most valid when followed with restitution or gesture of reparations.[79] The use of restitution (or lenient punitive actions) in the religious context is not entirely about the property, objects, or retribution. Instead, an important community and religious meaning stands behind the actions, reinforcing the sincerity and validity of the apology.[80]

Religious capacity-builders, peacebuilders, legalists, pragmatists, and traditionalists have all adopted different approaches to questions of peace, justice, and accountability depending upon their conception of justice, interest representation, organizational type, and worldview. Despite the diversity of the actors outlined in the typology and the wide range of strategies they employ, religious actors do share one critical element: a logic of faith underpins their overall approach to transitional justice. Although faith alone does not drive the strategies adopted by religious actors, the logic of particular faith doctrines is the linchpin that shapes core beliefs about accountability and informs the strategic choices of religious organizations. In practice, this means that the different attributes discussed in the typology are often not found exclusively in one type of actor, and the distinctions drawn here are less clear in practice. Moreover, actors may, over time, adapt the strategies they pursue and even revisit the principles that underpin their conceptions of justice, as illustrated by the discussions concerning peace and justice within the Catholic Church and CRS. More generally, though, the beliefs held by actors whose internal logic has its origins in faith, tradition, and emotion have led to a range of novel approaches to peace, justice, and accountability, many of which are notable for being distinctive from the legalist and pragmatic approaches more commonly associated with large international human rights organizations. Religious engagement with questions of peace, justice, and accountability spans the globe and encompasses diverse faith traditions, indicating a rich and influential landscape of religious actors engaged in transitional justice.

Conclusions

Religious organizations engaged in transitional justice form a pluralistic set of actors that have pursued a wide variety of approaches to transitional justice. Religious actors are diverse not only in their organization but also in their conceptions of justice, the interests they represent, and the strategies they pursue. The typology presented here is one attempt to categorize the universe of religious actors and, more generally, to elucidate the role of religious actors in transitional justice. The findings suggest that the identity of religious actors and the strategies they pursue are generally informed by beliefs that emerge from their faith, and that this effect is much stronger for some than for others.

Among religious actors, the divide between cosmopolitan and communitarian actors is pronounced. Religious cosmopolitan actors have viewed themselves as representing the interests of all individuals in the name of humanity. Religious cosmopolitan actors, especially capacity-builders, have been deeply influenced by an understanding of conflict that emerges from their faith and have pursued unique strategies in transitional justice. Actors in this category share a conception of justice that favors strategies of forgiveness, reconciliation, and healing over punitive justice. The conception of reconciliation held by religious cosmopolitan actors, and in particular capacity-builders, is comprehensive, placing emphasis on social justice issues such as inequality, social exclusion and discrimination as well as more traditional reconciliation mechanisms.[81] Although the religious dimension is central to the conceptions of justice held by cosmopolitan actors, it is also true that they tend to "wear their faith lightly" inasmuch as they are not missionary organizations but primarily are concerned with service to humanity, drawing on their faith and spiritual principles to guide social transformation and reconciliation without overt proselytizing.[82] Still, the cosmopolitan-communitarian divide should not be overstated. Religious actors form a pluralistic community with diverse conceptions of justice, but they also share an identity based in faith, and their specific strategies of accountability and justice are ultimately underpinned by their logic of faith. As Appleby observes, within each of the major world religious traditions, "notwithstanding their profound substantive differences, one can trace a moral trajectory challenging adherents to greater acts of compassion, forgiveness, and reconciliation."[83]

While religious actors, especially capacity-builders, are often less visible than their secular counterparts, for many, engagement in transitional justice emphasizes long-term reconciliation and local engagement and community-building at the grassroots level. This dual long-term and local focus combined with minimal participation in transnational networks may help explain the relatively minor role that has been attributed to many religious actors in transitional justice. Low visibility is not, however, tantamount to ineffectiveness. For many of these actors, a patient, grassroots approach grows out of a particular logic of faith and conception of justice centered on the importance of reconciliation.

More generally, the strategies pursued especially by religious capacity-builders but also by peacebuilders and pragmatists have both individually and collectively provided a significant counterweight to the legalism embraced by many large international human rights organizations. In particular, those religious actors with a cosmopolitan worldview have provided a critical counter-weight to pressure for high-profile trials or truth commissions, or other rapid attempts to reconcile warring populations. These actors have often done this by resisting pressure for trials and supporting amnesty agreements. The support of these organizations for amnesty stems not from an interest in a particular political bargain as might be the case for more strategic actors whose prefer-ences for the role of accountability in conflict are driven by an assessment of the consequences of accountability for securing a peace deal, but instead from the theological conceptions of mercy and grace that are fundamental to their view of long-term reconciliation.[84] In South Africa, the preferences of religious actors differed markedly from the push for trials emanating from the secular human rights community. Local and national faith groups helped shape the decision to pursue a policy that combined truth and amnesty.[85] More generally, Christian ethics of justice and reconciliation present a case for bal-ance between these two concepts that contrasts with the demands for trials and speedy reconciliation often advanced by the secular human rights community: "in the tension between justice in the present (e.g. imprisoning a perpetrator) and justice in the future (e.g. preventing a civil war) the decision should bend towards the latter."[86]

On the whole, nonstate actors have been crucial in shaping strategies of transitional justice. Religious actors have been central to these developments, but their role has remained underinvestigated. The discussion in this chapter provides an effort to differentiate among religious actors and also to compare these organizations with their secular counterparts. As such, it seeks to over-come tendencies to assume differences between secular and religious actors, as well as tendencies to assume similarities among religious actors. Several research agendas emerge from this analysis. First, scholars should devote attention to more systematic comparative work between secular organizations (especially human rights organizations) and religious actors. Do religious orga-nizations have a comparative advantage in transitional justice and peacebuild-ing more generally? There are indications that the sensitivity of many religious groups to long-term reconciliation may be an advantage, particularly in post-conflict situations charged with religious tension. In Bosnia and Herzegovina, an activist noted that international pressure to rebuild mosques in Bosnia's predominantly Serb cities such as Banja Luka led to disillusionment, riots, and death within the local communities: an activist from Banja Luka noted, "I had the impression that they were ordering us to reconcile. You do not do that on order."[87] These results contrast markedly with the relatively peaceful and suc-cessful efforts of interfaith dialogue and grassroots engagements pursued by some religious actors.[88]

Second, when is collaboration between secular and religious organizations likely to be productive? Other examples from Bosnia and Herzegovina suggest a niche or role for partnership and cooperation between secular human rights organizations and religious actors. A more precise understanding of the particular conditions conducive to cooperation, or those conditions that might lead to conflicting strategies, is needed to fully understand this dynamic.

Third, a more comprehensive understanding of the universe of religious actors, especially non-Christian actors, is needed. The religious actors discussed here have primarily been drawn from those working within the Christian faith tradition. However, scholars have emphasized the relevance of many religious traditions for peacebuilding and conflict resolution: "The elements extracted from religious traditions that could be used towards the drafting of a new conflict resolution theory include empathy, nonviolence, pacifism, sanctity of life, interiority, compassion (particularly the Buddhist version), religious discipline, messianism and imagination."[89] However, more concrete research into how actors inspired and informed by various religious traditions put these ideas into practice in peacebuilding and, specifically, transitional justice is needed. Since many conflict resolution situation also involve more than one faith tradition, such research should be attentive to the possibilities for interfaith collaboration (and tension) as regards nonstate religious actors and transitional justice.

Finally, the research presented here brings nonstate religious actors firmly into the mainstream study of nonstate actors in world politics. Future scholarship on nonstate actors is needed to continue this task by investigating the role of identity in underpinning network formation. Is collaboration limited to like-minded actors? To what extent are actors whose interests align, even temporarily, able to work together effectively absent shared beliefs about the role of justice in peacebuilding? Indeed, the influence that nonstate actors are able to exercise depends in part on their capacity to collaborate with other nonstate actors in transnational networks, thereby magnifying their impact. The typology presented here underscores potential symmetries among nonstate actors engaged in transitional justice and sheds light on potential networks available to each of these actors.

NOTES

We would like to thank Jonathan VanAntwerpen, R. Scott Appleby, Paige Arthur, Thomas Banchoff, Tatiana Carayannis, Nicolas Guilhot, Stephen Hopgood, Peter Katzenstein, Katherine Marshall, Kathleen R. McNamara, Jennifer Llewellyn, Juan Méndez, Daniel Nexon, Daniel Philpott, Jack Snyder, and the Social Science Research Council's Working Group on Religion, Reconciliation, and Transitional Justice, for their insightful comments on this chapter.

1. For an excellent account of the role of religious actors in transitional justice, see Daniel Philpott, "When Faith Meets History: The Influence of Religion on Transitional Justice," in *The Religious in Response to Mass Atrocity: Interdisciplinary Perspectives*, ed. Thomas Brudholm and Thomas Cushman. Forthcoming.

2. On logics of action, and the useful distinction between logics of appropriateness and logics of consequences, see James G. March and Johan P. Olsen, *Rediscovering Institutions: The Organizational Basis of Politics* (New York: Free Press, 1989), chap. 2. See also Leslie Vinjamuri and Jack Snyder, "Advocacy and Scholarship in the Study of Transitional Justice and International War Crimes Tribunals," *Annual Review of Political Science* 7 (2004): 345–362; Jack Snyder and Leslie Vinjamuri, "Trials and Errors: Principles and Pragmatism in Strategies of International Justice," *International Security* 28, no. 3 (2003–2004): 5–44.

3. On transnational advocacy networks, see Margaret E. Keck and Kathryn Sikkink, *Activists beyond Borders: Advocacy Networks in International Politics* (Ithaca, NY: Cornell University Press, 1998).

4. For an exceptional treatment of the role of religion in international politics, see Daniel Philpott, *Revolutions in Sovereignty: How Ideas Shaped Modern International Relations* (Princeton, NJ: Princeton University Press, 2001).

5. Actors emphasizing "social justice" are explicitly attentive to addressing economic, political, and social inequalities that are viewed as root causes of conflicts and thus key elements to long-term reconciliation.

6. See Martha Minow, *Between Vengeance and Forgiveness: Facing History and Genocide after Mass Violence* (Boston: Beacon Press, 1998); Martha Minow, ed., *Breaking the Cycles of Hatred: Memory, Law, and Repair* (Princeton, NJ: Princeton University Press, 2002); Nancy L. Rosenblum, "Justice and the Experience of Injustice," in *Breaking the Cycles of Hatred: Memory, Law, and Repair*, ed. Martha Minow (Princeton, NJ: Princeton University Press, 2002), 77–107; Jon Elster, *Closing the Books: Transitional Justice in Historical Perspective* (Cambridge: Cambridge University Press, 2004), chap. 8. Particularly in Christian ethics, retributive justice is underpinned by an "understanding of evil as an endemic human reality which cannot be overcome by mere dogged resolve." Charles Villa-Vicencio, "The Reek of Cruelty and the Quest for Healing: Where Retributive and Restorative Justice Meet," *Journal of Law and Religion* 14, no. 1 (1999–2000): 171.

7. See Minow, *Between Vengeance and Forgiveness*, chap. 5; see also Peggy Hutchison and Harmon Wray, "What Is Restorative Justice?" *New World Outlook*, 1999, http://gbgm-umc.org/nwo/99ja/what.html.

8. Restorative justice constitutes a comprehensive notion of reconciliation and justice that includes, but is not limited to, the more general notion of "reconciliation" espoused by many secular NGOs. Throughout this essay, the term "reconciliation" is used in this general sense, while "restorative justice" is used in the sense discussed earlier in the chapter. See Hutchison and Wray, "What Is Restorative Justice?"; Minow, *Between Vengeance and Forgiveness*. See also Donald W. Shriver Jr., "Forgiveness: A Bridge across Abysses of Revenge," in *Forgiveness and Reconciliation: Religion, Public Policy, and Conflict Transformation*, ed. Raymond G. Helmick, S. J., and Rodney L. Peterson (Philadelphia: Templeton Foundation Press, 2001), 151–167; Alex Boraine, *A Country Unmasked* (Oxford: Oxford University Press, 2000), 426.

9. The discussion of logics of action draws on distinctions among the logics of appropriateness, consequences, and emotions as outlined by Tory Higgens, as well as the discussion of logics in Snyder and Vinjamuri. See E. Tory Higgens, "Making a Good Decision: Value from Fit," *American Psychologist* 55, no. 11 (2000): 1217–1230; Christopher Camacho, E. Tory Higgens, and Lindsay Luger, "Moral Value Transfer from Regulatory Fit: 'What Feels Right *Is* Right' and 'What Feels Wrong *Is* Wrong,'" *Journal of Personality and Social Psychology* 84, no. 3 (2003), 498–510; Snyder and Vinjamuri, "Trials and Errors."

10. On the logic of emotions, see Vinjamuri and Snyder, "Advocacy and Scholarship."

11. Snyder and Vinjamuri, "Trials and Errors," 13.

12. Minow, *Between Vengeance and Forgiveness.*

13. Donald W. Shriver Jr., "Truth Commissions and Judicial Trials: Complementary or Antagonistic Servants of Public Justice?" *Journal of Law and Religion* 16, no. 1 (2001): 24–25; Shriver also more pointedly states: "However difficult it may be to make analogy from Jesus' ministry to ailing persons to a ministry to an ailing social system, it remains essential for Christians to remember that the words 'your sins are forgiven' and 'go and sin no more' often fell from his lips. We have little evidence that he ever said 'Go and suffer the consequences of your sins'" ("Forgiveness," 200).

14. Minow, *Between Vengeance and Forgiveness*, chap. 2. Though she does not refer to the logic of faith, Minow's general argument that religion itself may influence outcomes toward particular types of transitional justice reinforces the points made earlier.

15. Rosenblum, "Justice and the Experience of Injustice."

16. Ibid., 10; Rosenblum goes on to note that one of the constraining elements of retributive justice vis-à-vis memory is that "rules of evidence and norms of accountability dictated which memories are considered worthy of public acknowledgement and which are considered inadmissible, discounted as subjective and unreliable" (ibid., 80).

17. Sydney Tarrow, *Power in Movement: Social Movement, Collective Action and Politics* (Cambridge: Cambridge University Press, 1994); Fiona Adamson, "Global Liberalism vs. Political Islam: Competing Ideological Frameworks in International Politics," *International Studies Review* 7, no. 4 (2005): 547–556; Martha Finnemore, *National Interests in International Society* (Ithaca, NY: Cornell University Press, 1996).

18. Marc Galanter, "Righting Old Wrongs," in *Breaking the Cycles of Hatred: Memory, Law, and Repair*, ed. Martha Minow (Princeton, NJ: Princeton University Press, 2002), 107–131.

19. Cynthia Sampson, "Religion and Peacebuilding," in *Peacemaking in International Conflict: Methods and Techniques*, ed. William Zartman and J. Lewis Rasmussen (Washington, DC: United States Institute of Peace, 1997), 273–318; John Paul Lederach, *The Journey towards Reconciliation* (Scottdale, PA: Herald Press, 1999); R. Scott Appleby, *The Ambivalence of the Sacred: Religion, Violence and Reconciliation* (Lanham, MD: Rowman and Littlefield, 2000).

20. See note 6.

21. Recent activities of the ICC in Uganda highlight the logic of legalism in practice. The ICC, supported by many human rights organizations, has maintained

that warrants for the top leadership of the rebel Lords Resistance Army (LRA) are nonnegotiable despite LRA demands for an amnesty and signals from the Ugandan government that it was willing to consider such an amnesty.

22. For more on the logic of emotions, see Snyder and Vinjamuri, "Trials and Errors," 15–17.

23. Vinjamuri and Snyder, "Advocacy and Scholarship," 16.

24. See note 6.

25. *Gacaca*, or *Kinyarwanda*, translates roughly into "justice on the grass." See Amnesty International "Rwanda—Gacaca: A Question of Justice," December 17, 2002, http://web.amnesty.org/library/index/engafr470007202; see also Johns Hopkins University Center for Communication Programs, "Gacaca Program in Rwanda," http://jhuccp.org/africa/rwanda/gacaca.shtml.

26. For more on this strategy, see Snyder and Vinjamuri, "Trials and Errors."

27. See Leslie Vinjamuri, "Order and Justice in Iraq," *Survival* 45, no. 4 (2003–2004): 135–152.

28. For a summary of ICTJ work, see http://www.ictj.org; for a perspective from the Red Cross on pragmatism and transitional justice, see Jelena Pejic, "Accountability for International Crimes: From Conjecture to Reality," *International Review of the Red Cross* 84, no. 845 (2002): 13–33. For a general overview of recent pragmatic strategies, see Rachel Kerr, "Prosecuting War Crimes: Trials and Tribulations," review of *War Crimes: Confronting Atrocity in the Modern World*, by David Chuter, *War Crimes and Realpolitik: International Justice from World War I to the 21st Century*, by Jackson Nyamuya Maogoto, *Universal Jurisdiction: International and Municipal Legal Perspectives*, by Luc Reydams, and *Internationalized Criminal Courts: Sierra Leone, East Timor, Kosovo and Cambodia*, ed. Cesare P. Romano, Andrew Nollkaemper, and Jann K. Kleffner, *International Journal of Human Rights* 10, no. 1 (2006): 79–87.

29. See Keck and Sikkink, *Activists beyond Borders*, on the "boomerang effect."

30. We would like to thank Scott Appleby for his keen insights into the complexity of the evolving strategies and justice conceptions of many of the religious actors discussed in this chapter.

31. See Lederach, *The Journey towards Reconciliation*; and Cynthia Sampson and John Paul Lederach, eds., *From the Ground Up: Mennonite Contributions to International Peacebuilding* (Oxford: Oxford University Press, 2000).

32. United States Institute of Peace, *Catholic Contributions to International Peace*, Special Report 69, April 2001, http://usip.org/pubs/specialreports/sr69.html. The Mennonite movement from separatism to engagement in the world, and in peace and justice issues, stems from a realization in the 1960s that "Christians could no longer allow relief, development, and justice to be in tension because the Bible demanded a creative synthesis." See Joseph S. Miller "A History of the Mennonite Conciliation Service, International Conciliation Service, and Christian Peacemaker Teams," in *From the Ground Up: Mennonite Contributions to International Peacebuilding*, ed. Cynthia Sampson and John Paul Lederach (Oxford: Oxford University Press, 2000), 7.

33. John Paul Lederach, "Five Qualities of Practice in Support of Reconciliation Processes," in *Forgiveness and Reconciliation: Religion, Public Policy, and Conflict*

Transformation, ed. Raymond G. Helmick, S. J., and Rodney L. Peterson (Philadelphia: Templeton Foundation Press, 2001), 203. In addition: "The ability to learn from the people to whom they were offering relief is perhaps rooted in Mennonites' sense of Christian humility, as well as a theology and ecclesiology based on group discernment and a high view of community. They understood that respect for their own families and faith community also meant respecting the systems of community discernment and wisdom of other cultures" (Miller, "A History of the Mennonite Conciliation Service," 10).

34. Cynthia Sampson, "Local Assessments of Mennonite Peacebuilding," in *From the Ground Up: Mennonite Contributions to International Peacebuilding*, ed. Cynthia Sampson and John Paul Lederach (Oxford: Oxford University Press, 2000), 256–274.

35. Sally Engle Merry, "Mennonite Peacebuilding and Conflict Transformation: A Cultural Analysis," in *From the Ground Up: Mennonite Contributions to International Peacebuilding*, ed. Cynthia Sampson and John Paul Lederach (Oxford: Oxford University Press, 2000), 203–217.

36. Lederach, *The Journey towards Reconciliation*, 66.

37. Although the Mennonite framework for peacebuilding is highly distinctive, several other religious actors such as Quaker Peace and Social Witness, World Relief, World Jewish Aid, and moral rearmament share important elements such as long-term commitment and attention to social justice issues.

38. United States Institute of Peace, *Can Faith-Based NGOs Advance Interfaith Reconciliation: The Case of Bosnia and Herzegovina*, Special Report 103, March 2003, http://www.usip.org/pubs/specialreports/sr103.html.

39. See Sampson and Lederach, *From the Ground Up*; International Center for Transitional Justice, "Part 9: Community Reconciliation," in *Final Report of the Commission for Reception, Truth, and Reconciliation in East Timor*, 2006, http://www.ictj.org/cavr.report.asp#english.

40. United States Institute of Peace, *Can Faith-Based NGOs Advance Interfaith Reconciliation*.

41. Ibid.

42. An emphasis on social justice is not limited to capacity-building actors. Several other types of actors discussed in this chapter share this focus on social justice.

43. Merry, "Mennonite Peacebuilding and Conflict Transformation," 211.

44. Ibid., 120.

45. Ricardo Esquiva and Paul Stucky, "Building Peace from Below and Inside: The Mennonite Experience in Colombia," in *From the Ground Up: Mennonite Contributions to International Peacebuilding*, ed. Cynthia Sampson and John Paul Lederach (Oxford: Oxford University Press, 2000), 123.

46. Ibid., 135.

47. Mark Chupp, "Creating Space for Peace: The Central American Peace Portfolio," in *From the Ground Up: Mennonite Contributions to International Peacebuilding*, ed. Cynthia Sampson and John Paul Lederach (Oxford: Oxford University Press, 2000), 105.

48. United States Institute of Peace, *Catholic Contributions to International Peace*.

49. Quoted in Miriam Schulman, "Neighbor to the Assassin: Transitional Justice in Guatemala," *Issues in Ethics* 9, no. 3 (1998), http://www.scu.edu/ethics/publications/iie/v9n3/assassin.html. Importantly, the bishop who headed the REMHI project was murdered in 1998, two days after presenting the report. Although postconflict situations are complex, the example suggests that the church may also have been (understandably) unwilling to fully pursue retributive justice for fear of disrupting the negotiated peace in which it had played a role, and for fear of retribution.

50. United States Institute of Peace, *Catholic Contributions to International Peace.*

51. Our thanks to Scott Appleby for this important insight. See Catholic Relief Services, "Peacebuilding," http://crs.org/peacebuilding.

52. Philpott, "When Faith Meets History," 21.

53. United States Institute of Peace, *Catholic Contributions to International Peace.*

54. See Philpott, "When Faith Meets History," 22–23.

55. See Henry Wooster, "Faith at the Ramparts: The Philippine Catholic Church and the 1986 Revolution," in *Religion: The Missing Dimension of Statecraft*, ed. Douglas Johnston and Cynthia Sampson (New York: Oxford University Press, 1994), 164. Social justice themes also motivated the church to action, as the plight of the poor in the Philippines led the cardinal and local bishops to engage the regime in efforts to address growing economic inequality and social injustice. Ibid., and United States Institute of Peace, *Catholic Contributions to International Peace.*

56. Bartoli also cites a political dynamic emphasizing the power of war as something that overwhelms individuals and communities: "Hence, it was war and not specific individuals or parties . . . to be blamed for the massacres, destruction, and suffering. Therefore, when war ends, so does the need for revenge." Andrea Bartoli, "Forgiveness and Reconciliation in Mozambique," in *Forgiveness and Reconciliation: Religion, Public Policy, and Conflict Transformation*, ed. Raymond G. Helmick, S. J., and Rodney L. Petersen (Philadelphia: Templeton Foundation Press, 2001), 379.

57. Ibid., 369.

58. Ibid., 374.

59. Arieh J. Kochavi, *Prelude to Nuremberg: Allied War Crimes Policy and the Question of Punishment* (Chapel Hill: University of North Carolina Press, 1998).

60. Ibid., 140; quotation from A. L. Easterman of the WJC.

61. For statements and policy positions on various issues, see United States Conference of Catholic Bishops, "International Issues by Topic,"http://www.usccb.org/sdwp/international/topicissues.htm.

62. Organization of the Islamic Conference, "Homepage," http://www.oic-oci.org; and Organization of the Islamic Conference, "Press Release: OIC Attends Inauguration of National Consultation Days in Mauritania" October 27, 2005, http://www.oic-oci.org. For a more general discussion of Islamic and Muslim positions on the complex relationship between traditional values and culture and debates concerning universal human rights and justice, as well as points of agreement and dialogue, see Heiner Bielefeldt, "Muslim Voices in the Human Rights Debate," *Human Rights Quarterly* 17, no. 4 (1995): 587–617.

63. Organization of the Islamic Conference, "Resolution No. 1/9-P (IS): On the Cause of Palestine and the Arab Israeli Conflict," 9th Session of the Islamic Summit Conference, 12–13 November 2000, http://www.oic-oci.org.

64. The SACC home page notes: "As a National Council of Churches and Institutions, the SACC, acting on behalf of its member churches, is called by the Triune God to work for moral reconstruction in South Africa, focusing on issues of justice, reconciliation, integrity of creation and the eradication of poverty and contributing towards the empowerment of all who are spiritually, socially and economically marginalized." South African Council of Churches, "Homepage," http://www.sacc.org.za. See also South African Council of Churches, "About the SACC," http://www.sacc.org.za/about.html.

65. Bartoli, "Forgiveness and Reconciliation in the Mozambique Peace Process," 377.

66. This point is also observed by Minow, "Breaking the Cycles of Hatred."

67. International Center for Transitional Justice, "Part 9: Community Reconciliation," 2–3.

68. The Catholic Church was one of numerous stakeholders involved in the design of the CRP; others included representatives of the Council of East Timorese Resistance (CNRT), human rights NGOs, women's groups, youth organizations, the Association of Ex-Political Prisoners, Falintil (former guerrilla group), the UN Transitional Authority, and UNHCR. Importantly, the CRP process also reserves the right to send the most serious crimes to a formal trial process.

69. International Center for Transitional Justice, "Part 9: Community Reconciliation," 18, 19.

70. Ibid., 20.

71. Ibid., 42. In the wake of the Indonesian occupation and violence of 1999, the formal legal system in Timor-Leste was overwhelmed in dealing even with serious crimes and would not have been able to accommodate the caseload handled by the CRP. All told, 1,371 individuals completed the CRP process.

72. In 1991 more than 70 percent of South Africans indicated an affiliation with a major Christian church; correspondingly, the TRC process under Archbishop Desmond Tutu drew heavily on Christian symbols and practices. See Boraine, *A Country Unmasked*, 267.

73. Boraine, *A Country Unmasked*, 265–267. Boraine notes that TRC hearings were often opened with prayers and hymns. Even in cases when the commission "made no attempt to begin the day's proceedings with prayer or hymns, such action often came quite spontaneously from those who were attending" (ibid., 267).

74. Ibid., 268, 275; quoted material from Lyn S. Graybill, *Truth and Reconciliation in South Africa: Miracle or Model?* (Boulder, CO: Lynne Rienner, 2002), 61.

75. Boraine, *A Country Unmasked*, 362. *Ubuntu* is a concept shared across Africa, though consciously invoked by Archbishop Tutu in the South African reconciliation process. Tutu writes, "*Ubuntu* says I am human only because you are human. If I undermine your humanity I dehumanize myself. You must do what you can to maintain this great harmony, which is perpetually undermined by resentment, anger,

and desire for vengeance. That is why African jurisprudence is restorative rather that retributive" (quoted in Graybill, *Truth and Reconciliation in South Africa,* 47)

76. Boraine, *A Country Unmasked,* 268; Graybill, *Truth and Reconciliation in South Africa,* 47–48.

77. David R. Smock, "Conclusion," in *Religious Contributions to Peacemaking: When Religion Brings Peace, Not War,* ed. David R. Smock (Washington, DC: United States Institute of Peace, 2006), 38.

78. Johnston observes a process of "story-telling" to allow victims of religiously based conflicts (in the former Federal Republic of Yugoslavia) to gradually generate empathy, overcome the past, and work toward reconciliation; ecumenical projects emerged out of the interfaith workshop, held in Osijek, Croatia. This"story-telling" element approximates elements of restorative justice emphasized by cosmopolitan religious actors. Douglas Johnston, "Review: Religion: The Missing Dimension of Statecraft," *Islam and Christian-Muslim Relations* 10, no. 1 (1999): 81.

79. Shriver, "Truth Commissions and Judicial Trials," 164; Minow, *Between Vengeance and Forgiveness,* 114.

80. Minow, *Between Vengeance and Forgiveness,* notes the example of returning a sacred burial ground.

81. Smock, *Religious Contributions to Peacemaking.*

82. Gerard Clarke, "Faith Matters: Development and the Complex World of Faith-Based Organizations" (paper presented at the annual conference of the Development Studies Association, the Open University, Milton Keynes, 7–9 September 2005), http://www.devstud.org.uk/Conference05/papers/clarke.doc.

83. Appleby, *The Ambivalence of the Sacred,* 31

84. Lederach, *The Journey towards Reconciliation,* 68–69.

85. Boraine (*A Country Unmasked,* 298) notes his concern as to whether the South African decision not to prosecute represented a breach of international law and concludes that it does not. It is also important to note that the amnesty provided in South Africa was conditional upon review and full disclosure and was backed by the power of subpoena; this differs markedly from the blanket amnesties given in the wake of many conflict situations or dictatorships (e.g., in Latin America).

86. Shriver, "Truth Commissions and Judicial Trials," 24–25.

87. United States Institute of Peace, *Can Faith-Based NGOs Advance Interfaith Reconciliation.* The central role of time and local engagement is reinforced by the fact that the rebuilding of mosques in other Serb areas such as Prijedor did not experience such violence, despite a greater history of violence and atrocities in this area.

88. Ibid.

89. Marian Gh. Simion, Review of *Between Eden and Armageddon: The Future of World Religions, Violence and Peacemaking,* by Marc Gopin, *Boston Theological Institute Newsletter,* April 22, 2003, 2; see also Marc Gopin, "The Religious Component of Mennonite Peacemaking and Its Global Implications," in *From the Ground Up: Mennonite Contributions to International Peacebuilding,* ed. Cynthia Sampson and John Paul Lederach (Oxford: Oxford University Press, 2000), 233–255; Harvey Cox, with Arvind Sharma, Masao Abe, Abdulaziz Sachedina, Harjot Oberoi, and Moshe Idel,

"World Religions and Conflict Resolution," in *Religion: The Missing Dimension of State-craft*, ed. Douglas Johnston and Cynthia Sampson (New York: Oxford University Press, 1994), 266–282.

BIBLIOGRAPHY

Adamson, Fiona. "Global Liberalism vs. Political Islam: Competing Ideological Frameworks in International Politics." *International Studies Review* 7, no. 4 (2005): 547–569.

American Non-Governmental Organization Coalition for the International Criminal Court. "Faith and Ethics Network." 2002. http://www.aimcc.org/faith.htm.

Amnesty International. "Rwanda—Gacaca: A Question of Justice." http://web.amnesty.org/library/index/engafr470007202. December 17, 2002.

Appleby, R. Scott. *The Ambivalence of the Sacred: Religion, Violence and Reconciliation.* Lanham, MD: Rowman and Littlefield, 2000.

———. "Religion as an Agent of Conflict Transformation and Peacebuilding." In *Turbulent Peace: The Challenges of Managing International Conflict*, ed. Chester Crocker, Fen Osler Hampson, and Pamela R. Aall, 821–840. Washington. DC: United States Institute of Peace, 2001.

Bartoli, Andrea. "Forgiveness and Reconciliation in the Mozambique Peace Process." In *Forgiveness and Reconciliation: Religion, Public Policy, and Conflict Transformation*, ed. Raymond G. Helmick, S. J., and Rodney L. Peterson, 361–382. Philadelphia: Templeton Foundation Press, 2001.

———. "Mediating Peace in Mozambique: The Role of the Community of Saint'Egidio." In *Herding Cats: Multiparty Mediation in a Complex World*, ed. Chester Crocker, Fen Osler Hampson, and Pamela R. Aall, 245–274. Washington, DC: United States Institute of Peace, 2003.

Bass, Gary J. *Stay the Hand of Vengeance: The Politics of War Crimes Tribunals.* Princeton, NJ: Princeton University Press, 2000.

Bergey, Bonnie. "The 'Bottom-Up' Alternative in Somali Peacebuilding." In *From the Ground Up: Mennonite Contributions to International Peacebuilding*, ed. Cynthia Sampson and John Paul Lederach, 149–164. Oxford: Oxford University Press, 2000.

Bielefeldt, Heiner. "Muslim Voices in the Human Rights Debate." *Human Rights Quarterly* 17, no. 4 (1995): 587–617.

Boraine, Alex. *A Country Unmasked.* Oxford: Oxford University Press, 2000.

Camacho, Christopher, E. Tory Higgens, and Lindsay Luger. "Moral Value Transfer from Regulatory Fit: 'What Feels Right *Is* Right' and 'What Feels Wrong *Is* Wrong.'" *Journal of Personality and Social Psychology* 84, no. 3 (2003): 498–510.

Campbell, Joseph. "Partnering with Mennonites in Northern Ireland." In *From the Ground Up: Mennonite Contributions to International Peacebuilding*, ed. Cynthia Sampson and John Paul Lederach, 97–103. Oxford: Oxford University Press, 2000.

Catholic Relief Services. "Peacebuilding." http://crs.org/peacebuilding.

Chupp, Mark. "Creating Space for Peace: The Central American Peace Portfolio." In *From the Ground Up: Mennonite Contributions to International Peacebuilding*, ed. Cynthia Sampson and John Paul Lederach, 104–121. Oxford: Oxford University Press, 2000.

Clarke, Gerard. "Faith Matters: Development and the Complex World of Faith-Based Organizations." Paper presented at the annual conference of the Development Studies Association, the Open University, Milton Keynes, September 7–9, 2005. http://www.devstud.org.uk/Conference05/papers/clarke.doc.

Cochrane, James, John De Gruchy, and Stephen Martin, eds. *Facing the Truth: South African Faith Communities and the Truth and Reconciliation Commission*. Athens: Ohio University Press, 1999.

Cox, Harvey, with Arvind Sharma, Masao Abe, Abdulaziz Sachedina, Harjot Oberoi, and Moshe Idel. "World Religions and Conflict Resolution." In *Religion: The Missing Dimension of Statecraft*, ed. Douglas Johnston and Cynthia Sampson, 266–282. New York: Oxford University Press, 1994.

Cuffe, Jenny. "Uganda Torn over Price of Peace." *BBC News Online*, March 31, 2005. http://news.bbc.co.uk/go/pr/fr/-/2/hi/africa/4394923.stm.

De Gruchy, John W. *Reconciliation: Restoring Justice*. Minneapolis, MN: Fortress Press, 2002.

Elster, Jon. *Closing the Books: Transitional Justice in Historical Perspective*. Cambridge: Cambridge University Press, 2004.

Esquiva, Ricardo, and Paul Stucky. "Building Peace from Below and Inside: The Mennonite Experience in Colombia." In *From the Ground Up: Mennonite Contributions to International Peacebuilding*, ed. Cynthia Sampson and John Paul Lederach, 122–140. Oxford: Oxford University Press, 2000.

Finnemore, Martha. *National Interests in International Society*. Ithaca, NY: Cornell University Press, 1996.

———. *The Purpose of Intervention: Changing Beliefs about the Use of Force*. Ithaca, NY: Cornell University Press, 2003.

Fox, Jonathan. "Religion as an Overlooked Element of International Relations." *International Studies Review* 3.3 (2001): 53–73.

Gagnon, V. P. "Ethnic Nationalism and International Conflict: The Case of Serbia." *International Security* 19.3 (1994/1995): 130–166.

———. *The Myth of Ethnic War: Serbia and Croatia in the 1990s*. Ithaca, NY: Cornell University Press, 2004.

Galanter, Marc. "Righting Old Wrongs." In *Breaking the Cycles of Hatred: Memory, Law, and Repair*, ed. Martha Minow, 107-131. Princeton, NJ: Princeton University Press, 2002.

Gopin, Marc. *Between Eden and Armageddon: The Future of World Religions, Violence, and Peacemaking*. Oxford: Oxford University Press, 2000.

———. "The Religious Component of Mennonite Peacemaking and Its Global Implications." In *From the Ground Up: Mennonite Contributions to International Peacebuilding*, ed. Cynthia Sampson and John Paul Lederach, 233–255. Oxford: Oxford University Press, 2000.

Graybill, Lyn S. *Truth and Reconciliation in South Africa: Miracle or Model?* Boulder, CO: Lynne Rienner, 2002.

Greenstein, Laurie. "Evangelicals Are Growing Force in the Military Chaplain Corps." *New York Times,* July 12, 2005.

Hayner, Priscilla B. *Unspeakable Truths: Confronting State Terror and Atrocity.* New York: Routledge, 2001.

Hazan, Pierre. "Measuring the Impact of Punishment and Forgiveness: A Framework for Evaluating Transitional Justice." *International Review of the Red Cross* 88, no. 861 (2006): 19–47.

Helmick, Raymond G., S. J., and Rodney L. Peterson, eds. *Forgiveness and Reconciliation: Religion, Public Policy, and Conflict Transformation.* Philadelphia: Templeton Foundation Press, 2001.

Herr, Robert, and Judy Zimmerman Herr. "Building Peace in South Africa: A Case Study of Mennonite Programs." In *From the Ground Up: Mennonite Contributions to International Peacebuilding,* ed. Cynthia Sampson and John Paul Lederach, 59–76. Oxford: Oxford University Press, 2000.

Higgens, E. Tory. "Making a Good Decision: Value from Fit." *American Psychologist* 55, no. 11 (2000): 1217–1230.

Huntington, Samuel. *The Clash of Civilizations and the Remaking of the World Order.* New York: Simon and Schuster, 1996.

———. *Political Order in Changing Societies.* New Haven, CT: Yale University Press, 1968.

Hutchison, Peggy, and Harmon Wray. "What Is Restorative Justice?" *New World Outlook.* http://gbgm-umc.org/mwo/99ja/what.html. 1999.

International Center for Transitional Justice. "Homepage." http://www.ictj.org.

———. "Part 9: Community Reconciliation." In *Final Report of the Commission for Reception, Truth, and Reconciliation in East Timor.* 2006. http://www.ictj.org/cavr.report.asp#english.

Islamic Human Rights Commission. "Homepage." http://www.ihrc.org.

Johns Hopkins University Center for Communication Programs. "Gacaca Program in Rwanda." http://jhuccp.org/africa/rwanda/gacaca.shtml.

Johnston, Douglas. "Review: Religion: The Missing Dimension of Statecraft." *Islam and Christian-Muslim Relations* 10, no. 1 (1999): 77–81.

Johnston, Douglas, and Cynthia Sampson, eds. *Religion: The Missing Dimension of Statecraft.* New York: Oxford University Press, 1994.

Juergensmeyer, Mark. *The New Cold War? Religious Nationalism Confronts the Secular State.* Berkeley: University of California Press, 1993.

———. *Terror in the Mind of God: The Global Rise of Religious Violence.* Berkeley: University of California Press, 2003.

Keck, Margaret E., and Kathryn Sikkink. *Activists beyond Borders: Advocacy Networks in International Politics.* Ithaca, NY: Cornell University Press, 1998.

Kerr, Rachel. "Prosecuting War Crimes: Trials and Tribulations." Review of *War Crimes: Confronting Atrocity in the Modern World,* by David Chuter, *War Crimes and Realpolitik: International Justice from World War I to the 21st Century,* by Jackson Nyamuya

Maogoto, *Universal Jurisdiction: International and Municipal Legal Perspectives*, by Luc Reydams, and *Internationalized Criminal Courts: Sierra Leone, East Timor, Kosovo and Cambodia*, ed. Cesare P. Romano, Andrew Nollkaemper, and Jann K. Kleffner. *International Journal of Human Rights* 10, no. 1 (2006): 79–87.

Kochavi, Arieh J. *Prelude to Nuremberg: Allied War Crimes Policy and the Question of Punishment*. Chapel Hill: University of North Carolina Press, 1998.

Kraybill, Ron. "Reflections on Twenty Years in Peacebuilding." In *From the Ground Up: Mennonite Contributions to International Peacebuilding*, ed. Cynthia Sampson and John Paul Lederach, 30–44. Oxford: Oxford University Press, 2000.

Lederach, John Paul. "Civil Society and Reconciliation." In *Turbulent Peace: The Challenges of Managing International Conflict*, ed. Chester Crocker, Fen Osler Hampson, and Pamela R. Aall, 841–854. Washington, DC: United States Institute of Peace, 2001.

———. "Five Qualities of Practice in Support of Reconciliation Processes." In *Forgiveness and Reconciliation: Religion, Public Policy, and Conflict Transformation*, ed. Raymond G. Helmick, S. J., and Rodney L. Peterson, 193–203. Philadelphia: Templeton Foundation Press, 2001.

———. "Journey from Resolution to Transformative Peacebuilding." In *From the Ground Up: Mennonite Contributions to International Peacebuilding*, ed. Cynthia Sampson and John Paul Lederach, 45–55. Oxford: Oxford University Press, 2000.

———. *The Journey towards Reconciliation*. Scottdale, PA: Herald Press, 1999.

———. "Mennonite Central Committee Efforts in Somalia and Somaliland." In *From the Ground Up: Mennonite Contributions to International Peacebuilding*, ed. Cynthia Sampson and John Paul Lederach, 141–148. Oxford: Oxford University Press, 2000.

Liechty, Joseph. "Mennonites and Conflict in Northern Ireland, 1970–1998." In *From the Ground Up: Mennonite Contributions to International Peacebuilding*, ed. Cynthia Sampson and John Paul Lederach, 77–96. Oxford: Oxford University Press, 2000.

LoWilla, Emmanuel. "Intrafaith and Interfaith Dialogue in Southern Sudan." In *Religious Contributions to Peacemaking: When Religion Brings Peace, Not War*, ed. David R. Smock, 25–28. USIP: Peaceworks 55 (2006).

March, James G., and Johan P. Olsen. *Rediscovering Institutions: The Organizational Basis of Politics*. New York: Free Press, 1989.

Mennonite Central Committee. *Moving with Compassion: Annual Report 2004/2005*. 2005. http://www.mcc.org.

Merry, Sally Engle. "Mennonite Peacebuilding and Conflict Transformation: A Cultural Analysis." In *From the Ground Up: Mennonite Contributions to International Peacebuilding*, ed. Cynthia Sampson and John Paul Lederach, 203–217. Oxford: Oxford University Press, 2000.

Miller, Joseph S. "A History of the Mennonite Conciliation Service, International Conciliation Service, and Christian Peacemaker Teams." In *From the Ground Up: Mennonite Contributions to International Peacebuilding*, ed. Cynthia Sampson and John Paul Lederach, 3–29. Oxford: Oxford University Press, 2000.

Minow, Martha. *Between Vengeance and Forgiveness: Facing History and Genocide after Mass Violence*. Boston: Beacon Press, 1998.

Minow, Martha. "Breaking the Cycles of Hatred." In *Breaking the Cycles of Hatred: Memory, Law, and Repair*, ed. Martha Minow, 14–76. Princeton, NJ: Princeton University Press, 2002.

——, ed. *Breaking the Cycles of Hatred: Memory, Law, and Repair*. Princeton, NJ: Princeton University Press, 2002.

National Association of Evangelicals. *For the Health of a Nation: An Evangelical Call to Civic Responsibility*. 2004. http://www.nae.net.

——. "1 Year after Bush Administration Declared Darfur Violence a 'Genocide,' Progress Is Minimal, Evangelical Official Says." September 9, 2005. http://www.nae.net/index.cfm?FUSEACTION=editor.page&pageID=324&idCategory=1.

Nino, Carlos Santiago. *Radical Evil on Trial*. New Haven, CT: Yale University Press, 1996.

Organization of the Islamic Conference. "Homepage." http://www.oic-oci.org.

——. "Press Release: OIC Attends Inauguration of National Consultation Days in Mauritania." October 27, 2005. http://www.oic-oci.org.

——. "Resolution No. 1/9-P (IS): On the Cause of Palestine and the Arab Israeli Conflict." 9th Session of the Islamic Summit Conference, 12–13 November 2000. http://www.oic-oci.org.

Pape, Robert. *Dying to Win: The Strategic Logic of Suicide Terrorism*. New York: Random House, 2005.

Pejic, Jelena. "Accountability for International Crimes: From Conjecture to Reality." *International Review of the Red Cross* 84.845 (2002): 13–33.

Philpott, Daniel. *The Politics of Past Evil: Religion, Reconciliation, and the Dilemmas of Transitional Justice*. South Bend, IN: University of Notre Dame Press, 2006.

——. *Revolutions in Sovereignty: How Ideas Shaped Modern International Relations*. Princeton, NJ: Princeton University Press, 2001.

——. "When Faith Meets History: The Influence of Religion on Transitional Justice." In *The Religious in Response to Mass Atrocity: Interdisciplinary Perspectives*, ed. Thomas Brudholm and Thomas Cushman. Under review.

Posen, Barry. "The Security Dilemma and Ethnic Conflict." In *Ethnic Conflict and International Security*, ed. Michael Brown, 103–124. Princeton, NJ: Princeton University Press, 1993.

Presbyterian Church (USA). "Presbyterian Peacemaking Program: International Criminal Court." http://www.pcusa.org/peacemaking/un/icc.

Reychler, Luc. "Introduction: Towards a Religion of World Politics?" *International Journal of Peace Studies* 2.1 (1997): 19–38.

Risse, Thomas, Stephen C. Ropp, and Kathryn Sikkink, eds. *The Power of Human Rights: International Norms and Domestic Change*. Cambridge: Cambridge University Press, 1999.

Rosenblum, Nancy L. "Justice and the Experience of Injustice." In *Breaking the Cycles of Hatred: Memory, Law, and Repair*, ed. Martha Minow, 77–107. Princeton, NJ: Princeton University Press, 2002.

Ross, Will. "Peace before Justice." March 16, 2005. *BBC News Online*. http://news.bbc.co.uk/go/pr/fr/-/2/hi/africa/4352901.stm.

Rubin, Barry. "Religion and International Affairs." In *Religion: The Missing Dimension of Statecraft*, ed. Douglas Johnston and Cynthia Sampson, 20–34. New York: Oxford University Press, 1994.

Sampson, Cynthia. "Local Assessments of Mennonite Peacebuilding." In *From the Ground Up: Mennonite Contributions to International Peacebuilding*, ed. Cynthia Sampson and John Paul Lederach, 256–274. Oxford: Oxford University Press, 2000.

———. "Religion and Peacebuilding." In *Peacemaking in International Conflict: Methods and Techniques*, ed. William Zartman and J. Lewis Rasmussen, 273–318. Washington, DC: United States Institute of Peace, 1997.

Sampson, Cynthia, and John Paul Lederach, eds. *From the Ground Up: Mennonite Contributions to International Peacebuilding*. Oxford: Oxford University Press, 2000.

Schulman, Miriam. "Neighbor to the Assassin: Transitional Justice in Guatemala." *Issues in Ethics* 9, no. 3 (1998). http://www.scu.edu/ethics/publications/iie/v9n3/assassin.html.

Shriver, Donald W., Jr. "Forgiveness: A Bridge across Abysses of Revenge." In *Forgiveness and Reconciliation: Religion, Public Policy, and Conflict Transformation*, ed. Raymond G. Helmick, S. J., and Rodney L. Peterson, 151–167. Philadelphia: Templeton Foundation Press, 2001.

———. "Truth Commissions and Judicial Trials: Complementary or Antagonistic Servants of Public Justice?" *Journal of Law and Religion* 16, no. 1 (2001): 1–33.

Simion, Marian Gh. Review of *Between Eden and Armageddon: The Future of World Religions, Violence and Peacemaking*, by Marc Gopin. *Boston Theological Institute Newsletter* April 22, 2003, 1–2.

Smock, David R. "Conclusion." In *Religious Contributions to Peacemaking: When Religion Brings Peace, Not War*, ed. David R. Smock, 35–41. Washington, DC: United States Institute of Peace, 2006.

———. "Introduction." In *Religious Contributions to Peacemaking: When Religion Brings Peace, Not War*, ed. David R. Smock, 1–4. Washington, DC: United States Institute of Peace, 2006.

———. "Mediating between Christians and Muslims in Plateau State, Nigeria." In *Religious Contributions to Peacemaking: When Religion Brings Peace, Not War*, ed. David R. Smock, 17–20. Washington, DC: United States Institute of Peace, 2006.

Snyder, Jack, and Leslie Vinjamuri. "Trials and Errors: Principles and Pragmatism in Strategies of International Justice." *International Security* 28, no. 3 (2003–2004): 5–44.

South African Council of Churches. "About the SACC." http://www.sacc.org.za/about.html.

———. "Homepage." http://www.sacc.org.za.

Tarrow, Sidney. *Power in Movement: Social Movement, Collective Action and Politics*. Cambridge: Cambridge University Press, 1994.

United States Conference of Catholic Bishops. "International Issues by Topic." http://www.usccb.org/sdwp/international/topicissues.htm.

United States Institute of Peace. *Can Faith-Based NGOs Advance Interfaith Reconciliation: The Case of Bosnia and Herzegovina*. Special Report 103. March 2003. http://www.usip.org/pubs/specialreports/sr103.html.

United States Institute of Peace. *Catholic Contributions to International Peace.* Special
    Report 69. April 2001. http://usip.org/pubs/specialreports/sr69.html.
Villa-Vicencio, Charles. "The Reek of Cruelty and the Quest for Healing: Where
    Retributive and Restorative Justice Meet." *Journal of Law and Religion* 14, no. 1
    (1999–2000): 165–187.
Vinjamuri, Leslie. "Order and Justice in Iraq." *Survival* 45, no. 4 (2003–2004): 135–152.
Vinjamuri, Leslie, and Jack Snyder. "Advocacy and Scholarship in the Study of Transi-
    tional Justice and International War Crimes Tribunals." *Annual Review of Political
    Science* 7 (2004): 345–362.
Wooster, Henry. "Faith at the Ramparts: The Philippine Catholic Church and the 1986
    Revolution." In *Religion: The Missing Dimension of Statecraft*, ed. Douglas Johnston
    and Cynthia Sampson, 153–176. New York: Oxford University Press, 1994.
World Council of Churches. 2005. "WCC Central Committee 2005 Statement on the
    ICC." http://www.wcc-coe.org/wcc/what/international/impunity-icc.html.

8

Religion and Global Development: Intersecting Paths

Katherine Marshall

Over the past decade, important changes in visions and practical approaches about global poverty and equity have generated new connections among very different institutions. Initiatives by global institutions, the impact of new technologies, and the blurring of lines among hitherto segmented disciplines, sectors, and institutions (public and private, security and welfare), all part of the globalization revolution, are transforming relationships within the world of international development. New approaches to the roles that religion can and should play in development are an important part of that transformation, as religions also take on different forms and engagements. Faith-inspired organizations have become far more directly involved in development thinking and work, with roles ranging from global advocacy and mobilization on issues like poor-country debt and rights to health care to community-level programs such as education, water, and welfare. And secular development institutions, national and international, are today far more open than they were even fifteen years ago to cooperation with religious groups and to their ideas. This trend has provoked debates within the development world and tensions also within and among faith institutions, even as it promises to open new avenues for action and common engagement about global poverty.

The links between fighting poverty, development work, and religion appear strong and obvious to some observers, but for others the merits of yoking two historically differing fields and worlds in any systemic way are doubtful. And, indeed, wide gulfs have traditionally separated both intellectual and practical work by secular and faith institutions—even work directed to similar ends, like policies and programs for education, health, and water. The burgeoning of civil society, at global and national levels, and the broadening of national and international public sector approaches to encompass new disciplines and partnerships have radically changed the policy landscape. Still, specific links between faith and development practitioners have proved particularly complex to navigate. This is in part because deep historic, sociopolitical, and even emotional backdrops surrounding relationships between secular and religious worlds color contemporary debates and approaches.

This chapter explores this new terrain of faith development engagement and partnership. It focuses on the new trends and debates about these relationships, setting them against the backdrop of long-standing common concerns and interests around poverty and social justice. Recent debates about the benefits and risks of bringing faith and development work closer together highlight both these new dimensions, the product of contemporary world political forces and the increasing pluralism of many societies, and the core ethical issues that are evoked by global poverty and inequity. Perhaps the most explicit debates, illustrating graphically the underlying tensions that can arise, have transpired as a leading international development institution, the World Bank, embarked in 1998 on a high-level and visible effort to engage more actively with faith communities.[1] The World Bank's experience is an exemplary case study because many of the arguments advanced in discussions around the initiative have much broader application. The discussion highlights historical connections and disconnects, the initial impetus for exploratory discussions, criticisms and doubts along the way, current approaches, and agendas for future discussion and action.[2]

The chapter first introduces the major lines of controversy, setting out the historical developments that have brought faith and development institutions into closer contact in recent decades, on policy agendas and in practice, and the major responses, positive and negative, that this produced. It highlights how the broader global agendas that have sparked interest in issues of religion and public policy have affected the more specific debates about development work, and how on-the-ground experience has shaped discussions and action. It illustrates the discussion first with an account of the World Bank's outreach to faith communities and second through four short case studies describing faith development institution partnerships. The discussion then explores the hesitations and controversies within secular institutions in greater detail. The underlying argument is, first, that the changing roles of religion in the public sphere are linked above all to heightened global concerns about poverty and, more complex still, global balance, equity, stability, and social justice, and second that the global tendencies toward different forms of partnership change conventional sectoral and disciplinary approaches.

Main Lines of Controversy

The wide array of faith-inspired institutions and development agencies across the world share a central focus on poor people, concern about social exclusion, and a searing disappointment in the face of unfulfilled human potential. This common ground involves both communities in the strengthening global consensus that bolder and more concerted action is needed to address these issues. That common spirit and action engagement underlie the Millennium Declaration and the Millennium Development Goals (MDGs)—the centerpiece of the September 2000 United Nations Summit that grappled with the core issues facing humanity at the turn of the millennium—and they open opportunities even as they pose practical challenges.[3]

Religious and development institutions have traditionally operated largely in different spheres and have been cast in separate roles—even separate dramas. This generalization applies to widely different institutions (albeit with some noteworthy exceptions), including the array of institutions within the United Nations system working on development issues, most bilateral aid agencies, and the growing body of secular nongovernmental organizations. The World Bank, as a leading development institution working within the United Nations system, offers an interesting illustration of both separation and engagement. In its first half century (it began operations in 1946), it rarely engaged with faith institutions, and its extensive written record of research, policy making, and support for development projects contained barely a mention of religion or faith institutions, despite the on-the-ground reality of numerous intersections. However, the present global focus on fighting poverty and achieving social justice, and the rising roles of civil society broadly have, via rather separate paths, led to far more encounters between the two worlds—in both common cause and friction. For the World Bank, this new engagement raised unanticipated challenges. The experience offers a range of insights into the new policy environment that affects the way relationships between religion and public policy are changing in the contemporary world.

The common ground between faith and development institutions that arises from their shared concerns about poverty and equity was far from universally appreciated even at the time of the Millennium Summit held at the United Nations in September 2000. At the same time that common declarations of purpose and commitment pointed to an exciting new global engagement to address poverty issues, frictions came increasingly to the fore about the roles that religion played in development work. These were colored by many developments, including the evident resurgence of religion in many settings (including U.S. politics, in the Islamic world, and across Africa) and the heightened concerns about terrorism, especially after September 11, 2001. They were complicated by the growing and increasingly complex roles of global civil society institutions in development debates, fired by issues ranging from trade to environment to the role of women and indigenous peoples. Where did the vast world of religion, traditionally seen by secular organizations as operating in quite different domains, come into the complex new equations of relationships, including specifically the global effort to combat poverty?

Many practical and normative arguments support a sharper focus on faith roles in development. Faith institutions play (and have long played) large and varied roles in development work. Their pivotal roles in developing education and health services in many countries, their continuing roles in both fields, and their special roles in addressing specific threats to development like the world's major contemporary pandemic, HIV/AIDS, have great if often underappreciated importance for the central task of human development, widely recognized as lying at the core of development success. Faith institutions often play critical advocacy roles, mobilizing support for programs to fight hunger and poverty (witness Bread for the World in the United States) and, more broadly, to promote social justice (note the transforming role of the liberation theology movement within the Catholic community). Faith institutions have a wide range of insights and critiques about development strategies and programs that can translate into better policy formulation, debate, and action. They also have deep involvement in many if not most poor communities (faith institutions are omnipresent in communities across the world), and thus can contribute their knowledge and understanding about the needs and aspirations of poor people. There is a depth of experience with poverty born of centuries of experience and reflection about social issues, for both communities and individuals. In short, faith institutions have unique knowledge and experience, an often different set of insights and approaches to policy issues, and extensive operating networks deeply engaged at the community level. Their knowledge can help in laying a solid foundation for sustainable projects and programs and avoid a raft of potential pitfalls.

Historically, development institutions and practitioners, including specifically the World Bank, have lacked knowledge of the world's faith communities in general and about their development work. This blind spot has contributed in important instances to flawed project design and suboptimal community, sectoral, national, and transnational engagements. The failure, for example, to take sufficiently into account the knowledge of faith leaders working in communities in Africa affected by the policies undertaken to adjust economies in the 1980s, the insufficient dialogue about why girls should be enrolled in schools and why families keep them at home, and the missed opportunities related to local finance where faith-linked savings schemes offered potential are among countless examples of "might-have-beens" in development history.

Religion is a central part of global as well as local agendas and has an impact on a multitude of pressing development issues. Development institutions that fail to engage in dialogue and develop partnerships with faith groups risk missing opportunities to resolve social conflicts and advance effective governance and social cohesion. Prominent examples of areas where pressing contemporary issues on the global agenda take quite limited account of faith experience include transnational challenges such as corruption and migration. The topic of governance and corruption involves both issues of values and highly practical issues of processes and controls. Faith institutions can often offer insights into the motivations that lead to widespread corrupt practices in societies, and there are impressive examples of where faith leaders have helped to mobilize action to address the issues (Malawi, Kenya, for example). The extraordinary phenomenon of contemporary global migration has important religious dimensions, both in countries of origin of migrants and in the societies where they work and settle, yet knowledge about these dimensions is sparse.

Another important area of common concern where faith communities are playing vital roles is the effort to mobilize global support for the Millennium Declaration challenge of fighting poverty (especially in the rich countries that exercise disproportionate influence on trade policies and furnish much of the financial and technical support for development). Here again, moral and practical issues are intricately interwoven. There is increasing recognition that both the moral voice of compassion and the practical experience of working with poverty programs can combine to serve as a powerful and effective motivator in both global and national efforts to mobilize support for global development. Faith institutions have vast networks of engaged followers. Faith groups can be important allies in winning support for development work, while their opposition can be devastating. The Micah Challenge, an evangelical Christian alliance supporting the MDGs, the Religions for Peace (WCRP) "toolkits" for aid mobilization, and the strong faith voice that Bono, a leading advocate for development today, brings to his communications about the imperative of fighting poverty, are a few among many illustrations of new alliances involving faith communities. They address the challenge of heightening and sustaining public awareness about the significance of global poverty issues and the need for commitment to sustain support.

In short, strong arguments can be made, because of the many interconnections, that a development approach that ignores faith and religion is neither sensible nor viable.

Many arguments have also been raised *against* greater faith development engagement on poverty issues, especially when it takes on a formal dimension and when it operates at a global (as opposed to a national or community) level. These concerns have had practical implications, as they have translated into a raft of operational obstacles to policy and program cooperation. They are elaborated in greater detail later in the chapter, in relation to specific debates within the World Bank about its faith development initiative, where a wide range of objections from many national government representatives colored discussions over a period of several years.

The core arguments focus, in sum, on three sets of concerns. Perhaps the most important are those that reflect anxiety about trespassing too much on the sensitive boundaries between political and faith domains, fueled by a perception that religion today is highly politicized and related to many contemporary conflicts. The second relate to perceived tensions and contradictions between religion and modernization, especially reproductive health rights. Briefly (and in a somewhat caricatural fashion), the perception is that many religious organizations and leaders oppose important elements of modernization and social change and thus represent a negative force standing in the way of development. The third set of concerns reflect a largely unspoken but still widely held assumption that religion declines in importance as societies modernize and that engaging in any systematic fashion with faith organizations therefore deserves a low priority.

There is also a tension about how global and national approaches interplay. While there are well-established links in many countries between faith organizations (at least some of them) and public authorities, these often do not extend to global institutions overall and development institutions more specifically in any systematic fashion. Many governments, furthermore, are uneasy about the transnational dimensions of many faith organizations, which seem to elude their control or even knowledge. Some governments consider it expedient to deal with faith institutions simply as part of their engagement with civil society, though faith institutions are far larger and in many respects quite different from other groups that fall under the very broad and often amorphous heading of civil society. All these factors have served as important obstacles to thoughtful and systematic exploration of faith development issues and action to move in some new directions that seem fairly obvious.

The World Bank and Religion?

The World Bank embarked on a new initiative in 1998 to engage with the world of faith. The initiative took several forms, among them a series of four high-level meetings involving leaders from the world's major religions and leading development institutions, co-convened by James D. Wolfensohn (then World Bank president) and Lord Carey (then archbishop of Canterbury), where the common concerns about global poverty met great resonance. It also launched specific partnerships with several faith-inspired organizations, explored leading issues including understandings of poverty and the interplay of culture and development, and worked in three countries as a pilot experience in interfaith engagement on poverty issues (Ethiopia, Tanzania, and Guatemala). This experience is an interesting "case study" of how very different institutions have engaged together in practical ways. It thus illustrates several important global trends that are at play in relations between religion and global politics, including how secular public institutions engage with resurgent religion and how new partnerships that characterize the contemporary global scene can play out in practice. The World Bank's journey, far from a smooth one, has involved much learning and new understanding of both effective development work and the potential new partnerships that can strengthen its impact.

The World Bank is a major, if not the main, development institution today, directly involved in development work in some 120 countries (the bank is owned and led by its 185 member countries). It works on a wide variety of issues and with instruments ranging from development finance, policy analysis and research, and advocacy to its important "convening power." As a large and powerful global institution, it has attracted considerable controversy, especially over the past twenty years. As such, it is both a central and a somewhat special actor. One characteristic is that it is seen very differently by different people and institutions. This applies to many faith institutions, which see the World Bank variously as a positive force advocating for poverty eradiation, as an instrument of rich country interests and their power, as an institution with a powerful economic theology advancing market instruments, and as a unique voice for the poor. Above all, the World Bank is a complex institution mobilizing large resources, human, intellectual, and financial, with wide global reach and influence.[4] Its experience with faith institutions is thus both illustrative and a harbinger for the development community more broadly.

The World Bank's self-image is captured in the phrase, engraved in the marble at the front door of the World Bank's main building in Washington. D.C.: "Our dream is a world free of poverty." That mission unites people who engage in widely differing areas and may thus emphasize very different paths and priorities as they strive for a poverty-free world. The World Bank today is marked by a widening appreciation that the task of working for a more just world must enlist a range of interventions and actors, and that there is no magic bullet, no single recipe. A kaleidoscope of partnerships and a fundamentally interdisciplinary approach are vital if it is to attain its dream.

As frontline operational officers and international civil servants in a multilateral institution, World Bank staff work to address issues across a wide spectrum involving virtually all public policy issues, from AIDS to legal reform to zebras (i.e., biodiversity and environment). Debt, corruption, gender issues, and environmental assessments are the hourly fare. Bank staff work with villagers to raise crop yields, build pumps for water, and reduce maternal mortality. They work with urban slum communities on housing, with city administrators on sanitation, and with women's groups to confront the HIV/AIDS pandemic, expand promising microcredit schemes, and improve child nutrition. Education is a central concern, as are jobs and social safety nets. They deal all too often with the impacts of economic crises and mismanagement, including corruption, which siphons resources away from social services and development programs. Technology, trade, public institutions, and land rights affect these programs in many ways. The bank's staff aim is always directed to forge long-term visions and solutions that will yield better lives, even as they grapple daily with the practical consequences of strategic choices for countries as different as Bolivia, Cambodia, Mali, Morocco, South Africa, and Turkey. They are pragmatic visionaries and idealistic realists. The World Bank's central ethos is to serve as a catalyst and help bring the best of global experience to those who want and need to change.

Though this catalogue of development issues is familiar to any faith-based group or leader working in a poor community, the World Bank, over its sixty-year history, had remarkably little professional contact at either global or local levels with the world of faith and the people who work in it. Faith perspectives—including the myriad contributions of religious institutions that own land, run schools, assist poor people, and care for orphans and disabled people—were often invisible to development teams.[5] That oversight often resulted from simple lack of knowledge, preconceptions about differing roles, and, sometimes, suspicions that faith institutions stood against development goals. Project analysis and documentation, institutional vocabulary, research agendas, dialogue with individual countries, public speeches, and internal staff training rarely included glimpses of the world of faith. Even today the main World Bank Web site barely mentions religion or faith.[6] Some encounters with churches, temples, and mosques did occur, but these interactions were driven by individuals and proved patchy and ephemeral; they were also little documented.

A parallel portrait could be drawn of the views of many faith-based institutions regarding development institutions and specifically the World Bank. The former have often painted a rather dismal picture of the latter as large, difficult to understand, arrogant, driven by an agenda to create—and even concentrate—wealth, and removed from daily concerns of poor people. Some faith groups have portrayed development institutions as contributing to social and economic problems because of their advice to curtail subsidies, introduce or enforce taxation regimes, constrain civil service employment, work toward efficiency in expenditures on schools and health, and reduce barriers that protect farmers or local industry.[7] Tensions have mounted highest regarding the World Bank's advice to governments in handling their finances, including debt loads, economic crises, and extensive and often poorly managed public sectors. As an example, many faith groups have seen privatization of water systems as detrimental to the poor (Bolivia's El Alto and Cochabamba water reforms may be the best known examples); World Bank teams, in contrast, have regarded a combination of privatization of water management entities with regulation as the best—if not the only—way to attract investment and assure sound management, both essential for providing clean water at reasonable cost to all. Water remains a highly contentious issue with special concern for faith communities (both because it is so essential to people's lives and because of its spiritual significance for virtually all faiths). It was thus a central if somewhat ill-defined theme at the Parliament of the World's Religions in Barcelona in July 2004 and the World Council of Churches Assembly in Pôrto Alegre in February 2006.

The fact that the World Bank deals first and foremost with governments—which are its shareholders—and their core financial ministries, including central banks, attracts considerable attention from civil society organizations and especially faith institutions, who advance the critique that the path through government channels impedes understanding of and engagement with communities and nongovernmental organizations. This criticism comes with particular bite vis-à-vis countries where democratic institutions and traditions are not well developed, but it is echoed even in countries with vibrant public debate (India is a prominent example). For many decades, the multilateral development banks (including the World Bank) were indeed highly constrained in their relations with most nongovernmental entities, relating to them through the lens of government guidance. Meetings with civil society were in many countries rare and often stilted. This situation has, however, changed markedly in recent years. The World Bank fields a large network of specialists concerned primarily with civil society relations, and supports structured dialogue processes in many countries where the World Bank operates (Peru, Chile, Kenya, Senegal, India, and Indonesia are among many examples where such dialogue has influenced country operations over a period of decades). The World Bank also has partnerships (a term that often but not always implies a financing relationship) and a myriad of other relationships with an extraordinary range of institutions. Among the most dynamic are those with civil society organizations, which, of course, come in countless shapes and forms. What remains true, though, is that financing relationships for normal World Bank business are the province of governments, which decide when and for what purpose they will borrow or accept grants, and how the programs will be executed.

Many other forces have shaped the jarring perceptions and realities that divide faith and development institutions. Among the most important is a tendency for the development institutions to work in distinct silos and sectors, thus approaching issues quite distinctly as, for example, macroeconomic management, transport, water, or health. In contrast, many faith institutions, especially the core churches, temples, and mosques, tend to view social challenges as a whole and may be uncomfortable with the technical packaging of issues by sector. Thus the institutions often simply organize their work quite differently. This segmentation is one of the "cultural" differences that have contributed to significant tension among players who share a deep concern for the welfare of the world's poorest citizens and for the social, political, and environmental systems that affect them. Lack of understanding is another obstacle on both sides. Development institutions have few vehicles that help them navigate among faith institutions and learn from them, because they may be quite ignorant about religion generally and about the relevant institutions. And faith institutions often find the development institutions baffling and enigmatic in their complex and changing organizations and clipped, acronym-laden vocabulary. It would be naive not to recognize that some of the segmentation is fueled by a human tendency toward competition and a focus on one's own institutions, even in ventures whose aims are profoundly altruistic. However, significant differences in history, organization, and approach would seem to play a far greater part in the divides.

The long-standing tendency by the World Bank and many of its fellow institutions to employ dry, technical economics-speak contributes to an aura of exclusiveness. The bank recognizes that accessible language is critical for the public engagement that underlies development success, but it does not always put that precept into practice. World Bank circles also rarely use the language of ethics and values—of spirituality and the soul—which faith institutions expect to hear. This exacerbates misperceptions: development institutions are profoundly ethical in their origins, witness the passion of their staffs, and the elaborate rules governing financial management, procurement, and project evaluation, among other aspects of their work. But that is difficult to divine from institutional prose, which tends to be data-laden and "preachy" in the certainty of tone and tendency to prescribe.

Finally, faith institutions often describe a David-and-Goliath situation, wherein the mighty World Bank evinces little regard for poor countries and communities facing the Damocles sword of acute fiscal crisis with limited resources and voice, and for smaller institutions and actors. This is a common theme in the publications of the World Council of Churches as an example, but the underlying theme of imbalance of power is a common one in many commentaries about the World Bank. Such perceptions clearly play a role in relationships between faith and development groups.

James D. Wolfensohn, president of the World Bank from 1995 to 2005, took on such issues head-on early in his tenure, when he decided to embark on a series of significant efforts to address the World Bank's critics more directly and to work to bridge divides. His outreach drew in civil society, business, and cultural institutions, but the attempt to build links with communities of faith was among the most important and ambitious. Wolfensohn focused particular attention on a series of meetings between global faith and development leaders that aimed at creating a global alliance buttressed by policy consultations. He was also concerned to ensure the sustainability of the effort, both within the Bank and within the broader development community, and thus focused on the institutional links. As he argued in a major address in March 2004, the issue "of bringing the faiths together with the cause of humanity and the environment is something that is not just a dream, it's not something that cannot happen, but I suggest to you today is something that must happen."[8]

The main instrument through which the World Bank and the leaders who met to explore faith development issues sought to assure sustainability was the World Faiths Development Dialogue (WFDD). This autonomous institution was to serve as a bridge across the rather tension-filled waters separating faith and development institutions. Specifically, it was to engage in dialogue and action on poverty, culture and diversity, services to the poor, and equity.[9] The WFDD, for example, in its initial years examined the view of and involvement of faith institutions in the bank's Poverty Reduction Strategy Process (PRSP), which links debt relief to strategies for alleviating poverty. The WFDD also piloted interfaith explorations of development issues in Ethiopia, Guatemala, and Tanzania and engaged faith groups in programs to combat HIV/AIDS and preserve the environment. The bank also has maintained a small team (the unit is called the Development Dialogue on Values and Ethics) devoted primarily to fostering relationships with faith institutions that worked in tandem with WFDD.

Four global meetings between global faith and development leaders helped shape an agenda for action. At the first such meeting, held at Lambeth Palace in London in February 1998, a small group of leaders from the world's major faiths met under the leadership of James Wolfensohn and George Carey, then Archbishop of Canterbury, with His Highness the Aga Khan also present. Participants concluded that shared concerns about poverty were far more important than evident differences. A second meeting, held in Washington, D.C., in November 1999, concluded with an action plan for creating the WFDD. A larger group of leaders then met at Canterbury in October 2002 to link their dialogue to the Millennium Development Goals (MDGs).[10] The most recent meeting, held at Dublin Castle in January 2005,[11] chaired again by James Wolfensohn and Lord Carey with Archbishop Diarmuid Martin, reaffirmed the vital importance of faith development dialogue and action in advancing the fairly specific MDG agendas, and, more broadly, for working toward global equity.[12] The agendas that were defined there have guided dialogue and operational work and reflect a challenging agenda that is valid to this day.

Debates in the World Bank about Engaging with Faith Institutions

The initiative to bridge the gulf with faith institutions and to explore new forms of dialogue and partnerships began smoothly, and considerable support for this venture was evident in a growing network of supporters and interest among several country leaders (in Ethiopia and Kenya, for example) and global entities like the WCRP and the Parliament of the World's Religions. The World Bank participated in a major August 2000 summit at the United Nations that brought together hundreds of world religious leaders on the eve of the historic September 2000 UN Millennium Summit, and in other global and regional meetings. The WFDD seemed to be well launched and a promising path to operational dialogue well defined.

The overall initiative inspired by James Wolfensohn, however, soon encountered serious opposition from many of the World Bank's executive directors—representatives of its 185 member countries. It is significant that this controversy caught the bank's leaders and faith partners quite by surprise, as they had not expected that a modest initiative focused on dialogue could draw significant criticism. Nonetheless, for varying reasons, the engagement between faith and development institutions sparked a serious controversy in 2000, and it has remained an uneasy topic ever since. While several distinguished global leaders have characterized efforts to build bridges between the World Bank and faith institutions as profoundly visionary, one commentator illustrated another important current when he termed this World Bank program a "loony idea."[13]

The official discussions within the World Bank about the faith program took the form of two briefing meetings with the executive directors, followed by a lengthy series of individual meetings with all of their offices (twenty-four), focused in early 2000. As a result, Wolfensohn agreed to modify the plans for the World Bank's engagement with the WFDD (removing the World Bank from direct participation in its governance), to reorganize the World Bank unit responsible for the work (moving it from his office to the external affairs vice presidency), and to keep the issue of World Bank involvement under continuous review. The net result was that the Bank curtailed its planned effort and changed the form of its engagement with faith institutions to one that was more cautious, muted, and qualified. Agreements along these lines were reflected in two formal memorandums to the executive directors in early 2001. Wolfensohn made clear that he intended to continue with the initiative, which he considered to have vital importance both for the World Bank and for its work on poverty, but the period of controversy, in addition to providing a unique insight into the nature of concerns about the emerging roles of religion in public policy at a global level, left a cloud of doubt that has yet to lift.

Because the controversy about the faith dialogue took place at such a senior level within the World Bank, and put such a sharp spotlight on the issues, considerable attention was focused at the time and subsequently on the reasons its advocates believed that faith development dialogue makes sense and what form it could and should take, as well as to understanding and appreciating the detailed nature of the concerns and doubts that were raised about its pursuit. The protracted dialogue that the controversy sparked provided the chance to address the widely ranging concerns that surfaced in the process. That said, the dialogue was complicated by the significant political and intellectual revolution that resulted after September 11, 2001; terrorist attacks and other tensions exhibiting a religious element shone a new spotlight on the importance of religion in global affairs. The underlying and obviously complex questions about how poverty, violence, social justice, and terrorism were interrelated took on much greater prominence.

Changing political landscapes also affected the debates. For example, the approach of the U.S. representatives to the faith development discussions in 2000 was generally skeptical about explicit relationships with faith institutions and focused on what those representatives considered their relatively low priority. The tone shifted abruptly during the administration of President George W. Bush, whose representatives responded to the faith development work with enthusiasm. France took a particularly strong position opposing global engagement with faith institutions in 2000, a time when national debates about *laïcité* were at their height; subsequently the French government and institutions have evinced lively interest in faith issues, including those affecting the development agenda, above all in response to domestic relations with immigrant groups, many of them Muslim. All these factors cast in high relief the reality of complex interlocking interests.

A central debate turned around an issue with important global political ramifications: whether the focus of global policy and thus the work of global institutions should be on countries, or whether the globalization process had transformed international relations such that a broader, transnational focus was needed on many issues, including religion. The country representatives in the World Bank have tended powerfully to support an approach or response to a specific action proposal that centers on a sovereign government. Thus they tended to argue that relationships with national faith communities should have priority (though transnational Islamic politics in recent years has added nuance to this picture). If a government (say that of Zambia or Bolivia) chooses to engage with faith institutions, the World Bank and other development institutions would normally respect their decision and tailor programs accordingly. Thus church-run hospitals are engaged in health and HIV/AIDS programs in Uganda; Islamic charities were actively involved in programs in the Balkans, Indonesia, and Afghanistan; and the Bolivian Catholic Church was a major player in a complex process for devising a national poverty strategy in Bolivia. Various faith institutions have been important partners in social investment fund and community-driven development programs, proposing and implementing community-inspired programs across a wide range of social areas. The issues and objections tended to arise where transnational issues and global faith bodies became involved. This was the case when a broad development program was under review (for example, a multicountry AIDS training program focused on religious leaders) or in one instance where an initiative was proposed where the bank would lead a high level reflection on education issues across the Islamic majority countries. Since religion so often crosses national boundaries, this geography of religion became an important factor in the debates.

In many respects, the World Bank has yet to resolve fully its internal tensions and criticisms. These have in practice perturbed the WFDD's development, as well as the very evident need for the World Bank itself to expand staff knowledge about religious issues and interactions and approach faith partnerships more systematically. The faith development work has continued nonetheless; today faith organizations participate in the work of the World Bank at many levels, including the recently revamped Civil Society Forum, efforts to fight HIV/AIDS, and community approaches to the environment. Awareness of the importance of faith roles is embedded in some bank operations. However, the reach and depth of understanding remain patchy and fragile, and uncertainties regarding future directions persist. Following the World Bank's presidential transition in June 2005, a process of stocktaking began, to determine the level and direction of future engagement; this has persisted through the second (unexpected) presidential transition in July 2007, when Robert Zoellick replaced Paul Wolfowitz as president.

Drawing Lessons from Experience

The discussions and tensions just described reflect a specific debate in time and place, its features accentuated by circumstances, institutional characteristics, and personalities. But the issues at stake in forging new links among secular and faith institutions are far from abstract, and they have implications for the development process at many levels, from global to village and slum communities. Perhaps the best place to look for both inspiration and lessons is at the level of experience. Four cases are described briefly in the following. They reflect a broad range of engagements that demonstrate what can be achieved and some pitfalls and issues encountered; they also offer the basis for our working hypothesis: that the quality of development work, from basic understanding and honing of objectives through implementation and adaptation to fit local realities, is significantly improved when development and faith institutions engage together.[14]

The Community of Sant'Egidio and the Right to Health Care

A first case is the interaction between the Community of Sant'Egidio, the lay Catholic community best known for its remarkable work in supporting peace negotiations in Mozambique and elsewhere, and the World Bank. Sant'Egidio has emerged as a key actor in global debates about HIV/AIDS, and it was here that it determined that a partnership with the World Bank was essential. The World Bank at the level of the president was immediately enthusiastic, but the operating staff was reluctant, primarily because the Mozambique government was hesitant to use what it considered its scarce concessional funds from the World Bank to support an organization it viewed as a partner and donor. Both the bank and the Mozambique government were unprepared for the demanding moral arguments for action and the urgency of demands that Sant'Egidio presented. The issue of respective roles of public sector leadership and a private faith-inspired partner in addressing Mozambique's HIV/AIDS program also arose. The dialogue was transformational for policy and approach for the three actors concerned.

The backdrop was the growing conviction of the Community of Sant'Egidio that a central global challenge was not only to provide care for people affected by HIV/AIDS but to press its partners and the global HIV/AIDS community to assure the same standard of care in the poorest communities of Mozambique as in Rome. What began as a relatively straightforward effort to mobilize funding for treatment with antiretroviral therapy was thus framed over time as an issue of rights; a specific local program grew into an international advocacy campaign. For this lay Catholic community, based in Rome but now a global social movement, the links between working for peace, helping people in need, and supporting people with HIV/AIDS were obvious, and they cast the debate in a moral framework of rights and obligations. Sant'Egidio argued that no lowering of standards was morally acceptable, and that implicit acceptance that care of poor communities would be partial because of logistic or financial constraints was simply ethically wrong.

The World Bank, meanwhile, was at the time the leading international financier of HIV/AIDS programs in Africa and was focusing above all on prevention strategies and on supporting the development of national capacity. Its emphasis was on priorities and practical constraints. Relationships with governments were seen as critical because they alone could assure sustainability of programs. While the approach followed in an overall "blueprint" stressed the critical role of civil society, a category into which bank staff would place Sant'Egidio, funds and decisions on who would do what were the responsibility of governments, and direct negotiations with nongovernmental organizations had little place. When the Sant'Egidio issue arose, a long-gestating HIV/AIDS program supported by the World Bank in Mozambique, set in the framework of an Africa-wide program called the multisectoral AIDS program (MAP), was being negotiated, with some difficulty since the Mozambique government and the bank differed on some practical and strategic approaches. To reduce a lengthy and complex story to its central elements, the reluctance of the government to allocate MAP funds for the Sant'Egidio program led, or inspired, the bank to initiate a separate program called the Treatment Acceleration Project, which would support a learning-by-doing approach in three countries. The Sant'Egidio program was a centerpiece of this three-country project.

The lengthy discussions among the Community of Sant'Egidio, the Mozambique government, and the World Bank did not turn on religion, but many faith elements entered the picture, and the ethical imperatives that the different partners perceived, though they were framed in quite different ways by the different partners, were central. The proposal for the Treatment Acceleration Project met opposition from several bilateral donors, for example, who were concerned (among other issues) that the Catholic-inspired Sant'Egidio community was emphasizing treatment programs at the expense of prevention strategies that would involve condom promotion. What was most important, however, was the increasing focus over the life of the discussions on the underlying need to grapple with responsibilities and standards and, alongside very practical issues of procurement of drugs and financing channels, the ethical implications of the program.

Many lessons emerged from the negotiations and implementation of the Mozambique program, a complex learning venture that addressed the panoply of issues for the global AIDS program. Specifically in terms of faith development links, four facets are of particular interest. First, the complex and highly varied nature of faith-inspired organizations was significant. The Community of Sant'Egidio is sui generis in several respects, a movement, plainly faith-inspired and linked to the Catholic Church but in its technical operations highly professional in its outlook. Stereotypes about faith-based organizations held by many partners proved an important obstacle to understanding what the community did and wanted; inter alia, it led many to underestimate both its determination and its range of contacts; it also made costing difficult because Sant'Egidio relied heavily on volunteer inputs. Second, tensions between national and transnational organizations came into play. The Sant'Egidio AIDS program was born in Mozambique but expanded to other countries, and its advocacy campaign was Africa-wide. The World Bank's approach tended to be very country focused, and asymmetry in approaches to geography was difficult to handle. Third, tensions between secular and faith institutions around reproductive health rights came into play as various partners tended to cast Sant'Egidio into a "Catholic Church" role, leading to unease that a formula favoring the Sant'Egidio program could undermine AIDS prevention strategies that included condom use. Fourth, and most significant, the exchanges that led to the new treatment project were significant both in advancing technical consideration of AIDS treatment in poor-country settings and in sharpening the definition of the ethical issues involved. Issues were reframed with greater attention to the values that underlay proposed actions, including implicit trade-offs, long-term risks and commitments, and the links between rights and standards.

Sant'Egidio brings to its work on HIV/AIDS special personal and institutional qualities but also a community ethos inspired by deeply rooted but living spiritual traditions. The community has been part of a remarkable process of transforming global thinking about the HIV/AIDS pandemic and what can and above all what should be done. Its high standards, humane approach, and determination have won admirers and supporters for the programs it runs as a community, but they also have affected a wide range of approaches and programs that extend far beyond.

The Aga Khan Foundation and Early Education in the Muslim World

Not far away geographically from Mozambique, in Tanzania, Muslim communities concerned about both quality of education and the values imparted by the challenged government-run education system worked with another faith-inspired organization known worldwide for its standards of excellence and creative approach: the Aga Khan Foundation. Created by the Ismaili leader, the foundation works worldwide and is often at the forefront of new approaches and ideas. Again, its leaders and staff are inspired by a combined determination to accept nothing but the highest standards and a firm conviction that action against poverty is an imperative and is possible with sufficient will and resources.

The Tanzania story involves a modest effort to build on an Islamic school system (termed "madrasas" in East Africa) and facilities to launch a community-designed, state-of-the-art, preschool system for children in the area. The program took its cue from parents' practical worries about whether their children would succeed in school, their concerns about the values imparted to their children at school, and global research indicating that the most important educational interventions often come at a very early age. The Aga Khan Foundation provided financial support and helped in designing a structure that entailed careful monitoring of progress, highly efficient management, and full engagement of the community, especially women. The program was modest in its initial objectives, but its success has proved catching. Similar madrasa preschools are now operating in several East African countries, including Kenya and Uganda.

This experience offers a very different lens on faith development experience. First, it was primarily a community-led and local venture, which in practice is by far the most common. Second, the importance that the community gave both to its faith institutions (the madrasa system run by Islamic authorities) and to the values content of education for their children is indicative of a common thread that runs through many communities. And third, the practical partnership between the community and the global Aga Khan Foundation worked in an exemplary fashion, supporting a program that engaged the community effectively, responded to its specific concerns, and eventually moving its successful elements to a larger scale.

Fe y Alegría and Education Reform in Latin America

In Latin America, the challenge of providing quality education in the poorest communities has inspired another remarkable partnership, between the Jesuit order and its education institutions and a private foundation whose focus is on social entrepreneurship and leadership—the Avina Foundation. These improbable partners have together designed a bold and far-ranging program, known as Centro Magis (Center of Excellence), whose goal is to combine and build on the educational movement that Jesuits have led in poor communities in some sixteen Latin American countries, the Fe y Alegría system. The scope of this effort is reflected in the parallel effort of Centro Magis to strengthen networks and quality within the Jesuit-run and Jesuit-inspired universities of Latin America—there are some twenty-eight—and Jesuit social work.

The core of the Centro Magis program is a dual conviction—first, that leadership cannot succeed in failing societies, so education must be tied to social action and progress; and second, that the remarkable schools of Fe y Alegría, with a powerful community basis and impetus, stood to benefit from a gamut of modern management tools and approaches that were difficult to secure without focused support. Thus, the Avina Foundation is supporting a long-term program of learning and modernization, one that is determinedly true to the spirit of the Fe y Alegría movement yet open to transformation and change in what it hopes is the best of the "modern" spirit.

The Avina Fe y Alegría experience suggests three observations relevant to faith development dialogue and partnerships. First, it highlights the vital role that faith institutions are playing in practice in the field of education, with special reference to education in the poorest communities. Fe y Alegría educational institutions serve more than 1 million people across Latin America. Their contribution and experience are broad and could and should be better reflected in educational debates than they currently are. Second, the emphasis on values, leadership, and social change in the Fe y Alegría system reflects the ethical foundations of, in this instance, the Jesuit educational mission. The parallel concerns of Avina, a secular organization also powerfully driven by explicit focus on ethics and leadership, produced a significant synergy even as they sparked some lively debates. Third, the blend of traditional, long-proven approaches to education in the Fe y Alegría system and the ultramodern inspiration of the business methods and ethics introduced by Avina proved more compatible than many expected.

Jubilee 2000 and Global Debt Relief

A fourth example of the alchemy of unusual partnerships is the story of the Jubilee 2000 campaign, highlighted earlier in the chapter. The poor-country debt problem was long a source of worry, to bankers, to ministers of finance of countries rich and poor, and to development workers concerned about the welfare and sustainability of programs they saw languishing on the ground because of mounting financial shortfalls. Efforts to change the "rules of the game" of debt relief and cancellation were changing to meet evident needs in countries facing financial crises, but at an agonizingly slow pace, with a slowly moving consensus painfully negotiated behind closed doors when finance ministers met. The language of dialogue was highly technical, and a succession of painstakingly crafted efforts to meet the many divergent interests involved seemed endless and served to dampen any bold ideas and initiatives.

But in this seemingly unpromising soil a global social movement was planted, which in a remarkably short space of time took the technical, figures-driven discussions of debt ratios and repayment terms to an entirely different plane, where clarion calls for action were made on moral grounds. Debt burdens were tied directly to the dual sins of corruption and self-interest, and the consequences of heavy debt service obligations for poor countries were starkly presented as eating into funding available and thus spending on health and education for the poor. The core inspiration for the movement, however, was a call to ancient wisdom as reflected in the Bible: the teaching on Jubilee, which called for periodic forgiveness of debts, especially in "jubilee" years, to allow people struggling under burdens of debt to make a fresh start. The application to poor countries struggling under so many burdens of poverty seemed obvious, and many rallied to the cause who had barely considered international development issues before.

The movement that was aroused by the calls for a Jubilee by the year 2000 grew from these early seeds of reflection primarily within faith institutions. Mothers' unions, students, development activists, preachers, imams, all alike mobilized with demands for action from world leaders whenever they met, especially at the G8 meetings that gather the heads of state of the wealthiest and most powerful nations. Changes that were deemed absolutely impossible two years earlier became policy, and a range of new mechanisms were designed that allowed debt burdens to be sharply reduced in the world's poorest countries.

The specific actions on debt are in themselves a remarkable story, but what is still more inspiring is the impact of the Jubilee mobilization on broader thinking about and coalitions supporting work against poverty. The remarkable Millennium Declaration at the United Nations in September 2000 took much inspiration from the movement, as have strategic visions and practical action plans in many countries. Perhaps most important, the language of discussion of poverty has been reinfused with a sense of the ethical issues at stake, which both humanizes complex issues and offers avenues to address them.

Why Engage with Faith Institutions? The Arguments
against and Lessons Learned

Over the period 1998–2007, the engagement with faith institutions changed
in fundamental ways in many development institutions, the World Bank among
them. There is far more awareness of issues of faith today than a decade ago.
The lessons of practice highlighted in this chapter have produced an array
of experiences and demonstrated what can be achieved when new norms of
partnerships are explored and new partners engaged. Ironically, this awareness tends to be focused at two levels: institutional leadership and staff on
the ground, with considerable reticence evident at the middle management
level, in particular. Thus the engagement remains fairly limited. Perhaps most
significant, efforts to institutionalize such work and relationships, within the
World Bank but also in institutions like the United Nations Development Program (UNDP) and the British bilateral development agency, have made limited
progress.

The main reasons for limited progress are that the secular culture skeptical of religion has proved difficult to overcome, while at the same time many
faith institutions have faltered in their efforts to work with and come fully to
grips with the approach and workings of the development institutions. Briefly,
the arguments and doubts within secular organizations can be summarized
by three "D" words: religion is seen variously as dangerous, divisive, and largely
defunct. An "E" word also applies, as approaches to issues of religion often tend
to be infused with emotional, personal overtones, making debates quite unlike,
for example, those involving railroad reform. Somewhat more politically, the
three major categories of concerns can be described as the politics surrounding
religion; perceptions about generic and deep-seated approaches of some religious institutions to development; and questions about whether a systematic
dialogue with faith institutions should be a priority or is even relevant.

This discussion focuses on the reactions and "culture" of secular institutions as they have grappled with issues and institutions of religion. The reticence
of faith institutions also has played a role. Again in a simplifying formula, the
hesitations of many faith partners can be summarized by three "E" words, and
a "D" word. For many faith institutions, development institutions are seen as
part of what some describe as the "empire" of wealthy and powerful nations and
institutions that approach poverty from the vantage point of their own interests. The dominance of the governance structure of the World Bank by wealthy
countries accentuates this perception. Faith partners also point to the "effects" of
development programs, which many perceive as negative: prominent examples

are environmental damage, displacement of populations, and perceived negative consequences of economic policy reforms. Third, for many, the development institutions remain an "enigma," complex, powerful, hard to understand
and approach. For many, a summary judgment would be that the institutions
are not, as they themselves believe, altruistic and beneficial but "dangerous."[15]

The following discussion focuses on the secular institution perceptions.
Given their importance and their tenacity in development circles, they are elaborated here in some detail.

Religion is divisive. The international financial institutions, particularly the
World Bank, operate under strict injunctions to avoid political interference in
the affairs of member countries. Questions have been raised as to whether
engagement with interfaith and faith organizations could run up against that
injunction. World Bank engagement with leading faith figures and participation in global debates involving faith communities have been seen to threaten
an age-old and often hard-won separation between church and state (the *laïcité*
defended so keenly by France, in particular). And, indeed, religious politics can
be ferociously complex and even ferocious, so it is not surprising that those
who are not immersed in these worlds would hesitate to engage. Competition between faith systems seems hardwired, given the ultimate stakes (who is
saved) and shorter-term stakes (financial survival). Polite rhetoric and solemn
ritual can merely mask disdain and intolerance in some instances. And the
interplay of interfaith relations in increasingly plural societies presents new
challenges that many in the World Bank and other institutions have been hesitant to engage.

Critics have expressed concern that work with faith groups might draw the
World Bank into tensions and risks underlying fundamentalist movements.
Where religion contributes to civic conflict, the concern is that involvement—
even well intentioned—might accentuate those tensions and even promote violence. The keenest sensitivities have involved engagement by the World Bank
with Islamic leaders, but questions have also been raised as to how far the
World Bank should engage with the Catholic Church at an institutional level,
or whether faith leaders should be invited to participate in major policy consultations, and partnership arrangements in sensitive postconflict and postcrisis
situations (for example, following the 2004 tsunami).

Religion is dangerous. Deep down, many development actors see religions
as working toward a fundamentally different agenda—one largely driven by
tradition and immutable theology. These, they argue, lead faith leaders and
institutions to stand against modernization and social change in general, and
to oppose change and flexibility in the roles of women and men in particular,
especially where reproductive health is concerned. Many development workers

are also concerned that faith institutions—even if they focus on health and education—serve a limited segment of the community, excluding nonfollowers. The fact that faith groups often serve the whole community without quid pro quo is often either not known or ignored. Many cultural practices have a religious veneer, and vice versa, but disentangling the strands of culture and religion is difficult, the more so as both change—and often at different tempos. Female genital cutting is perhaps the most striking example where tightly knotted cultural and religious precepts are hellishly difficult to disentangle, but there are countless others.

Some development actors have also been reluctant to engage with faith institutions even in classic social services like health and education because of a concern that such work, however effective, is primarily motivated by a desire to gain converts. Development actors do not wish to be associated with such proselytizing activities in any fashion, while faith actors may view development agencies as undermining core cultural and religious values. The upshot has been a belief among development institutions that it was best not to engage at all with institutions so fundamentally opposed to what they see as key precepts and areas they consider of highest priority (the role of women, for example); they also see many issues like ancient traditions and rituals and approaches to sexuality as profoundly sensitive. This line of argument is especially difficult to address because these suspicions are often unspoken.

Religion is defunct. Another often-unspoken assumption among many development institutions is that as an economy grows and a society modernizes, religion becomes more peripheral and even retrograde. Taken to its extreme, this argument has contributed to a view that engagement with faith institutions is a low priority, and even unnecessary. The long-held view that prevailed in many secular institutions supported this belief in the declining role of religion, and it has taken development institutions some time to catch up with the paradigm shift that points instead to a religious resurgence at the global level and an increasing focus on religion in the public sphere. Long-held habits of thought and organization die hard. When combined with the hesitations about engaging with faith institutions because of their political character and the concern that religion might be incompatible with core development agendas, the sense that after all religion was less important than other topics facilitated a culture of neglect.

Each of these areas of doubt poses important questions and highlights areas of risk that deserve to be addressed. Indeed, dialogue on their implications has proved both sobering and enlightening, suggesting more sophisticated ways to approach the issues and highlighting important areas where research is needed. However, in recognizing the significance of the issues, it is equally important that the tensions apparent in approaches between faith and development institutions should not detract from the many real opportunities and that they should not obscure the enormous diversity that characterizes both the faith and development landscapes.

Development is at its heart political, so religion's political dimensions are hardly novel. Despite the frictions and religious fault lines that capture headlines today, the vast majority of people across the world for whom their faith plays important roles in their lives, despite widely different beliefs, live side by side in peace. The array of ecumenical and interfaith initiatives and institutions in today's world is extraordinary, and their rising number reflects the potent force of plural societies and leaders committed to respect, tolerance, and interfaith harmony. The institutions range from the global interfaith institutions like the Parliament of the World's Religions, United Religions Initiative, and Religions for Peace to a multitude of local interfaith groups, among them the Interfaith Conference of Metropolitan Washington and student interfaith groups. The assumption that faith groups cannot work together and that friction is inevitable is demonstrably false. Faith groups gain much by working together for a common end (two examples among many are interfaith efforts to build new houses organized by Habitat for Humanity and an interfaith initiative in Tanzania that has pressed for health policy reform). Such work can enhance social cohesion while diversity arguably stimulates creativity and long-term social development.

Legal and social norms guiding separation of church and state reflect both wisdom and hard politics. Yet important efforts are afoot to explore how to shift the boundaries in various contemporary settings. The development world has tended to hold highly simplified views of how religions work, and many are patently unaware of the enormous numbers of faith institutions and practices and wide differences among them. For example, international education and health targets—notably the Millennium Development Goals—barely note the major roles played by faith institutions in providing education and health services. Simply maintaining that "church" and "state" are separate is often impractical, unrealistic, unnecessary, and unwise. Debates on the evolving boundaries between church and state that rage everywhere from villages to the United Nations have implications for development programs from the micro to the macro level. These profoundly complex and sensitive issues, with roots far back in history, should enjoin us to great care and humility but need not lead us to neglect important institutions and their work.

Respect for norms regarding the roles of church and state needs to be grounded in an understanding of history and sociopolitical context country by country and even community by community, avoiding presuppositions and "models." France affords an interesting example. Centuries of religious wars have shaped contemporary approaches to immigrant communities and religious symbolism in schools (including, of course, the headscarf debates). Debates on accountability, governance, and change in many Muslim societies are colored by national and local narratives. India's creative models for building on social and faith traditions and institutions in the domain of personal law—within the bounds of basic rights—appear to work well. Morocco's pathbreaking new family code brings ancient faith traditions and modern concepts of rights together in a creative new pattern. A central conclusion is that in many, if not most, countries and in many domains of policy and practice, the intersections between faith and development and public and private spheres are numerous, and rigid efforts at separation are unrealistic and damaging. Different formulas are emerging in different places; one size does not fit all.

In response to criticisms that even well-intentioned engagement with specific faith leaders implies a political choice or judgment, the pitfalls should be recognized, but it would be foolish to allow the perceived impossibility of including all at the table to stifle relationships. Among the most practical and difficult challenges is determining who—of the host of possible choices— should participate in a dialogue, whether about health, corruption, or policies toward children. It is patently impossible to hear *all* voices, and there should be no pretense of doing so. Groups such as Religions for Peace and the Parliament of the World's Religions have invested decades in developing the understanding and consensus that enables them to aspire to representativity (as they term it). It is important to make no claims to all-inclusiveness but always to be prepared to hear new voices. That said, development practitioners do need to carefully avoid associating with advocates of violence or bitter critics of other faiths.

A more sensitive issue, perhaps, is where and how far it is wise and useful for development institutions to engage in conflict situations directly and to sit with controversial faith groups. On one side, the argument is that most conflict issues involve important socioeconomic dimensions, and cutting through vicious circles that prevent job creation and sound education is an essential element in resolving conflicts. That would argue for broad-based engagement with the parties across various sectors in search of solutions (including faith actors). The opposing argument would posit that the development institutions are poorly qualified to engage directly in conflictual negotiations. There are situations where the development institutions can play an honest broker role, putting socioeconomic issues at the center and working to establish an environment where the objective is to listen, not to judge; to understand, not to preach. A more controversial and complex issue arises when the objective is to reach beyond the circles of the "converted"—those who are already part of global interfaith networks—to include groups at the boundaries of tensions and conflicts. Generalization here is perilous, as each situation is different. Both an openness to possible new roles and great care and professionalism in such engagement would seem essential.

Development institutions can learn much by engaging with interfaith institutions and gatherings. Although deep traditions underlie theological differences, a host of dynamic leaders are working to build respect for those differences while also bridging them. Indeed, at a recent interfaith meeting, Sulak Sivaraksa, a wise Buddhist leader, commented that theologians today are increasingly open and flexible, and it is the economists who now are the least flexible in understanding other realities. This active reaching out across boundaries is essential in a globalized society because it works not for superficial harmony but for world peace and a genuine transformation in attitudes and practices springing from respect and understanding. Interfaith dialogue can lead to common ground among unlikely allies. In the United States, these alliances have allowed different faith traditions to work together to fight international trafficking of women, and advocate for sharply increased support for global programs to combat HIV/AIDS. Interfaith dialogue also offers a large ground for practical exchange and direct input, as it touches a wide range of development issues. Witness the core agenda of the 2004 Parliament of the World's Religions—debt, water, refugees, and religiously motivated violence—and the continuing Community of Sant'Egidio focus on HIV/AIDS.

Religion is complex, and countless faith institutions are at least as passionately dedicated to human development and social justice as the secular development institutions. The concerns that are summarized under the heading of "religion is dangerous" above all point to the need to raise the levels of "faith literacy" in development institutions. These institutions need to move beyond stereotypes and a veneer of passing reference to faith. There is much to learn, given the vast diversity and complexity of the religious landscape. And despite large areas of common ground, the "religious agenda" is not the same as the "development agenda." Religions are not, as Archbishop Anastasios of Albania reminded participants in one dialogue, "just other NGOs." Development and faith institutions will always confront differences, and it is important sometimes to "agree to disagree." In engaging with faith groups, development institutions have much to learn, both about the positive aspects of religion and about the clear tensions that exist. Nonetheless, it is useful to recall that most religious communities live side by side in harmony and respect. India, for example, is marked by a high degree of religious coexistence despite outbreaks of violence. Africa, too, is profoundly pluralistic, with relations among faith communities largely amicable.

The importance of religion in global and community relations is growing, not declining. The "liberal" assumption that religion will decline as incomes rise is a gross oversimplification; religion is patently not dying out. Battling this often deeply held assumption requires evidence because it often reflects personal experience: someone with a personal atheist code or bitter personal experience with the Catholic or Muslim faith may approach religion very differently from someone who finds insight and solace in a faith-based congregation.

Different agendas, visions, vocabulary, and fields of action of faith groups offer a wealth of insight from which development programs can benefit. How do faith groups experience globalization? How can development institutions reach those who feel excluded from the benefits of modernization? What do faith perspectives suggest for achieving equity and addressing national and personal indebtedness? What can development institutions learn from movements with similar agendas? Religious media also offer vast and powerful channels of communication, and development institutions can learn from how they communicate. The dynamics of change in religion reflect increasingly pluralistic societies and the potential for more personal religious practice ("bricolage," or combining beliefs in personal ways). More attention to the changing geography and demography of religion can help development institutions understand how societies change and modernize or fail to do so. Religion and human behavior are tightly associated in most societies.

Reiterating Positive Motivations for Faith Development Partnerships

Five main reasons can be advanced for working systematically to expand the faith development dialogue. Faith organizations have earned high levels of community trust. Faith institutions also work directly on key facets of socio-economic development—most significantly in education, the environment, and health. Faith institutions not only fuel many conflicts but also offer and work through a myriad of peacemaking channels, sustaining communities and spearheading the rebuilding and healing process. Such institutions often promote links among communities across national boundaries. Faith institutions also spur people to grapple with ethical issues ranging from corruption to equity. And they promote public support for development assistance and help forge consensus around hard choices.

Presence and trust. Poor communities around the world often trust faith leaders and institutions more than many other entities.[16] Given the centuries of engagement by faith groups in many dimensions of people's lives, development institutions need to hear their views and draw lessons from their experience. Religions also give hope and meaning to the lives of millions of people, and religious teachings on core values are essential to human relationships. This means that a development strategy or scheme is far more likely to succeed when faith leaders are engaged.

Active engagement in development. Some see faith as primarily about Sunday, Friday, Saturday—days set aside for worship—or funerals, marriage, baptism, and other rituals. The practical roles of religions, however, extend far beyond these pastoral activities, important as they are. Faith organizations play major roles in communities and together constitute the world's largest distribution system. We do not know precisely how many hospitals and schools faith institutions operate, how many hectares of forests and watersheds they protect, or how many orphans they care for. However, the numbers are large; some estimates put the share of faith-run hospitals in Africa at more than 50 percent. Given the primary focus of the MDGs and development agendas on health and education, dialogue and common engagement are critical in all these areas. The HIV/AIDS pandemic has particular importance. Faith institutions, leaders, and communities play major roles in both accentuating and defeating stigma—a primary vector of the disease—and are vital to devising viable strategies to combat it.

Conflict resolution, prevention, and humanitarian support. In many conflict-affected countries and regions, faith institutions are often the only surviving institutions. They run schools and hospitals even when bullets are flying and when all that is left is rubble. They rebuild after calamities; witness their key role after the December 2004 tsunami and in New Orleans after Hurricane Katrina. Whether individually or as part of interfaith alliances, faith communities also constantly engage in peacemaking activities, and their voice, consolation, and moral leadership promote healing.

Ethics and values. Faith institutions and leaders often stand as courageous leaders who "speak truth to power" and help with difficult moral transitions. Witness the role of Archbishop Desmond Tutu in fighting apartheid in South Africa, and of faith groups in confronting child soldiers, trafficked girls, female genital cutting, persecution of witches, and oppression of excluded groups. Thinking deeply about such issues is central to the calling of religious leaders, and they rely on centuries-old traditions to do so.

Global support for development agendas. Through alliances with faith communities, development leaders stand to benefit greatly from faith leadership, communication skills, and commitment to fighting poverty. Faith leadership drove the Jubilee 2000 campaign, and such moral and conceptual leadership will be essential in reaching the MDGs and achieving an even broader social justice agenda.

At its heart, the arguments for encouraging an active dialogue between faith and development institutions turn on growing recognition of enormous areas of overlap, convergence, shared concern and knowledge, and a core common purpose. Both faith and development institutions seek to work *with* poor communities to improve their lives and ensure a better future. Among their joint passions and challenges is a determination to focus on Africa and recommit the institutions and broader community to Africa. Growing awareness of critical challenges at the global level also demand such alliances. At the broadest level, we face a complex and dangerous road ahead in world affairs, and we need to travel it, where we can, together.

Dialogue and alliance are far from easy. Development circles often confuse dialogue with debate, which involves marshaling and explaining facts and hypotheses, scoring points, and even preaching. However, there is much to learn from ancient processes engrained in faith traditions, where dialogue means remaining open to learning and transformation. These traditions and that spirit will be especially important in addressing contentious areas such as gender roles, sexual ethics, contrasting visions of globalization, and approaches to global warming.

Critiques by religious leaders and institutions of the World Bank and other development institutions have helped awaken them to new ways of seeing problems and programs. The Internet and burgeoning civil society have facilitated extraordinary exchanges. We are, nonetheless, at an early stage of dialogue and common engagement. Just to give one example, while the Jubilee campaign helped bring important change to policy and approaches to poor countries, unanswered questions remain about how much debt to reschedule and forgive, and the implications of such adjustments for future financing.

Faith institutions have also promoted negative images of structural adjustment, globalization and free markets, privatization, user fees, and cash crop projects, among other knotty topics. These views are often based on what faith groups witness and experience but may lack a broader context. Constructive, experienced-based critiques are invaluable; confrontation and oversimplification are not. Participants in faith development dialogue have often advanced beyond mutual condemnation and misunderstanding to an emerging appreciation of why different views of these policies and approaches have taken hold. But there is far to go along this road.

At the Dublin meeting of faith and development leaders in early 2005, the community spoke of a covenant for action, and the global partnership of leaders from different sectors which met there expressed the fervent hope that concerted efforts could bring real results for poor communities around the world. In the words of Archbishop Diarmuid Martin, "Development is about real people, people in concrete situations; they possess one great asset, their dignity."

Conclusion

Faith and development institutions strongly agree that humanity's most critical challenge is to end acute poverty and fight for social justice. Poverty in the world today is an outrage, not only because of the misery it causes but also because we so clearly have the means to defeat it. From ancient times, wise religious leaders have taught compassion and love, have seen the faces of poor people, and have heard their voices (even when they were silent). Faith institutions have a wealth of experience, an array of instruments, infinite compassion and love, and a community of believers.

The good news is that for perhaps the first time in human history, a powerful consensus unites the global community in seeking to ensure that all people everywhere enjoy a minimally decent standard of living. The Millennium Development Goals challenge the global community to overcome the scourge of poverty, based on a covenant that involves trade reforms, more development assistance, honest use of development funds, and better governance, including citizens' participation in determining their own destinies. As James Wolfensohn, former president of the World Bank, says, "There is no place to hide" because everyone has clearly agreed to tackle poverty.

Despite this positive framework, many time-bound targets embodied in the MDGs are simply not on track. Recent reports from the UN secretary general, the World Bank, Jeffrey Sachs, head of Columbia University's Earth Institute, and others show a mixed picture and far still to go. The reasons include competing priorities among major leaders and countries (terrorism, Afghanistan, Iraq, humanitarian crises) and a failure to capture the imagination of many citizens. Faith leaders can bring special insight and conviction to the ethical dimensions of this challenge.

An important goal is to build a new kaleidoscope of alliances and partnerships between development and faith-based organizations. This effort needs to build on two major lessons from recent history: the problems we face in today's troubled world, and the motivations of human beings and institutions, are far more intricate that we often imagine. This means that all of us need to see this as our common fight and work as allies. Only then can we achieve the potential in which we have so much faith.

There is much to learn from the rich experience offered by existing faith development partnerships. These include the explorations of poverty and culture led by the WFDD; work on HIV/AIDS by Religions for Peace, Christian Aid, and Caritas; the two-year dialogue on economic models for development involving the World Council of Churches, the World Bank, and the International Monetary Fund; determined work across continents and faiths by Islamic Relief; and the work of the Alliance of Religions for Conservation. Many colleagues in the development community share a hope that these partnerships can make real the common interest in fighting poverty, protecting the environment, and building on plural cultures within global ethics and values.

At the risk of oversimplification, four dimensions are essential to the success of these partnerships: mind, heart, soul, and hands.

First, we need to look facts in the face and use them to clarify and learn. This intellectual dimension entails its own dangers, including intellectual arrogance, bogs of complexity, and cylindrical divisions among professions such as economics and business. Development leaders need to avoid the temptation to follow conventional wisdom and theory blindly, while faith leaders need to think through how ancient sources of wisdom apply to the modern world.

Second, the mind is not enough: no human endeavor can succeed without caring and compassion for those who face destitution. A focus on charity alone can lead us astray, and an emphasis on misery can lead to despair, fatalism, and romanticizing the past—perhaps the worst enemies of the heart. We need to retain the human face as an image and a sense of caring as we try to solve technical problems. We need, even in moments of crisis, to keep the causes front and center even while we help our brothers and sisters. We need to focus on relationships built on respect as well as trust. Development institutions and faith institutions alike need wise hearts.

Third, we cannot fight poverty without tending to people's spiritual dimension and its many manifestations in religious institutions, leaders, and movements. A focus on the soul can give us the wisdom to reflect more deeply on what we are trying to achieve. Soul also gives hope and meaning to daily actions and struggles, and unites faith and development communities. We need to beware of false certainty, exclusiveness, and overabstraction in the face of real problems, such as the suffering of women and children. Without this dimension, our work can be arid. The call to consider soul is a call to courage, integrity, and a sense of stewardship.

Finally, we live in times rich with rhetoric, yet too many critical aspects of human life suffer from an immense gap between rhetoric and reality. This is perhaps the most significant challenge we face: to translate our words and commitments into sustained action in the face of setbacks and competing priorities. We need to bring our hands (and our financial resources) to bear on this effort—to make sure that words lead to action. Traps abound: competing mandates, duplication of effort, lack of follow-through, and failure to respect and engage with the people affected. But the core battle entails using the many means at our disposal to translate ideas and ideals into reality.

For too long the world has parceled its challenges among head, heart, soul, or hands. As we work to create new faith development alliances, all four elements need to be engaged and intertwined. The temples are not only about heart and soul; the international institutions are not only about mind and brawn. There is far more in common, far more to share.

These are dangerous times, with dangerous roads ahead; such roads are best traveled together by those whose direction and path are essentially the same. This is a world with phenomenal opportunities, where the ancient assumption that "the poor shall always be with us" can and must be disproved. This demands urgent new thinking and action by different partners as it casts new light on ancient approaches, assumptions, and roles. Efforts to bridge the silos of work against poverty hold special importance, and none, perhaps, deserve greater attention than the areas where the worlds of religion and development coincide.

NOTES

1. The author was the officer at the World Bank responsible for the faith dialogue during the period described.

2. Two articles recount the earlier history of this story: Katherine Marshall, "Religion and Development: A Different Lens on Development Debates," *Peabody Journal of Education* 76, nos. 3/4 (2001): 339–375; and Scott Thomas, "Faith and Foreign Aid: How the World Bank Got Religion and Why It Matters," *Brandywine Review of Faith and International Affairs* 2, no. 2 (Fall 2004): 21–29.

3. http://ddp-ext.worldbank.org/ext/MDG/home.do provides background and many links describing the Millennium Declaration and Goals and their practical significance and status.

4. For a broader discussion about the World Bank, see my book, *The World Bank: From Reconstruction to Development to Equity* (London: Routledge, 2008).

5. In a review article about religion and development, Sabina Alkire notes that while the literature on religion and development is patchy, development institutions' staff often are not cognizant of material that does exist and so rediscover wheels or miss knowledge time and time again. Sabina Alkire, "Religion and Development," prepared for *The Elgar Companion to Development Studies*, ed. David Clark (Northampton, MA: Edward Elgar, 2006).

6. An exception is the Web site of the Development Dialogue on Values and Ethics, which includes a wide range of materials on the topic. See www.worldbank.org/developmentdialogue.

7. See, for example, the World Council of Churches publication *Lead Us Not into Temptation* (Geneva: WCC, 2002), prepared as a reflection on possible dialogue with the World Bank and the International Monetary Fund.

8. James Wolfensohn, "Millennium Challenges for Faith and Development," Third Annual Richard W. Snowdon Lecture at Trinity College, Interfaith Conference of Metropolitan Washington, March 30, 2004.

9. www.wfdd.org.uk. The WFDD was established as a UK charity in 2000 and reconstituted in the United States as WFDD International (a nonprofit organization) in 2006.

10. See Katherine Marshall and Richard Marsh, *Millennium Challenges for Faith and Development Leaders* (Washington, DC: World Bank, 2003).

11. Katherine Marshall and Lucy Keough, *Finding Global Balance: Common Ground between the Worlds of Development and Faith* (Washington, DC: World Bank, 2005).

12. A meeting in Uganda was planned for July 2007, but the controversy around Mr. Wolfowitz's tenure at the World Bank and his resignation in May 2007 delayed the meeting.

13. Michael Maccoby, *The Productive Narcissist: The Promise and Peril of Visionary Leadership* (New York: HarperCollins, 2003).

14. These summary accounts of experience are elaborated in greater detail in Katherine Marshall and Lucy Keough, *Mind, Heart and Soul in the Fight against Poverty* (Washington, DC: World Bank, 2004); and Katherine Marshall and Marisa Van Saanen, *Development and Faith: Where Mind, Heart and Soul Work Together* (Washington, DC: World Bank, 2007).

15. These perceptions are described in greater detail in Marshall and Van Saanen, *Development and Faith.*

16. A series of surveys led by the World Bank affirmed these high levels of trust. See Deepa Narayan, *Voices of the Poor: Can Anyone Hear Us?* (Washington, DC: World Bank, 2000).

BIBLIOGRAPHY

Alkire, Sabina. "Religion and Development." Prepared for *The Elgar Companion to Development Economics*, ed. David Clark. Northampton, MA: Edward Elgar, 2006.
Maccoby, Michael. *The Productive Narcissist: The Promise and Peril of Visionary Leadership.* New York: HarperCollins, 2003.
Marshall, Katherine. "Religion and Development: A Different Lens on Development Debates." *Peabody Journal of Education* 76, nos. 3/4 (2001): 339–375.
———. *The World Bank: From Reconstruction to Development to Equity.* London: Routledge, 2008
Marshall, Katherine, and Lucy Keough. *Finding Global Balance: Common Ground between the Worlds of Development and Faith.* Washington, DC: World Bank, 2005.
———. *Mind, Heart and Soul in the Fight against Poverty.* Washington, DC: World Bank, 2004.
Marshall, Katherine, and Richard Marsh. *Millennium Challenges for Faith and Development Leaders.* Washington, DC: World Bank, 2003.

Marshall, Katherine, and Marisa Van Saanen. *Development and Faith: Where Mind, Heart and Soul Work Together*. Washington, DC: World Bank, 2007.

Narayan, Deepa. *Voices of the Poor*. Washington, DC: World Bank, 2000–2003.

Thomas, Scott. "Faith and Foreign Aid: How the World Bank Got Religion and Why It Matters." *Brandywine Review of Faith and International Affairs* 2, no. 2 (Fall 2004): 21–29.

Wolfensohn, James. "Millennium Challenges for Faith and Development." Third Annual Richard W. Snowdon Lecture at Trinity College, Interfaith Conference of Metropolitan Washington. March 30, 2004.

World Council of Churches. *Lead Us Not into Temptation*. Geneva: WCC, 2002.

9

Peaceful Movements in the Muslim World

Thomas Michel, S. J.

Since the attacks of September 11, 2001, academicians, politicians, and journalists have tended to focus on movements within the Muslim world that promote and carry out acts of violence against civilian populations. While this concern with violence-oriented groups of Muslims is understandable, it has tended to overshadow some of the more dynamic and significant developments taking place today within the international Islamic community. In particular, it obscures the importance of transnational Muslim movements and organizations that are actively working for peace, interreligious dialogue, minority rights, education and development, religious freedom, and gender justice in the Islamic world.

Precisely because such transnational movements unequivocally and emphatically reject and condemn violence and even incline toward a radical Qur'anic pacifism, they tend to be overlooked in analyses of contemporary Islamic currents of thought, organization, and activity. Yet such movements shape the vision, motivate the commitment, and inspire the social and educational projects of millions of Muslims in many countries of the Middle East, Asia, Europe, and North America. They represent some of the most energetic and influential forces that are shaping the outlook and vision of Muslims, and point the direction that the worldwide Islamic community is heading far more accurately than do the increasingly isolated circles of those who are involved in terrorist fringe organizations.

This essay analyzes three such transnational Muslim movements and indicates the role they are playing as agents of personal and social transformation in today's globalized culture. The first is the global network, some 9 million strong, of the students of the *Risale-i Nur*, the voluminous commentary on the Qur'an authored by the twentieth-century Kurdish/Turkish thinker Said Nursi. The second movement, which is spiritually and historically related to the first, is the educational and cultural community centered about the person of the contemporary Turkish scholar Fethullah Gülen. The third is the Asian Muslim Action Network (AMAN), an organization with members in more than eighteen Asian countries that is involved in a variety of social projects and causes.

Admittedly, these phenomena are asymmetrical. The first two are communities of individual Muslims united by a common religious vision and purpose rather than organizations with bylaws and membership lists. The bond among them is reinforced by a common life lived in residences of study and formation and by the common practice of exercises of spiritual growth. They derive their inspiration, respectively, from the sermons and writings of the charismatic figures of Said Nursi and Fethullah Gülen. They began as national, and perhaps nationalist, movements in the Turkish context but have become transnational and appeal today to Muslims in many parts of the *umma*, particularly to those living in Western Europe and North America.

The third association, the Asian Muslim Action Network, is a quite different type of organization, with an intellectual background in social justice activism and progressive Islamic thought. AMAN is a young but fast-growing organization that has no single individual as founder or mentor, no national origin or ideological center. Although it has administrative offices in centrally located but predominantly Buddhist Bangkok, there is no institutional center. The norm of acting by mutual consent has a nonbinding moral force upon AMAN constituents.

This chapter explores these similarities and differences across the three movements, with particular attention to historical evolution, organizational structure, and concrete initiatives across development sectors—often in cooperation with secular states, nongovernmental organizations, and international organizations. Together, the three movements—and others like them—point to new, plural forms of Islamic action and interaction in the context of globalization and world politics.

A. Said Nursi and the *Risale-i Nur* Movement

It is impossible to understand the first movement under consideration, and perhaps also the second, without knowing something of the background of

Said Nursi (1877–1960), an outstanding Muslim thinker of the twentieth century referred to by many of his followers as "Bediuzzaman" (the Wonder of the
Age).[1] Born in the village of Nurs in the predominantly Kurdish-speaking
province of Bitlis in eastern Turkey, Nursi began his religious formation with
the study of the religious sciences in various *medreses* in eastern Turkey, where
he claims to have been influenced especially by Islamic reformers such as
Namik Kemal, Jamal al-Din Afghani, and Muhammad Abduh.[2]

As someone born in the final decades of the Ottoman Empire and reaching
maturity in the first years of the new Turkish Republic, Nursi lived and wrote
in a period of rapid social change. The national issue remained a burning one
for Turks throughout the twentieth century. What form should the successor
state to the Ottoman Empire take in the wake of World War I? What should be
the attitude of believing, practicing Muslims to secularist reforms introduced
during the early 1920s by Kemal Atatürk? What role should Islam play in the
emerging, evolving republic that was in the process of formation and solidifica-
tion? Modern Turkey has been characterized as a nation "full of the obsession
of dichotomies":[3] secularity or religiosity, modernity or tradition, science or revelation, reason or faith, state or *umma*, authority or democracy. The way that
Turks addressed these questions and responded to these dichotomies affected
their political and social position, their circle of friends and acquaintances, and
often their careers and professional life. Once having made their choices, many
Turks felt they were "trapped" in a set of ideological expectations not of their
making and were looking for a way to move forward.

In his teaching and writing, Said Nursi offered disciples a way to proceed
beyond these dead-end dichotomies in order to build a less fragmented future.
After his early experience of fighting with the Ottoman army on the Russian
front in World War I, when he was taken captive and interred in a prisoner-of-
war camp in Russia at the time of the 1917 October Revolution, Nursi ultimately
rejected both military and political solutions to the problems of the *umma*.
After early involvement at the local and national level in the politics of the
young Turkish Republic, he abandoned interest in both national politics and
geopolitical relations and devoted his life to a study of the Qur'an in the light
of modern sciences. He was to emphasize personal transformation through
study of the Qur'an as the path to regeneration of the Muslim community. In
formulating his reflections on the Qur'an in relation to the needs of modern
society, he eventually organized his extensive writings in the form of a 6,000-
page commentary on the Qur'an that he and his disciples call the *Risale-i Nur*,
the "Message of Light." In doing so, he reformulated Qur'anic teaching in such
a way as to foster a spiritual transformation in the individual Muslim that was
to be the basis for the renewal of the Muslim community.[4]

In his scholarship and teaching, Nursi's starting point was a perceived clash of worldviews represented, on the one hand, by positivist philosophy and, on the other, by religious faith. For most religious scholars of his time—and not just within Islam—modern science was a godless exercise in human pride that led people away from divine guidance into a tangle of human selfishness and ultimate damnation, whereas secular scholars coming from the philosophical tradition of the Enlightenment tended to view religion as an obscurantist mix of superstition and fairy tale, perhaps harmless of itself but dangerous when applied to politics, economics, and society. In this climate of either-or, Nursi tried to determine the role of faith in providing a needed corrective to a positivist approach to reality. He believed that the natural sciences, if divorced from a moral vision that could alone hold them together and give them direction, would lead inevitably to egoism, violence, and both destructive and self-destructive behavior. It was the role of revealed truth to help modern society to avoid spiritual disaster by forming people with a moral vision in which, as he states: "Conscience is illuminated by the religious sciences, and the mind is illuminated by the sciences of civilization. Wisdom occurs through the interaction of these."[5]

Serif Mardin argues that the task Nursi set himself was to reformulate the popular explanations of the cosmos that abounded in Ottoman literature in ways that would confirm and reinforce modern scientific discoveries. The challenge went beyond finding intimations in Qur'anic verses of airplanes, bacteria, and subatomic particles, and other modern scientific and technological phenomena, a preoccupation of some of his colleagues. Rather, Nursi sought to use traditional imagery in order to create a readiness among Muslims to appreciate scientific discoveries and to accept the results of empirical data. By framing natural phenomena in a mythic and poetic setting, in keeping with the Muslim mystic tradition, and stressing "the creative power of God," Said was able to create the feeling that the contents of the Qur'an opened up a view of a universe in movement and that this could be used to build a new image of the cosmos. Through affective resonances that fastened on the evocative power of the style of the Qur'an, such a new resource was made available to persons who, in the past, would have been passive participants in the "miracle" of the Qur'an."[6]

Nursi's effort to reconcile religious faith with scientific knowledge helps account for the disproportionate number of those trained in the secular sciences, particularly in engineering and medicine, within contemporary movements inspired by Nursi's thought. This interest in and respect for the natural sciences can also be seen in the strong emphasis on the sciences in the schools later set up and administered by his followers. Nursi's conviction of the need to build a united body of knowledge compiled both from the study of the religious disciplines and from the "sciences of civilization" led him to reformulate traditional Islamic thought in terms of the demands of modernity. The approach had enduring consequences. His writings have been translated into more than thirty languages and are studied and discussed systematically in schools and study groups that now constitute a transnational network.

Three themes within Nursi's thought are particularly relevant to contemporary issues around religious pluralism, globalization, and world politics: his views on *peace*, his *critique of modern civilization*, and his call to *Muslim-Christian unity*. These elements distinguish Nursi and his followers from many other modern Muslim movements.

Toward a Qur'anic Pacifism

Although in his youth Nursi's understanding of jihad led him to defend the Ottoman state against the Russian invasion of the Caucasus, Nursi later declared that the time of the "*jihad* of the sword" was over, and the pressing need of the modern age was a "non-physical *jihad*," or what he called "the *jihad* of the word." He concluded that the resort to violence showed a lack of self-confidence in the truth brought by Islam.[7] It is tempting to speculate that his pacifist position was strongly influenced by the traumatic experience of World War I, which was even more severe in Turkey than for the "lost generation" of western Europe and resulted in a net 30 percent decline in the population of Anatolia.[8] Nursi's reflections on the debacle led him to reformulate the Islamic concept of "martyr" to include all those innocent victims of violence, Christian as well as Muslim, who perished in the slaughter.[9]

Nursi articulated a sophisticated critique of militarism and nationalism that still resonates today. In his writings Nursi accused modern governments of consciously fomenting a kind of false nationalism, which amounts to a type of racism, by picturing those of another nationality or religion as the enemy against whom war must be waged. Meanwhile, the governments concentrate on providing amusements to distract people by promoting sense gratification and favoring consumerist market policies to "create needs." The result, for Nursi, was a sort of superficial happiness for the elite few while casting the rest into distress and poverty. Nursi further observed that ruling parties and cliques often actually *foment* conflicts and wars in an attempt to increase their popularity and rally support for what otherwise would be unpopular or incompetent regimes. He held up the Qur'an as a superior model of behavior, an alternative to the use of force to resolve conflicts centered on negotiation, compromise, and uprightness, rather than the employment of brute force oriented toward the very shortsighted goal of "winning the war."

Nursi's criticism of materialist tendencies in society and politics and his opposition to Turkey's engagement in wars and unholy alliances caused him to be imprisoned repeatedly. His opposition to war as an inhumane and ultimately useless endeavor aroused much opposition for, in the Turkish Republic as elsewhere, citizens were expected to support whatever wars were being waged, and anyone opposing the war was accused of disloyalty. His critics claimed that war against foreign incursions provided an opportunity to revive Islamic zeal and to assert the moral strength of the nation. They charged Nursi, who proposed prayers for peace and negotiated settlement, with indirectly supporting the invaders' aims.[10] Nursi clarified that he opposed foreign aggression, but that he rejected the practice of opposing force by force, holding that religion teaches people to seek truth and uprightness, not to try to achieve their aims through violence. Nursi was convinced that students of the *Risale-i Nur* could make better use of their time by studying the Qur'an than by engaging in military service. As he put it toward the end of his life: "I swear that if one of you were to insult me terribly and entirely trample my honor but not [make me] give up serving the Qur'an, belief, and the *Risale-i Nur*, I would forgive him, make peace with him, and try not to be offended."[11]

Critique of Modern Civilization

One of the most difficult challenges facing the modern Muslim in twentieth-century Turkey was how to grapple with a secular, modern civilization. Atatürk had adopted the institutions of European civilization; the Islamic practices and way of life that had been handed down for centuries were regarded as relics of the past and obstacles to progress. The spontaneous reaction of many religious leaders was simply to condemn the Republic as atheist and depraved and to call for a return to traditional religious values. Nursi's analysis was more subtle and articulated. He acknowledges that modern life is a bewildering mix of contradictions. There is much in modern civilization that is attractive, much that is useful and that makes life easier, more comfortable, and more enjoyable. At the same time, anyone who takes seriously the gift of religious faith is aware that modern civilization often sets itself in opposition to a life of faith and obedience to God.

For believers, it is not simply that modern civilization tends to exile God to the margins of daily consciousness and activity. Modern civilization also offers a value system that is at odds with that of faith. It defines happiness differently from religious thought; success and failure are counted in different terms. Selffulfillment is regarded as a basic human motivation, and possession of consumer goods is considered a mark of personal achievement. It follows that competition becomes the moving force of modern life, and the world comes to be divided into the winners and the losers. Those for whom God is the beginning, the center, and the end of existence, and for whom God's will is the criterion of good and evil, need a way to sort out what is valuable in modern civilization from what is ephemeral and destructive. Perhaps the greatest achievement of Said Nursi and the *Risale-i Nur* was to provide modern Muslims with the interpretive tools needed to analyze modern civilization and distinguish the genuine and lasting value in modern life from its harmful and self-destructive tendencies.

In numerous passages in the *Risale-i Nur*, Nursi points up the contrast between the societal values proposed by modern civilization and the vision of society presented by the Qur'an. To Nursi the Qur'anic vision differs only in details from what had been proposed by all the prophets before Muhammad; hence it is a vision that Muslims share with "true Christians" who genuinely follow the teachings of the prophet Jesus. Jesus' Christian followers sought to build Europe on these prophetic values, but this effort was sabotaged from the beginning by their reliance on Greco-Roman philosophy. This insight into a spiritual affinity with committed Christians, rare among Muslim scholars, is the basis of Nursi's call for "Muslim-Christian unity," which has had profound effects on the thinking and practice of his disciples.

The Need for Muslim-Christian Unity

Said Nursi's advocacy of an intellectual and spiritual dialogue between Muslims and Christians dates back to 1911, a half century before the Catholic Church's Second Vatican Council urged Christians and Muslims to move beyond the conflicts of the past to build relations characterized by respect and cooperation. It is a sad fact of human history that Christians and Muslims, despite their nature as communities called to worship and obey the one and same God, have often been in conflict and even at war with one another. Energies that should have been employed to cooperate in the establishment of God-centered societies have been dissipated in mutual suspicion, domination, and bloodshed. Nursi's repeated promotion of Muslim-Christian dialogue was even more striking in that his recommendations frequently date from periods of tension and even warfare between Muslim and Christian communities.

At the end of World War I, for example, he affirmed the right of Christian Greeks and Armenians to liberty as something commanded by the *shari'a* and called upon both Muslim and Christian to recognize the deeper problem as a state of moral and spiritual degradation.[12] The real enemies facing Muslims and Christians, he held, were not one another but the prevalence in the modern world of ignorance, poverty, and disunity.

Ultimately, for Nursi, the opponent of human happiness and ethical uprightness was unbelief. Unbelief is not only theoretical but practical, manifested in people choosing to find their own path through life, not seeking divine guidance, not caring about God's will or wise design for humankind, not wishing to give up their own pet desires and ideas to submit to God's teaching about human nature and destiny. Nursi held that in seeking to affirm a divinely guided way of life in the modern age, Muslims find their natural partners in those Christians who are committed to following the teachings of Jesus. Facing the challenge of "aggressive atheism," he states, "Muslims should unite not only with other Muslims, but also with the truly pious Christians."[13] For such a common effort to succeed, Christians and Muslims would have to refrain from disputes between these two families of believers. Said Nursi was not denying theological differences between Muslims and Christians or their significance. His point is that concentrating obsessively on differences can blind both Muslims and Christian to the more important common task they share, that of offering the modern world a vision of human life and society in which God is central and God's will informs moral values and action.

Nursi articulated these themes with increasing intensity during the post–World War II decades. On many occasions he warned of efforts to destroy both Muslims and Christians by alienating them from the source of spiritual and moral values and by creating enmity between them. In 1945–1946, for example, he underscored the joint danger posed for pious Christians and Muslims by atheistic communism. "The current from the North," he warned, in a clear reference to the Soviet Union of Josef Stalin, "would try to destroy the accord of Islam and the missionaries."[14] Over the next decade, until his death in 1960, Nursi was adamant that Christian-Muslim relations should move in the direction of peace, reconciliation, and even friendship. To this end, in 1950 he sent a collection of his works to Pope Pius XII in Rome and received in reply, in February 1951, a personal letter of thanks.[15] A few years later, in 1953, Nursi visited the Ecumenical Patriarch Athenagoras in Istanbul to pledge friendship and seek cooperation between Muslims and Christians in facing the challenges of the modern age.

Said Nursi held that if they seek to root their mutual relations in love, Muslims and Christians together can build a civilization according to God's plan in which human dignity, justice, and fellowship are the norm. "That which is most worthy of love," he wrote, "is love, and that most deserving of enmity is enmity. It is love and loving that render people's social life secure and that lead to happiness."[16] He concluded: "The time for enmity and hostility is finished."

Influence upon His Followers

When Nursi died at the age of eighty-four, he was buried in Urfa near the traditional birthplace of the prophet Abraham. The military, fearing that if his place
of burial were known, the tomb would become a site of pilgrimage and mobilization among his followers, secretly disinterred his body during the night.
While Nursi's final burial place remains unknown, his followers have grown
in the decades since his death. They refer to themselves as the students of the
Risale-i Nur, although outsiders often use, in a somewhat pejorative sense, the
term "Nurcu." Those in the movement dislike the term because they do not
consider themselves a sect or the followers of an individual, but rather orthodox
Muslim students of the Qur'an, guided by Nursi's commentary. Moreover, the
movement has split into various communities, each with its own activities, methods, and circles of influence. "The center of the religious market in Turkey,"
Massimo Introvigne explains, is occupied by "the greatest novelty in Turkish
religious history: a dozen Nurcu communities claiming the heritage of Said
Nursi's reformism."[17]

The *Risale-i Nur* students were kept under close surveillance by the military
in Turkey until the mid-1980s. Some were arrested, others were blacklisted
and prevented from entering universities or obtaining jobs. Their homes and
dormitories were raided for handwritten copies of the *Risale-i Nur*, which was
forbidden to be published and passed from hand to hand as a kind of samiz-
dat. Today the movement is no longer persecuted in Turkey and carries out its
activities openly. The *Risale-i Nur* has been published in its entirety in Turkish,
and parts have been translated into many languages.

In the 1980s, the movement spilled out of Turkey, mainly by means of
Turkish immigrants to northern and Western Europe. In the 1990s it reached
the former Soviet nations of the Caucasus and Central Asia, and most recently
is extending its activities into Southeast Asia. In two regions of the Muslim
world, namely, the Arab world and the countries of South Asia, the *Risale-i Nur*
has not met with considerable success.

A reliable estimate of the number of adherents to the Nur movement falls
somewhere between 5 and 6 million members,[18] although some estimates run
as high as 9 million. The students of the *Risale-i Nur* meet twice a week in
more than 5,500 *dershanes* (study hall) worldwide to study and discuss the
Risale-i Nur. Study groups have grown up as far afield as Manila in the Philippines, Kuala Lumpur in Malaysia, Makassar and Palembang in Indonesia, and
New Jersey and Texas in the United States. The movement is propagated on

the Internet by a variety of independently run Web sites (e.g., www.nur.web.tr/
english/, www.risale-inur.com.tr/rnk/eng/risale_eng.htm, www.saidnursi.com/
symposium/s21.html) and conducts seminars on the thought of the *Risale-i
Nur* in many predominantly Muslim countries.

What is significant is the influence that the ideas of Said Nursi have had
in shaping the attitudes of the members of this movement. Their measured
critique of modern civilization, their peace activism, and their openness to dialogue with Christians can all be traced to key themes of the *Risale-i Nur*. I con-
clude this section with an e-mail I received on the occasion of the death of
Pope John Paul II, from a young Turkish member of the movement who was
doing his year of compulsory military service. The letter clearly expresses the
way Said Nursi's central areas of concern have formed the thinking of a typical
disciple. I have not revised his broken English:

> I read in newspaper that Papa John Paul II was past a way. . . .
> I was so sorry . . . I started to pray for him, "*Inna lillahi wa inna
> ileyhi raciun*" (we came from God and to Him we will return). He
> returned to Him. . . . He returned to Him with thousands of good
> deeds . . . and for me, the most important thing he worked for peace,
> that means he worked for children, innocent people . . . for us . . . for
> dialogue, for tolerance . . . for understanding . . . for unity . . . during
> his life time, he was always with God and I hope that after this life
> God always will be with him.
>
> Please pray for me also . . . I wanna get out from army as soon as
> possible. . . . I don't wanna carry gun, I wanna carry my books, *Risale-i
> Nur*, Qur'an, Holy Bible, instead of bomb and guns. . . . I hope I can
> meet and talk with you again. . . . I need your prayers. . . . Sincerely,
> your brother Muhammed.

In the long run, Nursi concluded, a preoccupation with international crises was
less important than seeking the personal, interior transformation that comes
through the study of scripture. This attitude, which places a higher value on
the transformational power of the study of God's Word than on current events,
presents a challenge to modern people for whom the daily newspapers and
evening news on television are fixed appointments in their daily schedules.
However, one can see in Said Nursi's position the freedom of the honest individual who renounces an obsession with transitory events that will be forgotten
in a few years in favor of the search for eternal, unchangeable truth presented
in the Word of God.

The Gülen Movement

The second transnational Islamic movement to be studied is that associated with the name of Fethullah Gülen, who is simultaneously the founder, leader, and teacher of the movement. Like that of the readers of the *Risale-i Nur*, the Gülen community is also inspired by the thoughts and writings of Said Nursi, but there are some significant differences between the two movements.

Like Said Nursi, Fethullah Gülen was born and educated in the far eastern region of Anatolia, in the city of Erzurum. He began his career as a teacher of religion and a preacher in the mosques, first in eastern Anatolia and then in Izmir. In 1958, at the age of twenty, Gülen became aware of the writings of Said Nursi, which had a formative influence upon his thinking.[19] Another scholar has noted that the encounter with Nursi's thought enabled Gülen to transcend the Anatolian issues that had previously dominated his thinking: "He [Gülen] became aware of Nursi's writings in 1958, which facilitated his shift from a particular localized Islamic identity and community to a more cosmopolitan and discursive understanding of Islam. Nursi's writings empowered him to engage with diverse epistemological systems."[20]

Gülen became a teacher of Qur'an studies in the Mediterranean city of Izmir, and it was in that modern, cosmopolitan environment that the movement had its origins. In the 1970s, by means of lecturing in mosques, organizing summer camps, and erecting "lighthouses" (dormitories for student formation), Gülen began to build a community of religiously motivated students trained in both the Islamic and the secular sciences. In the highly polarized atmosphere of the time, the community took on an anticommunist stance and espoused a conservative brand of Turkish nationalism.

The importance that the lighthouses (*ışık evler*), residences (*yurts*), and *dershanes* play to this day in the formation and cohesion of the movement must not be underestimated. Students not only supplement their secular studies in high school and prepare for university entrance examinations but also form friendships and a network of social relations; in addition, they receive spiritual training through the study of the Qur'an and the *Risale-i Nur* and pursue their educational goals in a social environment free from the use of alcohol, drugs, smoking, premarital sex, and violence.

The Gülen community gradually began to move in a direction distinct from the original thrust of the *Risale-i Nur* movement, as Gülen himself produced new *ijtihads* that distinguished the community from that of the original students of the *Risale-i Nur*. Nursi had focused on personal renewal of the Muslim through the study of the Qur'an and wanted to help the modern believer move beyond the dichotomies omnipresent in Turkish society of his day through a spiritual transformation that would come about by the study of the *Risale-i Nur*.

By contrast, for Gülen and the community associated with his name, personal transformation is secondary to social transformation. In both cases personal transformation is oriented toward reforming and reshaping society, but while for Nursi the emphasis is on the individual Muslim who must be changed through an enlightened encounter with the Qur'an in the *Risale-i Nur*, in Gülen's vision it is the social effect of conscientious, dedicated, committed Muslim social agents that is the key to renewal of the Islamic *umma*. Whereas for Nursi the key term is "study," the central idea of Gülen is "service." Members of the Gülen community hope to change society through a holistic pattern of education that draws from and integrates disparate strands of previous pedagogical systems. Although Nursi was already aware of the limitations of traditional systems of education available to Muslims in Turkey, it was Gülen and his movement that gave their time and energy to working out an effective alternative.

From Turkish Student Initiative to Transnational Movement

In the new social and economic climate that emerged in Turkey during the presidency of Turgut Özal, the Gülen movement grew from a small number of students in a few cities like Izmir to a huge educational endeavor with important business and political links. Although stemming from a broadly conceived religious motivation, the schools are not traditional "Islamic" schools but secular institutions of high quality, as shown by the performance of students in science olympiads and the like.

In the 1980s, the community moved beyond its schools into the media with the publication of a daily newspaper, *Zaman*, and a television channel, Samanyolu. Today *Zaman* is published in twenty countries with an average circulation of a half million. In all, about thirty-five newspapers and magazines in various languages are projects of the Gülen community. The monthly journal in Turkish, *Sizinti*, the longest continuously published Islamic magazine in Turkey, with a circulation of more than 500,000, has enjoyed uninterrupted publication since 1979; the English version, *Fountain*, has worldwide circulation in the tens of thousands. The influential weekly newsmagazine *Aksiyon* is a Turkish equivalent of *Time* or *Newsweek*. In addition, the community puts out a number of professional journals, for doctors, engineers, teachers, and so forth.

The movement has addressed the thorny question of the secular state in Turkey. The Writers' and Journalists' Foundation, which is associated with the

Gülen movement, set up in the 1990s the Abant Workshops in which Turkish intellectuals, politicians, and journalists from every ideological stance were brought together to study and discuss issues related to Turkish state and society. These Abant sessions were intended to "head off sociopolitical polarization and to search for a new social consensus in Turkey. The annual workshops have included about fifty Turkish intellectuals from sharply different ideological backgrounds."[21]

After the fall of communism in the Soviet Union and Eastern Europe in 1989, the Gülen community was a key player in filling the gap in the educational system. Hundreds of schools and universities were set up throughout the former Soviet republics, both within the Russian Federated Republic (particularly in its predominantly Muslim regions such as Tatarstan, Yakutia, and Chechnya), in the newly independent nations of the Caucasus and Central Asia, and in the predominantly Muslim and pluralist regions of the Balkans such as Albania, Macedonia, Bosnia, Moldova, Bulgaria, and Kosovo. Television programs were prepared that were destined to be aired in the vast reaches of Central Asia, and scholarships were granted for study in Turkey.

The new century saw a further expansion of the educational activities of the Gülen community as it moved beyond the boundaries of Muslim-majority regions into China, Western Europe, North and South America, Africa, and Southeast Asia. The primary but not exclusive focus was on educating migrants from Turkey and other Muslim countries. Here the pedagogical approach underwent some adaptation. In many parts of Western Europe, the economic and bureaucratic difficulties of opening and supporting new schools discouraged and often prevented this activity. Moreover, in these regions, the movement often encountered a level of education of high quality. The educational task became not so much one of competing with the existing national public school systems but that of ensuring that immigrant Turks and others would have an adequate educational background to be able to compete and succeed in the government schools. Thus, in many parts of Western Europe, the Gülen community in its educational efforts has focused on weekend classes and tutorials aimed at supplementing the instruction given in the state schools and at preparing for standardized exams.

In the schools associated with the movement in the United States, located mainly in regions with a high concentration of Turkish Americans, the challenge has been to provide an opportunity for students to attain a high level of academic achievement. In fact, particularly in scientific fields, in states like New Jersey and Texas, educational institutions run by members of the Gülen movement have been among the most highly awarded schools in the state. These are not "Islamic schools" in that even though their inspiration is found in enlightened Islamic ideals, both the teaching and administrative staff and the student body are made up of the followers of other religions as well as of Muslims. In some cases, religious instruction is offered once a week, whereas in other cases religion is not taught in the schools.

The most recent figures show more than 600 schools and six universities,[22] in seventy-five countries on five continents.[23] The schools do not form a centralized "school system." Each school is established and run by individual members of the Gülen community in a privately registered and funded foundation. The teachers receive a common spiritual training and are sent to wherever the need is considered the greatest, but there is no central governing board that sends out instructions on educational policy, curriculum, or discipline. Rather, each school is "twinned" with a particular city or region in Turkey, which undertakes financial responsibility for the new school.

Gülen's genius does not lie so much in reinterpreting the teaching of the Qur'an as in applying traditional Islamic prescriptions in entirely new ways to respond to constantly changing social needs. According to the Albanian scholar Bekim Agai:

> The schoolteacher becomes a prophet who fulfills Islamic principles
> by imparting knowledge. The key point for Gülen is that the Islamic
> principles are unchanging, and yet must be given concrete form in
> each new era. Once, a Qur'an course might have been the best way
> to invest Islamic donations, but [today] other Islamic activities take
> precedence. He succeeds in gaining support in conservative Islamic
> circles for new Islamic fields of action by using traditional Islamic
> terminology and defining his terms conventionally, but at the same
> time furnishing them with innovative implications for the present
> day. He argues that questions of morality and education are more
> essential for today's Islam than are political issues, and that present-
> day Muslims are confronted with entirely different problems than the
> question of whether or not to introduce the *shari'a*.[24]

Commitment to Dialogue

The community inherited its commitment to interreligious dialogue and cooperation from the writings of Said Nursi in the *Risale-i Nur*, but this commitment has been renewed and given new impetus in the writings of Fethullah Gülen. In his speech in 1999 at the Parliament of the World's Religions in Capetown, Gülen presented an optimistic vision of interreligious harmony: "It is my conviction that in the future years, the new millennium will witness unprecedented religious blooming and the followers of world religions, such as Muslims, Christians, Jews, Buddhists, Hindus and others, will walk hand-in-hand to build a promised bright future of the world."[25]

Already beginning in 1911 and repeatedly down to his death in 1963, Said Nursi called for "Muslim-Christian unity" to oppose godless tendencies in modern societies. While endorsing Nursi's appeal, Gülen goes beyond Nursi's view in two important respects. First, dialogue and unity are not limited to "the good Christians," as Nursi had proposed, but are now to be extended to the conscientious followers of all religions. Second, the motivation for this dialogue is not simply a strategic alliance to oppose atheistic and secularizing tendencies in modern life, as Nursi had held, but is called for by the nature of Islamic belief itself:

> The goal of dialogue among world religions is not simply to destroy scientific materialism and the materialistic worldview that has caused such harm. Rather, the very nature of religion demands this dialogue. Judaism, Christianity, and Islam, and even Hinduism and Buddhism pursue the same goal. As a Muslim, I accept all Prophets and Books sent to different peoples throughout history, and regard belief in them as an essential principle of being Muslim.[26]

To further its pursuits of interreligious dialogue, the Gülen movement has created the Intercultural Dialogue Platform (IDP) as a project of the movement's Istanbul-based Writers and Journalists Foundation. The IDP has been particularly active in sponsoring and organizing "Abrahamic" encounters with high-ranking representatives of Judaism, Christianity, and Islam. The Gülen movement also organizes associations for the promotion of interreligious activities at the local and regional level, such as the Cosmicus Foundation in the Netherlands, the Australian Intercultural Society in Melbourne, the Friede-Institut für Dialogue in Vienna, the Interfaith Dialog Center of Patterson, New Jersey, Houston's Institute of Interfaith Dialog, and the Niagara Foundation of Chicago, all of which take independent initiatives toward promoting interreligious understanding and cooperation.

The Asian Muslim Action Network

The third organization under consideration is the Asian Muslim Action Network (AMAN). In structure and orientation, AMAN is quite different from both the followers of Said Nursi, and the movement associated with Fethullah Gülen. By contrast with those communities, AMAN does not focus on the teaching of a charismatic individual, nor does it arise out of the historical and cultural experience of being Muslim in a single nation or culture.

AMAN has been, from its inception, an international network of progressive Muslims in eighteen Asian countries, bringing together "individuals, groups and associations of Muslims in Asia subscribing to a progressive and enlightened approach to Islam."[27] It was founded in October 1990 by a small but influential group of Muslim scholars and social activists in order to respond, as is stated in the AMAN charter, to the numerous challenges faced by the peoples of Asia "ranging from mass poverty to elite corruption, materialistic life style, increasing ethnic, religious, and communal conflict, violence against women and children, and environmental degradation."[28] From this list of concerns, it can be seen that the scope of the organization is quite wide, addressing both structural issues and those requiring personal renewal.

At the Second Plenary Assembly of AMAN, held in Dhaka, Bangladesh, in the year 2000, on the tenth anniversary of the organization's founding, Dr. Asghar Ali Engineer of Bombay, India, the chairman of AMAN, noted the motivation for creating the network: "With the advent of democracies in South and Southeast Asian nations, awareness about democratic rights, human rights, and women's rights has been growing fast. However, although there was a great deal of secular theorizing on the issue, there was a lack of Islamic theorizing, and still less of activism."[29] In other words, AMAN is responding to the need felt by progressive Muslims in Asia to reflect on questions of poverty, democracy, civil rights, human rights, and the rights and status of women from an explicitly Islamic point of view, as well as the need for Muslim activists to work for those rights.

In the fifteen years since its creation, the organization has grown quickly. In addition to individual memberships in eighteen Asian countries, seventy-six local and national Muslim organizations in Asia have become members of AMAN. Local chapters have been established in Afghanistan, Bangladesh, Cambodia, Indonesia, India, Malaysia, Pakistan, the Philippines, and Sri Lanka, and its programs include the active participation of Muslims in China, Iran, and the republics of Central Asia.

The plenary assemblies, held every three years, are not business meetings so much as a convergence of workshops and study sessions. At the Third Plenary Assembly, held in Bangkok in December 2003, participants from twenty-one Asian nations took part. The program included workshops titled "The Culture of Peace" (with 1,300 national and international participants), "Multi-ethnic Asia" (260 participants), "Interfaith Dialogue" (2,600 participants), "Women and Peace" (56 participants), "Youth for Peace" (370 participants), "Poverty and Peace" (42 participants), and "HIV/AIDS" (670 participants).

AMAN has published more than twenty books on topics of concern, mainly focusing on themes of peace and Islamic renewal in Asia. Its publications include *Culture of Peace, New Visions for Peace, Understanding Peace and Conflict Transformation: A Religious Perspective, Islam and Modern Challenges*, and a *Resource Book on HIV/AIDS Prevention*. Its latest project is the monthly AMANA news service, which has, up to now, produced fifteen issues.

AMAN is quite open to working together in shared programs with other organizations, as well as with bodies linked with one or another religion in Asia. As such, AMAN has undertaken joint initiatives with Christians on peace education and on questions of justice for ethnic minorities; with the Federation of Asian Bishops' Conferences, a continental association of seventeen Catholic bishops' conferences in Asia; and with the Christian Conference of Asia, an ecumenical body composed of more than 120 churches and synods, of Orthodox and Reformation origin, in Asia.

AMAN's approach to Islamic practice is what a senior council member of the organization, the Malaysian political scientist Chandra Muzaffar, calls a "values approach to Islam," which he contrasts to a *fiqh* (i.e., jurisprudential) approach, with its "rigid religious-secular dichotomy." Muzaffar states: "It is only too apparent that a non-dogmatic approach to Islam which recognizes the primacy of eternal, universal spiritual and moral values while acknowledging the importance of rituals, symbols and practices is the most sane and sensible way of living religion in today's world. I describe this as the values approach to Islam."[30]

AMAN activists can trace their roots to figures in Islamic history who emphasized the values of "justice, honesty, sincerity, compassion, and simplicity of life" over legalistic and ritualistic prescriptions. It is instructive to see the individuals whom Muzaffar holds up as models of Islamic life for modern Muslims. Among the forerunners to be emulated by value-oriented Muslims today he mentions Ali ibn Abi Talib, the son-in-law of Muhammad who refused to engage in battle against other Muslims; the caliph Umar ibn Al-Khattab, noted for his commitment to just governance; the early ascetic Abu Dharr al-Ghiffari; the twentieth-century educational reformer Muhammad Abduh; more recent Muslim thinkers such as the Indo-Pakistani Muhammad Iqbal, the Algerian Malik Benabi, and the Pakistani American Fazlur Rahman; mystics like Mevlana Jalal al-Din Rumi, Ibn Arabi, and Shabistari; and distinguished Muslim scholars like Fakhr al-Din Razi, Ibn Sina, Ibn Rushd, and Ibn Khaldun, who "came into conflict with religious elites who derived their authority from perpetuating an Islam built around rituals, symbols, and practices." In modern times, Abdul Ghaffar Khan, the Pathan nationalist and educator, Gandhian organizer, and committed Islamic pacifist who died in 1988, has provided inspiration for the movement.

One of the most effective projects of AMAN is its educational work with Asian youth. The organization conducts training courses and youth camps focused on developing Muslim leadership that can address the principal AMAN concerns of poverty; social justice; environmental degradation; human rights; questions of peace, harmony, and reconciliation; and development issues and advocacy on behalf of "marginalized and vulnerable sectors of society such as women, children, and ethnic and religious minorities." Recent seminars and workshops have included the following topics: "Community-Based Peace Education," "Preventive Education on HIV-AIDS," and "Human Rights from an Islamic Perspective." In 2003, AMAN instituted the School of Peace Studies and Conflict Transformation, an annual course to train peace advocates in the techniques of conflict analysis and reconciliation. AMAN undertakes "training for trainers" workshops to prepare local and national animators and, through its Asian Resource Foundation subsidiary, annually awards scholarships for researchers working on questions in the previously mentioned fields; almost 500 activists have taken part in these leadership training courses. In recent years, AMAN's Research Fellowship Program has funded the research of twenty-two young Muslims on topics related to the general theme "Islam in Southeast Asia: Views from Within."

The stated concern for the "marginalized and vulnerable" has brought AMAN into the area of human rights. In 2001, in response to the decision of the General Assembly in Dhaka, the organization set up AMAN Watch as a regional Muslim expression of human rights concerns, which monitors human rights violations in predominantly Muslim regions of Asia, as well as the violation of the civil rights of Muslims in both majority and minority situations. AMAN Watch is one of the cooperating associations in the Hong Kong–based Asian Human Rights Commission (AHRC) and the Religious Groups for Human Rights (RGHR) association, which is an Asian coalition of Buddhist, Muslim, and Christian organizations advocating human rights.[31]

AMAN has given particular attention to the situations of ethnic and religious minorities. Most countries of Asia have minority groups distinguished from the majority by language, religion, race, or cultural background. Almost invariably, such groups suffer various forms of discrimination: the minority groups are often mistrusted and unwelcome in the dominant national society, treated with bureaucratic resistance and indifference, and in some instances subjected to violence and persecution. The fact that their native language and religion are usually not those of the dominant majority (Hindus in Pakistan, Christians and indigenous in India, Buddhists in Bangladesh, Muslims in

China, Christians in Myanmar, Muslims and indigenous in the Philippines, etc.) further isolates the ethnic minorities. AMAN championed the cause of the minorities by publicizing their plight and complaints at both the Dhaka and the Bangkok assemblies. Together with their Christian partners—the Federation of Asian Bishops' Conferences (FABC) and the Christian Conference of Asia (CCA)—AMAN has proposed an Asia-wide consultation on the situation of ethnic minorities and has announced plans for a joint study of the forms of discrimination experienced by Bangladesh's Chittagong Hill Tract tribes.

In contrast to the persuasive influence that Said Nursi and Fethullah Gülen have played in the movements they inspired, AMAN has no single intellectual mentor but is guided by a constellation of prominent Asian Muslim scholars. A survey of some of the more important figures will give an idea of the intellectual background and orientation of AMAN leadership.

Asghar Ali Engineer, AMAN chairman, is an Indian Muslim. The son of a religious scholar of a prominent Bohra (Ismaili) family, Asghar Ali was trained in the religious sciences and also in engineering, hence the name. He has been a fervent advocate of reform in the Bohra community (for which he was once set upon by paid thugs and beaten severely) and has written extensively on communal violence, women's rights, liberation theology, pluralism, and the role of Islam in secular societies.

Other leaders of AMAN are of varied background but are united in the conviction of the need for progressive Muslims in Asia to speak with one voice and to act in concert. Chandra Muzaffar is a political scientist from Malaysia who is president of the International Movement for a Just World or simply, as it is usually called, JUST. Professor Azyumardy Azra, rector of the Islamic State University of Indonesia, Dr. Carmen Abu Bakar, director of University of the Philippines' Institute of Islamic Studies, and Dr. Suzaina Abdul Kadir of the National University of Singapore are serving as advisers for the Research Fellowship Program. Imtiyaz Yusuf, a British Muslim of Indo-Pakistani origin with a doctorate in Islamic studies from Princeton University, is director of AMAN's School for Peace Studies and Conflict Transformation. Professor Chaiwat Satha-Anand is a Thai professor of political science and a well-known professor of peace studies; for some years, he has directed the International Peace Research Association's (IPRA) commission on nonviolence. Habib Chirzin is an Indonesian community organizer and human rights activist based in Jakarta and president of the Islamic Millennial Forum. The general secretary, Abdus Sabur, is a Bangladeshi activist with a background in alternative community organizing.

Although AMAN is predominantly a Muslim organization based on Islamic principles, the organization accepts non-Muslim members who agree to its ideals and goals. Its various programs are open to non-Muslim participants and speakers, not only to Christians, which would not be unusual among Muslim associations, but also to Hindus and Buddhists, which is somewhat more uncommon.

Conclusion

These examples of Muslim transnational movements are making their impact on the international Islamic *umma*. They are, for the most part, young movements dating back to the past thirty to forty years, growing very quickly by attracting bright, idealistic, highly motivated young people. They have developed an esprit of living and promoting an enlightened understanding of Islamic faith and tradition, and their enthusiasm is attracting others to these movements. They understand Islam as a religion that teaches peace, love, justice, cooperation, human rights, and equality of human dignity and see the mission of the Islamic community in the world to be that of *rahmat lil-alamin*, to be a blessing to the universe. Movements of this kind are likely to chart the course that the Islamic community will take during the coming century.

NOTES

1. Nursi has sometimes been claimed by Kurdish nationalists as a forerunner. For example, Hamit Bozarslan calls Nursi a "long-standing Kurdish nationalist," inferring that this was the reason for his frequent incarcerations by the Turkish authorities; see Bozarslan, "Political Aspects of the Kurdish Problem," in *The Kurds: A Contemporary Overview*, ed. Philip G. Kreyenbroeck and Stefan Sperl (London: Routledge, 1992), 103. Said Nursi admits that he has been accused of being a Kurdish nationalist, but he rejects all such nationalism as an un-Islamic European "infection" that brings about disunity in the *umma*. Said Nursi, "Sixteenth Word," in *The Words* (Istanbul: Sözler Publications, 1997), 85.

2. Namik Kemal's argument that constitutionalism and representative government were wholly compatible with Islamic teaching and, in fact, demanded by it, influenced not only the early thought and writings of Said Nursi but also the leading scholars of the Asian Muslim Action Network. Sükran Vahide, *Islam in Modern Turkey: An Intellectual Biography of Bediuzzaman Said Nursi* (Albany: State University of New York Press, 2005), 34.

3. Ahmet Turan Alkan, "Entellektüel ile Arifin Kesisme Noktasi," in *Fethullah Gülen Hocaefendi Ufuk Turu*, ed. Eyüp Can (Istanbul: Milliyet Yayinlari, 1996), 203–204, cited in Ahmet T. Kuru, "Reinterpretation of Secularism in Turkey," in *The Emergence of a New Turkey*, ed. M. Hakan Yavuz (Salt Lake City: University of Utah Press, 2006), 117. Samuel Huntington concurs, describing Turkey as "the most profoundly torn nation." Samuel Huntington, "A Clash of Civilizations?" *Foreign Affairs* 72, no. 3 (Summer 1993): 43.

4. The structure of this enormous work (6,000 pages) is unique. Although his earliest writings date back to about 1908, Nursi began in the 1930s to make a collection of these works, which he called *The Words*. This collection was followed by three others: *The Letters*, *The Flashes*, and *The Rays*, whose compilation was completed in 1949. All these works have been translated into English. Several additional collections, entitled the *Barla Lahıkası*, *Kastamonu Lahıkası*, and *Emirdağ Lahıkası*, have not yet been translated.

5. Sukran Vahide, *Bediuzzaman Said Nursi: The Author of the Risale-i Nur* (Istanbul: Sözler Publications, 1992), 39.

6. Serif Mardin, *Religion and Social Change in Modern Turkey* (Albany: State University of New York Press, 1989), 207.

7. Said Nursi, *The Damascus Sermon* (Istanbul: Sözler Publications, 1996), 9.

8. Justin McCarthy, *Muslims and Minorities: The Population of Ottoman Anatolia and the End of the Empire* (New York: New York University Press, 1983), 120–121.

9. Said Nursi, *Kastamonu Lahıkası* (Istanbul: Sinan Matbaası, 1960), 75, cited in Thomas Michel, S. J., "Muslim-Christian Dialogue and Cooperation in the Thought of Bediuzzaman Said Nursi," *Muslim World* 89, nos. 3/4 (July–October 1999): 325–335.

10. Said Nursi, "Sixteenth Flash," in *The Flashes* (Istanbul: Sözler Publications, 1996), 144.

11. Said Nursi, "Fourteenth Ray," in *The Rays* (Istanbul: Sözler Publications, 1998), 510, cited in Thomas Michel, S. J., "The Ethics of Pardon and Peace," in *Globalization, Ethics and Islam: The Case of Bediuzzaman Said Nursi*, ed. I. Markham and I. Özdemir (Burlington, VT: Ashgate, 2005), 46.

12. Nursi indicated two main factors that produced this degradation: despotism and distorted religion. Vahide, *Islam in Modern Turkey*, 161.

13. Said Nursi, *Lem'alar* (Istanbul: Sözler Publications, 1986), 146; Said Nursi, *Sincerity and Brotherhood* (Istanbul: Sözler Publications, 1991), 13, cited in Michel, "Muslim-Christian Dialogue," 325–335.

14. Said Nursi, *Emirdağ Lahıkası* (Istanbul: Sinan Matbaası, 1959), 156.

15. Ibid., 316.

16. Nursi, *The Damascus Sermon*, 49.

17. Massimo Introvigne, "Turkish Religious Market(s): A View Based on the Religious Economy Theory," in *The Emergence of a New Turkey*, ed. M. Hakan Yavuz (Salt Lake City: University of Utah Press, 2006), 42.

18. M. Hakan Yavuz, *Islamic Political Identity in Turkey* (Oxford: Oxford University Press, 2003), 11.

19. Aras and Caha trace two major influences on Gülen's thinking: the liberal, parliamentary Turkish Islamic tradition represented by Namik Kemal and the writings of Said Nursi. Bülent Aras and Ömer Caha, "Fethullah Gulen and His Liberal Turkish Islam Movement," *Middle East Review of International Affairs* 4, no. 4 (December 2000): 30–31.

20. M. Hakan Yavuz, "The Gülen Movement: The Turkish Puritans," in *Turkish Islam and the Secular State*, ed. M. Hakan Yavuz and John L. Esposito (Syracuse, NY: Syracuse University Press, 2003), 22.

21. Kuru, "Reinterpretation of Secularlism in Turkey," 141.

22. Fatih University in Istanbul, Turkey; Qafqas University in Baku, Azerbaijan; Ataturk-Alatoo University in Bishkek, Kyrgyzstan; Black Sea University in Tbilsi,

Georgia; Suleyman Demirel University in Almaty, Kazakhstan; International Turkmen-Turk University (ITTU) in Ashgabat, Türkmenistan. New universities are being planned in Africa and in the Balkans.

23. Ahmet T. Kuru, "Fethullah Gülen's Search for a Middle Way between Modernity and Muslim Tradition," in *Turkish Islam and the Secular State*, ed. M. Hakan Yavuz and John L. Esposito (Syracuse, NY: Syracuse University Press, 2003), 116.

24. Bekim Agai, "Fethullah Gülen: A Modern Turkish-Islamic Reformist?" *Qantara.de Dialogue with the Islamic World*, 28 December 2004, http://www.quantara.de/webcom/show_article.php/_c-575/_nr-2/_p-1/i.html?PHPSESSID=133099777

25. Fethullah Gülen, "At the Threshold of a New Millennium," in *Parliament of the World's Religions* (Capetown: n.p., 1999), 12.

26. Fethullah Gülen, "The Necessity of Interfaith Dialogue: A Muslim Perspective," in *Parliament of the World's Religions* (Capetown: n.p., 1999), 14.

27. AntiRacismNet, http://www.antiracismnet.org/directory/search.html?orgnum=1050.

28. AntiRacismNet, "Introduction to AMAN," in *New Visions for Peace*, ed. M. Abdus Sabur and Lisa Schenk (Bangkok: Asian Muslim Action Network, 2003), 11, http://www.antiracismnet.org/directory/search.html?orgnum=1050.

29. Asghar Ali Engineer, "Opening Remarks," in *Interfaith Conference on the Culture of Peace* (Bangkok: AMAN, 1991), 6.

30. Chandra Muzaffar, "AMAN: The Challenges Ahead," in *Interfaith Conference on the Culture of Peace* (Bangkok: AMAN, 1991), 25.

31. The commission publishes a bimonthly journal, *Human Rights Solidarity*, as well as almost daily online statements and urgent appeals on Asian human rights issues.

BIBLIOGRAPHY

Agai, Bekim. "Fethullah Gülen: A Modern Turkish-Islamic Reformist?" *Qantara.de Dialogue with the Islamic World*. December 28, 2004. http://www.quantara.de/webcom/show_article.php/_c-575/_nr-2/_p-1/i.html?PHPSESSID=133099777.
Alkan, Ahmet Turan. "Entellektüel ile Arifin Kesisme Noktasi." In *Fethullah Gülen Hocaefendi Ufuk Turu*, ed. Eyüp Can. Istanbul: Milliyet Yayinlari, 1996.
AntiRacismNet. "Introduction to AMAN." In *New Visions for Peace*, ed. M. Abdus Sabur and Lisa Schenk. Bangkok: Asian Muslim Action Network, 2003. http://www.antiracismnet.org/directory/search.html?orgnum=1050.
Aras, Bülent, and Ömer Caha. "Fethullah Gülen and His Liberal Turkish Islam Movement." *Middle East Review of International Affairs* 4, no. 4 (December 2000).
Bozarslan, Hamit. "Political Aspects of the Kurdish Problem." In *The Kurds: A Contemporary Overview*, ed. Philip G. Kreyenbroeck and Stefan Sperl, 95–114. London: Routledge, 1992.
Engineer, Asghar Ali. "Opening Remarks." In *Interfaith Conference on the Culture of Peace*. Bangkok: AMAN, 1991.
Gülen, Fethullah. "At the Threshold of a New Millennium." In *Parliament of the World's Religions*. Capetown: N.p., 1999.

————. "The Necessity of Interfaith Dialogue: A Muslim Perspective." In *Parliament of the World's Religions*. Capetown: N.p., 1999.

Huntington, Samuel. "A Clash of Civilizations?" *Foreign Affairs* 72, no. 3 (Summer 1993): 22–49.

Introvigne, Massimo. "Turkish Religious Market(s): A View Based on the Religious Economy Theory." In *The Emergence of a New Turkey*, ed. M. Hakan Yavuz, 23–48. Salt Lake City: University of Utah Press, 2006.

Kuru, Ahmet T. "Fethullah Gülen's Search for a Middle Way between Modernity and Muslim Tradition." In *Turkish Islam and the Secular State*, ed. M. Hakan Yavuz and John L. Esposito, 115–130. Syracuse, NY: Syracuse University Press, 2003.

————. "Reinterpretation of Secularlism in Turkey." In *The Emergence of a New Turkey*, ed. M. Hakan Yavuz, 136–159. Salt Lake City: University of Utah Press, 2006.

Mardin, Serif. *Religion and Social Change in Modern Turkey*. Albany: State University of New York Press, 1989.

McCarthy, Justin. *Muslims and Minorities: The Population of Ottoman Anatolia and the End of the Empire*. New York: New York University Press, 1983.

Michel, Thomas, S. J. "The Ethics of Pardon and Peace." In *Globalization, Ethics and Islam: The Case of Bediuzzaman Said Nursi*, ed. I. Markham and I. Özdemir, 37–47. Burlington, VT: Ashgate, 2005.

————. "Muslim-Christian Dialogue and Cooperation in the Thought of Bediuzzaman Said Nursi." *Muslim World* 89, nos. 3/4 (July–October 1999): 325–335.

Muzaffar, Chandra. "AMAN: The Challenges Ahead." In *Interfaith Conference on the Culture of Peace*. Bangkok: AMAN, 1991.

Nursi, Said. *The Damascus Sermon*. Istanbul: Sözler Publications, 1996.

————. *The Letters*. Istanbul: Sözler Publications, 1997.

————. *Emirdağ Lahıkası*. Istanbul: Sinan Matbaası, 1959.

————. *The Flashes*. Istanbul: Sözler Publications, 1996.

————. *Barla Lahıkası*. Istanbul, Sinan Matbaası, 1960.

————. *Kastamonu Lahıkası*. Istanbul: Sinan Matbaası, 1960.

————. *Lem'alar*. Istanbul: Sözler Publications, 1986.

————. *The Rays*. Istanbul: Sözler Publications, 1998.

————. *Sincerity and Brotherhood*. Istanbul: Sözler Publications, 1991.

————. *The Words*. Istanbul: Sözler Publications, 1997.

Vahide, Sükran. *Bediuzzaman Said Nursi: The Author of the Risale-i Nur*. Istanbul: Sözler Publications, 1992.

————. *Islam in Modern Turkey: An Intellectual Biography of Bediuzzaman Said Nursi*. Albany: State University of New York Press, 2005.

Yavuz, M. Hakan. "The Gülen Movement: The Turkish Puritans." In *Turkish Islam and the Secular State*, ed. M. Hakan Yavuz and John L. Esposito, 19–47. Syracuse, NY: Syracuse University Press, 2003.

————. *Islamic Political Identity in Turkey*. Oxford: Oxford University Press, 2003.

10

Trans-state Muslim Movements and Militant Extremists in an Era of Soft Power

John O. Voll

"The battle today cannot be fought on a regional level without taking into account the global hostility." The conflict is now in "the stage of the global battle." This proclamation by Ayman al-Zawahiri, the second in command to Osama Bin Laden in Al-Qaeda, is a forceful reminder of the development of powerful movements of transnational contention in the contemporary world.[1] The globalization of jihad in the visions and activities of militant Muslim extremists is one part of the broader trends in the development of "new transnational activism" in recent decades.[2] It is also an inescapable dimension of the new religious pluralism in world politics.

Religious movements, networks, and organizations are an important and visible part of the current worlds of transnational activism. However, much of the scholarship examining the emergence of international advocacy networks and transnational social movements concentrates on more secular groups and activities. Religious transnational advocacy is viewed most frequently in the historical contexts of missionary activity and the influence of religious organizations on early international advocacy campaigns like the one to abolish slavery in the nineteenth century.[3] The main focus of attention is on the development of national and international nongovernmental organizations (NGOs) as secular international organizations. "The NGO world in the second half of the twentieth century," William DeMars reminds us, "simply took for granted that the public discourse of any mainstream international NGO would be secular, universalistic, and progressive"—this despite the fact that "many of the historical forerunners to post–World War II NGOs were deeply religious in social origin and motivation."[4]

Since the end of the cold war, religious actors have emerged as a prominent transnational force across a range of global issue areas, including peacemaking, transitional justice, and development, topics covered elsewhere in this volume. As Thomas Michel argues in his chapter, peaceful Muslim groups are a crucial, if often overlooked, part of a new religious pluralism in world politics evident in increasing interactions with governments, international organizations, NGOs, and national and transnational civil society. At first glance, the movements and organizations of Islamic extremism and militancy might appear to fall outside these categories altogether. They are radical, violent, and engaged in a global conflict against the United States, its allies, and various state and substate authorities. They are analyzed mainly in literatures on security, terrorism, and counterterrorism. This chapter argues that such groups should, in fact, be studied alongside other transnational advocacy networks. One can acknowledge their particular characteristics—the glorification and perpetration of violence—while still applying the analytical categories developed for other kinds of transnational groups.

Militant extremists in the Muslim world such as Osama Bin Laden and Al-Qaeda are neither throwbacks to medieval modes of operation nor Luddite opponents of modernity. They share many characteristics with other transnational advocacy networks, including global communications and targeted appeals. Examining extremist religious movements through this optic sheds light on their operations and their persistence. In particular, it highlights two of their most salient characteristics: their transnational nonstate character and their use of "soft power" to build constituencies and recruit militants. These aspects will be examined after a somewhat more general description of the global contexts within which all groups of transnational activism and advocacy operate. A concluding section will return to the implications of the analysis for frameworks being put forward by scholars in a number of different fields examining the dynamics of world politics at the start of the twenty-first century.

The Changing World of Activism and Advocacy

The world in which activists and advocates operate changes daily. The transformations of many basic aspects of human life change the opportunities open to social movements and constantly redefine the resources available for mobilization by activists in their efforts to change conditions and policies around the world. Changing technologies of communication present new opportunities and challenges for framing and articulating the programs and agendas of advocacy. Analysts examining these changes and the developing nature of transnational activism have concentrated on the more secular causes and NGOs, and not as much attention has been given to the experiences of transnational religious activists and their organizations and movements.

In the middle of the twentieth century, some important dichotomies defined salient dimensions of global affairs and how those affairs were understood. Analytical polarities set the framework for interpreting international developments. First, with the growing importance of internationalization of business and economics, the distinctions between global and local, between international and domestic, became an important part of operational and analytical explanations of economic, political, and cultural affairs. Second, in the midcentury peak of influence of classical modernization theory, the distinction between "modern" and "traditional" was another important analytical polarity shaping how world affairs were understood. Third, sharp distinctions were made between societies variously identified as industrial, developed, or first world (northern) and those described as underdeveloped, developing, or third world (southern).

Remarkably, by the beginning of the twenty-first century, although there are conceptual echoes of these concepts in programs and policies, these three sharp polarities have been replaced in many studies by conceptualizations that combine the extremes and assume the dissolution of the sharp contrasts between national/international, traditional/modern, and North/South. Newer perspectives reflect changing realities in a world of increasingly intense interactions. In these changing global contexts, transnational activism plays important roles that are shaped by the complex realities that have replaced the polarities of the mid–twentieth century.

Globalization has challenged the familiar national/international polarity by transforming relationships between what were considered "global" and "local" aspects of politics, culture, and society. Increasingly, distinctive local developments are influenced by global elements to an extent that the "local" cannot be understood without at least some reference to the global. Similarly, "global" is not a separate, homogeneous category but is always reflecting some mode of "local" activity. This interactivity creates an interpretive difficulty relating to the "global-local problematic": "There is a widespread tendency to regard this problematic as straightforwardly involving a polarity, which assumes its most acute form in the claim that we live in a world of local assertions *against* globalizing trends, a world in which the very idea of locality is sometimes cast as a form of opposition or resistance to the hegemonically global."[5] In this context, Roland Robertson argues that "the local is not best seen, at least as an analytic or interpretive departure point, as a counterpoint to the global. Indeed it can be regarded, subject to some qualifications, as *an aspect* of globaliza- tion."[6] This interaction involves processes that might be better understood as "glocalization."

In simplistic terms, the traditional processes of globalization as understood in the mid–twentieth century have been transformed in many dimensions into the processes of glocalization, in which "global" and "local" are interacting aspects of inclusive dynamics. In this new world, as Mike Featherstone and Scott Lash have argued, "the global begins to replace the nation-state as the decisive framework for social life." They point to a "framework in which global *flows*—in mediascapes, ethnoscapes, finanscapes and technoscapes—are com- ing to assume as much, or greater, centrality than *national institutions.* Inter- national social, political, and cultural (for example the media) organizations are standing alongside and beginning to replace their national counterparts."[7] At the same time, local and national responses to these globalizing forces are framing and generating new patterns of transnational activity. In many different cases, what might have, in an earlier day, been local movements of contention or advocacy have become global in a variety of ways. One well-studied example of glocalized transnational advocacy is the Zapatista movement in Mexico.[8]

A second polarity that has been transformed is the traditional/modern opposition. There are many continuing debates about the nature of the rela- tionship between premodern and modern societies and the processes of "mod- ernization." Those debates are not particularly relevant for the discussion of movements and activism in a global context in which all peoples and societies are in some ways basically "modern." However, some of the older debates have now taken on a different cast.

In the middle of the twentieth century it was still possible to argue whether or not the end result of "modernization" would be a homogeneously modern world. However, by the twenty-first century it was clear that modernity has taken many different forms. Divergent and diverse historic processes of moderniza- tion make it possible for scholars like S. N. Eisenstadt to speak of "multiple modernities."[9] In a discussion of Muslim societies and modernity, Ira Lapidus argued already in the 1980s that the "events of the last two decades . . . have forced us to recognize that, whatever the universal elements in European politi- cal domination, and in the international capitalist system, there is in fact . . . no single form of modern society."[10]

In this contemporary world of multiple modernities, transnational move- ments of advocacy are not engaged in opposition to "modernity" so much as they are fighting for one mode of modernity as opposed to a different mode. One of the great tensions involves opposition to "globalization." Globalization has been defined by many people specifically in terms of a particular mode of global interactions: a global capitalist market system dominated by the economies of the United States, Western Europe, and Japan. In important ways, this form of globalization fits into the conceptualizations involved in understanding "modernity" as a homogeneous transforming force.

By the 1990s a strong movement opposed to "globalization" developed, with a major event being the protests against the meeting of the World Trade Organization (WTO) in Seattle in 1999 ("the Battle of Seattle"). These demonstrations illustrated that the activist movement of opposition to "Globalization" was itself an effective advocate of alternative visions of globalization. The two sides in Seattle did not represent "modernity" and its opponents; they represented two alternative modes of twenty-first-century glocalized modernity. If the movements of opposition were "antimodern," they were "antimodern" in the framework of being opposed to the dominant modes of modernity and were framed in terms of postmodern opposition to modernity (rather than a primitive Luddite style of opposition).

The third polarity—between the "developed" and the "underdeveloped" worlds, between the first and third worlds, or between the North and the South in global affairs—has also been transformed by the start of the twenty-first century. While the great gaps between rich and poor have not disappeared, the worlds of the rich and the poor are now global and interactive. Economies and cultures are more transnational and "glocal." Integrated processes of production may not reduce inequalities of wealth, but they illustrate the global nature of major enterprises. By the 1990s, analysts could legitimately speak of the "end of the third world," even though it did not mean the end of global poverty.[11] The old terminology that divided the world into the nations and societies of the "North" and the "South" has become obsolete. The old "underdeveloped world"/"third world"/"South" is no longer as identifiable territorially as it once was. At the beginning of the twenty-first century, important parts of the global economic and political elite groupings are drawn from the old "South." The world of the rich and powerful is now more global and diverse than at any time in world history.

By the beginning of the twenty-first century it is possible to speak of the emergence of "global civil society" in which both transnational activism and global economic processes flourish.[12] Many people in the old "first world" continue to have difficulty in recognizing the reality in which it is possible to argue, as Thomas Friedman does, that the "world is flat" as a level playing field for economic competition and collaboration.[13]

The dissolving of familiar polarities—international/national, traditional/ modern, and North/South—has changed the contexts within which international and transnational activists operate, and the nature of their operations.

Globally active movements and organizations are increasingly transnational in identity. Nongovernmental organizations that mobilize modern technologies of communication and organization are increasingly significant forces and actors in world affairs. The changing nature of transnational relationships across what was once the North/South divide provides new opportunities and resources for activists and advocates around the world. These dynamics are evident in multiple contexts, including the complex history of the human rights movement and advocacy network in Latin America and elsewhere.[14]

It is important to recognize that these NGOs and the broader movements of advocacy of which they are parts are not confined to the more usually noted secular groupings, but that there are also nongovernment advocacy networks and organizations that are fundamentally religious. Many, if not most, of these religious groupings are activist but neither militant nor advocates of violence as a tactic or strategy for achieving their goals. These religious groupings, like their more secular counterparts, operate within the new conditions of global activism at the beginning of the twenty-first century. While it is important to understand all types of transnational religious activism, this chapter concentrates on radical Muslim groupings within the contexts of the changing world of transnational activism and advocacy. It will provide a perspective different from those concerned primarily with issues of counterterrorism and security and add to our understanding of religious activism in the contemporary world.

Nongovernmental Muslim Transnational Activism

In the modern Muslim world, the emergence of transnational and trans-state movements of Muslim activism has important historical roots. As Muslim societies interacted and fought with European imperialists, hopes of a grand unification of Muslims were expressed. In the late nineteenth century, Jamal al-Din al-Afghani, a Muslim activist intellectual, advocated a Pan-Islamic movement to counter European expansion, and Pan-Islam was one of the elements of the foreign policy of the Ottoman sultan Abd al-Hamid II. However, these activities had little impact and were tied to specific states and their policies. Al-Afghani, for example, was more active in trying to enlist the support of rulers than in working to create a nongovernmental mass movement.

During the twentieth century, many important movements of Islamic renewal and reform emerged, and important organizations were created. However, reflecting the political dynamics of the time, even the nonstate, nongovernmental organizations tended to be defined by the national boundaries of their states and societies. In this way, some of the largest Muslim organizations in the world were basically "national" in their framework. In Indonesia, for example, Muhammadiyya (founded in 1912) and Nahdatul Ulama (founded in 1926), each with many millions of members, have remained virtually exclusively Indonesian in operation and perspective.

Some important movements that gained reputations for militant transnational activism by the 1990s were also primarily "national" throughout most of the twentieth century. The Muslim Brotherhood was established in Egypt in 1928 and gained a reputation in the Arab world as a leading voice advocating activist Islamic renewal. However, as an organization it remained Egyptian. Throughout the twentieth century, students who came to Egypt from other parts of the Muslim world sometimes came into contact with the Brotherhood and its teachings and were influenced by them. However, even when they established organizations in their homelands that they called the "Muslim Brotherhood," there was little continuing organizational coordination, and the various Brotherhoods became basically nationally identified. The largest such "national" organizations are the Muslim Brotherhoods in Syria, Jordan, and Sudan.[15]

The "transnationalization" of the Brotherhood by the 1990s was part of broader developments in the worlds of transnational advocacy and militancy in the final years of the twentieth century. Even in that context, the Muslim Brotherhood organizations remain remarkably national in orientation, and the transnational elements of the Brotherhood tradition are defined by militants who have left both the mainstream Brotherhood organizations and their theological and ideological positions. For example, Ayman al-Zawahiri, the leading ideologue of Al-Qaeda, may have begun his career as an activist within the Egyptian Brotherhood, but he soon left the Brotherhood, working first in the extremist Islamic Jihad organization. The evolution of organizations formed by dissidents from the mainstream Muslim Brotherhood reflects the broader trends of what many call the "Islamic resurgence" in the final quarter of the twentieth century. The first generation of movements in the resurgence had both a strong political dimension and state-oriented programs. During the 1980s, these major movements were often described as manifesting "political Islam." Such movements aimed at gaining control of the state or transforming the state. Olivier Roy even described the Islamist ideology of political Islam as being "obsessed with the state."[16] One of the most visible movements of political Islam was the Iranian Revolution of 1978–1979, but other movements across the Muslim world had the creation of "Islamic states" as the main goal of their programs. The local movements represented a wide range of definitions of what such a state would be, with some like the Islamic Tendency Movement in Tunisia emphasizing the democratic nature of the proposed Islamic state while others, like the Partai

Islam Se-Malaysia in Southeast Asia, advocated a relatively strict implementation of a conservative understanding of Islamic law (Sharia).

While Political Islam appeared to be global as a general movement, its actual manifestations were local in definition and basically state-oriented in perspective. Some, like the new Iranian Islamic Republic, hoped that they might be a model, but the Shiite character of the Iranian movement limited its appeal. Most of the major movements that were identified as being part of political Islam were defined by national boundaries and were oriented toward the states that were defined by those boundaries.

This situation began to change in the 1990s. For a variety of reasons, it became possible to announce the "failure of Political Islam."[17] This did not mean the end of the Islamic resurgence but, rather, a change in the nature of the movements involved. "The retreat of political Islamism has been accompanied by the advancement of Islam as a social phenomenon."[18] The new militant movements, called "neofundamentalists" by Olivier Roy, "try to re-Islamize society on a grassroots level, and no longer through state power" and are increasingly transnational and trans-state in their visions and activities.[19]

This shift to "grassroots levels" among militant Muslim groups was supported by the dynamics of the new world of transnational activism. In a global context in which "think global, act local" is the mantra of both NGO activists and "companies of all shapes and sizes that have global aspirations,"[20] the emerging global jihad style of the militant groups was not unusual. Until the late 1980s, movements of militant Muslim activism tended to be location specific, with little overlap in personnel. The war in Afghanistan in the 1980s was an important transitional experience. What began as a movement of local Afghan opposition to the Soviet invasion in 1979 became a "jihad" that attracted recruits from throughout the Muslim world. The specific cause was local, but the call was global.

This new type of call to action involved an important shift in definition of the obligation of Muslims to participate in jihad as a war effort. This obligation is generally seen as taking two forms, depending on the historical circumstances of the Muslim community. Usually the obligation is understood as being placed on the community as a whole, for the defense of the community and the faith. In this context, the obligation is on the community to provide a sufficient effort, and it is identified as the "sufficiency duty" (*fard kifayah*). Historically, this responsibility was in the hands of the rulers and the state, with the believers obligated to provide whatever support was necessary and sufficient. The duty is collective, and not every individual is obligated to participate directly. However, under extreme conditions of danger to the faith, it may be judged that it is necessary for all believers as individuals to participate in the jihad, and this participation becomes an "individual duty" (*fard 'ayn*). In this circumstance, the state becomes at best irrelevant and may be seen as part of the problem.

In Afghanistan, among the militants who were establishing the organization that was to become Al-Qaeda, the doctrinal shift was made by the end of the 1980s to viewing the jihad as an individual rather than a communal duty. A key figure in this shift was Abdullah Azzam, a Palestinian scholar who had completed graduate studies at the major Islamic university in Cairo, al-Azhar, and taught Islamic law in Jordan before he moved to Afghanistan to participate in the war effort against the Soviets. He is described as "both the ideological godfather and the global recruiter par excellence of Muslims drawn to the Afghan jihad" and was a major influence in shaping the thinking of Osama Bin Laden.[21] Before Azzam was murdered in 1989, he defined the doctrinal shift clearly: "Some scholars consider jihad today in Afghanistan and Palestine to be *fard kifayah*. We agree with them in that jihad in Afghanistan for the Arabs was initially *fard kifayah*. But the jihad is in need of men and the inhabitants of Afghanistan have not met the requirement which is to expel the Disbelievers from Afghanistan. In this case, the communal obligation (*fard kifayah*) is overturned. It becomes individually obligatory (*fard 'ayn*) in Afghanistan."[22]

After the end of the anti-Soviet phase of the war in Afghanistan, people like Osama Bin Laden shifted the emphasis, conceiving of jihad as being global. As al-Zawahiri argues, the conflict is now in the stage of "global battle," and participation in jihad is an individual obligation for all true Muslims around the world. In his letter to Abu Musab al-Zarqawi released in October 2005, al-Zawahiri makes it clear that all of the local jihads, whether in the far-flung regions of the Islamic world, such as Chechnya, Afghanistan, Kashmir, and Bosnia, or in the heartlands of Islam, like Iraq and Palestine, are part of the broader global jihad.[23] In the terms of the broader developments of transnational activism, in the Azzam-Zawahiri tradition, jihad has become glocalized.

This development was disputed, even among the militant-activist organizations. Important and vigorous debates took place within some of the key organizations. During the 1980s and early 1990s, the major militant groups were "religious nationalists," in the terminology of Fawaz Gerges, who worked to defeat their local governments, the "near enemy" and establish local "theocratic states."[24] By the late 1990s, the Azzam-Zawahiri tradition articulated a competing transnational mode of militancy that became in many ways the most visible manifestation of the militant jihadi movement at the beginning of the twenty-first century.

In the glocal jihad, there is little place for state or government action. Terrorist networks by the early 1990s were moving beyond the state identifications of earlier organizations. This reflects similar transnational organizational

trends in business and other fields. The broader transition is described in a
RAND volume from 2001: "What has been emerging in the business world is
now becoming apparent in the organizational structures of the newer and more
active terrorist groups, which appear to be adopting decentralized, flexible network structures. The rise of networked arrangements in terrorist organizations
is part of a wider move away from formally organized, state-sponsored groups
to privately financed, loose networks of individuals and subgroups."[25]

In this aspect as in many others, Osama Bin Laden and Al-Qaeda are the
best-studied and possibly the leading operational examples. Bruce Hoffman,
a leading expert on terrorist organizations, notes, "Osama bin Laden is perhaps best viewed as a terrorist CEO. He has essentially applied the techniques
of business administration and modern management. . . . In the 1990s he did
what the executives of transnational companies did throughout much of the
industrialized world—namely, design and implement a flexible new organizational framework and strategy incorporating multiple levels and both top-down
and bottom-up approaches."[26] Peter Bergen notes that Al Qaeda "has successfully turned itself from an organization into a mass movement," and that "Al
Qaeda the group has been morphing into Al Qaeda the ideological movement."[27]
In this organizational structure, there is no connection with a state, nor does a
state government define the boundaries of Al-Qaeda's actions and visions.

Nongovernmental Muslim transnational activism is assuming important
new forms at the beginning of the twenty-first century. The high visibility of the
violent actions of some of these transnational groupings strengthens concerns
about their material destructive capacity. Attention is frequently given to the
democratization of technologies of destruction, which, as Joseph Nye notes, has
"created a new set of conditions that have increased the lethality and the difficulty of managing terrorism today." The fact that "technological progress is putting into the hand of deviant groups and individuals, destructive capabilities that
were once limited primarily to governments and armies," for Nye, marks "the
'privatization of war' and a dramatic change in world politics."[28] Much attention
has been focused on this security dimension of transnational militancy. However, an important and too-frequently ignored aspect of these groups' effectiveness is their capacity to mobilize instruments of "soft power" so important in
the contemporary era of shifting global and transnational relationships.

Militant Transnational Activism and Soft Power

The structure of world affairs and global interactions is in the midst of a
major change. Both in terms of actual operations and in the ways that those

operations are conceived and understood by analysts, the old systems of relationships are passing rapidly. At the end of World War II, the nature of global
relations, as reflected in the way that the United Nations organization was
structured and conceived, primarily involved relations among sovereign territorial states. In these relationships, military might and control of material
economic resources are usually seen as the foundations for the power of these
sovereign states. This system was basically the system of Realpolitik.

By the end of the twentieth century, major scholars were revising the state-
centric conceptualizations of world relations. Some critiques concentrated on
the weakness of the "nation-state" itself as an effective structure in the contexts
of intensifying globalizations in many areas. Peter Drucker, a respected analyst
of economic organization, wrote in the early 1990s that the "nation-state is not
going to wither away. It may remain the most powerful political organ around
for a long time to come, but it will no longer be the indispensable one. Increasingly it will have to share power with other organs, other institutions, other
policy-makers."[29]

Other scholars looked at the changing nature of power itself. Already in the
early 1970s, before he served as national security adviser for President Jimmy
Carter, Zbigniew Brzezinski noted the shifting nature of power and the foundations of society. He spoke of the opening of the Technetronic Age in which
the "industrial process is no longer the principal determinant of social change"
and "knowledge becomes a tool of power and the effective mobilization of talent an important way to acquire power."[30] The end of the cold war signaled the
beginning of an era in which attention needed to be given to the wide range of
sources of power. By the beginning of the twenty-first century, a RAND study
stated that "'information' and 'power' are becoming increasingly intertwined.
Across many political, economic, and military areas, informational 'soft power'
is taking precedence over traditional, material 'hard power.'"[31]

The concept of soft power was developed by Joseph Nye and has been
adopted by many analysts. The starting point in the conceptualization of soft
power is that "information is power and modern information technology is
spreading information more widely than ever before in history."[32] Basically,
power is the ability to do things or to get things done. Hard power is the ability
to make people do things, regardless of whether or not they want to. Soft power,
for Nye, "rests on the ability to shape the preferences of others" and to get them
to want to do the things that you want them to do.[33]

Hard power was frequently the foundation for the power of states in the
modern era of sovereign nation-states. It is possible to see some of the dramatic moments in the history of that system in Europe as being efforts by existing states to set limits on soft power—at the Congress of Vienna in 1815, for

example, to set limits on the appeal of the radical (and appealing) visions stirred up by the French Revolution or the continent-wide hard-power responses to the revolutions of 1848. In the twentieth century, the two world wars were major exercises of hard power, but the victory of the United States in the cold war is at least partially built on the great soft-power appeal of the alternative to the Soviet communist system that was presented by the West in general and the United States in particular. That power involved lifestyles and aspirations—the fact that many people around the world would like to have a way of life similar to that of most Americans. Other societies, cultures, and states have soft-power appeal as well, to varying degrees.

How might the concept of soft power be applied to understand the growth of militant transnational activism? Most obviously, it is worth noting that these groups are, by definition, cut off from—and opposed to—the hard-power resources available to states. It is often noted that terrorism is the weapon of the "weak." Under such circumstances the creation of a base of support and the survival of an international network depend crucially on appeals centered on core beliefs and cultural practices. As Nye points out, "Terrorism depends crucially on soft power. It depends on its ability to attract support from the crowd at least as much as its ability to destroy the enemy's will to fight." It is through soft power "that terrorists gain general support as well as new recruits."[34]

In his discussion of soft power, Nye mentions religion only in passing. He notes that "for centuries, organized religious movements have possessed soft power" but centers most of his attention on secular organizations and forces.[35] However, in the contemporary context, and in world historical terms, the soft power of religious traditions deserves greater attention. One significant but not frequently noted historic competition between hard power and religion's soft power occurred in Southeast Asia. At the beginning of the fifteenth century C.E., two major global dynamics intersected in the islands of the region that now constitute Indonesia. Islam had only recently been brought in a significant way by merchants and itinerant teachers to the islands of Sumatra and Java. At the same time, western Europeans arrived in the form of Portuguese and then Dutch and British military forces and business enterprises. In the following four centuries, the basic hard-power resources were in the hands of Christian Europeans who militarily dominated the region. Muslim merchants and teachers tended to have only soft-power resources available. However, in the middle of the twentieth century, when Indonesia became independent, it was the largest Muslim country in the world. Despite four centuries of hard-power control, European imperialism was effectively defeated by the soft power of the Muslim merchants and teachers.

The soft power of religion has become increasingly visible in the contemporary world as religion has emerged as a more potent force in national and

international affairs. Militant transnational religious movements have benefited from this trend. They have become significant agents in world politics—
not simply through their violent acts but also through their appeals. In a world
where information and knowledge are bases for power, the ability of Al-Qaeda
and related groups to operate in the new world of cyberinformation is a major
asset, and perhaps the most visible reminder that soft power is not simply a
benevolent element but is rather a source of strength for violent extremism as
well as humanitarian efforts.

Many people in the West have great difficulty in understanding the appeal
of the call to Bin Laden's style of jihad and martyrdom, but that appeal exists.
This appeal is not a Luddite exhortation to oppose modernity and restore a
medieval life. The vision of Bin Laden and those like him is framed in terms of
the hard-power realities of the contemporary world. Many people in the Muslim world feel oppressed and are poor, and Bin Laden presents to overcome
the hard power of those seen as the oppressors—soft power designed to mobilize a transnational constituency and recruit militants. An Al-Qaeda recruit-
ment videotape that circulated around the Middle East in the summer of 2001,
before the destruction of the World Trade Center, provides a good example of
this appeal. The film emphasizes that poorly armed but dedicated people can
fight and defeat better-equipped adversaries, like the Soviet Union. Throughout the film, strong pictures of the hard power of the enemy being used to
oppress poor people are contrasted with the calm dignity of the warriors. Bin
Laden's clearly stated conclusion is: "Using very meager resources and military
means, the Afghan mujahidin demolished one of the most important myths
in human history and the biggest military apparatus. We no longer fear the so-
called Great Powers."[36]

In the long-term conflict between Al-Qaeda and the United States, this
theme of the contrast between hard power and soft power remains an important core part of the way that Bin Laden frames his message. A good example
is the narrative describing a significant battle in Tora Bora, Afghanistan, late
in 2001. In that battle, a major allied military attack failed to defeat, capture, or
kill a small Al-Qaeda force (including Bin Laden), and in the propaganda of the
militants, Tora Bora has become a symbol of the weakness of the hard power
of "The Superpower."[37] In the days before American forces went into Iraq in
2003, for example, Bin Laden's message to the Iraqi people on the lessons
of Tora Bora was: "In that great battle, the forces of truth triumphed over all
the evil forces by remaining true to their principles." From his point of view,
the battle culminated with the resounding, devastating failure of the global
alliance of evil, with all its supposed power, to overcome a small group of mujahidin, numbering no more than 300, in their trenches within one square mile.

Bin Laden concluded: "If all the forces of global evil could not even achieve their objective over one square mile against a small number of *mujahidin* with such modest capabilities, how could they expect to triumph over the entire Islamic world?"[38]

It is clear that soft power, evident in the capacity to circulate such communications to a wider audience, is an important resource now available to militant religious transnational activists like Al-Qaeda. The basic contexts of the new world of transnational activism make this possible. Glocal activism can mobilize dedicated warriors at the local level while providing these militants with a global support system in terms of both ideology and material goods. The nonstate nature of much transnational activism, whether violent or humanitarian, gives added flexibility to such networks in an era of increasing availability of the technologies of mobilization of supporters and means of destruction. This flexibility makes it possible to mobilize many diverse forces and gives the movements and networks greater internal vitality and external influence.

Pluralism Turned Upside Down

Supporters of religious and cultural pluralism are the most visible and best-known groups in the new world of transnational activism. The concept of "transnational" itself implies both going beyond a "national" identification and an acceptance of the fact of necessarily dealing with people who are not from your own "nation." "The fundamental sociocultural change that has increased transnational activism," according to Sidney Tarrow, "is the growth of a stratum of individuals who travel regularly, read foreign books and journals, and become involved in networks of transactions abroad."[39] Anthony Appiah, in his contribution to this volume and elsewhere, describes these people as "cosmopolitans." They literally fulfill the dictionary definition of "cosmopolitan" as "having constituent elements from all over the world or from many different parts of the world."[40]

In the worldview of the "cosmopolitans," diversity is accepted as a resource, and pluralism is part of the conceptual framework. However, in the world of glocalization, being purely "global" or purely "cosmopolitan" is difficult and a rare phenomenon. Instead, in a variety of ways cosmopolitans maintain connections with their societies and cultures of origin and upbringing. These roots provide the "local" in the "glocal" lives that they lead. The result is what Appiah and others have called "rooted cosmopolitanism."[41] For example, Appiah speaks of his father, a major Ghanaian nationalist, and his support for a "rooted cosmopolitanism" or "cosmopolitan patriotism."[42]

In much of the discussion of rooted cosmopolitanism, there is a positive tone. Just as DeMars noted that most discussions of NGOs "simply took for granted that the public discourse of any mainstream international NGO would be secular, universalistic, and progressive,"[43] there is a tendency to think of "rooted cosmopolitans" as being similarly "progressive." However, many of the leaders and activists in militant transnational networks fit the basic definition of "cosmopolitan" and clearly are also "rooted." Appiah speaks of "a new world-wide fraternity that presents cosmopolitanism with something of a sinister mirror image," and he identifies this with the emergence of groups of "young, global Muslim fundamentalists."[44]

Since Appiah, in his essay in this volume, identifies "cosmopolitanism" with a "combination of universalism and tolerance," he identifies this "sinister mirror image" as "countercosmopolitanism." In the sense of being transnational, transcultural, and global, whether one calls the militant extremists "cosmopolitan" or "countercosmopolitan," they are global actors able to operate effectively in a full spectrum of cultural contexts. Their hostility to cultural pluralism and their advocacy and practice of violence set them apart from Appiah's cosmopolitans.

There is, however, an important way in which Al-Qaeda accepts and works with cultural and religious pluralism. While hostile to non-Muslim traditions, both religious and secular, Osama Bin Laden and his lieutenants embrace and exploit the global diversity *within* Islam. As Olivier Roy has pointed out, they respond to local and national contexts by espousing a "'universal' Islam, valid in any cultural context." Globalization proves "a good opportunity to dissociate Islam from any given culture and to provide a model that could work beyond any culture."[45] Bin Laden's vision of global (glocal) jihad incorporates a diversity of themes and priorities from different parts of Islamic history—the conflict between radical Arab socialism and the Islamists, for example, or the split between Sunnis and Shiites. The flexibility of diverse appeals within an overall transnational vision for the global *umma* is one of the keys to understanding Al-Qaeda's survival and success.

Bin Laden's message to the Iraqi people on the eve of the U.S. invasion is illustrative. Bin Laden argued that joining with infidels in the fight against the United States was permissible, even if the infidels were the old radical socialist enemies of Islamic movements everywhere: "There is no harm in such circumstances if the Muslims' interests coincide with those of the socialists in fighting the Crusaders, despite our firm conviction that they are infidels," he argued. "The current fighting and the fighting that will take place in the coming days can be very much compared to the Muslims' previous battles. There is nothing wrong with a convergence of interests here, just as the Muslims' struggle against Byzantium suited the Persians but did not harm the Prophet's companions, may God be pleased with them."[46]

A similar flexibility of message and effective use of global communications was evident in the letter from al-Zawahiri to Zarqawi on the situation in Iraq, released in October 2005. Al-Zawahiri emphasized that the sectarian, Sunni-Shiite element was secondary to the struggle against the foreign aggressor and that the support of all of the people was essential in this larger conflict.[47] The letter called on Muslims to downplay a deep division that had been a major driver of Muslim politics for centuries. The outbreaks of violence between Sunnis and Shiites in February and March 2006, and the deepening civil war that ensued, manifested the continuing strength of these divisions and underscored the remarkable pragmatism of Al-Qaeda's stance.

For Appiah, the appeal of Islamic militants who see themselves as part of a global community and draw creatively on the Muslim tradition in crafting their appeals is evidence of the strength of countercosmopolitanism. However, it is difficult to draw too stark a distinction between the transcultural Islam of contemporary Muslim cosmopolitans and their countercosmopolitan counterparts. Tolerance by itself, Appiah writes, "is not what distinguishes the cosmopolitan from the neofundamentalist. There are plenty of things that the heroes of radical Islam are happy to tolerate. They don't care if you eat kabobs or meatballs or kung pao chicken, as long as the meat is halal." At the same time, Appiah continues, "there are plenty of things that cosmopolitans will not tolerate. We will sometimes want to intervene in other places because what is going on there violates our principles so deeply." For both groups, Appiah argues, "toleration has its limits."[48] The central difference between both groups, it would seem, is the *framework* for thinking about cultural and religious pluralism and the limits of toleration. For militants, some pluralism and tolerance *within* a tradition is acceptable, but pluralism across traditions is not. Cosmopolitans uphold peaceful interaction and cooperation across traditions, both religious and secular, as the ideal.

In the new world of transnational activism, religion is an important if sometimes overlooked element. Activist religious networks are increasingly visible, and the militant Muslim transnational groups are among the most prominent. These groups, most visibly represented by Al-Qaeda and Osama Bin Laden, have considerable soft-power resources at their disposal, including an ability to craft and communicate flexible appeals that draw on sacred texts, Muslim history, and the analysis of contemporary world politics. Like the major corporations that they may resemble, they "think global and act local" in a world arena marked by glocalization. The militant transnational activism of Al-Qaeda provides one important example of new trans-state and transnational forms of identity, engagement, and organization in the contemporary world.

NOTES

1. "Al-Sharq al-Awsat Publishes Extracts from Al-Jihad Leader Al-Zawahiri's New Book," *al-Sharq al-Awsat*, December 2, 2001, FBIS-NES-2002-0108, 5. Published by the Foreign Broadcast Information Service (FBIS).

2. Sidney Tarrow, *The New Transnational Activism* (Cambridge: Cambridge University Press, 2005), especially 124–126.

3. See, for example, the case studies chosen in two of the major volumes in the study of transnational advocacy: Jackie Smith, Charles Chatfield, and Ron Pagnucco, eds., *Transnational Social Movements and Global Politics: Solidarity beyond the State* (Syracuse, NY: Syracuse University Press, 1997); Margaret E. Keck and Kathryn Sikkink, *Activists beyond Borders: Advocacy Networks in International Politics* (Ithaca, NY: Cornell University Press, 1998); Peter Waterman, *Globalization, Social Movements and the New Internationalisms* (London: Continuum, 1998).

4. William E. DeMars, *NGOs and Transnational Networks: Wild Cards in World Politics* (London: Pluto Press, 2005), 64. Ironically, DeMars lists the 151 "Active NGOs Discussed in This Book" in the appendix, but identifies only eight of them as explicitly religious.

5. Roland Robertson, "Glocalization: Time-Space and Homogeneity-Heterogeneity," in *Global Modernities*, ed. Mike Featherstone, Scott Lash, and Roland Robertson (London: Sage, 1995), 29.

6. Ibid., 30.

7. Mike Featherstone and Scott Lash, "Globalization, Modernity and the Spatialization of Social Theory: An Introduction," in *Global Modernities*, ed. Mike Featherstone, Scott Lash, and Roland Robertson (London: Sage, 1995), 1–2.

8. See, for example, David Ronfeldt and John Arquilla, "Emergence and Influence of the Zapatista Netwar," in *Networks and Netwars: The Future of Terror, Crime, and Militancy*, ed. John Arquilla and David Ronfeldt (Santa Monica, CA: RAND, 2001), 171–199; Tarrow, *The New Transnational Activism*, 113–119.

9. See, for example, S. N. Eisenstadt, "The Reconstruction of Religious Arenas in the Framework of 'Multiple Modernities,'" *Millennium: Journal of International Studies* 29, no. 3 (2000): 591–611.

10. I. M. Lapidus, "Islam and Modernity," in *Patterns of Modernity*, vol. 2, *Beyond the West*, ed. S. N. Eisenstadt (New York: New York University Press, 1987), 89.

11. Nigel Harris, *The End of the Third World: Newly Industrializing Countries and the Decline of an Ideology* (Harmondsworth: Penguin, 1986).

12. Craig Warkentin, *Reshaping World Politics: NGOs, the Internet, and Global Civil Society* (Boulder, CO: Rowman and Littlefield, 2001).

13. Daniel H. Pink, "Why the World Is Flat" (interview with Thomas Friedman), *Wired Magazine* 13, no. 05, March 5, 2006, http://www.wired.com/wired/archive/13.05/friedman_pr.html.

14. See, for example, analysis in Keck and Sikkink, *Activists beyond Borders*, chap. 3.

15. Studies reflecting the "national" definitions of the movements in each of these three states are Umar F. Abd-Allah, *The Islamic Struggle in Syria* (Berkeley: Mizan Press, 1983); Quintan Wiktorowicz, *The Management of Islamic Activism: Salafis, the Muslim Brotherhood, and State Power in Jordan* (Albany: State University of New York Press, 2001); and Hasan al-Turabi, *al-Harakah al-islamiyyah fi al-sudan: al-tatawwur, wa al-kasb wa al-minhaj* (Cairo: al-Qari' al-Arabi, 1411/1991).

16. Olivier Roy, *The Failure of Political Islam*, trans. Carol Volk (Cambridge, MA: Harvard University Press, 1994), xi.

17. The most comprehensive presentation of this conclusion is Roy, *The Failure of Political Islam*.

18. Ibid., 78.

19. Ibid., 79.

20. See, for example, the discussions in Daniel Patrick Welch, "Think Global, Act Local: Rinse, Repeat, Die," *Scoop Independent News* [February 28, 2006]. (http://www.scoop.co.nz) on NGOs; and Mary T. Morgan, "Think Local, Learn Global, Act Glocal," in *Brandpapers* (http://www.brandchannel.com/ papers_review.asp?sp_ id=363) on companies.

21. Peter L. Bergen, *Holy War, Inc.* (New York: Touchstone, 2002), 54.

22. Imam Abdullah Azzam, *Join the Caravan*, Part 3: "Clarifications about the Issue of Jihad Today," (http://www.religioscope.com/info/doc/jihad/azzam_caravan_5_part3.htm). This is also published in *Islam in Transition: Muslim Perspectives*, 2nd ed., ed. John J. Donohue and John L. Esposito (New York: Oxford University Press, 2007).

23. See the Arabic text and English translation as released by the Office of the Director of National Intelligence, on October 11, 2005, http://www.dni.gov/release_letter_101105.html.

24. Fawaz A. Gerges, *The Far Enemy: Why Jihad Went Global* (Cambridge: Cambridge University Press, 2005), 43.

25. Michele Zanini and Sean J. A. Edwards, "The Networking of Terror in the Information Age," in Arquilla and Ronfeldt, *Networks and Netwars*, 32.

26. Bruce Hoffman, "The Leadership Secrets of Osama bin Laden: The Terrorist as CEO," *Atlantic*, April 2003, 26.

27. Peter Bergen, "The Dense Web of Al Qaeda," *Washington Post*, December 25, 2003, 29; and Peter Bergen, "Al Qaeda: The Movement," *Los Angeles Times*, March 17, 2004.

28. Joseph S. Nye Jr., *Power in the Global Information Age: From Realism to Globalization* (London: Routledge, 2004), 208–209.

29. Peter F. Drucker, *Post-Capitalist Society* (New York: HarperBusiness, 1993), 11.

30. Zbigniew Brzezinski, *Between Two Ages: America's Role in the Technetronic Era* (New York: Viking, 1970), 9, 12

31. John Arquilla and David Ronfeldt, *The Emergence of Noopolitik: Toward an American Information Strategy* (Santa Monica, CA: RAND, 1999), ix.

32. Joseph S. Nye Jr., *Soft Power: The Means to Success in World Politics* (New York: Public Affairs, 2004), 1.

33. Ibid., 5.

34. Ibid., 22, 25.

35. Ibid., 94.

36. The tape, with translations and analytical essays, is available on the site of Columbia International Affairs Online, http://www.ciaonet.org under "Case Studies: CIAO Responds to the Terrorist Attacks against the United States"; the quotation comes from reel 3, selection 10, of the tape.

37. For a discussion of this battle, see Mary Anne Weaver, "Lost at Tora Bora," *New York Times Magazine*, September 11, 2005, 54–60.

38. Usama Bin Laden, "To the People of Iraq," February 11, 2003, in *Messages to the World: The Statements of Osama Bin Laden*, trans. James Howarth, ed. Bruce Lawrence (London: Verso: 2005), 181–182.

39. Tarrow, *The New Transnational Activism*, 35.

40. The American Heritage Dictionary of the English Language, 4th ed. (Boston: Houghton Mifflin, 2000), 414.

41. For a discussion of the development of this terminology, see Tarrow, *The New Transnational Activism*, 42.

42. See, for example, Kwame Anthony Appiah, *The Ethics of Identity* (Princeton, NJ: Princeton University Press, 2005), 239

43. DeMars, NGOs and Transnational Networks, 64.

44. Kwame Anthony Appiah, "The Case for Contamination," *New York Times Magazine*, January 1, 2006, 35–36.

45. Olivier Roy, *Globalized Islam: The Search for a New Ummah* (New York: Columbia University Press, 2004), 25.

46. "To the People of Iraq," 84.

47. See the Arabic text and English translation as released by the Office of the Director of National Intelligence, on October 11, 2005, http://www.dni.gov/release_letter_101105.html.

48. Appiah, "The Case for Contamination," 36.

BIBLIOGRAPHY

Abd-Allah, Umar F. *The Islamic Struggle in Syria*. Berkeley, CA: Mizan Press, 1983.
Appiah, Kwame Anthony. "The Case for Contamination." *New York Times Magazine*, January 1, 2006, 35–36.
———. *Cosmopolitanism: Ethics in a World of Strangers*. New York: Norton, 2006.
———. *The Ethics of Identity*. Princeton, NJ: Princeton University Press, 2005.
Arquilla, John, and David Ronfeldt. *The Emergence of Noopolitik: Toward an American Information Strategy*. Santa Monica, CA: RAND, 1999.
Azzam, Imam Abdullah. *Join the Caravan*, Part 3: "Clarifications about the Issue of Jihad Today," (http://www.religioscope.com/info/doc/jihad/azzam_caravan_5_part3.htm) Selections in *Islam in Transition: Muslim Perspectives*, 2nd ed., ed. John J. Donohue and John L. Esposito. New York: Oxford University Press, 2007.
Bergen, Peter. "Al Qaeda: The Movement." *Los Angeles Times*, March 17, 2004.

Bergen, Peter. "The Dense Web of Al Qaeda." *Washington Post*, December 25, 2003, 29.
———. *Holy War, Inc.* New York: Touchstone, 2002.
Bin Laden, Usama. "Case Studies: CIAO Responds to the Terrorist Attacks against the United States." *Columbia International Affairs Online.* November 2001. http://www.ciaonet.org. Reel 3, excerpt 10.
———. "To the People of Iraq." February 11, 2003. In *Messages to the World: The Statements of Osama Bin Laden,* trans. James Howarth, ed. Bruce Lawrence, 181–182. London: Verso: 2005.
Brzezinski, Zbigniew. *Between Two Ages: America's Role in the Technetronic Era.* New York: Viking Press, 1970.
DeMars, William E. *NGOs and Transnational Networks: Wild Cards in World Politics.* London: Pluto Press, 2005.
Drucker, Peter F. *Post-capitalist Society.* New York: HarperBusiness, 1993.
Eisenstadt, S. N. "The Reconstruction of Religious Arenas in the Framework of 'Multiple Modernities.'" *Millennium: Journal of International Studies* 29, no. 3 (2000): 591–611.
Featherstone, Mike, and Scott Lash. "Globalization, Modernity and the Spatialization of Social Theory: An Introduction." In *Global Modernities,* ed. Mike Featherstone, Scott Lash, and Roland Robertson, 1–2. London: Sage, 1995.
Gerges, Fawaz A. *The Far Enemy: Why Jihad Went Global.* Cambridge: Cambridge University Press, 2005.
Harris, Nigel. *The End of the Third World: Newly Industrializing Countries and the Decline of an Ideology.* Harmondsworth: Penguin, 1986.
Hoffman, Bruce. "The Leadership Secrets of Osama bin Laden: The Terrorist as CEO." *Atlantic,* April 2003, 26.
Keck, Margaret E., and Kathryn Sikkink. *Activists beyond Borders: Advocacy Networks in International Politics.* Ithaca, NY: Cornell University Press, 1998.
Lapidus, I. M. "Islam and Modernity." In *Patterns of Modernity.* Vol. 2, *Beyond the West,* ed. S. N. Eisenstadt, 89. New York: New York University Press, 1987.
Morgan, Mary T. "Think Local. Learn Global. Act Glocal." In *Brandpapers.* http://www.brandchannel.com/papers_review.asp?sp_id=363.
Nye, Joseph S., Jr. *Power in the Global Information Age: From Realism to Globalization.* London: Routledge, 2004.
———. *Soft Power: The Means to Success in World Politics.* New York: Public Affairs, 2004.
Pink, Daniel H. "Why the World Is Flat." *Wired Magazine* 13, no. 05. March 5, 2006. http://www.wired.com/wired/archive/13.05/friedman_pr.html.
Robertson, Roland. "Glocalization: Time-Space and Homogeneity-Heterogeneity." In *Global Modernities,* ed. Mike Featherstone, Scott Lash, and Roland Robertson, 25–44. London: Sage, 1995.
Ronfeldt, David, and John Arquilla. "Emergence and Influence of the Zapatista Netwar." In *Networks and Netwars: The Future of Terror, Crime, and Militancy,* ed. John Arquilla and David Ronfeldt, 171–199. Santa Monica, CA: RAND, 2001.
Roy, Olivier. *The Failure of Political Islam.* Trans. Carol Volk. Cambridge, MA: Harvard University Press, 1994.

————. *Globalized Islam: The Search for a New Ummah*. New York: Columbia University Press, 2004.

"Al-Sharq al-Awsat Publishes Extracts from Al-Jihad Leader Al-Zawahiri's New Book." Published by the Foreign Broadcast Information Service. December 2, 2001. FBIS-NES-2002-0108. 5.

Smith, Jackie, Charles Chatfield, and Ron Pagnucco, eds. *Transnational Social Movements and Global Politics: Solidarity beyond the State*. Syracuse, NY: Syracuse University Press, 1997.

Tarrow, Sidney. *The New Transnational Activism*. Cambridge: Cambridge University Press, 2005.

al-Turabi, Hasan. *al-Harakah al-islamiyyah fi al-sudan: al-tatawwur, wa al-kasb wa al-minhaj*. Cairo: al-Qari' al-Arabi, 1411/1991.

Warkentin, Craig. *Reshaping World Politics: NGOs, the Internet, and Global Civil Society*. Boulder, CO: Rowman and Littlefield, 2001.

Waterman, Peter. *Globalization, Social Movements and the New Internationalisms*. London: Continuum, 1998.

Weaver, Mary Anne. "Lost at Tora Bora." *New York Times Magazine*, September 11, 2005, 54–60.

Welch, Daniel Patrick. "Think Global, Act Local: Rinse, Repeat, Die." *Scoop Independent News*, February 28, 2006. http://www.scoop.co.nz.

Wiktorowicz, Quintan. *The Management of Islamic Activism: Salafis, the Muslim Brotherhood, and State Power in Jordan*. Albany: State University of New York Press, 2001.

Zanini, Michele, and Sean J. A. Edwards. "The Networking of Terror in the Information Age." In *Networks and Netwars: The Future of Terror, Crime, and Militancy*, ed. John Arquilla and David Ronfeldt, 32. Santa Monica, CA: RAND, 2001, pp. 29–60.

al-Zawahiri, Ayman. "Letter from al-Zawahiri to al-Zarqawi." Published by the Office of the Director of National Intelligence. Released October 11, 2005. http://www.dni.gov/release_letter_101105.html.

11

Religious Pluralism and the Politics of a Global Cloning Ban

Thomas Banchoff

Life sciences revolutions in embryo, stem cell, and cloning research raise ethical questions that will be with us for decades to come. When does human life begin and deserve protection? How should the protection of the embryo be weighed against the promise of biomedical progress and the reduction of human suffering? Should frontier technologies including cloning and human genetic enhancement be allowed to develop and flourish? Such fundamental ethical questions engage the attention of the world's major religious traditions. And because they raise the questions of whether and how to regulate scientific activity, they have an irreducibly political dimension. Over the past decade, the parallel engagement of religion and politics with science has generated tremendous controversy in the United States, Western Europe, and beyond. But with one notable exception, that controversy has played out at the national, not the international, level. This chapter examines that exception: the unsuccessful drive for a global cloning ban within the United Nations in 2001–2005.

The failed effort to ban all forms of cloning in international law at the turn of the new millennium is an example of the new religious pluralism in world politics. The world's largest religious community, the Roman Catholic Church, together with the United States and its Evangelical Protestant president, George W. Bush, opposed all forms of cloning—for reproductive as well as for biomedical or therapeutic purposes. The anticloning coalition, which centered on Catholic-majority countries, faced a shifting array of states, including secular democracies in Europe and East Asian scientific powers. Ultimately, after some hesitation, the Organization of the Islamic Conference, a body of fifty-seven states with mainly Muslim-majority populations, came out against the ban effort and tipped the balance in favor of its opponents.

In the end this struggle did not have a primarily religious character. While the UN cloning controversy involved ethical claims and religious actors, it centered on other issues: national sovereignty, scientific freedom, and present and future economic advantage. Religion played a significant role, but only through interaction with other material and political forces. How did religion and religious-secular interaction shape the controversy? What accounts for the relatively limited impact of religious actors?

The answers advanced here center on institutional structures at the level of religious organizations and the UN system itself. On the one hand, the low level of institutionalization among religious communities—with important exceptions, including the Catholic Church—militated against the formulation of clear policy positions. In the context of ethically charged questions such as stem cells and cloning, internally diverse religious communities did not always speak with a clear voice. On the other hand, the dominant role of states and considerations of national interest within the UN marginalized the role of religious and other nonstate actors in the international political controversy. Religions do not have official representation within the General Assembly, with the exception of the Vatican, which enjoys permanent observer status. And the institutionalized norm of national sovereignty constrains the terms of debate; states can and do claim a right to oppose or ignore rules and norms that clash with perceived national interests. The weak institutionalization of transnational religious communities and the strong, state-centered cast of the UN prevented the emergence of a focused international debate about cloning governance in 2001–2005. As long as the national frame of reference for religious-political controversy remains predominant, global regulation of revolutionary, border-crossing life science technologies is unlikely to emerge.

This chapter proceeds in three sections. It first describes the international norms, national controversies, and religious voices that served as a backdrop for the cloning controversy of 2001–2005. The post–World War II decades saw the establishment of norms of human rights and human dignity in international law. Breakthroughs in embryo research and in vitro fertilization from 1968 to 1978 sparked controversies within leading Atlantic powers about the implications of human dignity in a new context. Debates about how to balance protection of the human embryo against the biomedical promise of embryo research sharpened in the wake of the cloning and stem cell breakthroughs of 1997–1998. Over the same period, leading religious traditions took up the ethical challenges posed by these life sciences breakthroughs and began, unevenly and with multiple voices, to articulate positions in national political controversies. A second section of the chapter traces and analyzes the 2001–2005 struggle that ended in a General Assembly deadlock, forcing the abandonment of efforts to establish a legally binding treaty and the recourse instead to the nonbinding Declaration on Human Cloning, passed by a slim majority in March 2005. Low levels of institutionalization within religious communities and the state-centered cast of the UN best account for the limited impact of religious actors in shaping the controversy and its outcome. A final section draws conclusions from the cloning case for a better understanding of religious pluralism, globalization, and world politics.

International Norms, National Controversies, Religious Voices

The UN cloning controversy was informed by a far-reaching religious and secular consensus around values of human dignity and human rights. This consensus was already evident in outline form in the Universal Declaration of Human Rights (1948), drafted by leading religious and secular thinkers of the day and endorsed by the General Assembly. It gained momentum in the 1960s when the Second Vatican Council threw the full weight of the Roman Catholic Church behind the ideas of human equality, religious freedom, and social justice—a path already taken by most mainline Jewish and Protestant groups and some Orthodox communities. The upsurge of religious interest in human rights and human dignity is also evident in a series of international declarations emanating from the Islamic world, beginning with the Universal Islamic Declaration of Human Rights (1981). These overlapping religious commitments are evident in statements such as the Declaration of the World Religions on a Global Ethic (1993), approved by the Parliament of the World's Religions at its centenary meeting. They find parallels in secular international legal instruments, including the International Covenant on Civil and Political Rights (1966) and the International Covenant on Economic, Social, and Cultural Rights (1967), and subsequent treaties and declarations ranging from the rights of women and children to those of indigenous peoples. Secular-religious convergence around human rights and human dignity is a big story of the past sixty years.

Parallel to this evolution of international norms, breakthroughs in the life sciences raised new questions about human rights and human dignity in an unprecedented way. Controversy about embryo research can be traced back to March 1969, when the Britain-based team of Robert Edwards and Patrick Steptoe announced the first verified case of in vitro fertilization (IVF), accomplished the previous year. There followed a first phase of embryo research focused on IVF as a fertility treatment that culminated in the birth of the first "test-tube baby," Louise Brown, in 1978. The decade that followed saw the routinization of IVF technology and the spread of clinics throughout Europe, North America, and Australia, and to Israel, India, and Japan. By the mid-1980s, scientists perfected embryo-freezing techniques that reduced the number of egg extractions patients would have to undergo, simultaneously creating a supply of surplus embryos for potential use in experiments both inside and outside the area of fertility medicine.

The next major scientific breakthroughs in this area were the cloning of Dolly the sheep, announced in March 1997, and the isolation of human embryonic stem cells, announced in November 1998. The success of cloning by nuclear transfer—the replacement of the genetic material in an egg cell with that of an adult mammal and subsequent development of an organism to birth—raised the specter of human reproductive cloning. The stem cell breakthrough the following year suggested another, therapeutic application of cloning technology. The ability of embryonic stem cells to grow into different kinds of tissue held out the promise of a new era of regenerative medicine. Cloning embryos with a patient's DNA provided a potential way to generate genetically matched stem cells for therapies to battle degenerative diseases such as Parkinson's and Alzheimer's. The reproductive versus therapeutic cloning distinction was born, and the stage was set for the controversy that unfolded within the UN in 2001–2005—whether to ban just reproductive cloning (which was universally condemned) or also to prohibit therapeutic cloning (which was not).

How exactly did cloning raise fundamental issues of human rights and human dignity, norms set down in international law? Was the governance of science something best left to UN member states, or was it, like many other human rights and dignity issues, from discrimination against women to the the exploitation of children, an area of international concern? What role should nongovernmental organizations, and religious communities in particular, play in framing the global debate? These were the vital questions at stake in the UN struggle. But the controversy, with its sharply opposed principled viewpoints, did not emerge at the international level out of nowhere. It grew out of value-driven controversies at the national level, particularly in the Atlantic democracies, which featured a wide range of religious and secular voices and culminated in a variety of contrasting regulatory regimes.[1]

National Controversies

Somewhat surprisingly in retrospect, national controversies about embryo research were slow to develop. Through the 1970s, ethical debates in the

United States, the United Kingdom, and Australia—the first centers of IVF technology—centered on the safety of the procedure, the "naturalness" of artificial procreation technology, and anxieties about a "Brave New World" of genetic engineering and enhancement. In the United States, the Department of Health, Education, and Welfare (HEW) imposed a ban on federal funding for IVF work with embryos in the mid-1970s, mainly out of a concern for the safety of mothers and children. The moral status of embryos used and discarded in IVF experiments did not play a significant role in public debates. At the time it did not even focus the attention of the Catholic Church, which centered its criticisms on IVF as an artificial intervention in the procreative process.

The success of IVF technology in the decade after 1978 and the stockpiling of surplus embryos and their use in experiments raised the political visibility of the issue. In the United States in 1979, a HEW panel made a recommendation to allow federal funding for embryo research, but successive Republican administrations refused to implement it. In the United Kingdom in 1984, an expert panel under the leadership of Mary Warnock, a moral philosopher, called for a regulatory regime to allow experiments with surplus embryos and to permit the creation of embryos expressly for research purposes under certain circumstances. The Warnock Committee's basic recommendations became UK law in 1990, the same year that the German Bundestag passed a more restrictive Embryo Protection Law that criminalized all embryo research. In 1994, the French government passed a similarly restrictive law, and in 1995 a Republican majority in the U.S. Congress outlawed any embryo research with federal funds—while letting it continue largely unregulated in the private sector.[2]

The national political controversies that culminated in these outcomes saw different constellations of religious and secular forces. In the United States, the Conference of Catholic Bishops linked embryo research to the abortion issue and successfully led opposition to President Bill Clinton's effort to loosen restrictions on federal funding for research in 1994. In the United Kingdom, the Anglican hierarchy was deeply divided, with most church leaders supporting the implementation of a liberal embryo research regime in order to advance medical progress. In Germany, against the historical backdrop of Nazi eugenics, the major parties and the Catholic and Protestant churches supported the total ban on embryo research. France, with its strong secular political culture, was an anomaly. The Catholic Church opposed research but was politically marginal. Considerable partisan support for a research ban was expressed mainly in secular, humanist arguments about the dangers of genetic manipulation and the instrumentalization of human life.

The breakthroughs of 1997–1998 transformed the policy debate and political constellation on both sides of the Atlantic and broadened the controversy internationally in the decade that followed. In the United States, a Catholic and Evangelical coalition opposed to all embryo research began to fragment under the impact of scientific discoveries and hoped-for biomedical progress. A Republican-controlled Congress repeatedly failed to pass legislation that would ban all cloning efforts, either reproductive or therapeutic. In the United Kingdom, a large Labour majority, with considerable Conservative support and the endorsement of most of the Anglican hierarchy, extended provisions of the 1990 law to allow for therapeutic cloning under strict regulations. In Germany, almost total opposition to embryo research remained in place; there was no move to relax the 1990 law. In France, by contrast, the strong secular coalition opposed to embryo research began to fragment under the impact of new discoveries and hopes for future cures, and work with surplus IVF embryos was legalized for a five-year period—even as all cloning remained banned.

The promise of stem cell research also broadened the governance discussion beyond the Atlantic democracies and Europe, where it had been concentrated. In Asia, where science and health ministries and professional associations tended to provide a looser regulatory framework, research generally went ahead with fewer restrictions and considerable infusions of public funding. South Korea, Japan, Singapore, China, and India began to emerge as international players in stem cell research. Through 2007, none of these countries had conducted extended public or parliamentary debates on permissible research. Beyond the Atlantic democracies, Israel, Australia, and New Zealand, religious communities remained generally unengaged with the stem cell and cloning issue. South Korea, with its large Christian and Buddhist communities, did see some public discussion of the compatibility of cloning research with religious traditions. And a national bioethics council in Singapore solicited the views of Christian, Buddhist, Hindu, and Muslim groups. But these cases were exceptional. Even in Iran, where Islamic authorities were generally supportive of stem cell and cloning research, the issue was rarely cast in religious or ethical terms. As in Asia, general support for scientific progress and national economic competitiveness provided the overriding rationale for national policy.[3]

Religious Voices

Starting in the 1980s, and increasingly since the late 1990s, transnational religious communities moved to formulate and advocate particular approaches to embryo, stem cell, and cloning research. There has been considerable substantive and institutional variation in bioethical perspectives and policy stances. Within the Christian tradition, the Catholic Church is both the strictest opponent of embryo research and the best-organized and most influential political actor around the issue. The general Islamic approach to stem cell and cloning research is permissive, but there is no central institutional authority to articulate a binding policy stance. Judaism is also generally favorable to embryo and cloning research but has fewer adherents and a limited public policy impact. The Buddhist and Hindu traditions, deeply diverse internally, have so far been least engaged around the stem cell and cloning controversy. Taken together, the responses of these transnational religious traditions to the same scientific and technological breakthroughs constitute a plural and varied landscape.

As noted previously, the Catholic Church was slow to seize upon the embryo research issue. Through the 1970s it directed its criticisms at IVF as an artificial reproductive technology. Only in 1982 did John Paul II identify the protection of embryos as part of a larger campaign against abortion. Five years later, in 1987, the church issued its first comprehensive statement on IVF and embryo research, a Vatican instruction entitled *Donum Vitae*—or the gift of life. The document reiterated the church's opposition to IVF as an infertility treatment and took up the moral status of the embryo in more detail. It argued that the embryo should be treated as a human person from the moment of conception—not because there was any scientific proof of personhood but because human life is a gift from God and should not be willfully destroyed. The document was one of the precursors of John Paul's notion of a "culture of life" from conception to death, set out in more detail in his encyclical *Evangelium Vitae* in 1995. Not all Catholic theologians followed this developing line of argument. Some invoked an older tradition, linked with Saint Thomas Aquinas and Aristotle, that postulated ensoulment after the forty-day mark. But the Church as an organization endorsed the absolute protection of embryos from the point of fertilization.

The Church's official response to the cloning and stem cell breakthroughs of the late 1990s was set out in two documents. An August 2000 letter from the Pontifical Academy for Life Sciences argued that a living human embryo from the point of fertilization is "a *human subject* with a well defined identity, which from that point begins its own *coordinated, continuous and gradual development*. The embryo could not be considered a "simple mass of cells" but as a "*human individual*" with the "*right* to its own life" (emphasis in original). It followed that the destruction of embryos to derive stem cells is a "gravely immoral" act. Anticipating pro-research arguments based on biomedical hopes, the letter continued: "A good end does not make right an action which in itself is wrong." By the same logic the letter condemned therapeutic cloning as the creation of embryos in order to destroy them. These arguments, while contested by some moral theologians, informed the Church's international stance on the issue.[4]

Most Orthodox churches and some Protestant communities—most notably the Lutheran Church in Germany—aligned themselves with this position.

Others took a more permissive stance toward stem cell and cloning research. Here the Anglican Church, part of a larger international Communion, was the most influential. As early as 1985, a majority of the church's Board for Social Responsibility had endorsed embryo research in the service of biomedical progress. The board developed several arguments then that would gain wide currency later—that the embryo, before the completion of the implantation stage at about fourteen days, has no nervous system, can still split and become twins, and is subject to natural mortality rates of greater than 60 percent. Under such conditions, the board argued, research in the service of noble ends such as the alleviation of human suffering was compatible with Christian teaching. A strong minority current of opposition to all destructive embryo research persisted within the church, represented by the current Archbishop of Canterbury, Rowan Williams. A 2001 paper endorsed by a synod of the church laid bare some of these internal tensions. The document referred to the embryo as "sacred" while at the same time endorsing stem cell and cloning research. Across other Protestant denominations, too, the moral status of the embryo is in tension with the promise of an "ethic of healing." Given these divisions, it is perhaps not surprising that the World Council of Churches has not endorsed a position on the issue.[5]

Jewish groups based in the United States, Europe, and Israel are among the most vocal supporters of stem cell research. Here the foundation is a Talmudic tradition that identifies the forty-day stage of gestation as the point at which the fetus becomes a human being. The longtime chief rabbi of the United Kingdom, Immanuel Jakobovits, pioneered efforts to apply this tradition to new scientific technologies. In the U.S. context, Rabbi Eliot Dorff set out the prevailing Jewish position in testimony before the U.S. National Bioethics Advisory Commission in 1998—that the embryo is unformed, "like water," for forty days.[6] This tradition does not, in the eyes of many interpreters, justify interventions to destroy the embryo in utero. But it holds that an embryo in the laboratory, without the potential to grow into a human being, does not deserve the same protection—especially when research holds the promise of alleviating human suffering. The issue of creating embryos expressly for research is controversial in the Jewish tradition. For most authorities, it is deemed permissible if necessary to advance biomedical knowledge. But others, including Jakobovits, have opposed the creation of life in order to destroy it as incompatible with the Jewish moral tradition. The first, less restrictive position on embryo creation has dominated across Orthodox, Conservative, and Reform currents of Judaism, in Europe, Israel, and the United States.

This has been evident in the specific response to the stem cell and cloning breakthroughs. Two major organizations based in the United States, representing Orthodox and Conservative Judaism, backed stem cell research in 2001, noting: "Our Torah tradition places great value upon human life; we are taught in the opening chapters of Genesis that each human was created in G-d's very image. The potential to save and heal human lives is an integral part of valuing human life from the traditional Jewish perspective." The same statement reflected some of the ambivalence within Judaism concerning the deliberate creation of embryos for research. "We believe it is entirely appropriate to utilize for this research existing embryos, such as those created for IVF purposes that would otherwise be discarded but for this research," the statement noted, but continued: "We think it another matter to create embryos ab initio for the sole purpose of conducting this form of research." Subsequent statements from the same organizations were more positive about the creation of embryos through cloning. Recalling that the Jewish tradition "states that an embryo *in vitro* does not enjoy the full status of human-hood and its attendant protections," a statement made on the occasion of a 2002 Senate cloning debate argued it should be encouraged if it "advances our ability to heal humans with greater success."[7] In a similar vein, a report of the Israel Academy of Science and Humanities underscored that "the commandment to save lives supersedes many other laws in Judaism."[8]

The debate within Islam has many parallels with that in Judaism. In Islamic law the fetus attains the status of personhood either at 40 or 120 days. Qur'an 38:72–73 suggests a gradual process of human formation: "And your Lord said to the angels: 'I am going to create human from clay. And when I have given him form and breathed into him of My life force, you must all show respect by bowing down before him.'" Collections of the sayings of Muhammad construe the attainment of personhood as a gradual process through which God infuses the fetus with form and spirit while in the womb: "Each one of you possesses his own formation within his mother's womb, first as a drop of matter for forty days, then as a blood clot for forty days, then as a blob for forty days, and then the angel is sent to breathe life into him."[9] As in the Jewish traditions the absence of full humanity from conception does not make its deliberate destruction licit; the embryo is considered a developing form of human life deserving of some protection. But full humanity, or fully formed personhood, is not yet present. As a seminar convened under the auspices of the Islamic Organization for Medical Sciences put it in 1983, an "embryo is a living organism from the moment of conception, and its life is to be respected in all its stages, *especially* after spirit is breathed in" (emphasis added).[10]

Islam lacks a central teaching authority such as the Catholic magisterium. It is also less institutionalized than Judaism, which has an array of national and international organizations that take positions on public policy issues. The legal pronouncements (fatwas) of respected imams carry considerable weight.

And over the past decade Islamic bioethicists have convened more often to hammer out joint positions on sensitive issues, including embryo, stem cell, and cloning research. The Organization of the Islamic Conference (OIC), an intergovernmental organization of predominantly Muslim countries, has provided a supportive institutional framework. In 1997, the OIC co-convened the Islamic Law Medical Seminar in Casablanca, which provided a general condemnation for cloning but remained open to future scientific applications. "Ordinary human cloning, in which the nucleus of a living somatic cell from an individual is placed into the cytoplasm of an egg devoid of its nucleus, is not to be permitted," the seminar communiqué, adding that "if exceptional cases emerge in the future, they should be considered to verify compliance with the Shari'ah."[11]

Subsequent rulings in favor of and opposed to therapeutic cloning have taken place, with the former prevailing in terms of numbers and influence. For example, the European Council for Fatwa and Research argued that "it is permissible to use the technologies of cloning in the fields of therapy by using stem cells to produce healthy organs that can replace the defective ones provided that this should not lead to damaging a fetus older than 40 days of age."[12] In Singapore a fatwa committee of the Islamic Religious Council endorsed the view that deriving stem cells from "embryos below 14 days for the purpose of research, which will benefit mankind, is allowed in Islam."[13] It was not until early 2003 that the OIC Standing Committee on Scientific and Technological Cooperation set up the International Committee on Bioethics. And in January 2005 the Islamic Organization for Medical Sciences endorsed therapeutic cloning at a meeting in Cairo. While it may be an exaggeration to argue that "therapeutic cloning is acceptable universally by all the Shia and the Sunni Muslims," it is true that "embryos don't have the same sanctity (that they do in the Christian faith)."[14]

It is even more difficult to find authoritative positions on embryo, cloning, and stem cell research within Hinduism and Buddhism. Both religious traditions are marked by a deep internal pluralism that extends to questions of early human life and its significance. Classical Hinduism placed the soul's rebirth at the moment of conception. An early Hindu text, the *Caraka Samhita*, vividly describes the beginning of life:

> Conception occurs when intercourse takes place in due season
> between a man of unimpaired semen and a woman whose genera-
> tive organ, (menstrual) blood and womb are unvitiated—when, in
> fact, in the event of intercourse thus described, the individual soul
> (*jiva*) descends into the union of semen and (menstrual) blood in the

womb in keeping with the (*karmically* produced) psychic disposition (of the embryonic matter).[15]

Later currents within Hinduism locate the presence of the soul at the three- to five-month range, or go as late as seven months.

In the context of stem cell and cloning research, this less restrictive standard has prevailed. In response to a query from the U.S. National Ethics Advisory Board in 1998, Mata Amritanandamayi of India—a leading Hindu representative at the Parliament of the World's Religions in 1993—argued, "The fuller understanding of cellular and reproductive processes can enhance the genetic engineering already underway and lead to new treatments for disease and the relief of suffering."[16] The Hindu group consulted by the government of Singapore noted, "According to our Faith (Hinduism) killing a foetus is a sinful act." But it further noted that "whether the 14 day old foetus is endowed with all the qualities of life is not well regarded. Therefore, there is no non-acceptance to use these ES cells to protect human life and advance life by curing disease."[17] Due both to the diversity of Hinduism and to the secular cast of the Indian state, where the vast majority of Hindus live, the religious tradition has had little impact on the transnational political and policy debate. This could conceivably change in years to come, as the National Bioethics Committee submits draft regulatory guidelines for political deliberation and approval.[18]

Buddhism, like Hinduism, encompasses a diversity of approaches to the embryo and the question of whether it is entitled to protection. As with Hinduism, scriptural traditions tend to emphasize the embryo as part of humanity (as distinct from any assertions about the presence of a unique individual soul). Damien Keown summarizes the position: "From conception onwards the spiritual and material components that constitute the new individual—what Buddhists call nama-rupa (mind and body)—evolve together."[19] Any deliberate harm to the embryo is deemed incompatible with the notion of *ahimsa*, or non-violence to living things. The Dalai Lama points to the *Abhidharma*, philosophical treatises written by the early Buddhist monks that argue that "consciousness enters the embryo through the meeting of the regenerative substances of the father and mother, and at that point it becomes a sentient being." He acknowledges that "from the classical Buddhist standpoint, it has become a sentient being and extermination of that would be morally equivalent, almost, to killing a human being."[20]

In the context of stem cell breakthroughs, and their biomedical promise, some thinkers have contended that the Buddhist emphasis on compassion points to the positive value of biomedical research. The Dalai Lama himself has argued for a reconsideration of the moral status of the embryo in the light of discoveries. Commenting on scientific knowledge about high levels of natural embryo loss, he has argued that "for the formation of life, for something to actually become a human, something more is needed than simply a fertilized egg." Embryo and stem cell research might be countenanced in the Buddhist tradition: "It may be that what you do to a conglomeration of cells that have the possibility of becoming human entails no negative or karmically unwholesome act." Without giving a precise cut-off point, the Dalai Lama concluded that "when you're dealing with a configuration of cells that are definitely on the track to becoming a human being, it's a different situation."[21] The diversity of perspectives within the Buddhist tradition, broadly defined, is exemplified by statements by leading Korean cloning researchers. Hwang-Woo Suk, the scientist whose research was discredited as fraudulent in late 2005, told an interviewer: "I am not versed in the creeds of Buddhism. But when I carry out research, I always check whether they square with the sublime spirit of the Buddha."[22] One of his collaborators told an American audience, "Cloning is a different way of thinking about the recycling of life."[23]

Transnational religious communities have developed clear positions on the ethics of stem cell and cloning research in only a handful of cases. The Catholic Church, like most all national Orthodox churches, is fundamentally opposed to any research destructive of embryos, while Protestant groups are divided on the issue. The overall Jewish position in favor of research is clearly articulated. The Muslim tradition is generally favorable to research but divided somewhat on the question of creating embryos for research or therapeutic cloning. The absence of clear institutional structures to formulate authoritative positions, within and across Muslim countries, distinguishes Islam from the other Abrahamic faiths. Hinduism and Buddhism are extremely diverse internally. Each incorporates scriptural traditions that suggest conception as the start of a particular human existence—as well as other views that emphasize the centrality of compassion and an "ethic of healing" supportive of research. Overall, the last decade has seen a variety of religious perspectives on stem cell and cloning research, their articulation across national borders, and their interaction within the context of national politics. In 2001, when the cloning issue moved onto the agenda of the UN, this religious pluralism shaped efforts to forge an international regime to govern reproductive and therapeutic cloning.

The UN and the Politics of a Cloning Ban

The years after the announcement of Dolly's birth saw a wave of national legislation outlawing reproductive cloning, as well as repeated calls for international regulation. It was not until 2001, however, that the cloning issue officially moved onto the United Nations agenda.[24] Concerned about the eugenic implications of the new technologies—salient against the backdrop of the Nazi past—France and Germany jointly proposed an international convention against reproductive cloning in August. Therapeutic cloning, a divisive topic in national politics on both sides of the Atlantic, was omitted from the proposal. The intention was to forge broad global consensus against a procedure that was universally condemned. A German Foreign Ministry official commented at the time, "Cloning is a worthwhile issue on which it's safe to find common ground, both with the French and the Americans."[25] The posited common ground did not materialize.

When the General Assembly's Legal Committee, the body charged with discussing mandates for international conventions, first took up the question in November 2001, the Vatican raised objections to the narrow focus on reproductive cloning. Archbishop Renato Martino, the Vatican's permanent UN observer, acknowledged to the committee the importance of "achieving universal agreement in the creation of a normative instrument, valid for all the world." But the proposed convention, he insisted, should also address therapeutic cloning and outlaw the destruction of embryos in research. "Before the moral norm which prohibits the direct taking of the life of an innocent human being, there are no privileges or exceptions for anyone," Martino asserted, quoting John Paul II's 1995 encyclical, *Evangelium Vitae*: "It makes no difference whether one is the master of the world or the 'poorest of the poor' on the face of the earth. Before the demands of morality we are all absolutely equal."[26]

In December 2001 the General Assembly voted to set up the Ad Hoc Committee on an International Convention against the Reproductive Cloning of Human Beings, effectively ignoring the Vatican's plea that therapeutic cloning also be considered. But two months later, the U.S. administration of George Bush backed the Vatican position in favor of a comprehensive cloning ban.[27] The U.S. stance was apparently an effort to placate conservatives upset about Bush's August 2001 decision to allow some federal funding for embryonic stem cell research with existing cell lines. It also clearly reflected Bush's own religious convictions and determination to hold the line at the creation of embryos for research. As he told conservative activists in April 2002, in the midst of a failed effort to pass a comprehensive cloning ban in the Senate, "Life is a creation, not a commodity." Addressing Evangelical audiences about the issue he would later refer to life as a "gift from God."[28]

With Bush's decision, battle lines were drawn. The United States came out in support of a proposal put forward by Costa Rica and backed by a group of mainly Catholic countries. It called for an international convention banning all forms of cloning. France and Germany threw their weight behind a Belgian proposal centered solely on reproductive cloning. Germany and France had both outlawed cloning on their territory. But they and their supporters insisted that it was important to achieve consensus where it was possible—on reproductive cloning—and effectively leave the question of therapeutic cloning to the UN member states to handle separately. India, China, South Korea, and Singapore, as well as a large number of European countries, also supported the Belgian proposal. Among the most outspoken was the United Kingdom, which had legalized therapeutic cloning in December 2001 and objected vehemently to the possibility that the issue might eventually be decided at the international level.

The issue came to a head in November 2003. To most observers it appeared as if the U.S.-backed proposal would win a clear majority; several smaller island nations and developing countries had swelled the ranks of those supporting a comprehensive ban. But on the verge of a climactic vote on the two proposals, Iran introduced a procedural motion to delay consideration of the issue for two years. Speaking on behalf of the Organization of the Islamic Conference, whose ambassadors had convened prior to the meeting, the Iranian representative suggested that in view of the lack of consensus, more time was needed to study the issue. Several of the countries aligned with the United States, Costa Rica, and the Vatican joined in the the call for more time, and the Iranian resolution passed by a vote of 80 to 79, with 15 abstentions. Some observers saw in the OIC move an effort to maintain a more liberal global research regime in accordance with Islamic precepts. Others saw an effort to put the issue off until after the 2004 U.S. presidential election. But given the divisions among Muslim countries on the issue, and the absence of fatwas considered universally authoritative, the declared reason for the motion—the need for more time to formulate clear positions—should not be dismissed. The U.S. representative put such a gloss on the vote at the time. Muslim countries, James Cunningham suggested, "have a fundamental need to integrate policy and views from their religious community and in many places that integration hasn't taken place yet."[29]

As it happened, supporters of a comprehensive ban were able to get the issue back onto the General Assembly agenda in fall 2004—but again failed to break the deadlock. The same two proposals, with only minor changes, confronted each other. And despite the best efforts of the Legal Committee staff to mediate, all signs pointed toward a showdown vote on which resolution to use as the basis for negotiations on an international convention. The October 2004 debates saw some sharp exchanges within the committee over the moral status of the embryo and the appropriateness of international regulation of cloning research. Closely following the Vatican's perspective on the early embryo, Costa Rica's foreign minister Roberto Tovar espied "no substantial difference" between an embryo and an adult. "We were all once embryos and blastocysts," he noted. His Honduran colleague was more explicit in invoking religious tradition: "We should not play God. Let us remember that we are simply dust after all."[30]

With few exceptions, opponents of a comprehensive ban did not take up the question of the moral status of the embryo. The UK ambassador was unusually blunt, referring to the early embryo as "a ball of unspecialized cells," but most of his colleagues emphasized two other arguments—the biomedical promise of the research and the principle of national sovereignty. They did not engage opposing philosophical and religious perspectives as much as they insisted on each country's right to decide the question for itself. The South Korean representative noted that "many different religious and moral views exist regarding when human life begins." Singapore's spokesman noted that views of when life begins "differ from one religion to another, and even within religions"; he accused supporters of a comprehensive ban of trying to impose "value judgments." In the same vein, the Chinese ambassador pointed to "a diversity of civilizations and cultures which should show mutual understanding and respect," and the Japanese ambassador underscored that "historical, ethical, cultural and religious traditions of each country should be respected in formulating a convention on this issue."[31]

With a divisive vote imminent in November 2004, the members of the OIC, represented by Turkey as chair, forcefully argued in favor of more time to reach broader consensus. At this point, the Italian delegation won support for the creation of a working group to draft a nonbinding Declaration on Human Cloning—effectively tabling the more ambitious plan of a convention under international law. The chairman of the Legal Committee, eager to uphold its tradition of striving for the deepest possible consensus, welcomed the proposal with relief. Noting fundamental issues of "good and evil" bound up with the cloning question, and its relevance for "belief and religions," he related his staff's concern that "it would be unbearable for the international community to be divided on an issue like cloning." The nonbinding resolution offered a way out of the conflict.[32]

The working group text sought to finesse the key issues by coming up with language that suggested a ban on all cloning but could also be construed as allowing for national decisions on therapeutic cloning. On March 8, 2005, the General Assembly voted on the text generated by the working group and endorsed by the Legal Committee. It called on member states "to prohibit all forms of human cloning inasmuch as they are incompatible with human dignity and the protection of human life." The word "inasmuch" created an opening for cloning that was not deemed incompatible with human dignity, but the resolution as a whole suggested a blanket condemnation. Not surprisingly, many of the supporters of the Belgian convention draft refused to go along. In the end the final vote was 84 to 34 in favor of the declaration, with 37 abstentions. Muslim-majority nations came down on different sides of the question. Saudi Arabia and Kuwait, for example, supported the resolution, while Iran, Turkey, and Jordan abstained. Most all Catholic-majority nations favored the resolution, with Brazil an important exception.

Conclusion

The UN cloning debate of 2001–2005 illustrated both the importance of religious actors in world politics and the limits of their influence. In the years before the UN took up the issue, religious communities staked out positions on stem cell and cloning research in national political controversies, particularly in Atlantic democracies. They also began to articulate positions at the international level, grappling with scientific and ethical questions that, by their very nature, crossed over national boundaries. The result was a diverse set of ethical stances within and across religious communities, ranging from the Roman Catholic Church's official opposition to all destructive embryo research, through the more permissive stances of Judaism and Islam, and a great diversity of views within Hinduism and Buddhism. Religious pluralism around the cloning issue not only reflected different scriptural and theological approaches to the moral status of the embryo and the promise of biomedical progress. It was also a function of the diverse configuration of religious organizations, some more international and institutionalized than others.

In the UN context, the international and political reach of religious actors became clear in November 2001, when the Vatican engineered a successful effort to place therapeutic cloning, and not just research cloning, on the global agenda. This initiative, backed by most Catholic-majority countries and by the United States of George W. Bush, changed the terms of debate and precipitated a deadlock at the international level. As the debate progressed, the other crucial voting bloc, the Organization of the Islamic Conference, sought to arrive at a consensus around the issue. The OIC's successful effort to defer a vote that might have resulted in a U.S. and Vatican victory in 2003 and again in 2004 reflected, in part, the more permissive approach to embryo research in the Muslim tradition. But OIC members did not articulate their position in religious terms; they referred instead to the need for more time to explore the issue and seek consensus. The diversity of views within Islam on cloning research, reinforced by the lack of a central teaching authority, contributed to the UN controversy not being cast primarily in terms of competing religious and ethical perspectives.

Ultimately, the dominant secular terms of the UN debate had more to do with the institutional culture of the organization than with the nature of the cloning issue. The organizing principle of national sovereignty constrained the terms of the deliberations. In the Legal Committee and the General Assembly there was some engagement with fundamental ethical and religious questions, including when life begins and deserves protection, and the moral imperative of healing the sick. But the decisive argument of supporters of therapeutic cloning was that the decision should be left to states. Given the existence of deep philosophical and religious differences, they insisted, national political communities should decide the issue for themselves. The norm of national sovereignty, institutionalized within the United Nations itself, framed the terms of the debate and contributed to the outcome: a toothless and ambiguous declaration with no practical implications for the future worldwide trajectory of stem cell and cloning research.

The cloning case suggests some broader implications for the way we think about religious pluralism in world politics. The vast majority of the world's population are members of religious communities—probably well over 80 percent. In the post–cold war world, religion has emerged as a more salient marker of individual and group political identity. Simultaneously we are seeing a growing number of global issues with ethical dimensions that intersect with religious traditions, including not just cloning but economic and social development, public health crises, humanitarian disasters, and human rights. In this emergent constellation it is critical that religious communities engage one another and secular actors and institutions—not to arrive at consensus about how to address these and other global challenges, but to learn more about opposing viewpoints so as to promote workable compromises and sustainable solutions.

The bioethical issues explored in this chapter provide some evidence of transnational intellectual and political mobilization. Roman Catholic, Protestant, and Orthodox Christian communities have taken up questions of human rights and human dignity raised by revolutions in the life sciences. Over the past decade the Organization of the Islamic Conference has become a framework for bioethical reflection among Muslims—and a platform for involvement in international controversies. Various currents of Judaism, concentrated in Israel, the United States, and Europe, have developed principled positions. And Hindu and Buddhist thinkers around the world have begun to explore ways to apply their diverse traditions to new discoveries. These conversations within and across traditions are not disconnected; they are framed by the commitments to human rights and human dignity enshrined in international law. But transnational interreligious and religious-secular debate about science and bioethics remains fragmented and uneven. The nation state remains the critical locus of political contestation and policy formation.

Over the period explored in this chapter (2001-2005), the world was reeling from September 11, 2001, and its aftermath, including the war in Afghanistan and the invasion of Iraq. Bioethical questions—including the cloning issue— were rarely in the media spotlight. In the years since, the life sciences revolution and its implications have remained overshadowed by issues of peace and war, democracy and justice, and economic and social development. Still, the UN cloning controversy was a critical juncture: the first time that religious and secular actors and arguments engaged, at a global level, the critical issue of how and whether to govern a scientific enterprise with tremendous potential for good or for ill. Because science has a transnational dimension and scientific breakthroughs raise universal ethical issues, religious and secular actors within the state and civil society will grapple with regulatory issues into the future—at the international, as well as the national level. How religious pluralism will shape the global governance of the life sciences remains an open question. But as long as religious communities remain institutionally weak and politics remains centered on national interests and national sovereignty, the prospects for transnational deliberation on—and governance of—revolutionary life science technologies will remain dim.

NOTES

1. Thomas Banchoff, "Path-Dependence and Value-Driven Issues: The Comparative Politics of Stem Cell Research," *World Politics* 57, no. 2 (January 2005): 200–230. Unless otherwise noted, "stem cell" refers throughout this chapter to cells derived from human embryos.

2. For background, see Thomas Banchoff, "Stem Cell Politics, Religious and Secular: The United States and France Compared," in *Democracy and the New Religious Pluralism*, ed. Thomas Banchoff (Oxford: Oxford University Press, 2007): 301–322.

3. Leroy Walters, "Human Embryonic Stem Cell Research: An Intercultural Perspective," *Kennedy Institute of Ethics Journal* 14, no. 1 (March 2004): 3–38.

4. Pontifical Academy for Life, "Declaration on the Production and the Scientific and Therapeutic Use of Human Embryonic Stem Cells," August 25, 2000, http:// www.vatican.va/roman_curia/pontifical_academies/acdlife/documents/rc_pa_acdlife_ doc_20000824_cellule-staminali_en.html.

5. Church of England, "Human Fertilisation and Embryology," http://www. cofe.anglican.org/info/socialpublic/science/hfea/. A 2003 report of the WCC Central Committee did take up the issue, noting the danger that with embryo research, "incipient human life is treated as a commodity, the value of which is being weighed over against the value of protecting other human life through new forms of treatment." But the WCC as a whole did not take a position on the issue. World Council of Churches, "Report of the General Secretary," Central Committee, Geneva Switzerland, August 26–September 2, 2003.

6. National Bioethics Advisory Commission, *Ethical Issues in Human Stem Cell Research* 3 (Washington, DC: NBAC, 1999), C1.

7. Union of Orthodox Jewish Congregations of America and the Rabbinical Council of America, "Letter to George Bush Regarding Stem Cell Research," July 26, 2001, http://www.ou.org/public/statements/2001/nate34.htm; Union of Orthodox Jewish Congregations of America and the Rabbinical Council of America, "Cloning Research, Jewish Tradition, and Public Policy: A Joint Statement by the Union of Orthodox Jewish Congregations of America and the Rabbinical Council of America," March 2002, http://www.ou.org/public/Publib/cloninglet.htm

8. Bioethics Advisory Committee of the Israel Academy of Science and Humanities, "Report: The Use of Embryonic Stem Cells for Therapeutic Research," August 2001, http://www.internationale-kooperation.de/doc/bioethic_600.pdf.

9. Cited in National Bioethics Advisory Commission, *Ethical Issues in Human Stem Cell Research*, G4.

10. Islamic Organization for Medical Sciences, "Recommendations of the Seminar on Human Reproduction in Islam," seminar held May 24, 1983, http://www.islamset. com/bioethics/firstvol.html.

11. Islamic Organization for Medical Sciences, "Recommendations of the 9th Fiqh-Medical Seminar," June 14–17, 1997, http://www.islamset.com/healnews/ cloning/view.html. The seminar recommendations noted "with regret that the Muslim world continues to follow blindly in the footsteps of the West in the fields of modern biological sciences. It called for the establishment of the necessary academic institutions to undertake this work according to the teachings of the Shari'ah."

12. The European Council for Fatwa and Research, "Final Statement of the 10th Ordinary Session," session held January 22–26, 2003, http://www.e-cfr.org/eng/ article.php?sid=36.

13. Singapore, Bioethics Advisory Committee (BAC) 2002., cited in Walters, "Human Embryonic Stem Cell Research," 22.

14. Wagdy Sawahel, "Muslim States Urged to Back Therapeutic Cloning," *SciDev. net*, January 5, 2005, http://www.scidev.net/News/index.cfm?fuseaction=readNews& itemid=1831&language=1; Abdulaziz Sachedina, an expert on the ethics of cloning in Islam, cited in Colum Lynch, "U.N. Postpones Debate on Human Cloning," *Washington Post*, November 7, 2003, A02.

15. Cited in Walters, "Human Embryonic Stem Cell Research," 24.

16. Satyakama Dhruv, "Cloning and the Human Soul," *Illuminations* 2, no. 2 (Fall 1997), http://illuminated.netfirms.com/a_cloning.htm.

17. Singapore, Bioethics Advisory Committee 2002, cited in Walters, "Human Embryonic Stem Cell Research," 22.

18. Draft guidelines made public in 2005 opposed therapeutic cloning in general, with a proviso: "In special situations where cloning is for therapeutic purposes with regard to cells, tissues or organs, the Committee will examine them on a case to case basis." Indian Council of Medical Research, *Draft Guidelines for Stem Cell Research/Regulation in India*, August 5, 2004, http://hinxtongroup.org/guidelines_stemcell_india.doc.

19. Damien Keown, *Buddhist Bioethics: A Very Short Introduction* (Oxford: Oxford University Press, 2005), 85.

20. "When Does a Stem Cell Become a Human Being? Scientific Perspectives from His Holiness the Dalai Lama," *Mandala* (March/May 2003): 14.

21. Ibid.

22. Cited in Kim Tae-gyu, "Stem Cell and Buddhism," *Korea Times*, May 24, 2005. http://www.dhammaweb.net/news/stemcell.html

23. Professor Yong Moon to a conference of the American Academy of Science, cited in Michael Horstman, "Buddhism at One with Stem Cell Research," *News in Science*, February 18, 2004, http://www.abc.net.au/science/news/stories/s1046974.htm.

24. For all the relevant documentation, see http://www.un.org/law/cloning/.

25. Cited in Steven Erlanger, "France and Germany Jointly Seek a Ban on Cloning Humans," *New York Times*, August 22, 2001.

26. The Holy See, "Intervention of H. E. Mons. Renato R. Martino at the United Nations Organization 'On International Convention against the Reproductive Cloning of Human Beings,'" November 19, 2001: http://www.vatican.va/roman_curia/secretariat_state/documents/rc_seg-st_doc_20011119_martino-vi-comm_en.html; John Paul II, *Evangelium Vitae*, March 25, 1995, http://www.vatican.va/holy_father/john_paul_ii/encyclicals/documents/hf_jp-ii_enc_25031995_evangelium-vitae_en.html.

27. Colum Lynch, "U.S. Seeks to Extend Ban on Cloning," *Washington Post*, February 27, 2002, A08.

28. White House Press Release, "President Bush Calls on Senate to Back Human Cloning Ban," April 10, 2002; White House Press Release, "Remarks Via Satellite by the President to the National Association of Evangelicals Convention," March 11, 2004.

29. United States Mission to the United Nations Press Release, "Remarks by Ambassador James B. Cunningham, Deputy United States Representative to the United Nations, on the Motion to Defer a Vote on the UN Resolution to Ban Human Cloning, at the Stakeout, November 6, 2003," *USUN Press Release 225 (03)* (November 6, 2003).

30. There is no official transcript of the proceedings. These citations are drawn from the webcasts of the October 2004 debates, available at the Ad Hoc Committee on an International Convention against the Reproductive Cloning of Human Beings, "Sixth Committee of the General Assembly Debate: Agenda Item Entitled 'International Convention against the Reproductive Cloning of Human Beings,'" October 2004, http://www.un.org/law/cloning/.

31. The Jordanian representative was most direct in invoking the principle of national sovereignty: "You cannot compel another nation to act against its national interest and positions and to ban embryonic stem cell research on the national level." Ibid.

32. Ibid.

BIBLIOGRAPHY

Ad Hoc Committee on an International Convention against the Reproductive Cloning of Human Beings. "Sixth Committee of the General Assembly Debate: Agenda Item Entitled 'International Convention against the Reproductive Cloning of Human Beings.'" October 2004. http://www.un.org/law/cloning/.

Banchoff, Thomas. "Path-Dependence and Value-Driven Issues: The Comparative Politics of Stem Cell Research." *World Politics* 57, no. 2 (January 2005): 200–230.

———. "Stem Cell Politics, Religious and Secular: The United States and France Compared." In *Democracy and the New Religious Pluralism*, ed. Thomas Banchoff, 301–322. Oxford: Oxford University Press, 2007.

Bioethics Advisory Committee of the Israel Academy of Science and Humanities. "Report: The Use of Embryonic Stem Cells for Therapeutic Research." August 2001. http://www.internationale-kooperation.de/doc/bioethic_600.pdf.

Church of England. "Human Fertilisation and Embryology." http://www.cofe.anglican.org/info/socialpublic/science/hfea/.

Dhruv, Satyakama. "Cloning and the Human Soul." *Illuminations* 2, no. 2 (Fall 1997). http://illuminated.netfirms.com/a_cloning.htm.

Erlanger, Steven. "France and Germany Jointly Seek a Ban on Cloning Humans." *New York Times*, August 22, 2001.

European Council for Fatwa and Research. "Final Statement of the 10th Ordinary Session." Session held January 22–26, 2003. http://www.e-cfr.org/eng/article.php?sid=36.

Holy See. "Intervention of H. E. Mons. Renato R. Martino at the United Nations Organization 'On International Convention against the Reproductive Cloning of Human Beings.'" November 19, 2001. http://www.vatican.va/roman_curia/secretariat_state/documents/rc_seg-st_doc_20011119_martino-vi-comm_en.html.

Horstman, Michael. "Buddhism at One with Stem Cell Research." *News in Science*, February 18, 2004. http://www.abc.net.au/science/news/stories/s1046974.htm.

Indian Council of Medical Research. *Draft Guidelines for Stem Cell Research/Regulation in India.* August 5, 2004. http://hinxtongroup.org/guidelines_stemcell_india.doc.

Islamic Organization for Medical Sciences. "Recommendations of the 9th Fiqh-Medical Seminar." Seminar held June 14–17, 1997. http://www.islamset.com/healnews/cloning/view.html.

———. "Recommendations of the Seminar on Human Reproduction in Islam." Seminar held May 24, 1983. http://www.islamset.com/bioethics/firstvol.html.

John Paul II. *Evangelium Vitae.* March 25, 1995. http://www.vatican.va/holy_father/john_paul_ii/encyclicals/documents/hf_jp-ii_enc_25031995_evangelium-vitae_en.html.

Keown, Damien. *Buddhist Bioethics: A Very Short Introduction.* Oxford: Oxford University Press, 2005.

Lynch, Colum. "U.N. Postpones Debate on Human Cloning." *Washington Post,* November 7, 2003, A02.

———. "U.S. Seeks to Extend Ban on Cloning," *Washington Post,* February 27, 2002, A08.

National Bioethics Advisory Commission. *Ethical Issues in Human Stem Cell Research* 3. Washington, DC: NBAC, 1999.

Pontifical Academy for Life. "Declaration on the Production and the Scientific and Therapeutic Use of Human Embryonic Stem Cells." August 25, 2000. http://www.vatican.va/roman_curia/pontifical_academies/acdlife/documents/rc_pa_acdlife_doc_20000824_cellule-staminali_en.html.

Reuters. "Bush Administration Proposes Human Cloning Ban at the UN." *Washington Post,* February 28, 2002.

Sawahel, Wagdy. "Muslim States Urged to Back Therapeutic Cloning." *SciDev.net.* January 5, 2005. http://www.scidev.net/News/index.cfm?fuseaction=readNews&itemid=1831&language=1.

Tae-gyu, Kim. "Stem Cell and Buddhism." *Korea Times,* May 24, 2005.

Union of Orthodox Jewish Congregations of America and the Rabbinical Council of America. "Cloning Research, Jewish Tradition, and Public Policy: A Joint Statement by the Union of Orthodox Jewish Congregations of America and the Rabbinical Council of America." March 2002. http://www.ou.org/public/Publib/cloninglet.htm.

———. "Letter to George Bush Regarding Stem Cell Research." July 26, 2001. http://www.ou.org/public/statements/2001/nate34.htm.

United States Mission to the United Nations Press Release. "Remarks by Ambassador James B. Cunningham, Deputy United States Representative to the United Nations, on the Motion to Defer a Vote on the UN Resolution to Ban Human Cloning, at the Stakeout, November 6, 2003." *USUN Press Release 225 (03).* November 6, 2003.

Walters, Leroy. "Human Embryonic Stem Cell Research: An Intercultural Perspective." *Kennedy Institute of Ethics Journal* 14, no. 1 (March 2004): 3–38.

"When Does a Stem Cell Become a Human Being? Scientific Perspectives from His Holiness the Dalai Lama." *Mandala* (March/May 2003): 14.

White House Press Release. "President Bush Calls on Senate to Back Human Cloning Ban." April 10, 2002.

———. "Remarks via Satellite by the President to the National Association of Evangelicals Convention." March 11, 2004.

World Council of Churches. "Report of the General Secretary." Central Committee, Geneva Switzerland, August 26–September 2, 2003.

12

U.S. Foreign Policy and Global Religious Pluralism

Elizabeth H. Prodromou

Any effort to understand, much less to manage, the role of religion in world affairs must address a single, overarching reality: a historically unprecedented pluralism evident in national religious demographies, internally diverse faith traditions, and transnational religious actors and activities. This multilevel and crosscutting global religious pluralism refutes the theories of secularization that dominated social science theory and international relations praxis for most of the twentieth century. It also poses new foreign policy challenges, as national leaders seek to combine the pursuit of material interests in wealth and security with attention to questions of cultural difference, religious freedom, and human rights in an era of globalization.

The case of the United States, the world's predominant power at the outset of the twenty-first century, illustrates the opportunities and risks for foreign policy at this new juncture of global religious pluralism. With its global reach and long-standing commitment to universal human rights, the United States is uniquely positioned to address two salient features of the new constellation—religious persecution in diverse national contexts and the threats posed by militant religious movements. American responses to this constellation since the late 1990s, I argue, have been defensive and reactionary, driven by qualitative change in the influence of religion in the formation and articulation of U.S. foreign policy. It may be premature to make a definitive case for a distinctively religious turn in U.S. foreign policy, given lack of access to the internal deliberations of recent administrations. Nonetheless, there is credible evidence, in the form of America's international actions and public rhetoric, and, equally important, in the domestic and international responses and interpretations of Washington's actions, to support the claim of a qualitative change in the role of religion in American foreign policy since the end of the cold war and, especially, over the last decade. This chapter explores the nature, as well as the consequences for world politics, of this qualitative difference from historical patterns in how religion matters in U.S. foreign policy.

This chapter is divided into four sections. I first offer a brief historical overview of the influence of religion as an animating force in American foreign policy. A historicized perspective on the place of religious discourse, ideas, and actors in America's role in the international arena highlights what is distinctive and particular about the contemporary relationship between religion and U.S. foreign policy. Two subsequent sections focus on policy turning points and their legacies: the International Religious Freedom Act (IRFA) of 1998 and the proclamation of the War on Terror after the attacks of September 11, 2001. These key junctures of 1998 and 2001 changed the profile of religion in U.S. foreign policy and national security strategy and help to explain the international perception of an unparalleled turn toward God in American statecraft and, at its source, the Executive Office.

A final, concluding section argues that the religious turn threatens to isolate the United States and, paradoxically, undermine its efforts to combat global religious persecution and to counter international terrorism. Washington's policy on religious freedom and against terrorism, especially over the last decade, is widely perceived as a cynical control-response to global conditions of unprecedented religious pluralism and challenges to American hegemony. Efforts to promote peace and toleration among different religious communities and within diverse civil societies—most visible, and least successful, in the ongoing occupation of Iraq—are widely perceived as the religious dimensions of an aggressive imperialism, mainly underpinned by a neoconservative ideology but also endorsed by proponents of liberal interventionism.[1] As a result, the religious factor in Washington's formulation and conduct of foreign policy has become securitized. By transforming religion into a source of risk and confrontation in foreign policy over the past decade, Washington has actually weakened America's capacity to advance religious freedom, human rights, and peace in a religiously plural world.

Historical Legacies: Religion, American Exceptionalism, and U.S. Foreign Policy

A periodization of U.S. foreign policy after the cold war shows a gradual yet discernible shift in the salience of religion, both domestically and internationally. Domestically, the rise of the Religious Right—a process that began under Ronald Reagan's presidency, continued under subsequent Republican and Democratic administrations, and has been cast into stark relief during the presidential terms of George W. Bush—enabled a bargain of convenience between religious and nonreligious groups whose shared concerns about religious persecution and human rights were not necessarily matched by a compatibility between their broader political interests. Internationally, the renewed influence of religious actors coincided with a growing willingness of U.S. foreign policy elites, mainly secular in orientation, to privilege force over diplomacy and unilateral over multilateral action—a trend most evident in Washington's declaration in September 2001 of the War on Terror and the U.S. invasion of Iraq in March 2003.

It would be a mistake to reduce the influence of religion in U.S. foreign policy to the G. W. Bush presidency and its immediate predecessors. The historical roots of that influence go far deeper. An expansive scholarly literature explores the origins and manifestations of a deep strain of religious messianism that runs through the master narrative of America's claims of exceptionalism as a nation-state. From the founding myth of Puritan settlement of the New World as a struggle for religious freedom, to the articulation of the doctrine of Manifest Destiny as a rationale for America's westward territorial expansion, to Wilsonian internationalism as a public service creed, and the definition of the cold war as a battle with atheistic communism, religion and a religious political culture have been a constant element in "the longstanding U.S. view of itself as morally superior, and therefore exceptional vis-à-vis other powers."[2] The pervasiveness of religious themes in U.S. foreign policy is unsurprising, given that America's political culture has been informed by what Robert Bellah aptly described as civil religion, wherein collective political identity has been expressed as a nation self-consciously "under God."[3]

Yet, even with such evidence of religious legacies, Douglas Johnston was right to observe in the mid-1990s that "American diplomacy has essentially placed religion beyond the bounds of critical analysis."[4] Within the post–World War II foreign policy establishment, deep skepticism about the inherent irrationality of religion, including its capacity to provoke violence, led to the marginalization of what Jean Bethke Elshtain refers to as "God talk" in American foreign policy.[5] References to religion, God, and transcendence have been rare in policy rhetoric, with the notable exception of presidential inaugural speeches or political party platforms.[6] And while Secretary of State John Foster Dulles condemned atheistic communism during the 1950s, secularist and materialist assumptions meant that U.S. foreign policy during the cold war was based on a "cognitive map of the field of international affairs"[that has been predicated on] "segregating religion from the 'normal' concerns of state."[7]

Within the dominant secular policy mind-set, religious freedom was a marginal issue. Absence of concern with religion in the cold war and, even, post–cold war era was evident in Washington's lack of foreign policy focus on violations of religious freedom—for individuals and groups—in both allied and rival states. As evidence, successive U.S. administrations made little effort either to publicize or to condemn violations of religious human rights in cases as wide-ranging as the Saudi theocracy, Iran under the Shah, communist China, and secular-authoritarian Turkey. Presidents and their administrations occasionally criticized violations of religious freedom in such cases, but the critiques were overwhelmingly rhetorical flourishes within the context of support for human rights in general. In practice, secular balance-of-power thinking and material interest considerations—the importance of stability in Iran, for example, or of Saudi oil, Chinese markets, and U.S. access to NATO bases in Turkey—tended to trump religious freedom concerns.[8]

Despite the indisputable hegemony of secularist and materialist assumptions over religious ideas and values in U.S. foreign policy for most of the twentieth century, a brief review of social science scholarship and public policy works, as well as public opinion polls and survey data conducted since the start of the third millennium, and especially since the events of 9/11, confirms the existence of a perception that religion matters in U.S. foreign policy.[9] More precisely, the aforementioned sources point to an overwhelming perception, at both the domestic and external levels, that there is something unique about the way that religion matters in the formulation, execution, and objectives of U.S. national security strategy. Accordingly, scholars, public policy makers, and media analysts in the United States and abroad express the view that there has been a decisive turn toward God, or, in the words of Madeleine Albright, toward "the Almighty,"[10] in the service of consolidating America's global hegemony in a post-biploar world. Religion, therefore, has become the handmaiden of a well-defined grand strategy "to expand an American imperium"[11] guaranteed by the state's unparalleled military might and dedicated to the projection of American culture and the preservation of American economic interests; simply put, contemporary U.S. foreign policy making combines the elements of a religious crusade with neomercantilist economic policy and military supremacy.

Some may dismiss out of hand the preceding perception as a vulgarized misunderstanding—either of the continuing dominance of "rational" interests of a materialist and secularist nature in U.S. foreign policy, or of an admirable shift toward the systematic analysis and incorporation of religion as leverage for a post–cold war U.S. foreign policy that is dedicated to spreading the realities of equality and freedom through encouraging democracy and markets around the world. However, there exists a pervasive perception, in both public and elite opinion around the world, that religion—in the form of a highly particularized religious perspective built on civilizational assumptions[12] and expressed in a collaboration of conservative ideological and religious interests[13]—is being used as an ethical, conceptual, and rhetorical instrument of support for U.S. foreign policy. This perception deserves serious consideration, given that it has generated measurable, if unanticipated, risk factors for American national security.[14]

The International Religious Freedom Act of 1998

Two factors help to explain the actual shift in the role of religion in U.S. foreign policy, as well as the strong perception of a turn toward God in American diplomacy. The first factor is the passage of the International Religious Freedom Act of 1998, which marked a new foreign policy departure—the institutionalization of an important human right as a priority for the United States.

The legislation, passed unanimously by both houses of Congress and signed into law by President Bill Clinton, had as its overall purpose "to strengthen United States advocacy on behalf of individuals persecuted in foreign countries on account of religion."[15] The act was intended "to authorize United States actions in response to violations of religious freedom in foreign countries." To that end, IRFA brought about institutional innovation: an ambassador-at-large for international religious freedom within the Department of State, the Commission on International Religious Freedom (USCIRF) to be appointed by Congress, and a special adviser on international religious freedom within the National Security Council. An administrative core of the new arrangement was the Office of International Religious Freedom within the State Department, which was meant to complement the work of the USCIRF, especially around the identification of "countries of particular concern" (on account of their egregious violations of religious freedom) and recommendation to the executive branch of U.S. foreign policy censures, sanctions, or other measures.

One might argue that IRFA's passage was not a sharp break with the previous course of American foreign policy—in three respects. First, IRFA might be construed as a natural international extension of national experience—the positive legacy through which religious freedom served to attenuate Old-World hostilities, in effect reconciling warring Protestant (and, later, Catholic) immigrants on the basis of the First Amendment consensus. "The right to freedom of religion," according to IRFA, "undergirds the very origin and existence of the United States."[16] Second, the act was broadly compatible with a range of international human rights documents and declarations already endorsed by the United States: the Universal Declaration of Human Rights (1948), the International Covenant on Civil and Political Rights (1966), and the Declaration on the Elimination of All Forms of Intolerance and Discrimination Based on Religion or Belief (1981).[17] Third, there was precedent for legislation linking religious freedom and American foreign policy. In 1974 the Jackson-Vanik Amendment created linkage between economic and cultural cooperation with the Soviet Union and Moscow's willingness to loosen its strictures on Jewish emigration.[18]

Despite the aforementioned elements of continuity, the IRFA was unprecedented in many crucial respects, and it is in these unique aspects that the perception of a turn toward religion in Washington's international relations gains traction. Above all, the legislation was unique because it legally formalized the relationship between American policy abroad and religion, and by mandating the promotion and protection of religious freedom as an official goal of U.S. foreign policy, the IRFA linked religion to American national security. Equally significant was the fact that the origins of the IRFA lay in an unprecedented domestic political mobilization, a multifaith political coalition, which has been characterized as the New Religious Right.

The New Religious Right is a heterogeneous constituency distinct from the traditional Religious Right, which had primarily been composed of socially conservative, frequently isolationist, Evangelical Protestant Christians; best exemplified by the Moral Majority of the early 1980s, with its high-profile focus on abortion, prayer in schools, and family values issues, these conservative Christians had largely failed in their efforts to use electoral politics to shape the country's domestic social policy during the Reagan years. The product of internal debate about the causes of previous electoral and policy failures, the New Religious Right cemented domestic concerns to foreign policy priorities. Emerging during the Clinton administration and congealing during the first administration of G. W. Bush, the New Religious Right was an amalgam of Evangelical Protestants, religiously and socially conservative Catholics, and politically conservative Jews, all of whom were committed to an activist, militarized U.S. foreign policy.

The centrality of Evangelical Protestantism to a grand strategic vision of a global Pax Americana was crucial to the New Religious Right. Evangelical Protestant groups enjoyed a history of public activism in U.S. domestic politics, the existence of significant organizational and capital resources for domestic and transnational mobilization, and an expressed commitment to develop a theological framework for global engagement based on principles of equality and freedom as God-given rights. The less-than-obvious affinities between Evangelical Protestants, on the one hand, and conservative Jewish groups, on the other, derived in large part from their shared support for the state of Israel, albeit with very different theological rationales whose political end points, paradoxically, are completely incompatible.[19] Where Evangelical Protestant and conservative Jewish groups found common cause on U.S. foreign policy in the Middle East, conservative Catholics and Evangelical Protestants combined support for religious freedom with a shared approach to many domestic social questions. All three groups shared an overall skepticism about the compatibility of Islam with Western norms of human rights and democracy.[20]

Given the heterogeneity and internal cleavages of the New Religious Right, it is unsurprising that a common vision for America in the world, including a commitment to spreading America's conception of liberty through the promotion of democracy, helped to hold it together through the 1990s.[21] Egregious examples of religious persecution in the post–cold war world, particularly attacks on Christians in southern Sudan carried out by the Muslim-dominated government based in the north, were picked up by the American media, and long-standing Evangelical Protestant and Jewish concerns about religious persecution under communist regimes in the Soviet Union and China began to capture the attention of a wider public expecting to see human rights improvements in the wake of the termination of bipolar rivalry. Consequently, an opportunity arose for political entrepreneurs to build a coalition for far-reaching, unprecedented legislation in support of religious freedom—a coalition anchored in the New Religious Right and also encompassing some secular human rights advocacy organizations. The IRFA, signed into law in October 1998, was the result.[22]

The IRFA was unique, above all, in that it legally formalized the relationship between U.S. foreign policy and religious freedom. However, the legislation also signaled a substantive, if not immediately consequential, shift in the American foreign policy establishment's traditional secularist bent, by virtue of recognizing the existence of links between religious pluralism, religious freedom, and political stability. According to the act, "more than one-half of the world's population lives under regimes that severely restrict or prohibit the freedom of their citizens to study, believe, observe, and freely practice the religious faith of their choice." Ultimately, IRFA was designed "to channel United States security and development assistance to governments other than those found to be engaged in gross violations of the right to freedom of religion."[23]

Nonetheless, despite the legal foundations and institutional mechanisms created by the legislation, critics have charged that religious human rights remain a second-order priority for America's foreign policy apparatus. Under Clinton, the State Department and the White House largely ignored the early policy recommendations of the USCIRF—a trend that has not improved significantly under the Bush administrations. Among the most incisive critics is none other than Robert Seiple, former U.S. ambassador-at-large for international religious freedom, for whom the failure to respond to egregious human rights and religious freedom violations suggested the "need to practice a more mature form of confessional foreign policy."[24] Even more direct criticism has been leveled by Thomas Farr, the first director of the Office of International Religious Freedom. Farr characterized the implementation of the IRFA as "anemic" and evidence of a continuing "secularist myopia." Despite the bipartisan consensus of 1998 and the continued salience of the religious freedom issue in world politics, national elites refused "to acknowledge religion as a factor requiring direct and immediate attention" in Washington's foreign policy calculations.[25]

Such criticisms are, arguably, overstated, since the IRFA's impact, at least, has increased the salience of religious freedom consideration in U.S. foreign policy deliberations in multiple contexts, indicating the substantive change in how religion factors into the American foreign policy-making calculus. However, the greatest impact of the IRFA, until now, may well be in the international *perception* of how religion matters in U.S. foreign policy. In the context of globalization, the sole superpower and a Christian-majority country placed singular emphasis on religious freedom in its public human rights and democracy agenda. In a world marked by increasing religious pluralism and intense competition for adherents, the U.S. government was perceived by many to be backing Christian proselytism and mixing in other states' domestic affairs. International policy elites and publics were aware of, and in some cases, misinformed about, the origins of the IRFA in the political alliance linking domestic electoral clout and policy goals to a vision for America's status as global superpower. The consequence was the same in terms of perceptions: as a Chinese foreign policy spokesman opined, the United States should "stop interfering in China's internal affairs under the pretext of religion"—a view echoed in other states as well.[26]

September 11, 2001, the War on Terror, and the Invasion of Iraq

Yet, the argument that there has been a religious turn in U.S. foreign policy does not rest solely on passage of the International Religious Freedom Act. It is the combination of IRFA with the post–September 11, 2001, War on Terror and U.S. invasion of Iraq that reinforces that case. With the attacks on the World Trade Center and the Pentagon, the United States was forced to confront Al-Qaeda and the phenomenon of international terrorism linked with Islamic radicalism. The U.S. response did not have to have a salient religious dimension. It could have centered on secular calculations of material interest—the importance of defeating the terrorist threat militarily and of political and economic reform designed to undermine Islamic radicalism across the Middle East and beyond.

This secular mind-set was, in fact, dominant among neoconservatives within the administration of G. W. Bush. Interestingly enough, the preceding administrations, of G.H.W. Bush and Bill Clinton, had also reflected skepticism about the possibilities for activating "the reconciling aspects of religious faith"[27] for purposes of making America strong in the world, and instead, conceived of the stability and opportunities of the post-bipolar system as driven by "powerful secular trends."[28] Yet, the political leaderships of both parties also recognized that, given the striking religious pluralization of American society generated by changing immigration patterns and demographic trends in the latter part of the twentieth century,[29] the country's religious map and, therefore, potential voter alignments[30] must be considered in foreign policy choices aimed at achieving a grand strategy of American hegemony.

Therefore, it was in the recognition of religion as a nexus between domestic policy concerns, electoral outcomes, and foreign policy that the faint indicators are evident in terms of the change in the historical pattern of how religion matters in U.S. foreign policy. Indicative was President G.H.W. Bush's celebration of victory in the first Gulf War in 1991 as the dawn of a "new world order,"[31] effectively recasting the human agency of America's military might in the transformative light of divine agency. Bush also drew on the myth of American exceptionalism, referring to the United States' "special responsibility to assist those in other countries who are now working to make the transition to pluralist democracies"—a statement consonant with the Manifest Destiny tradition. In a reference to its victory over communism in the cold war, Clinton placed the United States on "the right side of history" in the "fullness of time." For Clinton, Washington's policy of peacebuilding through promoting democracy and markets reflected America's "duty to be authors of history."[32]

Generally speaking, the first Bush and Clinton used religious language and allusions to deliberately cut across partisan lines, in order to appeal to a centrist electoral constituency whose isolationist impulses threatened to rear up in the absence of a Soviet threat.

However, the distinctiveness of the role of religion in U.S. foreign policy after the cold war, and more specifically, post-9/11 events was etched most starkly in the rhetoric of George W. Bush. Bush's personal faith, combined with religious flourishes in his rhetoric, put a strong religious imprint on his administration's foreign policy after September 11, 2001. The President's approach, shared by the then ascendant New Religious Right, confirmed the impression generated by the IRFA of a stronger religious orientation in America's engagement in international affairs.

One can draw a clear line between Bush's personal religiosity and his rhetoric once in office. Bush was a late convert to Evangelical Protestantism. By his own account, he found Jesus at the age of forty, under the guidance of the Reverend Billy Graham. When asked during the 2000 campaign to name his favorite philosopher, Bush's response was Jesus. Consistent with contemporary formulations of Evangelical Protestantism, Bush's personal theology centers on individual redemption through the victory of good over evil and involves an intimate relationship with Jesus Christ. In this optic, presidential leadership is an expression of God's will. "There is only one reason I am in the Oval Office and not in a bar," Bush wrote in his official biography. "I found faith. I found God."[33]

Bush laced his first inaugural address with Christian allusions that hinted at his vision for U.S. hegemony and America's responsibility to utilize foreign policy to carry out God's will. In one passage, Bush likened the United States to the Good Samaritan of the New Testament parable: "When we see that wounded traveler on the road to Jericho, we will not pass to the other side."[34] In another passage, he described "our nation's grand story of courage and its simple dream of dignity." That story, he insisted, was shaped by God's own hand: "We are not this story's author, who fills time and eternity with his purpose." For Bush, God had singled out America to be his chosen instrument—so that God's will "is achieved in our duty."[35]

The main tensions within Bush's first foreign policy team centered on the use of force and commitments to multilateralism—national security strategy was the issue, not the question of religion's role within it.[36] Bush's advisers included respected academics and proven military leaders, such as Condoleezza Rice and Colin Powell, both known to favor traditional diplomacy over the use of force. Secretary of State Powell emerged early as the champion of a foreign policy approach based on pragmatism. The risk-averse pragmatists followed in the spirit of Clinton's liberal interventionism. They insisted on the priority of multilateral over unilateral action, and on the value of stability over any aggressive promotion of democratization or the use of military force. Religious freedom mattered for Rice, Powell, and their associates, but mainly as one human right among others—significantly, an approach in continuity with that of the Clinton administration. This group's reaction to September 11, 2001, was not to launch an ambitious effort of regime change in the Arab-Muslim world but to build a coalition to defeat Al-Qaeda and destroy its base in Afghanistan by removing the Taliban.

This pragmatic group was outflanked by the more ideological neoconservatives concentrated in the Defense Department, on the National Security Council staff, and in the office of Vice President Dick Cheney. Deputy Secretary of Defense Paul Wolfowitz emerged as their leading representative. The neoconservative agenda as it developed during the 1990s aimed "to turn . . . a 'unipolar moment' into a unipolar era."[37] The idea was to expand and perpetuate America's post–cold war global dominion through an expansion of democracy and free markets. What distinguished this neoconservative generation from the previous one, also notable for its embrace of democracy and markets, was a readiness to apply military power to the global transformational project— power to be exercised with allies, where possible, and alone where necessary. Michael Mann has convincingly argued that the military background of many second-generation neoconservatives definitively shaped their foreign policy worldview.[38] Military might became the sine qua non for the universalization of American principles and was the essential support for "a principal aim of American foreign policy," to "bring about a change of regime in hostile nations" wherever "tyrannical governments acquire the military power to threaten their neighbors, our allies, and the United States itself."[39] As with the pragmatists, there was little or no reference to religion in this rhetoric, even if it rested on an implicit faith in the rightness of the American cause.

It is significant that neither of the two ideological factions in the Bush foreign policy team was particularly religious in its orientation. In their writings and speeches, Cheney, Powell, Rice, Rumsfeld, and Wolfowitz indicated little affinity for the president's religiosity. But the president, through the symbolic force of his office, was able to project a faith-based dimension onto the strategic calculations of others. His personal religiosity helped to build a bridge between the ascendant, neoconservative faction and the New Religious Right, a core source of Bush's domestic support. In the 2000 elections and again in 2004, Evangelicals and conservative Catholics responded positively to Bush's call for compassionate conservatism and faith-based initiatives. The idea of transforming the world in America's image resonated with those who identified with the United States as a Christian nation and with its president, a self-professed Evangelical. Bush's personal theology, then, not only informed his insistence on America's responsibility to secure the world against evil, but also played into the hands of neoconservatives, enabling them to "seize the policy initiative in Washington."[40]

It was the events of September 11, 2001, that crystallized the application of the president's personal theology to his view of America's place in the world.[41]

Where Bush was cautious during the 2000 presidential campaign about align-
ing his foreign policy ideas with any divine plan, the attacks on the World Trade
Center and the Pentagon catalyzed the transformation of his personal theology
of individual salvation into a religiously informed perspective on U.S. foreign
policy. In addressing the nation on his return to the White House on September 16, 2001, Bush cast himself as a crusader and an agent of Divine will:
"This crusade, this war on terrorism is going to take a while."[42] Several days
later he remarked in an address before Congress: "The course of this conflict
is not known, yet its outcome is certain. Freedom and fear, justice and cruelty
have always been at war, and we know that God is not neutral between them."[43]
Before the month of September 2001 had ended, the outlines of a policy of
"coercive democratization"[44] were in place—the combination of the unilateral
projection of American military might with the advancement of freedom and
democracy designed to counter both tyranny and terrorism.

The language that Bush used to explain the U.S. response to September 11,
2001, compellingly expressed the fusion between the worldview of the New
Religious Right and the secular neoconservative ideology. Bush painted a Man-
ichaean world of good versus evil and returned continuously to the discursive
theme of America's position on the side of good. "This will be a monumental
struggle of good versus evil," he told a national and international audience the
day after the attack. "But good will prevail."[45]

This ethical dualism was compatible with a secular neoconservative
approach. Yet, Bush went further. While careful to draw a distinction between
the terrorists and most peace-loving Muslims, his good versus evil frame, overlaid with his personal theology, injected a religious element into his response
to the attacks. Because terrorists constituted the very embodiment of evil—
"the evil ones" who "have no country, no ideology" other than "hate"—the War
on Terror was America's "responsibility to history," America's "calling."[46] For
Bush, that calling was linked to his own mission in elected office; he famously
told a reporter: "I'm in the Lord's hands."[47]

In the months that followed the terrorist attacks in New York and Washington, the United States and an allied coalition launched a successful military operation against the Taliban in Afghanistan, which had been harboring
Osama Bin Laden and other Al-Qaeda leaders. Still, the goals of U.S. foreign
policy were broader than retaliation against the perpetrators of the attacks and
went beyond what many of America's allies were willing to accept. At the level
of rhetoric, the January 2002 State of the Union address marked a critical turn.
Bush linked the War on Terror with a strategy to defeat the "axis of evil,"[48]
defined to include Iraq, Iran, and North Korea. Iraq had already emerged as
the paradigmatic case for the application of the neoconservatives' national

security strategy after the Al-Qaeda attacks—a push for regime change centered on democracy and human rights that, however selectively applied, resonated with the New Religious Right's own global vision of religious freedom and human rights. A recalibration of the map of power in the Middle East marked the fusion of otherwise incompatible secular and religious worldviews, through a collaboration of domestic political interests.

In the drive for war, Vice President Cheney, Secretary of Defense Rumsfeld, his deputy secretary Wolfowitz, and others brought a variety of arguments to bear—including alleged links between Saddam Hussein and Al-Qaeda and the Iraqi dictator's purported efforts to amass weapons of mass destruction. The largely secular neoconservatives also deployed ethical certainties that dovetailed with Bush's religious worldview. In this sense, the utopianism and ideological fundamentalism of the neoconservatives, while secular, resonated deeply with the New Religious Right,[49] which had responded positively to Bush's election slogan of compassionate conservatism. By the time that Bush ran for president, the traditional bloc of Christian conservatives that had been electorally ineffective and publicly discredited by the scandals of the 1980s had remade itself[50] along lines that were sympathetic to the neoconservative vision of U.S. foreign policy, as a chance to globalize a religious freedom and human rights agenda through a regime-change approach and security strategy articulated in unmistakably eschatological terms.

Quoting from the president's notable speech at West Point on June 2002, *The National Security Strategy of the United States of America, 2002*, rejected the charge that it was "somehow undiplomatic or impolitic to speak the language of right and wrong."[51] In an effort to mobilize public support for the war, Bush stepped up explicitly religious imagery in his January 2003 State of the Union address. Americans, he asserted, should be "confident in the ways of Providence, even when they are far from our understanding. Events aren't moved by blind change and chance. Behind all of life and all history there is a dedication and purpose, set by the hand of a just and faithful God."[52]

The controversial, American-led war launched in March 2003 to bring down the Saddam Hussein regime marked a new departure in the interplay of religion and U.S. diplomacy. The Bush Doctrine of preventive war embedded in *The National Security Strategy* of 2002[53] committed the United States to perpetuating its global military supremacy, designated democratic capitalism the "single sustainable model of national success," and, importantly, assigned to the United States a missionary obligation to "extend the benefits of freedom across the globe."[54] The document claimed for the United States the prerogative of enumerating what it termed "the nonnegotiable demands of human dignity" in the form of "the rule of law; limits on the absolute power of the state; free speech; freedom of worship; equal justice; respect for women; religious and ethnic tolerance; and respect for private property."[55]

If the passage of the IRFA had been suggestive of a shift in the historical pattern of religion's salience in U.S. foreign policy after the cold war, America's war in Iraq as the headline of Washington's post-9/11 security strategy became the focus of the shift and, above all, cemented an international perception that religion had become central to U.S. foreign policy actions. The devolution of conditions in Iraq has reinforced the perception abroad, and in some quarters in the United States, that religion's influence in American foreign policy has contributed to global disorder.

In particular, America's failure to envision and, then, inability to contain the insurgency that has led to a Sunni-Shia civil war in Iraq and the country's emergence as a theater of operations for Al-Qaeda have contributed to international views, especially in Muslim-majority countries, that America's claims about support for democracy are rhetorical coverage for a new crusade by the world's Judeo-Christian superpower. The fact that the IRFA has neither produced any visible change in America's ongoing alliance with authoritarian regimes in Pakistan, Egypt, and Saudi Arabia nor evoked any critique of Israel's human rights policies toward its Arab Christian and Muslim communities has intensified the aforementioned view among Muslims around the world.

By the same token, the dramatic deterioration of the situation in Iraq after 2005 has produced tensions and fragmentation in the alliance of convenience between neoconservatives and the New Religious Right, as well as within the latter group. Prior to the action in Iraq, an amalgam of liberal-moderate Christian ethicists publicly declared their opposition to the Iraq war. The Council of Bishops of the United Methodist Church, Bush's own denomination, publicly denounced his approach: "A preemptive war by the United States against a nation like Iraq goes against the very grain of our understanding of the gospel, our church's teachings, and our conscience."[56] With the deepening quagmire in Iraq, the internal divisions within the New Religious Right have led to a distancing of the group from the Bush administration's global agenda of democratization-*cum*-counterterrorism. Meanwhile, most of the neoconservative architects of Bush's post–September 11, 2001, strategy have left office, including Rumsfeld and Wolfowitz, and the pragmatists around Condoleezza Rice and Rumsfeld's successor, Robert Gates, have failed to design a multilateral strategy that can stabilize Iraq and lead to a U.S. withdrawal from that country.

In sum, the presidency of G. W. Bush leaves little doubt that religion matters in U.S. foreign policy. However, the Bush presidency, in response to the 9/11 events and the legislative event of the IRFA, clarified—and, for the moment, has eliminated the contingencies in—the historical particularities of the new nexus between religion and American foreign policy since the end of the cold war: a militaristic expression of the commitment to promote religious freedom abroad and to protect American national security against the threats of religious radicalism. The realities and, equally important, the perception of the causes, consequences, and possible future, or this nexus, have produced a paradox—an erosion in America's soft- and hard-power assets for improving religious human rights around the world and for protecting American security against the perils of religious extremism.

Conclusion

This chapter has analyzed the origins and implications of the relationship between religion and American foreign policy in a contemporary international system marked by unprecedented religious pluralism. My aims went well beyond making the case that religion matters in Washington's formulation and conduct of foreign policy. Instead, I aimed to support the argument that there has been a substantive change in the historical pattern whereby religion was salient to America's role in world affairs, as well as to explain how this change has occurred and to suggest the consequences of this new connection between religion and U.S. foreign policy.

The chapter shows that the *reasons* that religion matters in American foreign policy after the cold war stem from a new configuration of domestic interest groups in tandem with a fundamental paradigm shift in the post-bipolar international power structure. The chapter also explains the operational results of these two factors—in the form of the IRFA legislation and the post-9/11 War on Terror. Finally, the chapter provides suggestive evidence that the relationship between religion and U.S. foreign policy has created empirical realities and active perceptions which now function as confining conditions on America's capacity to engage with global religious pluralism in a manner that enhances human rights and diminishes religious totalitarianism. In short, the policy decisions taken after the cold war, and most intensely during the G. W. Bush presidency, have consolidated a relationship between religion and U.S. foreign policy that, at least in the short term, may be detrimental both to American national security and to forces for religious tolerance in international relations.

It bears emphasis that the initial post–bipolar decade had prefigured the shift in the salience of religion in American foreign policy, particularly insofar as the Clinton administration was willing to draw on religious interest groups for electoral support and, significantly, to justify America's unilateral use of force in cases of humanitarian crisis, nation-building through regime change, and military threat. The emergence of the multifaith and liberal secularist coalition that led to the passage of the International Religious Freedom Act was the first explicit policy indicator of the new turn toward religion in America's emergent foreign policy in a post-bipolar world order.

However, it is equally important to emphasize that, while the Clinton presidency opportunistically and somewhat grudgingly drew the general outlines of the new nexus between religion and U.S. foreign policy as a collaboration between "the mighty and the Almighty,"[57] the Bush presidency has lent credence to the view that the relationship between religion and American policy abroad amounts to God's choice on behalf of American initiatives—even when executed through unilateral force—to promote religious freedom and defeat religious extremists like those who attacked the United States on September 11, 2001. The past seven years, after all, have seen a decisive move by religious groups and religious ideas into the operational side of foreign policy. Religious rhetoric has become more than an abstract legitimation mechanism or a part of American civil religion, since convictions about America's divine calling to spread democracy and freedom have been articulated by an Evangelical president endorsing neoconservative ideas and the unilateral application of U.S. military might to respond to new security threats.

On the basis of IRFA alone, then, it would be difficult to explain the widespread perception, abroad and in the United States, of a religious thrust in Washington's foreign policy. Viewed in isolation, IRFA marked an important departure, but its uneven implementation suggests the importance of religion as a rhetorical mantra, rather than a key priority area, in American politics. Only in combination with the 9/11 attacks and the subsequent War on Terror did religious considerations advance to more prominence in U.S. foreign policy, particularly with reference to the Muslim world. The campaign against Al-Qaeda, the war on the Taliban in Afghanistan, and the invasion of Iraq have demonstrated a reliance on military solutions to complex political, socioeconomic, and cultural problems, and have lent serious traction to the view that America's declared commitment to democracy, human rights, and religious freedom is part of a strategy of global hegemony built on the protection of the frontiers and outposts of the West. Under Bush's presidency, Samuel Huntington's "Clash of Civilizations" thesis, unfortunately, has been enlivened.

As a concluding observation, it is important to be clear that this chapter does not argue that U.S. foreign policy after the cold war has been essentially and exclusively religious. Of course, presidents Bill Clinton and G. W. Bush brought personal faith convictions to their views about America's transformative role in the post-bipolar world., and G. W. Bush has obviously interpreted the War on Terror and democracy-promotion as part of God's plan for the

United States and the world. Yet, most of the primary architects of U.S. foreign policy since the collapse of the Soviet Union have been driven by a more secular vision of America's role in the world and the importance of shoring up American national interests, unilaterally and with military force, where necessary.

It is the uneasy juxtaposition of these two strands of thought, one more religious, the other more secular, expressed in a shared vision of American transformative power in international affairs, that has analytical implications worth considering for their intellectual richness and policy urgency when it comes to global religious pluralism.

What are some of the analytical implications of this confluence of the religious and the secular? We are, it is often argued, living in a desecularizing world, in which religion is finding its way back into the public sphere, politics, and the dynamics of government. Resurgent religion, in this view, marks the rise of a postsecular era. Yet, such a zero-sum analysis misses ways in which religious and secular forces, often inextricable, combine to shape political and policy outcomes in world affairs. The multidimensional coalition of religious and secular interests and ideas at work in U.S. foreign policy supports Martin Marty's notion of the world as a religio-secular reality characterized by the sustained, fluid, and above all pluralized presence of religion.[58] This religio-secular reality implies a range of possible arrangements when it comes to the relationship between religious pluralism and world politics—for example, situations where the salience of religious freedom issues may be folded into secular conceptions of universal human rights, or alternatively, where both perspectives are trumped by calculations of material interest. These different perspectives, difficult to disentangle, intersected within the second Bush administration.

Furthermore, in a world marked by growing religious pluralism and complex political-ethical dilemmas (for example, whether to push for democracy and free elections that might bring illiberal forces to power), either the conviction or perception of an identity between U.S. foreign policy and Divine Providence will almost certainly provoke a defensive reaction against what will be seen as an arrogant effort to impose American beliefs on the rest of the world. A similar reaction is likely as a response to the secularist blinders that overlook the diversity and elasticity that is the hallmark of the contemporary religio-secular reality. Emphasis on force as a means of regime change will miss the salience of religious factors in sustainable political solutions after the execution of force.

It is the power of the presidential office and its pulpit, together with the bluntness, boldness, and lack of nuance that characterize the incorporation of religion as a variable in American national security strategy, that underscores the importance of understanding religio-secular interactions, linkages, contradictions, and compatibilities. The failure to appreciate the religio-secular nature of world affairs accounts for the perception that God has captured the White House and U.S. foreign policy since the end of the cold war, and September 2001, in particular.[59] Since the Bush administration's decision to invade Iraq, and in light of the terrorist violence and civil war that have marked the occupation phase, arguably the most controversial question in world politics has become whether or not the United States stands within the order of international law. Signals in 2006–2007, and more recently, that the United States might repeat its Iraqi adventure with a military engagement with Iran have provoked intense domestic and international debates about whether the United States has placed itself outside the international legal structures it has helped to create and sustain through the end of the bipolar era. Overall, the future world role of the United States, especially its will and capacity to contribute to structures of global governance that help to temper the rigidities of the Westphalian order (a system of sovereign states increasingly challenged in their capacity to address both the material and normative aspects of equity and justice) is under intense, critical scrutiny. Within this broader context, the relevance and role of religion in America's evolving foreign policy and national security strategy deserve further, careful analysis.

Looking ahead, a more effective U.S. foreign policy in the present age will have to incorporate what Alfred Stepan describes as the multivocality, the internal diversity, of all religious traditions, and the complexity of their interactions with the secular order.[60] In the context of the democratization literature, Stepan called for the integration of religion into a sustainable democratic politics built on the "twin tolerations"—that is, the minimal boundaries of freedom of action that must somehow be crafted for political institutions vis-à-vis religious authorities, and for religious individuals and groups vis-à-vis political institutions.[61] In the context of U.S. foreign policy, the relationship between the religious and the political must also be carefully managed. Under Bush the military promotion of democracy and human rights, including religious freedom, has proved counterproductive. The juxtaposition of the IRFA and the War on Terror, overlaid by the faith-laden rhetoric of George Bush, gave credence to the view that support for democracy was a cover for American imperialism. The capacity of U.S. foreign policy to contribute multilateral global governance and sustainable democratization strategies that advance human rights requires moving beyond a crusading stance toward a more pragmatic embrace of multilateral diplomacy and international institutions.

Almost two decades since the end of the cold war, the idea of the United States as a benevolent hegemon and guarantor of world order has lost adherents. However, there remains loose consensus in the United States and abroad in favor of such an order, grounded in respect for basic human rights, including religious freedom. And there is an acknowledgment, often grudging, that only the United States has the economic, political—and ultimately, military— resources to play a leading role in securing such an international order, not in isolation, but in collaboration with others. However weakened its moral authority, the United States possesses material resources that could serve to strengthen international law and global governance in a post–bipolar order marked by a resurgence of ethnic and religious differences and greater cultural and religious pluralism. The religious political culture of the United States, anchored in its Christian majority, expressed in its civil religion, and articulated in its presidential rhetoric, is not going to disappear. It will continue to create tensions with the rest of the world. But a positive redirection of the role of religion in American foreign policy—in the service of durable forms of global governance and robust democratic regimes—is possible. This presupposes a break with the destructive combination of religion, unilateralism, and resort to force that have characterized U.S. foreign policy under the presidency of George W. Bush.

NOTES

1. Richard Falk provides a sobering treatment of the implications of the securitization of religion for global governance. See, for example, Richard A. Falk, *The Declining World Order: America's Imperial Geopolitics* (New York: Routledge, 2004).

2. David M. Malone, "A Decade of U.S. Unilateralism?" in *Unilateralism and U.S. Foreign Policy: International Perspectives*, ed. David M. Malone and Yuen Foong Khong (Boulder, CO: Lynne Rienner, 2003), 24.

3. Richard De Zoysa, "America's Foreign Policy: Manifest Destiny or Great Satan?" *Contemporary Politics* 11, nos. 2/3 (June–September 2005): 133–156; Robert N. Bellah, "Civil Religion in America," *Daedalus* 96 (Winter 1967): 1–21.

4. Douglas Johnston, "Introduction: Realpolitik Expanded," in *Faith-Based Diplomacy: Trumping Realpolitik*, ed. Douglas Johnston (New York: Oxford University Press, 2003), 3.

5. Jean Bethke Elshtain, "Against Liberal Monism," *Daedalus* 132, no. 3 (Summer 2003): 78–79.

6. For a discussion of trends in presidential rhetoric, see Madeleine K. Albright, *The Mighty and the Almighty: Reflections on America, God, and World Affairs* (New York: HarperCollins, 2006), 15–32.

7. A thoughtful exploration of the (im)balance between ideals and material interests in U.S. foreign policy is provided in Michael Ignatieff, ed., *American Exceptionalism and Human Rights* (Princeton, NJ: Princeton University Press, 2005).

8. Robert A. Seiple, "Why Brandywine Review?" *Brandywine Review of Faith and International Affairs* 1, no. 1 (Spring 2003): 1.

9. See the footnotes and bibliography for this chapter.

10. Albright, *The Mighty and the Almighty*.

11. Andrew J. Bacevich, *American Empire: The Realities and Consequences of U.S. Diplomacy* (Cambridge, MA: Harvard University Press, 2002), 2–3. One of the most caustic assessments of the view that American militarism and religious fundamentalism have become the marker of U.S. foreign policy during the presidential tenure of George W. Bush is David Domke's *God Willing? Political Fundamentalism in the White House, the "War on Terror" and the Echoing Press* (London: Pluto Press, 2004).

12. Samuel Huntington, "The Clash of Civilizations?" *Foreign Affairs* 72, no. 3 (Summer 1993): 22–49.

13. See Andrew Kohut, *The Diminishing Divide: Religion's Changing Role in American Politics* (Washington, DC: Brookings Institution Press, 2000).

14. See, for example, http://www.gordon.edu/ccs/usaspeakers/elizabethprodromou; Andrew Kohut and Bruce Stokes, *America against the World: How We Are Different and Why We Are Disliked* (New York: Times Books, 2006); Kevin Phillips, *American Theocracy: The Peril and Politics of Radical Religion, Oil, and Borrowed Money in the 21st Century* (New York: Viking Penguin, 2006); Julia E. Sweig, *Friendly Fire: Losing Friends and Making Enemies in the Anti-American Century* (New York: Public Affairs, 2006); Pew Research Center, "America's Image Slips, but Allies Share U.S. Concerns over Iran, Hamas," June 13, 2006, http://pewglobal.org/reports/display.php?ReportID=252; and Pew Research Center, "The Great Divide: How Westerners and Muslims View Each Other," June 22, 2006, http://pewglobal.org/reports/display.php?ReportID=253.

15. The International Religious Freedom Act, http://uscirf.gov/about/authorizing legislation.html.

16. See "Authorizing Amendments and Legislation," for the full text of the IRFA, at http://uscirf.gov/about/autohrizinglegislation.html.

17. Useful references on foundational human rights documents and the evolution of human rights architectures with regard to religious rights include Tore Lindholm, W. Cole Durham Jr., and Bahia G. Tahzib-Lie, eds., *Facilitating Religious Freedom or Belief: A Deskbook* (Leiden: Martinus Nijhoff, 2004); and Tad Stahnke and J. Paul Martin, eds., *Religion and Human Rights: Basic Documents* (New York: Center for the Study of Human Rights, Columbia University, 1998).

18. See "Jackson-Vanik and Russia Fact Sheet," http://www.whitehouse.gov/news/releases/2001/11/20011113-16.html.

19. Significantly, the theology of dispensational eschatology that is dominant among Evangelical Protestant groups supports the return of Jews to Israel as the precursor for Jews to "either convert to Christianity or be killed off" before the Second Coming of Christ. Dennis Hoover discusses the interface of eschatology and national security for Evangelical Protestant views on Israel in "Is Evangelicalism Itching for a Civilizational Fight? A Media Study," *Brandywine Review of Faith and International Affairs* 2, no. 1 (Spring 2004): 11–16. The quotation is from Andrew Bacevich, *The New American Militarism: How Americans Are Seduced by War* (New York: Oxford University Press, 2005), 132. What Dennis Hoover discusses as the theology of dispensational eschatology is discussed by Bacevich as the doctrine of premillennial dispensationalism. For a superb summary, with useful citations,

of the recent history of the militarized view of American foreign policy that binds Evangelical Protestants and conservative Jews, see Bacevich, *The New American Militarism*, 122–146.

20. Hoover, "Is Evangelicalism Itching for a Civilizational Fight?" Also see the various surveys of the Pew Forum on Religion and Public Life located on the Religion and World Affairs page, http://pewforum.org/world-affairs/.

21. There is a small but growing literature on the role of religious interest groups in U.S. foreign policy; the internal heterogeneity of the New Religious Right, as well as the commitment to democracy-promotion and human rights as the glue that cements the various actors in the New Religious Right, can be culled from a review of some of these by-now standard references. For example, see Rosalind I. J. Hackett, Mark Silk, and Dennis Hoover, eds., *Religious Persecution as a U.S. Policy Issue* (Hartford, CT: Center for the Study of Religion in Public Life, 2000); Allen D. Hertzke, *Freeing God's Children: The Unlikely Alliance for Global Human Rights* (Oxford: Rowman and Littlefield, 2004); and Hertzke, *Representing God in Washington: The Role of Religious Lobbies in the American Polity* (Knoxville: University of Tennessee Press, 2004). More recently, see Elliot Abrams, ed., *The Influence of Faith: Religious Groups in U.S. Foreign Policy* (Lanham, MD: Rowman and Littlefield, 2001); the chapter "Onward," in Bacevich, *The New American Militarism*; and John J. Meirsheimer and Stephen M. Walt, *The Israel Lobby and U.S. Foreign Policy* (New York: Farrar, Straus and Giroux, 2007).

22. Madeleine Albright acknowledges the centrality of this coalition in *The Mighty and the Almighty*, 96.

23. *The International Religious Freedom Act.*

24. Robert A. Seiple, "Confessional Foreign Policy," *Brandywine Review of Faith and International Affairs* 2, no. 2 (Fall 2004): 1.

25. Thomas F. Farr, "Retooling the Middle Eastern Freedom Agenda: Engaging Islam," *Review of Faith and International Affairs* 4, no. 2 (Fall 2006): 15.

26. "China Opposes Being Listed on U.S. Religious Freedom Blacklist, November 20, 2006," http://news3.xinhuanet.com/english/2006-11/20/content_5354574.htm.

27. Johnston, "Introduction," 5.

28. Condoleezza Rice emphasized the relevance of secular trends for the sustainability of American hegemony as the linchpin of global order after the cold war. Quoted in Bacevich, *American Empire*, 34.

29. Diana Eck, *A New Religious America: How a "Christian" Country Has Become the World's Most Religiously Diverse Nation* (San Francisco: HarperCollins, 1999).

30. Ibid.

31. George W. Bush, "Address before a Joint Session of the Congress on the Cessation of the Persian Gulf Conflict," http://bushlibrary.tamu.edu/research/papers/1991/91030600.html [March 6, 1991].

32. Quoted in Bacevich, *American Empire*, 32, 1, 33. Clinton's interpretation of the end of the cold war within the context of the Pauline letters to the Galatians occurred in his "Remarks at the World Trade Organization in Geneva, Switzerland," May 18, 1998. On the importance of Christian themes in U.S. foreign policy, see also Bacevich, *The New American Militarism*, 69–96, 122–146.

33. Quoted in David Frum, *The Right Man* (New York: Random House, 2003), 283.

34. George W. Bush, "President George W. Bush's Inaugural Address," January 20, 2001. For more on this point, see Laurie Goodstein, "A President Puts His Faith in Providence," *New York Times*, February 9, 2003.

35. Ibid.

36. On these foreign policy cleavages and eventual hegemony of the neoconservative wing in the first administration of George W. Bush, see James Mann, *Rise of the Vulcans: The History of Bush's War Cabinet* (New York: Viking, 2004).

37. Ibid. According to Mann, the neoconservatives in the Bush foreign policy team labeled themselves "the Vulcans," after the Roman god of fire, the forge, and metalwork. "That word, *Vulcans*, captured perfectly the image the Bush foreign policy team sought to convey, a sense of power, toughness, resilience and durability." See ibid, x.

38. Ibid. Bacevich offers a succinct and compelling analysis of the intergenerational differences in neoconservative ideology, elucidating the gradual turn toward emphasis on the buildup and projection of force, such that "one aspect of the neoconservative legacy has been to foster the intellectual climate necessary for the emergence of the new American militarism." See *The New American Militarism*, 71.

39. Robert Kagan and William Kristol, eds., *Present Dangers: Crisis and Opportunity in American Foreign and Defense Policy* (San Francisco: Encounter Books, 2000), 17.

40. Falk, *The Declining World Order*, viii.

41. I have explored this theme elsewhere in my work. See Andrew J. Bacevich and Elizabeth H. Prodromou, "God Is Not Neutral: Religion and U.S. Foreign Policy after 9/11," *Orbis* 48, no. 1 (Winter 2004): 43–54.

42. Bush described the War on Terror as a crusade on September 16, 2001. Although this politically charged term, deemed offensive to Muslims, did not reappear in the president's lexicon, one former Bush speechwriter believes that the war on terror had made Bush "a crusader after all." Frum, *The Right Man*, 265.

43. White House Press Release, "Remarks by the President upon Arrival," September 16, 2001; George W. Bush, "Address to a Joint Session of Congress and the American People," September 20, 2001.

44. Joseph P. Nye later coined this term to describe the administration's approach. See, for example, his "Foreign Policy after Iraq," *San Francisco Chronicle*, March 14, 2007.

45. White House Press Release, "Remarks by the President in Photo Opportunity with the National Security Team," September 12, 2001.

46. White House Press Release, "President Rallies Troops at Travis Air Force Base," October 17, 2001; and White House Press Release, "President Unveils Most Wanted Terrorists," October 10, 2001.

47. Cited in Bob Woodward, *Bush at War* (New York: Simon and Schuster, 2002), 46.

48. George W. Bush, "State of the Union Address," January 29, 2002.

49. An excellent summary of the analytic failure to move beyond "the fixed idea that the Christian right was moribund" by the 1990s is provided by Mark J. Rozell, "What Christian Right?" *Religion in the News* 6, no. 1 (Spring 2003): 2–3, 22. Equally

useful in analyzing the effects on domestic social policy and foreign policy of the reconstructed Christian Right, grounded in Evangelical Protestant groups, is the article by Dennis R. Hoover, "Choosing Up Sides in the Middle East," *Religion in the News* 5, no. 3 (Fall 2002): 8–10, 20–21.

50. The secular, neoconservative vision of a Pax Americana appealed to an electoral constituency that included the traditional Religious Right but that had metamorphosed into a New Religious Right, which some describe "as a 'religious center'—moderate Evangelicals and Catholics, along with a substantial portion of black Protestants" that swung away from supporting the Clinton Democrats' faith-friendly social agenda to Bush's signature domestic policy of faith-based initiatives. As noted earlier in this chapter, also finding a place under the umbrella of the New Religious Right, on account of their foreign policy affinities, were ultraconservative Evangelical Protestants and conservative Jews. For the quotation, see Dennis Hoover, "Faith Based Administration," *Religion in the News* 5, no. 3 (Fall 2002): 12. Hoover offers insights into the main dimensions and evolutions of faith-based initiatives, as more than "a single policy, but rather a broad movement to make government tax, regulatory, and funding policies friendlier to faith-based organizations (FBOs) that deliver social services." See ibid.

51. *The National Security Strategy of the United States of America, 2002,* September 17, 2002 (Washington, DC: White House, 2002), www.whitehouse.gov.

52. George W. Bush, "Remarks by President George W. Bush at National Prayer Breakfast," February 6, 2003.

53. *The National Security Strategy of the United States of America, 2002.*

54. George W. Bush, cover letter to ibid.

55. *The National Security Strategy of the United States of America, 2002.*

56. Joe Feuherherd, "Opinions Clash on Just War: Christian Opposition to Attack on Iraq Is Widespread, but Not Universal," *National Catholic Reporter,* February 7, 2003.

57. Albright, *The Mighty and the Almighty.*

58. Martin E. Marty, "Our Religio-Secular World," *Daedalus* 132, no. 3 (Summer 2003): 42–48.

59. For a related argument, see Bacevich and Prodromou, "God Is Not Neutral."

60. Alfred Stepan, "Religion, Democracy, and the 'Twin Tolerations,'" *Journal of Democracy* 11, no. 4 (October 2000): 44.

61. Ibid., 37.

BIBLIOGRAPHY

Abrams, Elliot, ed. *The Influence of Faith: Religious Groups in U.S. Foreign Policy.* Lanham, MD: Rowman and Littlefield, 2001.

Albright, Madeleine K. *The Mighty and the Almighty: Reflections on America, God, and World Affairs.* New York: HarperCollins, 2006.

Atlas, James. "A Classicist's Legacy: New Empire Builders." *New York Times,* May 2, 2003.

Bacevich, Andrew J. *American Empire: The Realities and Consequences of U.S. Diplomacy.* Cambridge, MA: Harvard University Press, 2002.

————. *The New American Militarism: How Americans Are Seduced by War*. New York: Oxford University Press, 2005.

Bacevich, Andrew J., and Elizabeth H. Prodromou. "God Is Not Neutral: Religion and U.S. Foreign Policy after 9/11." *Orbis* 48, no. 1 (Winter 2004): 43–54.

Bellah, Robert. "Civil Religion in America." *Daedalus* 96 (Winter 1967): 1–21.

Boot, Max. "American Imperialism? No Need to Run Away from Label." *USA Today*, May 5, 2003.

Brookhiser, Richard. "The Mind of George W. Bush." *Atlantic Monthly*, April 2003.

Bush, George H. W. "Address before a Joint Session of the Congress on the Cessation of the Persian Gulf Conflict." March 6, 1991. http://bushlibrary.tamu.edu/research/papers/1991/91030600.html.

Bush, George W. "Address to a Joint Session of Congress and the American People." September 20, 2001.

————. *A Charge to Keep*. New York: William Morrow, 1999.

————. "Commencement Address." U.S. Military Academy at West Point Commencement, Annapolis, Maryland, June 1, 2002, http://www.whitehouse.gov/news/releases/2002/06/20020601-3.html.

————. "Commencement Address." Yale University Commencement, New Haven, Connecticut, May 21, 2001.

————. "President George W. Bush's Inaugural Address." January 20, 2001.

————. "Remarks by President George W. Bush at National Prayer Breakfast." February 6, 2003.

————. "State of the Union Address." January 29, 2002.

————. "Statement by the President in His Address to the Nation." September 11, 2001.

Carlson, John D., and Erik C. Owens, eds. *The Sacred and the Sovereign*. Washington, DC: Georgetown University Press, 2003.

"China Opposes Being Listed on U.S. Religious Freedom Blacklist." November 20, 2006. http://news3.xinhuanet.com/english/2006-11/20/content_5354574.htm.

Clinton, William J. "Remarks at the World Trade Organization in Geneva, Switzerland." May 18, 1998.

De Zoysa, Richard. "America's Foreign Policy: Manifest Destiny or Great Satan?" *Contemporary Politics* 11, nos. 2/3 (June–September 2005): 133–156.

Domke, David. *God Willing? Political Fundamentalism in the White House, the "War on Terror" and the Echoing Press*. London: Pluto Press, 2004.

Eck, Diana L. *A New Religious America: How a "Christian" Country Has Become the World's Most Religiously Diverse Nation*. San Francisco: HarperCollins, 2002.

Elshtain, Jean Bethke. "Against Liberal Monism." *Daedalus* 132, no. 3 (Summer 2003): 78–79.

"Evangelize Elsewhere." *Washington Post*, April 15, 2003.

Falk, Richard. *The Declining World Order: America's Imperial Geopolitics*. New York: Routledge, 2004.

————. "United Nations: Rule of Law." *Le Monde Diplomatique (English Version)*, December 2, 2002.

Farr, Thomas F. "Retooling the Middle Eastern Freedom Agenda: Engaging Islam." *Review of Faith and International Affairs* 4, no. 2 (Fall 2006): 11–19.

Feuherherd, Joe. "Opinions Clash on Just War: Christian Opposition to Attack on Iraq Is Widespread, but Not Universal." *National Catholic Reporter*, February 7, 2003.

Fineman, Howard. "Bush and God." *Newsweek*, March 10, 2003.

Foot, Rosemary. "Credibility at Stake: Domestic Supremacy in U.S. Human Rights Policy." In *Unilateralism and U.S. Foreign Policy*, ed. David M. Malone and Yuen Foong Khong, 95–116. Boulder, CO: Lynne Rienner, 2003.

Frum, David. *The Right Man*. New York: Random House, 2003.

Goodstein, Laurie. "A President Puts His Faith in Providence." *New York Times*, February 9, 2003.

Green, John C. "The Undetected Tide." *Religion in the News* 6.1 (Spring 2003): 4–6.

Hackett, Rosalind I. J., Mark Silk, and Dennis Hoover, eds. *Religious Persecution as a U.S. Policy Issue*. Hartford, CT: Center for the Study of Religion in Public Life, 2000.

Hehir, Brian. "Experts: Religion Affects Foreign Policy." *Washington Times*, February 5, 2003.

Hertzke, Allen D. *Freeing God's Children: The Unlikely Alliance for Global Human Rights*. Oxford: Rowman and Littlefield, 2004.

———. *Representing God in Washington: The Role of Religious Lobbies in the American Polity*. Knoxville: University of Tennessee Press, 2004.

Hoover, Dennis R. "Choosing Up Sides in the Middle East." *Religion in the News* 5, no. 3 (Fall 2002): 8–10.

———. "Faith Based Administration." *Religion in the News* 5, no. 3 (Fall 2002): 12–14.

———. "Is Evangelicalism Itching for a Civilizational Fight? A Media Study." *Brandywine Review of Faith and International Affairs* 2, no. 1 (Spring 2004): 11–16.

Huntington, Samuel. "The Clash of Civilizations?" *Foreign Affairs* 72, no. 3 (Summer 1993): 22–49.

Ignatieff, Michael, ed. *American Exceptionalism and Human Rights*. Princeton, NJ: Princeton University Press, 2005.

Ikenberry, G. John. "America's Imperial Ambition." *Foreign Affairs* 81.5 (September/October 2002): 44–60.

The International Religious Freedom Act. http://uscirf.gov/about/authorizing legislation.html.

"Jackson-Vanik and Russia Fact Sheet." http://www.whitehouse.gov/news/releases/2001/11/20011113-16.html.

Johnston, Douglas. "Introduction: Realpolitik Expanded." In *Faith-Based Diplomacy: Trumping Realpolitik*, ed. Douglas Johnston, 3–10. New York: Oxford University Press, 2003.

Kagan, Donald, and Frederick W. Kagan. *While America Sleeps: Self-Delusion, Military Weakness, and the Threat to Peace Today*. New York: St. Martin's Press, 2000.

Kagan, Robert, and William Kristol, eds. *Present Dangers: Crisis and Opportunity in American Foreign and Defense Policy*. San Francisco: Encounter Books, 2000.

Keller, Bill. "God and George W. Bush." *New York Times*, May 17, 2003.

Kennedy, Paul M. *The Rise and Fall of the Great Powers: Economic Change and Military Conflict from 1500 to 2000*. New York: Vintage Books, 1989.

Klein, Joe. "The Blinding Glare of His Certainty." *Time*, February 24, 2003.

Kohut, Andrew. *The Diminishing Divide: Religion's Changing Role in American Politics.* Washington, DC: Brookings Institution Press, 2000.

Kohut, Andrew, and Bruce Stokes. *America against the World: How We Are Different and Why We Are Disliked.* New York: Times Books, 2006.

Kristoff, Nicholas D. "Following God Abroad." *New York Times,* May 21, 2002.

Kupchan, Charles A. *The End of the American Era: U.S. Foreign Policy and the Geopolitics of the Twenty-first Century.* New York: Knopf, 2002.

Lake, Anthony. "From Containment to Enlargement." *Vital Speeches of the Day* 60, no. 1 (October 15, 1993): 13–19.

Lieber, Robert J. "The Neoconservative-Conspiracy Theory: Pure Myth." *Chronicle Review,* May 2, 2003.

Lindholm, Tore, W. Cole Durham Jr., and Bahia G. Tahzib-Lie, eds. *Facilitating Religious Freedom or Belief: A Deskbook.* Leiden: Martinus Nijhoff, 2004.

Malone, David M. "A Decade of U.S. Unilateralism?" In *Unilateralism and U.S. Foreign Policy: International Perspectives,* ed. David M. Malone and Yuen Foong Khong, 19–40. Boulder, CO: Lynne Rienner, 2003.

Malone, David M., and Foong Khong, eds. *Unilateralism and U.S. Foreign Policy: International Perspectives.* Boulder, CO: Lynne Rienner, 2003.

Mann, James. *Rise of the Vulcans: The History of Bush's War Cabinet.* New York: Viking, 2004.

Marty, Martin E. "Our Religio-Secular World." *Daedalus* 132, no. 3 (Summer 2003): 42–48.

———. "The Sin of Pride." *Newsweek,* March 10, 2003.

Meirsheimer, John J., and Stephen M. Walt. *The Israel Lobby and U.S. Foreign Policy.* New York: Farrar, Straus and Giroux, 2007.

Mitchell, Mark T. "A Theology of Engagement for the 'Newest Internationalists.'" *Brandywine Review of Faith and International Affairs* 1, no. 1 (Spring 2003): 11–19.

The National Security Strategy of the United States of America, 2002. Washington, DC: White House, 2002. September 17, 2002. www.whitehouse.gov.

Nye, Joseph P. "Foreign Policy after Iraq." *San Francisco Chronicle,* March 14, 2007.

Patrick, Stewart, and Shephard Foreman, eds. *Multilateralism and U.S. Foreign Policy: Ambivalent Engagement.* Boulder, CO: Lynne Rienner, 2002.

Pew Research Center. "America's Image Slips, but Allies Share U.S. Concerns over Iran, Hamas." June 13, 2006. http://pewglobal.org/reports/display.php?ReportID=252.

———. "The Great Divide: How Westerners and Muslims View Each Other." June 22, 2006. http://pewglobal.org/reports/display.php?ReportID=253.

Phillips, Kevin. *American Theocracy: The Peril and Politics of Radical Religion, Oil, and Borrowed Money in the 21st Century.* New York: Viking Penguin, 2006.

Regular, Arnon. "Road Map Is a Life Saver for Us." *Haaretz,* July 3, 2002).

Romano, Lois, and George Lardner Jr. "Bush's Life-Changing Year." *Washington Post,* July 25, 1999.

Rozell, Mark J. "What Christian Right?" *Religion in the News* 6, no. 1 (Spring 2003): 2–3.

Seiple, Robert A. "Confessional Foreign Policy." *Brandywine Review of Faith and International Affairs* 2, no. 2 (Fall 2004): 1–2.

————. "Why Brandywine Review?" *Brandywine Review of Faith and International Affairs* 1, no. 1 (Spring 2003): 1–2.

Seiple, Robert A., and Dennis R. Hoover, eds. *Religion and Security: The New Nexus in International Relations*. Oxford: Rowman and Littlefield, 2004.

Silk, Mark. "The GOP Gets Religion." *Religion in the News* 6.1 (Spring 2003): 1.

Snyder, Jack. "Imperial Temptations." *National Interest* 71 (Spring 2003): 29–40.

Stahnke, Tad, and Martin, J. Paul, eds. *Religion and Human Rights: Basic Documents* New York: Center for the Study of Human Rights, Columbia University, 1998.

Stepan, Alfred. "Religion, Democracy, and the 'Twin Tolerations.'" *Journal of Democracy* 11, no. 4 (October 2000): 37–57.

Sweig, Julia E. *Friendly Fire: Losing Friends and Making Enemies in the Anti-American Century*. New York: Public Affairs, 2006.

White House Press Release. "President Rallies Troops at Travis Air Force Base." October 17, 2001.

————. "President Unveils Most Wanted Terrorists." October 10, 2001.

————. "Remarks by the President in Photo Opportunity with the National Security Team." September 12, 2001.

————. "Remarks by the President upon Arrival." September 16, 2001.

Wohlforth, William C. "The Stability of a Unipolar World." *International Security* 24.1 (Summer 1999): 5–41.

Wolfowitz, Paul. "Statesmanship in the New Century." In *Present Dangers: Crisis and Opportunity in American Foreign and Defense Policy*, ed. Robert Kagan and William Kristol, 307–336. San Francisco: Encounter Books, 2000.

Woodward, Bob. *Bush at War*. New York: Simon and Schuster, 2002.

Index